# Political Violence and the Authoritarian State in Peru

## Silencing Civil Society

Jo-Marie Burt

palgrave
macmillan

POLITICAL VIOLENCE AND THE AUTHORITARIAN STATE IN PERU

Copyright © Jo-Marie Burt, 2007.

First published in hardcover in 2007 by
PALGRAVE MACMILLAN® in the United States – a division of
St. Martin's Press LLC, 175 Fifth Avenue, New York, NY 10010.

Where this book is distributed in the UK, Europe and the rest of the world,
this is by Palgrave Macmillan, a division of Macmillan Publishers Limited,
registered in England, company number 785998, of Houndmills,
Basingstoke, Hampshire RG21 6XS.

Palgrave Macmillan is the global academic imprint of the above companies
and has companies and representatives throughout the world.

Palgrave® and Macmillan® are registered trademarks in the United States,
the United Kingdom, Europe and other countries.

ISBN: 978–0–230–62117–6

Library of Congress Cataloging-in-Publication Data is available from the
Library of Congress.

A catalogue record of the book is available from the British Library.

Design by Newgen Imaging Systems (P) Ltd., Chennai, India.

First PALGRAVE MACMILLAN paperback edition: February 2010.

10   9   8   7   6   5   4   3   2   1

Printed in the United States of America.

*To the Lamas-Espejo family*
*Y, sobre todo, a Teresa, César, y Simón*

# CONTENTS

# LIST OF FIGURES

# LIST OF TABLES

# ACKNOWLEDGMENTS

The Chinese character for the word "person" is made up of two mutually supporting strokes leaning on one another; if one stroke is taken away, the other collapses, symbolizing the interdependence we as human beings share with one another.

Nothing more aptly describes the way an author leans on multiple others in the course of researching and writing a book. Taking credit for sole authorship seems a violation of the myriad kindnesses, collaborations, and friendships that sustained me during this project and were essential to its culmination. Without the many people who assisted me, shared their insights with me, and collaborated in various ways in this project, the book you hold in your hands would simply not exist. My debts are many, because in researching and writing this book I relied not only on the support and encouragement of family, friends, and colleagues, but also on the kindness of strangers, those who without knowing me willingly shared their time and knowledge so that I could better comprehend Peruvian politics. To my joy, many of these strangers are now dear friends.

This book is based on field research in Peru that stretches over more than a decade. Extended periods of fieldwork in the early and mid-1990s were possible thanks to the generous support of the Inter-American Foundation, the Institute for the Study of World Politics, the United States Institute of Peace, and The Aspen Institute. Follow-up visits in 1996, 1997, and 1998 were possible thanks to support from the North American Congress on Latin America, where I worked as editor of *NACLA Report on the Americas* between 1995 and 2000. Fieldwork conducted for a book project on Peru's human rights movement by my good friend and fellow *peruanista*, Coletta Youngers, allowed me to observe firsthand the dramatic social protests that emerged in 2000 to contest the fraudulent electoral process mounted by the Fujimori regime to assure its continuance in power. Further research on civil society and its role in the collapse of the Fujimori regime was conducted in the summers of 2001 and 2003 with generous funding from the Department of Public and International Affairs and the Office of the Provost at George Mason University. I also conducted research on the causes and consequences of political violence in Villa El Salvador for the Peruvian Truth and Reconciliation Commission in 2002, which permitted me to carry out follow-up interviews of individuals I had interviewed in 1993–1994 as well as conduct new interviews.

That any of this even happened is due to the generosity of the Thomas J. Watson Foundation, which awarded me an independent study and travel grant in 1986 that launched my life-long fascination with and love for Peru. Nancy Bekavac, who was director of the foundation during my Watson year, was especially supportive of my project and my process. I am especially grateful to Maurizio Vannicelli, my professor at the College of the Holy Cross, for it was his encouragement that motivated me to apply to the Watson, which—as I am certain he foresaw—would prove to be such a formative experience. His vision, compassion, and concern for all of humanity fundamentally shaped my view of intellectual life as part of a broader struggle for social justice. His presence is sorely missed.

At Columbia University my advisor, Douglas Chalmers, was a supportive and judicious guide as well as tough critic. That I am also able to call him friend is a testament to Doug's grace and goodwill. I am grateful to Lisa Anderson, Margaret Crahan, Robert Kaufman, and Alfred Stepan, also my intellectual mentors, for their invaluable advice and support during different stages of this project. A special mention is due to Paolo Sérgio Pinheiro, who was a Visiting Tinker Professor at Columbia during my second year of graduate work there, and whose groundbreaking scholarship-activism inspired me and a number of my colleagues to pursue scholarly research on the effects of violence and authoritarianism in Latin America. At the Institute of Latin American and Iberian Studies at Columbia University, Ana María Bejarano, Marc Chernick, Katherine Hite, Rayda Márquez, Scott Martin, Kerianne Piester, Monique Segarra, and Melina Selverston, were exceptional colleagues and friends, and their camaraderie and intelligence continue to inspire me.

Several people read parts or all of this manuscript at different stages and provided critical feedback and suggestions to improve it, and I am deeply grateful to each of them: Julio Carrión, Margaret Crahan, Nena Delpino, Lesley Gill, Francisco Gutiérrez, Eric Hershberg, Steve Heydemann, Billie Jean Isbell, Robert Kaufman, Charles Kenney, Nelson Manrique, Philip Mauceri, Cynthia McClintock, J. Patrice McSherry, Luis Pásara, Carlos Reyna, Karen Sosnoski, Steve Stern, Charles Tilly, Carlos Vilas, and Coletta Youngers. I am also indebted to Carlos Iván Degregori, whose writings on Shining Path have been prolific and insightful, for his valuable comments on earlier versions of the chapters on Shining Path, and to Ariel Armony for stimulating my thinking on civil society.

Discussions about Peruvian politics with numerous other colleagues and friends over the years have also helped shape my thinking on many issues addressed in this book and deserve special mention: Alberto Adrianzén, Carlos Basombrío, César Bedoya, Maxwell Cameron, Baltazar Caravedo, Pilar Coll, Ernesto de la Jara, Susan Eckstein, Marcial Godoy-Anativia, José Gonzales, Kevin Goonan, Gustavo Gorriti, Jane Henrici, Josefina Huamán, Robin Kirk, Amy Lind, José López Ricci, Enrique

Mayer, Enrique Obando, David Scott Palmer, Ponciano del Pino, Guillermo Rochabrún, Isaías Rojas, Fernando Rospigliosi, Jorge Salazar, Francisco Soberón, Orin Starn, Lucía Vásquez, and Robert Weiner. My work benefited enormously from the collaborations, insights, and assistance of these and many other colleagues and friends, though of course I alone am responsible for the contents of this manuscript and whatever failings lie within.

Over the course of my years of research in Peru I have enjoyed affiliations and collaborations with a variety institutions that greatly facilitated my research and initiated new and enduring friendships. Colleagues at DESCO offered thought-provoking debate and enduring support, and I am especially grateful for the continued friendship of Nelson Manrique, Carlos Reyna, and Gustavo Riofrío. The Instituto Diálogo y Propuesta (IDS) also provided a supportive environment for my research, and I am deeply indebted to Rolando Ames for his friendship and solidarity. Pilar Coll, Susana Villarán, and Sofía Macher, each of whom led the National Human Rights Coordinator in the 1980s and 1990s, were especially generous, and I am grateful to them for sharing their time and insights with me on many occasions over the years. The Asociación Pro-Derechos Humanos (APRODEH) and the Instituto de Defensa Legal (IDL) provided me with critical data, resources, and assistance at various points throughout this project. Special thanks are due to Francisco Soberón, Miguel Jugo, and Charo Narváez at APRODEH, and Ernesto de la Jara, Carlos Basombrío, Isaías Rojas, Nélida Gandarillas, and Cecilia Narváez at IDL. Giovanna Peñaflor and Manuel Córdova at the polling company IMASEN were a delight to work with, and they and their staff proved extremely competent in carrying out the surveys and focus groups of residents in Villa El Salvador and San Juan de Lurigancho. I am also grateful to several others who helped me establish contacts for my interviews, including Emma Aguirre, Cecilia Bravo, Julio Calderón, Diana Miloslavich, Néstor Ríos, and Eudosio Sifuentes.

Several people were very directly involved in the research and production of this book, and I would like to express to them my deepest appreciation for their hard work, humor, and friendship. José López Ricci, Liliana Miranda, Rodrigo Portales, and Rosario Romero provided invaluable research assistance at different stages of my fieldwork. Carlos Reyna provided me with information and feedback throughout the project. Gustavo Riofrío assisted me with the map of Lima's *barriadas*. Vera Lentz, a courageous photographer who has documented Peru's brutal civil conflict since the early 1980s, graciously allowed me to use her amazing photographs for this book, including the cover image. I am also grateful to *Caretas* and *El Peruano* for the use of images from their archives. At Palgrave Macmillan I would like to especially thank editors Gabriella Georgiades and Luba Ostashevsky, assistant editor Joanna Mericle, and production editor Erin Ivy. They provided critical editorial assistance through all stages of preparing the manuscript and have been kind, supportive, and a pleasure to work with. Finally, Maran Elancheran did an exceptional job copyediting the final manuscript.

Many people from Villa El Salvador have shared their lives, struggles, and hopes with me throughout the years. I am especially grateful to former mayors of Villa, Michel Azcueta, Johny Rodríguez, and Martín Pumar, and former city councilman Néstor Ríos, who helped me in numerous ways to better understand the political dynamics in the district. The Rev. Eugenio Kirke, the Rev. Gregory Chisholm, and Sister Vicky Dorrego, who each made Villa their home for long periods of their lives, shared with me their invaluable insights into the district's history and dynamics. Though I never formally interviewed María Elena Moyano, I met her first in 1987, and spoke with her on several different occasions about women's organizations and human rights in the district. Her brutal death at the hands of Shining Path was a terrible loss.

There are many others in Villa El Salvador I would like to thank who discussed politics and life and so much more with me, but prudence requires that I do not. Their friendship and their faith in me and in my work have sustained me throughout this process. Villa El Salvador is the heroic creation of its 350,000 residents, whose labor, solidarity, and faith in the future transformed a piece of barren desert into a beautiful, bustling city that now has 20-foot trees and gardens and playgrounds, markets, schools, and clinics. This city is my second home, and I remain forever grateful to the *vecinos* of Grupo 17, and most especially to the loving Lamas-Espejo family, who took me in many years ago and made me part of their family. I dedicate this book to them, and especially to Teresa, who is the heart of it all, to César, whose brilliance and thirst for justice inspired me from the moment I met him, and to Simon, our little addition to this transnational family.

Finally, I am deeply thankful to my parents, Arnold and Lucia Burt; to my brother Tim and his wife Tammy; and to my sister Nancy and her husband Charley for their steadfast love and support. César, thank you for our years of learning and being together. And Simon thank you for never letting me forget the most important thing in life: spending time with the ones you love. And yes, Mommy is now done with the book. Let's go get some chocolate ice cream to celebrate!

# LIST OF ACRONYMS

| | |
|---|---|
| AP | Popular Action |
| APEMIVES | Association of Small Entrepreneurs of Villa El Salvador |
| APRA | American Popular Revolutionary Alliance |
| CADE | Annual Conference of Entrepreneurs |
| CGTP | General Confederation of Peruvian Workers |
| CNDH | National Human Rights Coordinator |
| CTP | Confederation of Peruvian Workers |
| CUAVES | Self-managing Urban Community of Villa El Salvador |
| CVR | Peruvian Truth and Reconciliation Commission |
| DESCO | Center for the Study and Promotion of Development |
| DINCOTE | National Directorate against Terrorism (later DIRCOTE) |
| FARC | Revolutionary Armed Forces of Colombia |
| FEPOMUVES | Popular Women's Federation of Villa El Salvador |
| FONCODES | National Fund for Social Compensation and Development |
| FUCOMIVES | Federation of Vendors and Micro Entrepreneurs of Villa El Salvador |
| IDESI | Institute for the Development of the Informal Sector |
| IPSS | Social Security Institute of Peru |
| IS | Socialist Left |
| IU | United Left |
| MIR | Revolutionary Left Movement |
| MRTA | Túpac Amaru Revolutionary Movement |
| NGDOS | Nongovernmental Development Organizations |
| OAS | Organization of American States |
| ONPE | National Office of Electoral Processes |
| PAD | Direct Assistance Program |
| PAIT | Temporary Income Support Program |
| PC | Communist Party |
| PC-Unity | Peruvian Communist Party-Unity |

| | |
|---|---|
| PCP-SL | Communist Party of Peru (Shining Path) |
| PCR | Revolutionary Communist Party |
| PPC | Popular Christian Party |
| PMR | Revolutionary Mariateguista Party |
| PROEM | Emergency Employment Program |
| PUM | United Mariateguista Party |
| SIN | National Intelligence Service |
| SINAMOS | National System for Social Mobilization |
| SUNAD | National Superintendency for Customs |
| SUNAT | National Superintendency for Tax Administration |
| SUTEP | Peruvian Education Workers' Union |
| UNCP | National University of the Center |
| UNIR | National Union of the Revolutionary Left |
| VR | Revolutionary Vanguard |

PERU

N

COLOMBIA

ECUADOR

Tumbes

Loreto

Piura

Amazonas

Lambayeque

Cajamarca

San Martin

BRAZIL

Ancash

Huanuco

Pasco

Ucayali

PACIFIC OCEAN

Lima

Junin

Huancayo

Madre de Dios

Callao

★Lima

Huancavelica

Cusco

Ayacucho

☐ Cusco

Abancay

Apurimac

Ica

Ayacucho

Puno

B O L I V I A

Arequipa

--- International Boundary
— Department Boundary
★ National Capital
☐ Department Capital

Moquegua

Tacna

Map not to Scale
Copyright © 2007 www.mapsofworld.com

CHILE

# Introduction

*The state threatened our leaders by detaining them and sending them to prison. The Shining Path threatened them too, accusing them of being traitors and a series of other things. The social activist hid, avoiding positions of public responsibility, seeking refuge in silence.*

Community leader, Villa El Salvador

On February 15, 1992, a Shining Path hit squad murdered Maria Elena Moyano, an Afro-Peruvian community leader from Villa El Salvador, a poor district in southern Lima. Shining Path, a Maoist guerrilla movement that launched its revolutionary war against the Peruvian state in 1980, was stepping up its attacks in Lima, Peru's capital city, as part of its strategy to topple the Peruvian state. Moyano had become an outspoken critic of Shining Path, particularly as it sought to expand its influence in Villa El Salvador. Shining Path accused Moyano of being a stooge of the state, emphasizing her role as deputy mayor of the town and ignoring the fact that she was also an implacable critic of the government for its failure to address the pressing needs of poor Peruvians and for human rights violations committed in the context of the war against Shining Path. In a brutal display of violence, Shining Path militants shot Moyano in front of her children and then obliterated her body with a stick of dynamite. In the aftermath of Moyano's murder, community leaders dispersed, fearful that they would be the next victims.

Less than a year later, Pedro Huilca, secretary general of the Confederation of Peruvian Workers (CGTP), was gunned down in the streets of Lima. Government officials accused Shining Path of the crime, and the charge reverberated in the media as another example of Shining Path's savage war against Peruvian society. Shining Path had previously assassinated trade union leaders; in 1989, for example, the Maoists claimed responsibility for the killing of Enrique Castilla, a union activist, in Lima. Yet several observers, including Huilca's wife, believed the government was responsible. Shortly before Huilca's murder, President Alberto Fujimori had publicly fustigated Huilca for challenging the government's neoliberal economic policies, and insinuated that he and the CGTP leadership were in cahoots with the Shining Path. This would not be the first time a trade unionist was attacked by government forces: in February 1989, Saúl Cantoral, a leader of the miners' union, was kidnapped and later killed by a paramilitary death squad. Several years after Huilca's murder, international investigators concluded that the Fujimori government was in fact responsible *for the crime. The violence inflicted upon trade unionists by Shining Path and government forces throughout the 1980s and 1990s undermined the basis of collective solidarity, contributing to the erosion of the organizational capacity of the workers' movement and of its political significance.*

★ ★ ★

In modern warfare, civilians are often the primary victims of violence. This was certainly the case in Peru, which was consumed by a brutal internal conflict in the 1980s and a good part of the 1990s. The Peruvian Truth and Reconciliation Commission (CVR), a government-appointed body created in 2001 and charged with investigating the causes and consequences of political violence in Peru between 1980 and 2000, has documented the murder of 69,000 Peruvians at the hands of insurgent groups and state security forces and their proxies. Some 12,000 of these murders include the forced disappearance of individuals primarily at the hands of state security forces.[1] More than 600,000 Peruvians were displaced from their homes, and at least 40,000 children were orphaned. Countless people were victims of torture by state security forces, and both insurgents and state agents routinely committed sexual violence, predominantly against women. Draconian antiterrorist legislation put in place after President Alberto Fujimori's 1992 coup d'état, which eviscerated constitutional rule with the backing of the armed forces, also led to the incarceration of hundreds if not thousands of individuals innocent of any wrongdoing, who endured long and painful years in prison. In addition to outright murder, Shining Path also forcibly recruited young people to fight in its guerrilla army, and held natives from the Ashaninka tribe in the central jungle captive, confining them to virtual slavery (CVR 2003).

In contrast to Argentina, Chile, Uruguay, and other Latin American nations that endured military regimes that engaged in massive human rights violations against civilians and presumed opponents to terrorize the population into silence and compliance, in Peru political violence had multiple fonts. In Argentina and Uruguay, for example, while left-wing violence predated the dictatorships, once the military took power, the state exercised a perverse monopoly of violence, and the vast majority of political killings were at the hands of government forces.[2] In the Central American nations of El Salvador and Guatemala that, like Peru, experienced internal conflict and had highly structured and mobilized guerrilla armies, it is also true that the bulk of political violence came at the hands of the state and its proxy forces (such as paramilitary groups).[3] In Peru, on the other hand, violence was committed on a massive scale by *both* the state and insurgent groups. According to the CVR, insurgent groups were responsible for the majority of atrocities: Shining Path committed 54  percent of politically motivated killings, while the smaller Tupac Amaru Revolutionary Movement (MRTA) is responsible for 1.5 percent. The state and its proxies were responsible for nearly 40 percent of the killings, with the authorship of the remaining percentage unknown. These numbers do not attribute responsibility for nor do they quantify other forms of violence used during the conflict, such as torture, including sexual violence, that did not lead to death; the forced displacement of individuals and communities; and arbitrary detention, which became a central feature of counterinsurgency operations particularly after the 1992 coup.

This book examines the emergence and expansion of political violence in Peru in the 1980s and 1990s. It is concerned with understanding how political violence shapes and reorders state-society relations, its impact on civil society, and how these evolving dynamics effect democratic governance. In the course of this analysis, I examine two of the most complex and enigmatic phenomena to emerge in Latin America in recent decades: the extremely violent Shining Path guerrilla movement, and the decade-long regime of political outsider-turned-dictator Alberto Fujimori (1990–2000). After describing the context in which these two authoritarian political projects flourished in Peru, I analyze their effects on civil society and on contemporary Peruvian democracy. In pursuit of their objectives—revolutionary overthrow of the state in the case of Shining Path, the reassertion of state power and the consolidation of an authoritarian political project in the case of the Fujimori regime—both actors visited violence upon civil society actors in ways that contributed to the severe erosion of community, solidarity, social trust, and communication, and thus the ability of such actors to organize to contest power.

My concern with civil society is not rooted in a naive belief in a direct causal relationship between civil society and democracy.[4] As Armony (2004) has noted, civil society consists of a wide array of groups and associations, some of which may contribute to democratic development, but it may also include groups (such as the Ku Klux Klan) that are antidemocratic, racist, and even violent and do little to enhance tolerance, civility, and democratic coexistence or that may even undermine democracy. There may be no simple or direct relationship between civil society and democracy, but as John Keane (1996:51) has argued, state power without "social obstacles"—by which he means a robust, democratic, and nonviolent civil society—is "always hazardous, a license for despotism."[5]

As in most contemporary conflicts, Peru's internal war is not only a story of violence waged between two armed groups. It was also a conflict waged upon the terrain of civil society itself. In the case of Shining Path, the movement's ideological dogmatism led it to frame its struggle for state power in juxtaposition to existing social movements, whose affiliation to other left-wing parties made them ideologically impure. Constrained by its own ideological framework from building alliances with existing grassroots movements, Shining Path sought to generate its own organizations and neutralize competing social movements. Shining Path thus deployed a strategy of moral and physical assault on existing social movement leaders it perceived as obstacles, while seeking to co-opt and intimidate others into submission. At the same time Shining Path sought to compete with other sectors of the Left for legitimacy and support among the civilian population, leading to deep conflicts within Peruvian civil and political society about the nature of social transformation in Peru, the legitimacy of violence as a tool for social change, and human rights.

The state, meanwhile, particularly in the 1990s, also sought to galvanize support within civil society for its project of reestablishing state authority, defeating the insurgency, and reorganizing state-society relations. The state's early approach to counterinsurgency in the 1980s was more confrontational, marked by mistrust of the urban and rural poor, an inability to distinguish between legitimate social protest and the insurgency, and a militaristic approach to combating the insurgency that resulted in the indiscriminate use of violence, massacres of civilians, and forced disappearances. It was not until the late 1980s that strategic elites within the state apparatus began to understand that this approach was fundamentally counterproductive, and that shifting the terrain of the conflict toward building support in civil society was crucial to defeating the insurgency, reasserting state power, and restoring stability. This project, rooted in traditional understandings of national security that viewed the armed forces as the only actor capable of guiding the nation and the state toward stability, was fully deployed under the Fujimori regime. Efforts to develop alliances between the state and society were accompanied by strategies to neutralize and intimidate oppositional elements in society from emerging to contest the regime's concentration of power as well as its social and economic policies.

Both Shining Path and the Fujimori regime thrived in the context of weak state institutions and of profound individual and collective insecurity. In order to sustain local support for their projects, both sought to provide poor urban and rural communities with concrete material aid and new structures of security. Both also deployed violence, fear, and intimidation to destroy the material and moral basis of civil society organization; the fragmentation of civil society was both the condition for and result of the expansion of these authoritarian projects. The Fujimori regime vanquished Shining Path with the 1992 arrest of the group's principal leader and ideologue, Abimael Guzmán; yet rather than building on this victory to reestablish democratic governance, it sought to keep civil society fearful and disorganized, so that it could not challenge the regime's authoritarian reconfiguration of power and privilege. The consequences of political violence and the authoritarian state for Peruvian civil society, and hence Peruvian democracy, were dire and profound.

The analysis developed here is grounded in a Gramscian conceptualization of power, which insists on the symbiotic relationship between consensus and coercion. It thus seeks to draw out elements of both that are underrepresented in the existing literature in an effort to contribute to our understanding of how such authoritarian and violent political projects were able to develop and thrive in Peru. The conventional answer to this question is that Peru is an historically authoritarian society, thus it is not surprising that such authoritarian projects took root and flourished. This view is too simplistic. It fails to take into account efforts at both the grass-roots level and in political society to strengthen and deepen Peruvian democracy in the 1980s. It also neglects the ways in which political violence reordered political and social meanings in Peru, contributing to collective insecurity and fear, and thus to the likelihood that local communities were willing to support highly authoritarian and violent political projects. It also fails to account for the way political entrepreneurs, whether these were nonstate actors or ruling elites, can manipulate and exploit fear to justify authoritarian projects. Finally, such a view neglects the degree to which coercion and consensus can be mutually reinforcing. In the case of Shining Path, for example, the literature and the media emphasizes the group's violence and authoritarianism, but often downplays the ways Shining Path was able to generate sympathy and support in local contexts. Similarly, analysis of the Fujimori regime focuses on popular support for the regime and often neglects the coercive dimension of power that sustained its authoritarian project. I was particularly dissatisfied with the lack of reflection on the ways in which support for the Fujimori regime was rooted in new understandings generated by political violence and the crisis of the state itself, and of the way state power was being deployed by the Fujimori regime to inhibit civil society organization through intimidation, fear, and repression. This book aims to analyze these dimensions of power that have been underemphasized in the existing literature, in the hopes of contributing to our understanding of civil society, political violence, and the authoritarian state in Peru.

## Political Violence in Peru

The Shining Path guerrilla movement launched its revolutionary war in 1980 not in a context of political repression or exclusion, but at the precise moment that Peru was making a transition from military to civilian rule, providing new opportunities for citizen participation through elections, local government, and other mechanisms. For Shining Path, electoral democracy was merely window dressing for the "bureaucratic-capitalist state," and it did not participate in elections for a constituent assembly in 1978 or in national elections in 1980. Shining Path thus distinguished itself from the plethora of other left-wing political parties that had emerged in the context of the struggle against the military regime in the late 1970s and that agreed to participate in elections, though not without some degree of ambiguity vis-à-vis what some of the more radical among these groups viewed as "merely" political democracy.[6] Thus, in sharp contrast to most other revolutionary movements in Latin America, which emerged to contest exclusionary political *and* socioeconomic arrangements, in Peru the Shining Path launched its revolution at a time of political opening, even though socioeconomic exclusion (poverty, inequality) remained sharp.

Though Peru was a democracy, its leaders proved incapable of finding lawful and democratic ways to address the challenge of insurgent violence. The first reaction of the government of Fernando Belaúnde (1980–1985) was to ignore the insurgency, then to employ state terror to counter insurgent terror. The state's response to the mounting insurgent challenge, rooted in colonial mentalities that view indigenous peasants as subhuman and ultimately dispensable, was based on brute force.[7] The result was massive killings, massacres, and forced disappearances. Indiscriminate violence proved counterproductive, however, creating new recruits for Shining Path and fueling the spiral of violence.

Insurgent violence and state terror thus grew in the context of political democracy—another important factor distinguishing the Peruvian experience of political violence from the rest of the region.[8] But an important qualifier is necessary, for though Peru retained important aspects of democracy—including regular elections, separation of powers, a free press, dynamic opposition parties—large swaths of territory were declared emergency zones and handed over to the military. At the height of the war, "Political-Military Commands" ruled in one-third of the national territory and over half of the population: in these areas, citizens were governed not by elected authorities but by military generals; civilian officials and authorities were sidelined, and civil and political liberties were suspended.[9] Not surprisingly, it was in these areas that state-sponsored human rights violations increased at alarming levels. In 1984 Human Rights Watch aptly criticized the militarization of Peru's counterinsurgency strategy as an "abdication of democratic authority."

It was a remarkable achievement that, in the midst of the unfolding conflict, national elections were held and on July 28, 1985, Alan García, of the centrist American Popular Revolutionary Alliance (APRA), was sworn in as president, marking the first time in Peruvian history that one democratically elected government succeeded another. García's initial efforts to address the insurgency using democratic methods and respecting human rights were soon abandoned in the face of strong military pressure, and the regime resorted to the same tactics of terror and violence as its predecessor. But Shining Path was not deterred; on the contrary, by the late 1980s the insurgency was active in 22 of Peru's 24 departments. It had consolidated its hold in important regions of the countryside, the jungle, and was making a push to establish a presence in the sprawling urban shantytowns, or *barriadas*, that surround Lima and are home to two-thirds of its population.

Rather than uniting democratic forces from diverse political parties to buttress Peru's fledgling democracy, as some theorists postulated as a possibility in the late 1980s,[10] political violence deepened and exacerbated social *and* political polarization in Peru. In response to the growing threat of a Shining Path takeover, in the late 1980s the armed forces developed a plan to take power through a coup d'état and rule Peru for 20–30 years in order to defeat insurgents, restore stability, and restructure state-society relations to prevent future conflict and breakdown.[11] A different kind of coup took place, however, in 1992, when President Alberto Fujimori dissolved constitutional rule and concentrated power in the executive with the backing of the armed forces. (Fujimori's coup is often referred to as the *autogolpe*, or self-coup, since the president remained in power even as other democratic institutions were dissolved.) Fujimori's coalition of technocrats, sectors of the economic elite, and the armed forces sought to consolidate state power, reassert government control over the national territory, and restructure state-society relations along neoliberal lines.[12]

Democratic governance was thus fully eviscerated in the context of expanding political violence, the incapacity (or perhaps unwillingness) of state elites to protect citizens and establish legitimate authority, and the growing desire for a return to normalcy among the citizenry. This desire for normalcy—which scholars have identified as common in societies in extreme situations of violence, economic breakdown, and state paralysis[13]—was manipulated and exploited by state elites to bolster support for

**Figure I.1**  Soldiers Patrol Villa El Salvador after 1992 Coup d'état

Soldiers in an army truck patrol the streets of Villa El Salvador in the days after the April 5, 1992 *autogolpe*, in which President Fujimori dissolved congress, suspended the constitution, and intervened in the judiciary with the backing of the military. Such emergency measures were necessary, he claimed, to combat Shining Path, drug trafficking, and corruption.

*Source*: Photograph by Vera Lentz.

an authoritarian political project that promised to bring an end to terrorism and restore stability, but at the expense of individual rights and democratic governance. Many citizens accepted the trade-off as a necessary one in the context of more than a decade of failed counterinsurgency and extreme personal and collective insecurity—a reaction also seen in societies such as Chile and Argentina facing situations of extreme conflict and volatility (Lechner 1992). At the same time, the Fujimori regime instrumentalized fear to keep civil society weak and unable to articulate itself in the public realm as it sought to consolidate its authoritarian political project and its neoliberal economic agenda.

## State Formation and Deformation

Conceptually this book draws from the literature on state formation to explore the ways in which states shape and structure the social arena in which different actors compete for political power, as well as the ways in which contentious social processes shape and constitute state action. Some of this literature, which was first developed in reference to the European experience, portrays state formation as an almost teleological process of movement from weak and fragmented power centers toward the creation of centralized state institutions. Scholars analyzing the experience of Third World nations have noted that state making is in fact a continuous, ongoing process, and the affirmation of central state institutions is one among many possible outcomes.[14] State formation is thus best viewed as a process rather than an outcome. Indeed, as Migdal (1988, 2001) and others have noted, states are one among many sets of institutions vying for dominance. An impasse between state makers and the leaders of socially based institutions competing for local, regional, or even national dominance may block the centralization of state power. Alternatively, alliances between such social groups and state makers may result in hybrid systems in which the state performs some but not all of the roles states are supposed to engage in.

The literature on failing states, which is primarily based on the African experience, points to the inverse trend analyzed in the literature on state formation based on the European experience.[15] In these cases, patrimonial systems of domination, such as in Mobutu's Zaire, collapse into Hobbesian-like anarchy with the withdrawal of cold war political and financial support. A failing state is one which is unable to maintain authority and guarantee law and order and the rule of law in a large portion of its national territory. It is unable to manage macroeconomic policy and evaluate policy options; to mediate conflict between social groups; and to respond to citizen demands for basic services. It has lost its monopoly of the legitimate use of force, giving rise to the privatization of conflict and violence. The public sphere collapses, and the sense of belonging to a broad political community wanes. With no legitimate sovereign to impose order, restore confidence in state institutions, and provide the legal and normative framework for ordinary citizens to go about their daily lives, failing states become Hobbesian prototypes of a war of "all against all." With increasing alarm, scholars and policymakers have highlighted the problem of failing states, but often fail to analyze the historical process of state formation that led to the observed outcomes.

In the case of Latin America, and the Andean region in particular, state making efforts have not resulted in the creation of Weberian-style states that regulate the market and society, extract resources to maintain a functioning bureaucracy, control the national territory, and hold a monopoly on the legitimate use of violence. Nor are they failing states (with the possible exception of Haiti). Rather, Latin American and especially the Andean states exercise only incomplete control over the national territory; they often lack the capacity to fully regulate their societies and often encounter societal resistance at the hour of extracting resources through taxation and other mechanisms; they do not maintain a monopoly on violence, and the state's use of violence is often contested and viewed as illegitimate; and these states often fail to guarantee the exercise of citizenship rights for all members of the political community. Adelman (2006) has termed these "unfinished states," though this is problematic in the sense pointed out by Midgal: by measuring existing states against the Weberian ideal-type, it assumes that the European model is the standard, and can only conceptualize divergences from the ideal-type as deviations. This book approaches the study of states and state-society relations in the sense Migdal, Tilly, and others have argued for, suggesting that states are a field of power marked by the use and the threat of violence, and that state authority is often fragmented and state legitimacy is often contested.[16] Where state power is weak, and particularly where it is exercised in a nondemocratic fashion, opportunities exist for nonstate actors to create alternative structures of power and—in some instances—to contest state power at the center.

Beginning with a brief analysis of the formation of an historically weak state in Peru, the book examines the dramatic social, political, and economic crises that submerged this Andean nation in the 1980s and contributed to a dramatic breakdown of public authority and state capacity. In this context, Shining Path expanded its activities from the hinterlands of the south-central Andes to the very center of power in Lima by the late 1980s. The state's inability to stop insurgent violence, its use of indiscriminate terror against the rural and urban poor, and the downward spiral of the economy contributed, in a recursive process, to further delegitimize the state and open up the field of contestation over the very nature of the state. Shining Path exploited this situation to its advantage, particularly in the *barriadas* of Lima. This process of violent contestation of state power produced a reaction among elite groups, who supported an authoritarian solution to the crisis under the personalistic leadership of Alberto Fujimori. The book examines the process of state breakdown, expanding political violence, and the authoritarian reconstitution of the state under Fujimori. The resulting analysis is a historical, relational analysis of state formation and deformation, the structuring of social conflict, and the impact of social conflict and civil society organization on the state.

## The Gray Zones and the Politics of the Local

While the early literature on transitions to democracy largely neglected the realm of the state, new scholarship has begun to address the relationship between the state and democracy.[17] In a seminal piece, O'Donnell (1993) highlighted the problematic nature of democracy in societies in which states do not exercise full control over their national territory and/ or perform expected functions, such as policing and rule adjudication. O'Donnell observed that the presence of nondemocratic nonstate actors in areas of low state presence/functionality—areas that Alain Minc (1993) has referred to as "gray zones"—may further limit the state's operative capacity and thus provide opportunities for nonstate actors to privatize state functions (as in regional party bosses who use state resources for private gain or to oil their patronage networks), thereby undermining democracy and the full exercise of citizenship rights for all members of the political community.[18] In many ways, O'Donnell's insights about social forces contesting state power echo arguments developed by Migdal (1988) in which he examined "traditional" and other social networks in developing societies that challenged and often blocked the efforts of state makers to centralize state power, but Migdal's work did not draw connections between these processes and democratic governance as O'Donnell has sought to do in this and other works.[19]

In some cases, the existence of gray zones may be a long-standing phenomenon; the state may have lacked the ability or the incentive to establish its presence in certain areas of the nation, allowing for other institutions, groups, or individuals to dominate local politics. In other instances, areas that had some level of state presence and functionality may see a withering of state capacity. State institutions may have been forced to retreat due to fiscal crisis, political disarray, insurgent or other violence, or other factors, creating new opportunities for nonstate actors to establish their own structures of domination and legitimacy. If they succeed in doing so, these actors may begin to contest power locally and, at some point, they may even challenge power at the center.[20] Thus the expansion of gray zones may present a challenge to democratic governance as well as to the legitimacy of the political system itself. In the Peruvian case, nonstate actors—specifically, the Shining Path guerrilla movement— emerged and operated in the expanding gray zones of weak state presence and functionality.

Through an ethnographic analysis of the gray zones in Lima's *barriadas*, which examines the ways Shining Path was able to leverage sympathy from the urban poor, this book aims to contribute to the emerging body of scholarship that seeks to develop tools and concepts to theorize about such processes of contestation and competing claims of power and authority. Anthropologists and political scientists have written about the "political vacuums" in the Peruvian countryside in the aftermath of the 1969 land reform and the ability of the Shining Path to develop support networks and expand its operating capacity in these gray zones.[21] Most scholars agree that the Shining Path was not a mass-based peasant movement, yet it was able to establish a presence and operate in vast regions of the country, particularly in those areas where the state was absent or largely ineffective, building alternative structures of authority (but not mass-based support networks) that sometimes challenged, sometimes replaced, the state itself. This was not multiple sovereignty in the sense Tilly (1978) defines it, since Shining Path never fully controlled a defined territory. However, Shining Path did exercise extensive influence throughout much of the Peruvian countryside, in parts of the jungle, and in the barriadas of Lima. In these spaces, the Shining Path contested state authority and contributed to the erosion of the state's legitimacy, particularly in the late 1980s after the onset of hyperinflation, the collapse of the economy, and the retreat of the state as the central entity regulating daily life and the normative frameworks that sustain it. In this way, political violence was both a result of the crisis of the Peruvian state and a constituent element of it.

It is in this context that Shining Path made a push to extend its traditional zones of influence into the more complex terrain of urban politics. Few observers believed Shining Path would be successful in Lima, where left-wing parties, nonprofit and church groups, trade unions, and community organizations had been active for more than a decade, and where the state had a significant if not always unproblematic presence. Yet by the early 1990s, Shining Path's advance into Lima had even the U.S. State Department warning of an impending insurgent takeover. In part two of the book, I describe the role of Lima in Shining Path's overall strategy, and analyze the way in which Shining Path exploited the crisis of the state and of organized politics to advance its revolutionary struggle in the city, particularly in Lima's barriadas. I document how Shining Path exploited the situation of increasing crime, public insecurity, and weak state response to generate sympathy and build alliances with the urban poor by providing them with concrete goods or services the state was no longer providing or had never provided in the first instance. Shining Path played upon the state's incapacity to provide basic security to its citizens by developing alternative structures of authority to mete out justice in cases of crime and other violations, and to reestablish local order. In the barriadas, this translated into campaigns to intimidate thieves, delinquents, and drug addicts into desisting from their activities and, when such warnings were not heeded, the physical elimination of such "deviants." These campaigns generated currents of sympathy for the Maoist organization among important segments of the urban poor who had grown weary of crime and insecurity and the failure of the police and the judiciary to address these problems. Shining Path also attempted to construct an image of itself as a harsh but fair imparter of justice in a country in which justice was routinely bought and sold, and where conflict resolution mechanisms at the grassroots were sorely lacking. It "punished" local authorities, vendors, and community leaders who it claimed were corrupt, and in many instances successfully manipulated popular outrage at often petty acts of corruption in its favor.

By examining the way the Shining Path sought to exploit the "gray zones," the book seeks to go beyond simplistic understandings of Shining Path as little more than a group of demented psychopaths engaged in violence for violence's sake. Such views do little to advance our understanding of why this group emerged and how it was capable of mobilizing the support structures it did for so long and throughout such a large part of Peruvian territory. The analysis developed here suggests the need to understand the political strategies the insurgency pursued with the objective of gaining local support, neutralizing opponents, and advancing its "revolutionary" cause. This by no means is an attempt to downplay Shining Path's resort to brutal and terrorist violence against civilians.[22] Rather, it challenges us to understand why such an authoritarian and violent group was able to build levels of support to sustain its authoritarian project of social change. Constructing local forms of governance—the provision of security, vigilante justice, punishment of corruption, and so on—was a strategy pursued by Shining Path to build support in local communities. These were the political strategies that accompanied Shining Path's use of terrorist violence against civilian targets—a method Shining Path developed early on and perfected as a way to eliminate its opponents, neutralize potential foci of resistance, and assert its dominance over local communities. The brutality and extent of Shining Path violence has often obscured the political strategies the group pursued to win local support and without which it would have been unable to sustain its push into Lima.

At the same time, my research also challenges Shining Path's claim to command the massive support of the urban poor. While Shining Path's provision of locally desired goods helped create sympathy and passive support for the insurgency, particularly in areas where the state's presence was weakest, my research demonstrates that this support was contingent and utilitarian rather than ideological. When Shining Path was forced to retreat from microlevel governance after the arrest of its top leadership in 1992 and 1993, support for the movement dissipated quickly. Unlike the Salvadoran insurgency analyzed by Wood (2003), which built legitimacy not only through the provision of concrete goods to constituents but also by mobilizing extensive ideological support in civil society through appeals to the justness of its struggle against a violent and exclusionary state, Shining Path was unable, by virtue of its own dogmatism, to develop a sustained basis of ideological support in civil society. When its ability to provide concrete services to local communities collapsed, so did its networks of support, making the group vulnerable to the new state offensive after the arrest of the movement's top leadership in late 1992.

## The Silencing of Civil Society

Political violence is directed against individual bodies: it is meant to silence, punish, or repudiate individuals. But violence also has a social objective. While its ultimate victim is an individual or a group of individuals, violence is also directed at the body politic.[23] In the case of Peru, violence was deployed by a variety of armed actors who sought to silence civil society, eliminating any organized effort to challenge the authoritarian and violent projects they were seeking to impose.

Both Shining Path and state security forces deployed violence to neutralize their presumed opponents. Violence was directed not only at the bodies of the immediate victims, however. Violence was intended to convey a message to the broader social body that opposition would not be tolerated. In many cases, individuals, families, and even entire communities found themselves literally caught between the crossfire of two powerful and ruthless armed actors. In this context, solidarity and trust were destroyed; this undermined collective identities and social mobilization in a broader sense. Organizations such as trade unions, peasant federations, community kitchens, and neighborhood associations were regarded suspiciously by the state, while these same groups were under assault by Shining Path if they failed to submit to the Maoists' vision of revolutionary violence. This multidirectionality of violence meant that fear had multiple and often reinforcing dimensions. For civil society activists in particular, the fear of being suspected of terrorism by the state, on the one hand, and of incurring Shining Path's wrath for not supporting its revolutionary war, on the other, forced many to abandon their role in the public sphere. As one community activist from Villa El Salvador stated,

> The state threatened our leaders by detaining them and sending them to prison. Shining Path threatened them too, accusing them of being traitors and a series of other things. The social activist hid, avoiding positions of public responsibility, seeking refuge in silence.[24]

Fear thus became embedded in the Peruvian psyche. In a society in which social segmentation by race and class is already acute, fear exacerbated suspicion of the "other" and became a defining feature of daily life.[25] This book analyzes this culture of fear and its impact on civil society organization. In contrast to the Southern Cone and Central America, where the state was the primary agent of violence, in Peru the combination of state and insurgent violence was a two-pronged assault on collective identities and destroyed the material and moral bases of civil society organization. Violence thus contributed to the creation of a culture of fear that immobilized people and undermined civil society.

Despite this culture of fear, some individuals and groups in civil society sought to actively denounce violence and human rights violations and defend their local communities from insurgents and the state. In Peru, as in many societies experiencing internal conflict, violence intimidated people into inaction and paralysis, but it also galvanized others into resistance. A vibrant, though small and largely middle class, human rights community emerged to contest state violence and, increasingly, insurgent violence as well.[26] Despite persistent attacks from the state, which accused rights groups of being the "stooges" of Shining Path, and from Shining Path itself, which criticized these groups as defending "bourgeois rights" rather than "rights of the people" (social, economic, cultural rights), human rights organizations struggled in the face of great danger to document rights abuses, defend victims, and appeal to the international community. In local communities, resistance to state and insurgent violence took many forms. Victims and family members of victims sought to publicly denounce government abuses.[27] Several authors have documented the resistance of peasant communities in some parts of rural Peru to Shining Path violence.[28] Here I document the efforts of local activists in Lima's *barriadas* to resist both state and insurgent violence, as well as their attempts to impose their political projects on local communities.

The book examines the head-on collision between Shining Path and other models of social organization that were developing elsewhere in the nation, most notably in local and regional level governments where the parties of the democratic Left, grouped together in the United Left (IU) coalition, sought to build participatory grassroots democracy and a more responsive state. It does so through an ethnographic case study of Villa El Salvador, a squatter settlement established in 1971 that is today the second-largest district in Lima. The IU had mobilized a vast network of community organizations to develop in Villa El Salvador a model of peaceful social change. For Shining Path, this was a revisionist project that only detained the inevitable social revolution; such obstacles needed to be destroyed. As a result, Shining Path launched a frontal assault against the democratic Left and the social organizations that supported it through campaigns of intimidation, slander, and selective assassinations. The most emblematic—but by far not the only—case is that of María Elena Moyano. This relentless and brutal resort to violence effectively neutralized opposition and contributed to the creation of a culture of fear. Yet it also undermined Shining Path's ability to build solid and lasting alliances among the urban poor. With the arrest of Shining Path's top leaders in late 1992, the organization retreated and lost its influence in the district (as elsewhere in Lima). But the damage was substantial: civil society remained cowered by fear, a process that intensified during the authoritarian years of the Fujimori regime.

This complex story reveals the extent to which there was in fact a battle underway upon the terrain of civil society itself that was not being fully represented in the diverse literature emerging on Shining Path and Peru's civil conflict.[29] In situations of conflict, civilian populations are often the "targets of terror," but they are also often protagonists in the conflict: they may organize to resist violence, and sometimes to participate in it. In modern conflicts, civilian populations are "the templates on which power contests are carved, the fonts of resistance, and the architects of new social orders and disorders."[30] In other words, insurgent groups and state actors seek to mobilize support—logistical, moral, and otherwise—from groups in civil society to sustain their political, ideological, and military battles. Thus civil society is not simply acted upon by armed groups; it is also often an active participant in conflict, as collaborators, as resistors, or otherwise. This complicates much of the current understanding of Peru's internal conflict, which views civil society simply as a passive recipient and victim of violence, or as its mirror image, as valiant resistor of armed violence. Civil society groups often *are* the victims of insurgent and/or state violence, as was the case with María Elena Moyano, who was victimized by Shining Path, and Pedro Huilca, who was the victim of state terror. But both were also active members of civil society who sought to resist violence. And they were both embedded in communities—in the case of Moyano, in the urban shantytowns that surround Lima, and in the case of Huilca, in the trade union movement—that were victims of terror, sought to resist terror, and at times were complicit with terror. This book seeks to explore some of these complex relationships between civil society and insurgent and state terror.

### State Making versus Democracy

Constructing a democratic regime requires more than free and fair elections; it also implies the construction of a democratic state in which leaders have the capacity to exert authority over society and economy, but in which mechanisms of accountability exist at different levels to protect citizens against arbitrary action by state makers. In this sense, state making and democracy building can be mutually reinforcing processes, but this is not necessarily the case. As the literature on state formation has established, state building has often been a nondemocratic and bloody process concerned with concentrating state power rather than building norms and mechanisms of democratic accountability.[31] Indeed, some authors have described state making as "organized crime" and a "protection racket."[32] It was through later processes of social mobilization and protest demanding rights and inclusion in the polity that helped broaden definitions of citizenship and redefine the terms of democratic accountability that helped make states more democratic.[33] In examining state making in Peru in the 1990s, this analysis concentrates on the way in which reaffirming state power in the context of state breakdown, economic crisis, and political violence worked against the affirmation of democratic institutions.

As Shining Path expanded its zone of influence into Lima, elite groups came to see the insurgency no longer as a far-away problem afflicting rural Peru only; it was now perceived as a fundamental threat to the dominant structure of authority and to relations of production. In response, a new elite coalition emerged in an attempt to revert the process of state decay, subdue the insurgent challenge, and restore state authority over society. This new coalition of technocratic state elites, the armed forces, and the domestic business elite (with the implicit support of transnational capital) sought to reconstitute the state, but it did not seek to establish a state structured along democratic principles. Instead, this coalition supported the centralization of power in the hands of a powerful executive that ruled in close alliance with the armed forces. I examine this process, with special emphasis on the reordering of state power after the 1992 *autogolpe* to suggest that even after international pressure forced Fujimori to hold new legislative elections, and democratic institutions were presumably reinstated, these became mere window dressing for the consolidation of an authoritarian regime. The postcoup reordering of power remained intact. In effect, the Fujimori regime's state-building project worked at cross-purposes to the affirmation of democratic processes and procedures. The regime's concentration of power in the executive, and the institutional reordering that followed the *autogolpe*, effectively eviscerated horizontal accountability. The weakness of civil society meant that there was little vertical accountability. Violence and the culture of fear undermined civil society's ability to challenge the authoritarian reconstitution of the state under Fujimori. They also reordered political and social meanings, so that Peruvians were increasingly willing to accept heavy-handed measures to detain the violence and restore order. The book thus emphasizes the relationship between expanding political violence, a weakening civil society, and growing societal acceptance of authoritarianism.

But this was not simply a societal demand: elites played on these deep societal anxieties to justify their authoritarian project and reproduce social demands for authoritarianism. I argue that the Fujimori regime deployed the discursive and the coercive powers of the state to perpetuate the weakness of civil and political society in order to maintain its hold on power. Through interviews, archival research, and discourse analysis, I document how the Fujimori regime systematically instrumentalized fear to keep a weak civil society on the defensive and unable to organize, even after the defeat of the Shining Path in 1992. Any opposition to the regime was characterized as an act of subversion. In a country in which suspected terrorists were assassinated, disappeared, or tortured, this had a profoundly chilling effect on civil society organization. As one community activist who opposed the Fujimori government's policies said when asked why she did not protest openly against the Fujimori regime, *"Quien*

INTRODUCTION 17

*habla es terrorista"* (He who speaks out is considered to be a terrorist). Occasional displays of state violence against social movement leaders, such as the 1993 murder of Pedro Huilca, Peru's top trade union leader, reinforced this culture of fear. The result was a cowered, demobilized civil society unable to challenge an authoritarian regime; and the degeneration of that regime—precisely because of the absence of social obstacles to state power—into despotic rule based on crony capitalism and massive corruption. The use of state power to perpetuate a culture of fear effectively blocked the reemergence of civil society and eviscerated democratic governance in Peru. It also contributed to the reproduction of social inequalities, as workers, peasants, and other groups in civil society were too weak to challenge the neoliberal model that, despite nearly two decades since its application, has failed to substantially improve poverty levels, create new and sustainable jobs, or reduce inequalities.

Finally, the relational approach to state-society relations adopted here permits an analysis of shifts in the political process such that small groups within civil society began to challenge the dominant narrative of fear. It was only after a long process of failure and learning that organized groups in civil society became more unified in their effort to challenge the regime. Growing societal resistance to the regime's worst abuses—particularly in light of the fraudulent electoral process of mid-2000—threw into question its legitimacy especially vis-à-vis the international community, exacerbated existing fissures within the ruling coalition, and contributed decisively to its ultimate demise in November when Fujimori fled to Japan and faxed his resignation as president. Contrary to those who argue that the regime's collapse was the result primarily of civil society resistance, or of factors within the regime itself, a relational approach helps us understand the dynamic, interactive, and contentious process of political change at play in Peru's efforts to recuperate democracy and the rule of law.

The Peruvian case offers many lessons for the study of state-society relations in the developing world. As efforts to strengthen the Peruvian state in the late 1960s and early 1970s were abandoned (as they were elsewhere in the world), the neoliberal model of state-society relations began to take hold in Latin America and elsewhere. After the dramatic failure of the state-led development model promoted by APRA's Alan García, a more aggressive model of neoliberalism was pursued after 1990 under the leadership of Alberto Fujimori. The state-building project of the Fujimori regime has been largely neglected in the literature, which instead has focused on whether the regime was democratic or authoritarian, or on the mafia-like quality the regime acquired in its latter years in power. This book seeks to refocus attention on the initial intention of the Fujimori regime: to restructure state-society relations along authoritarian *and* neoliberal lines. The weakening and partial collapse of state institutions in the late 1980s, coupled with the debilitation of political and civil society, created the conditions for the reaffirmation of state power by an extremely personalistic, anti-institutionalist, and authoritarian leadership. The result was an inherently unstable process that, by 2000, also collapsed as evidence of mafia-like behavior and extreme corruption emerged. Shifts in the composition and power correlations between elite groups leading the state-building process during the 1990s led to two distinct phases of state building: in the early period (1990–1997), elites focused on reasserting state power by reorganizing the economy, subduing guerrilla movements, and reordering social relations; by the late 1990s, however, a small clique had assumed near total control of the state apparatus, using it for personal enrichment and to assure, in mafia-like fashion, its continued power and impunity until the regime's collapse in late 2000. This book attempts to explain this process, and to highlight why analyses focusing on regime type alone are inadequate to explain the nature of political change in Peru over the past two decades and the ambiguous regime that was constructed over the course of the decade of the 1990s under Fujimori's rule.

The book's analysis of the Fujimori regime and the challenges facing Peru's transitional democracy raises important theoretical questions about the nature of the state, the absence of effective mediations between state and society, and the capacity of political society to effectively represent and mobilize civil society. Each of these, in turn, has implications for the prospects for democratization in Peru, and for democratic theory in general. The Peruvian case also offers lessons for other nations experiencing similar problems of state formation and insurgent violence such as Colombia. The fact that the Fujimori model is widely lauded today in Colombia (and some may argue is being selectively applied there) suggests the importance of critical analysis of this model. While Shining Path was indeed contained under the Fujimori regime, the negative consequences of the exercise of authoritarian state power for human rights, civil society, and democratic governance have been profound. Rebuilding the state is a necessary but insufficient condition for achieving democracy, respect for human rights, and a lasting peace. State making without horizontal accountability creates opportunities for abuse of authority, malfeasance, and corruption. State making absent an independent civil society capable of demanding (vertical) accountability and ensuring limits to state power is similarly a recipe for authoritarianism, cronyism, and corruption. As noted above, this is not to suggest any simple equation or causality between civil society and democracy. Yet, as Fujimori's Peru so dramatically illustrates, state power without social obstacles is, as Keane has observed, "a license for despotism."

## Methodological Issues

Political violence is not a topic that lends itself easily to research using public opinion polls or surveys. Little hard data exists that reliably represents the attitudes of the urban poor vis-à-vis Shining Path, aside from a handful of public opinion polls carried out in the early 1990s that specifically asked people their opinion of Shining Path and their activities. In any case, though such methods may be useful to provide supporting data, other methods are necessary in order to more fully tease out the complex motivations and rationales that underlie popular attitudes toward actors engaged in political violence. Ethnographic research is a useful tool that allows the researcher to develop a more engaged relationship with the community under study and develop relationships that might allow him or her to probe into highly sensitive issues such as attitudes toward violent actors. I thus set out to do ethnographic research that would permit me to understand popular responses and reactions to the Shining Path and its activities in Lima's *barriadas*, as well as to the Fujimori regime.

I began by doing a general survey of existing research and data sets on political violence in general and in Lima in particular. This included interviews with researchers at private think tanks and human rights organizations who were engaged in research on political violence. Based on this initial inquiry I selected four research sites, consisting of four popular districts in Lima in which Shining Path had established an active presence and which it considered strategic zones of influence: San Juan de Lurigancho, Ate-Vitarte, El Agustino, and Villa El Salvador.

The next phase of research consisted of constructing the political history of each of these communities, as well as a chronology of Shining Path activity in each district. I first reviewed existing scholarly literature on Lima's *barriadas* as well as any literature on each of the individual communities produced by scholars, community activists, and nongovernmental development organizations (NGDOs). I reviewed newspaper coverage of political events within each district using DESCO's database on political violence. These chronologies had some important limitations, since newspaper coverage in Peru is incomplete and occasionally inaccurate, and because much of Shining Path's activities were not visible and thus remained unrecorded by the media. Nevertheless the chronologies established an important baseline from which to develop an understanding of Shining Path activity in each district, and from which to formulate questions for my interviews.

The next phase involved direct interviewing. For each district, I began interviewing at minimum five informed observers—individuals who had several years of experience working in the area and with local organizations, such as development workers, religious leaders, local school officials, and municipal government authorities. I then conducted extended, semistructured interviews with at least two dozen residents within each district.[34] These interviews were supplemented with focus groups (two in San Juan de Lurigancho and six in Villa El Salvador), which permitted a survey of popular attitudes among *barriada* residents who did not necessarily have any experience in community or other types of grassroots organizations. In addition, I participated in dozens of local meetings, as well as workshops and informal meetings organized by different Lima-based NGDOs, during the period of formal fieldwork in Lima.[35] Finally, I conducted a survey of 300 residents each in Villa El Salvador and San Juan de Lurigancho for a more representative sample of popular perceptions of the state, political parties, local organizations, and Shining Path.[36] This combination of archival research, surveys, in-depth interviews, workshops, and focus groups offers a revealing glimpse at the complex, changing, and often contradictory nature of popular attitudes toward Shining Path in areas in which the guerrilla organization had some degree of influence and activity.

I chose to do an ethnographic case study of Villa El Salvador given the district's importance as a symbol of alternative forms of participatory and grassroots democracy and Shining Path's efforts to establish a foothold there. This also made sense in terms of my broader questions on the impact of political violence on civil society, since Villa El Salvador was one of the best-organized districts in Lima. I conducted more extensive interviewing in Villa El Salvador during the period of formal fieldwork in 1992–1995, including in-depth interviews with over 60 residents of the district; more than a dozen with outside observers; six focus groups; participant-observation of numerous meetings, forums, and other public events; and the survey research mentioned previously. I made yearly visits to the district between 1996 and 2000, and conducted follow-up research in 2002, when I was asked to write a report on the causes and effects of political violence in Villa El Salvador for the CVR.[37]

Research on the Fujimori regime was conducted throughout the 1990s. I began to systematically interview opposition leaders and activists in 1998, and was a participant-observer to numerous meetings of student leaders, community groups, and human rights and other nongovernmental organizations during my research trips to Lima. I also interviewed government officials and members of the ruling party in congress. I wrote extensively about the Fujimori regime's authoritarian practices as well as the emerging civil society protests in *NACLA Report on the Americas*, which I had the privilege of contributing to as editor from 1995 to 2000. In 2000 I observed the three days of protests leading up to Fujimori's swearing in as president on July 28, 2000, including the massive "March of the Four Suyos." I conducted follow-up interviews and archival research in Lima in 2001 and 2003.

## Organization of the Book

The book is organized into three parts. The first part explores the history of weak state formation in Peru, the crisis of the state, and of organized politics in the 1980s, and how the unfolding violence furthered weakened state capacity and strained state-society relations. This provides the necessary framework for analysis of the next two parts of the book focusing on the expansion of Shining Path into Lima and the emergence of the personalistic authoritarian leadership of Alberto Fujimori. Part two examines the ways in which the state's incomplete control over national territory, uneven service provision, and nondemocratic use of power to control social unrest created political opportunities for societal power contenders—in this case, a radical Maoist guerrilla movement—to contest state power at the local level. It focuses on the Shining Path in poor urban shantytowns in Lima, and analyzes the frontal battle between Shining Path and the democratic Left through a detailed case study of one shantytown, Villa El Salvador. Part three analyzes the reconstitution of the state under the Fujimori regime, during which state power was centralized and restructured along neoliberal and authoritarian lines. The use of state power to keep civil society in fear and disorganized is explored in detail. Also analyzed are the factors that contributed to the demise of the Fujimori regime in 2000, particularly the way despotic power undermined the coherence of the regime's state-making project, gave rise to massive corruption and influence peddling, and prompted a resurgence of civil society activity against the regime.

Chapter one describes that the process of state formation in Peru, which resulted in a weak state that failed to integrate the nation and extend citizenship to all its members, and explores the factors contributing to a deeper and more extended crisis of the state in the late 1980s. Chapter two analyzes the dire social consequences of the retreating state, measured in dramatically increased levels of poverty, heightened inequality, and growing distance between a corrupt and neglectful state and an increasingly fragmented society. Insurgent action and the state's use of indiscriminate violence to contain it, and the way in which this contributed to a further weakening of state power and authority at the local and national levels, is examined in chapter three. Chapter four examines the failure of democratic political parties to mediate these multiple crises and how this contributed to the crisis of organized politics.

In the late 1980s and early 1990s, this retreat of the state and the crisis of organized politics created new opportunities for Shining Path to expand its presence, most notably in the urban shantytowns that ring Lima, Peru's capital city and center of economic and political power. Drawing on extensive ethnographic research in four Lima shantytowns, the second part of the book examines how Shining Path—following similar methods deployed in rural areas in the early 1980s—advanced its presence and authority in society by fulfilling functions the state never provided or, in the context of the extreme crisis of the late 1980s, had ceased providing. Chapter five sets the stage by exploring the process of urbanization in Peru, and the role the city, and particularly the *barriadas* of Lima, played in Shining Path's imaginary of revolutionary change. Chapter six explores the ways in which Shining Path exploited the retreat of the state by providing concrete goods and services to local populations in Lima's *barriadas*. Chapter seven provides a detailed case study of Villa El Salvador, examining the history of Shining Path organizing in the district, its attempt to establish its dominance there, and the shifting popular responses to Shining Path's actions.

The third part of the book explores the response to these contentious processes by elite groups and the shifting terrain of state-society relations that followed. Chapter eight examines the process of authoritarian state reconstitution under the Fujimori regime. The 1992 coup was the defining moment in this endeavor, and the postcoup reordering of power is examined to sustain the argument that despite the return of elections the Fujimori regime remained fundamentally an authoritarian one. It also examines the regime's successful containment of the Shining Path insurgency, which permitted the state to restore some semblance of order and to reassert its authority over society. Chapter nine examines the way ruling elites deployed state power to perpetuate fear in order to reduce the opportunities for civil society mobilization to emerge to challenge the regime's authoritarian project.

The final chapter explores the factors contributing to the *denouement* of the Fujimori regime in November 2000. As the machinery of the state was deployed to assure a third term in power for President Fujimori, contradictions within the regime surrounding what critics dubbed the "re-reelection project" began to grow, creating opportunities for challengers to become more vocal in their opposition to the regime. This culminated in the wave of protests that swept Peru in the context of the contested 2000 electoral process, and ended in November 2000, when Fujimori fled to Japan and faxed his resignation as president. Special attention is focused on the process by which civil society was able to overcome fear and organize in the context of the 2000 electoral process, and how these protests and mobilizations contributed to Peru's transition to democracy.

# PART 1

*State Formation and State Deformation*

# CHAPTER ONE

# The Weak State

*For a long time it was said that there was a war against Chile. They say Chile won and then left and no one has heard of him since. . . . The comuneros [indigenous peasants] believed that Chile was a general until the arrival of the damned blues [police]. The chief of the blues heard people talking about General Chile one day and chastised them. "Ignoramuses! Chile is a country, and we are Peruvians."*

Ciro Alegría, *Broad and Alien is the World*

The historically exclusionary nature of the Peruvian state, its limited presence and authority throughout the national territory, and its narrow basis of social legitimacy have been widely analyzed.[1] Peruvian historians and sociologists have traced the formation of what has been referred to as the oligarchic state in Peru at the turn of the twentieth century, which was based on alliance between the owners of large landed estates, known as *gamonales*, in the rural highlands; the commercial and financial elites of the coast; and foreign capital, which extracted raw materials for the international market. These elites maintained a tightly controlled system that restricted citizenship and resorted to repression and traditional forms of clientelism to contain and delimit challenges to their rule (Cotler 1978a; Burga and Flores Galindo 1981). In Peru's oligarchic society, "political power was privatized and monopolized by a small group of families."[2] The state was primarily an instrument for these elites to advance their economic interests—expanding capitalism on the coast and selected regions where mining was developing, maintaining feudal-like relations in rural areas. The state remained anemic, subject to regionally based *gamonales* who carefully protected their fiefdoms from state encroachment. As historians Burga and Flores Galindo (1981:89) have noted, "The limits of the haciendas were also the limits of [the oligarchic state's] power."

The mass-based, antioligarchic political parties that emerged in the 1930s—the populist APRA and the Communist Party (PC)—were substantially weakened by repression and, particularly in the case of the Communists, by factional and ideological splits. Neither APRA nor the

PC was able to challenge the deeply entrenched forms of clientelism that dominated state-society relations, and oligarchic rule endured in Peru well into the 1960s (Cotler 1978a; Stokes 1995). But this was an oligarchy that never concerned itself with establishing a national project that would incorporate the masses and establish the basis for a modern nation-state. According to Burga and Flores Galindo (1981:94), "Rather than seek the incorporation of other social classes into their project, the oligarchy kept the masses marginalized, as demonstrated by the persistent exclusion of illiterates from political life." The next reformist challenge emerged in the 1950s, this time spearheaded by new middle-class parties, including Popular Action (AP), under the leadership of Fernando Belaúnde Terry, who would twice be elected president, and the Christian Democratic Party. However, these groups were similarly unable to culminate their efforts to reform the oligarchic state.

## Reform from Above: Peru's
## Military Experiment

It was not until the military intervention of 1968 that the power of the oligarchic state was broken with the implementation of a broad reformist program under the leadership of General Juan Velasco Alvarado (1968–1975). In the context of a deeply divided ruling elite, the Velasco regime sought to expand the power of the Peruvian state to regulate foreign capital, promote industrial development, and develop a more encompassing notion of national identity and citizenship. Strengthening state capacity and broadening the reach of the state throughout the national territory were seen as key to developing Peru's economy and therefore to its social development, while overcoming the historic racism and structures of exclusion were seen as necessary to broaden state legitimacy and authority. Mindful of the lessons of the 1959 Cuban Revolution, the Peruvian military viewed these nation- and state-building efforts as vital to undercutting popular support for potential revolutionary projects. Unlike other military regimes in Latin America at the time, which sought to remove radical challenges to the status quo by violently repressing working and lower-class movements, Velasco's regime was a state-led project of social incorporation whose ultimate goal was to undercut more radical options and to extend and deepen the legitimacy of the Peruvian state (Quijano 1971; Stepan 1978; Huber Stephens 1983). The Velasco regime thus endeavored to create new mechanisms of representation based on a direct relationship between the state and society organized in specific functional groups (peasants, industrial workers, urban squatters).[3] In effect, the Velasco regime sought to promote social inclusion by incorporating lower-class groups into new state-chartered associational groups, effectively extending citizenship through social and economic rights rather than civil and political rights.

Velasco's experiment was the most ambitious state-building and nation-building project in modern Peruvian history. Velasco's reforms constituted an effort to dramatically alter state-society relations by redefining the role of the state vis-à-vis the economy, its capacity to influence and integrate society, and to modernize the country. Taken together, they comprised a two-pronged effort to construct the nation by promoting a greater sense of "Peruvianness," in part by incorporating those sectors of society that had largely been excluded from modern politics, and to build the state, by creating new public agencies, increasing the state's role in directing the economy, and by decreeing reforms that would ameliorate the country's growing distributive conflicts (Cotler 1978a, 1983; Stepan 1978).

Ultimately, however, Velasco's reformist program floundered. While the reforms had succeeded in dramatically expanding the state sector, the contradictions of governing were wreaking havoc on the military as an institution, which was growing increasingly divided over the course of the reforms.[4] Growing popular mobilization, and especially labor conflict, was increasingly seen by more traditionalist sectors as a cause of concern. An "institutionalist" sector of the military was growing increasingly wary of Velasco's personalistic rule and the politicization of the military, which they saw endangering the interests and unity of the military institution itself. Meanwhile, the regime's attempt to construct vertical channels of integration of popular groups faltered as these groups increasingly sought to carve out more autonomous spheres of action, which also alarmed the traditionalists within the armed forces as well as economic elites. The private sector, already alienated by the military regime's reforms, had virtually ceased investing in the country. In the face of declining receipts and growing balance of payments crises, the regime grew dependent on financing public sector projects with foreign debt. This would create major problems after 1974, when the skyrocketing of international petroleum prices and the collapse of copper and other key Peruvian exports caused major imbalances in the economy.

As the economic crisis of 1974 worsened and labor conflict increased, divisions within the military over the course of Velasco's reforms hardened. The outcome of a police strike for a wage increase on February 5, 1975, which degenerated into rioting mobs that looted downtown Lima, seemed to highlight the growing aimlessness of the Velasco regime and stiffened the resolve of the institutionalists within the military. In August, General Francisco Morales Bermúdez replaced an ailing Velasco in a bloodless coup. In this so-called second phase of the military government, pro-Velasco officers were ousted, reforms were scuttled, and economic orthodoxy was implemented. The Velasco regime had left the country severely indebted, prompting the International Monetary Fund (IMF) to condition future loans on austerity measures and revealing the structural constraints to economic policy imposed by international actors (Mauceri 1996).

The austerity measures—which included the elimination of subsidies on basic food items such as milk, the freezing of wages, and reductions in state spending—fueled growing popular unrest. The language of "rights" and "social justice" so widely used during the Velasco period emboldened popular sectors in the cities and countryside to demand what they considered rightfully theirs. A class-based discourse, rooted in the labor communities founded under Velasco, spread into the university and urban *barriada* movements and gave the emerging opposition to the military regime's new conservatism an ideological grounding.[5] In 1977, a wide range of social movements, including trade unions, *barriada* organizations, student groups, and regional federations, called for a general strike against the austerity measures, effectively shutting down the country for 24 hours. Ongoing labor militancy, including two additional general strikes in 1978, prompted the Morales regime to speed up its timetable for a return to civilian rule. The strikes were not an all-out victory for labor, however, as Morales dismissed nearly 5,000 unionized workers, many from the public sector, crippling the union movement. The politically motivated dismissals of public sector employees would also have a negative effect on state capacity, as it deprived key state bureaucracies of competent and experienced personnel (Pastor and Wise 1992). Despite the massive social protests, in the final instance, the military retained firm control over the transition process. Military leaders engaged in secret negotiations with conservative and centrist parties, primarily the Popular Christian Party (PPC) and APRA, in order to circumvent the direct participation of the Left and trade unions in the transition process (Lynch 1992; Mauceri 1997).

The Velasco regime's reforms left Peru with an ambiguous legacy. The state's role in the economy and society had expanded dramatically. Previously an insignificant actor in the Peruvian economy, the state had become a predominant player: the public sector share of total investment jumped from 16 percent in 1965 to 51 percent by 1975.[6] But most analysts agree that rather than strengthening the state as an instrument to promote autonomous development and to integrate Peruvian society, Velasco's experiment actually further debilitated the state by overextending its role in the economy, creating a larger but often inefficient civil service, amassing a huge foreign debt, and promoting policies that tended to hinder rather than promote private investment.[7] Indeed, the state remained weak in many respects: it was more dependent than ever on international capital; its extractive apparatus remained underdeveloped; centralization of state presence of the national territory was still incomplete; and it remained fundamentally unembedded in society.

Nor did the Velasco regime's reforms resolve Peru's distributive conflicts. In addition, the Velasco regime's ultimately unsuccessful efforts to resolve the citizenship question by incorporating the lower classes into state-chartered organizations had other unintended consequences for state-society relations in Peru. The Velasco regime's promotion of labor unions, peasant federations, and urban community organizations stimulated grassroots and labor organizing to an unprecedented degree and gave them a new language of rights and struggle to press for their demands. New social and political groups that incubated in the womb of Velasquismo grew more radical in the wake of the Velasco regime's failures and the Morales regime's conservatism. Many of these organizations effectively co-opted the regime's reformist rhetoric and demanded the social changes the military regime had promised when it came to power in 1968 (Tovar 1985; Mauceri 1996; Stokes 1995). The state thus helped constitute new social actors who, in the wake of the retreat of the state under the Morales Bermúdez government and later under Belaúnde, would challenge state policies. The stage was thus set for a stalemate between a still weak state and an increasingly emboldened civil society.

## Transition to Democracy

After 12 years of military rule, in 1980 Peru returned to democratic rule. Weary of military rule and eager for promised social changes to be ful-filled, Peruvians greeted the return to democracy with great enthusiasm. The military's handpicked candidate for the presidency was Víctor Raúl Haya de la Torre, the founder and principal leader of APRA. That the military and APRA had reached a sort of modus vivendi after so many decades of hostility reflected changes within both the armed forces and Peru's oldest mass-based party. Haya's sudden death, just months before the elections, opened the political playing field. Fernando Belaúnde, who had been ousted by Velasco in 1968, played up his distance from the mil-itary regime and the refusal of his party, AP, to participate in the 1978 constitutional assembly. He won the elections and was sworn in as presi-dent on July 28, 1980.

Belaúnde inherited a state that, Velasco's corporatist efforts aside, remained stubbornly distant from society. The new constitution, for-mally adopted in 1979, finally gave illiterates the right to vote, and it recognized a series of social and economic rights. Yet mechanisms to develop and promote more democratic state–society relations were still lacking. There was barely any discussion of reforming political parties to make them more representative and internally democratic, for example, thus perpetuating authoritarian leadership styles even within mass-based parties like APRA and the IU, as we shall see in chapter four. Belaúnde did promote a decentralization process, including direct elections for mayors, but without a broader process of reform this often resulted in strengthening local networks of bossism and corruption. Nor was there an attempt to reform the state bureaucracy to make it more efficient and responsive to citizens' needs.

In fact, rather than address these deficiencies, Belaúnde's policies often exacerbated them. His government's embrace of orthodox neoliberalism and economic austerity exacerbated the distance between the state and society (Malloy and Conaghan 1995). The antistatist bias of Belaúnde's neoliberal advisors prevented them from seeing the importance of strengthening state institutions and building support for Peru's new democratic regime by devising ways to integrate Peruvian society and incorporate new social actors. Groups in civil society, fueled by the Velasco regime's discourse of rights and social justice, had acquired both the discursive and the organizational tools necessary to challenge Belaúnde's neoliberal model.

Powerful business sectors as well as international actors such as the IMF championed this model as an alternative to the state-led model of development common in much of Latin America in the 1950s and 1960s. For the neoliberals, it was the heavy-handed statism that was responsible for the region's economic decline, and reducing the role of the state in the economy and society (via privatization, reductions in public spending, liberalization of the economy, and so on) was the preferred solution to both improving economic performance and reducing the historic poverty and inequality that characterized the region. In any case, given Peru's huge and growing debt-servicing difficulties, Belaúnde had little room to leverage vis-à-vis the IMF, whose offer of debt rescheduling required the adoption of monetarist policies (Mauceri 1996). The program consisted of privatizing state-owned enterprises, stimulating private investment and liberalizing the economy by eliminating government intervention in pricing, marketing, and the financial system; reducing tariff and trade barriers; reductions in social spending; and currency devaluations (Pastor and Wise 1992).

The historic weakness of the state bureaucracy, coupled with the massive layoffs of 1977 and the persistence of interinstitutional conflict among state agencies, seriously constrained effective policy implementation. Belaúnde's highly autocratic governing style further undermined bureaucratic capacity (Pastor and Wise 1992; Mauceri 1996). Policymaking came to rely almost solely on executive decree, while little concern was paid to how and whether implementation would take place. This reflected the delegative nature of Peruvian democracy. O'Donnell (1992) defines delegative democracy as noninstitutionalized democracy in which the president treats his elected mandate as a delegation to run the country as he or she sees fit, without concern for accountability or consensus building. The president is the embodiment of the nation; democratic accountability is seen as an impediment to the full authority delegated to the president; and congress and the judiciary are seen as nuisances (O'Donnell 1992). The autocratic governing style that emerges further undermines the state bureaucracy, and effective policy implementation is gutted.

In the Peruvian case, policy implementation was severely hampered as key state institutions failed to coordinate their activities or oversee policy implementation and neglected long-term planning, a process that Richard Webb has described as the "balkanization"[8] of state policymaking. The result was policy incoherence and increasing reliance on external debt.

The extreme antistatism of the neoliberal policymakers led them to discount the importance of creating and reinforcing key state institutions and agencies that are critical for effective policy implementation (Pastor and Wise 1992; Mauceri 1996). Moreover, because it held a majority in congress, the Belaúnde administration did little to build a governing consensus among opposition parties, a basic characteristic of delegative democracy (O'Donnell 1992). As the crises deepened, opposition parties began to more forcefully challenge the pace and extent of the neoliberal reforms amidst growing labor conflict. As a result, the administration's efforts to mediate between capital and labor floundered.[9]

By 1983, Belaúnde's neoliberal program had collapsed. Trade liberalization policies, which were implemented with the expectation that resources would shift toward Peru's traditional production of mineral and other commodity exports and make the domestic industrial sector more competitive, resulted in little more than an influx of foreign products, especially luxury items. The liberalization effort also increased the price of credit, forcing many local industries into the red and increasing unemployment.[10] The privatization process was not able to attract higher levels of domestic and foreign private direct investment, and only a handful of insignificant state-owned enterprises were sold off.[11] At the same time, the program was undercut as ministers overseeing the privatization drive were reluctant to erode their power base by privatizing state-owned enterprises (Pastor and Wise 1992).

Other policy inconsistencies were evident, particularly around election time when fiscal policy was "softened" to benefit the incumbent administration's party (Pastor and Wise 1992). Exogenous difficulties further crippled the model: price shocks from the international economy, the cutoff of international credit, and bad weather conditions caused by El Niño current. In the 1980–1985 period, GDP stagnated, inflation doubled, debt rose by 70 percent, and real wages declined by more than 35 percent (Pastor and Wise 1992).

Economic adjustment sharpened social divisions and fueled popular unrest against the Belaúnde administration. Between 1982 and 1985, real wages fell over 35 percent (Cuánto 1990a). The informal sector saw its income fall by nearly 20 percent during this period, and the deteriorating terms of trade between agriculture and manufacturing undercut rural incomes (Pastor and Wise 1992). Discontent exploded as workers and shantytown dwellers took to the streets to protest the government's economic policies. The level of discontent was stunningly revealed in the 1983 municipal elections, when the entire weight of the political system seemed to shift to the center-left: the centrist APRA party took 33 percent of the total vote, while the leftist IU coalition won 29 percent at the national level, and its candidate, Alfonso Barrantes, was elected as mayor of Lima, the capital city and home to one-third of the country's population. In the south-central highlands, a more ominous indicator of discontent was evident in the high abstention rates and in some cases the outright disruption of elections, leading some observers to suggest that unrest in these regions was, at least in part, being channeled by the Shining Path insurgency (McClintock 1984). The Belaúnde administration's failure to stop the insurgency—and its brutal repression of Andean peasants between 1983 and 1985—further undermined popular confidence in the regime, as we shall see in chapter three.

## The Rise and Fall of Populism
## and the Crisis of the State

Growing discontent against austerity and economic malaise was ably channeled by a charismatic young APRA leader, Alan García, in the 1985 national elections. García, who won the elections with just under 50 percent of the popular vote, promised to reverse the previous regime's recessionary policies and implement a mix of populist and social-democratic policies, including inflation reduction, economic growth, and income redistribution in favor of the poor (Graham 1992). García positioned this as an alternative to the "Washington Consensus," the orthodox economic model being advanced by Washington, the IMF, and other international financial institutions. His fiery rhetoric, particularly on the issue of Latin American foreign debt, which had cast a heavy shadow on the social and economic development of the region since Mexico defaulted on its loans in 1982, sought to forge a new, region-wide consensus based on a revival of some aspects of the old statist model of development.

In many ways, García was the embodiment of traditional Latin American populism. Through his charismatic leadership, he sought to carve out a coalition of industrial national elites and the urban and rural poor, whom he promised to benefit by creating new jobs and investing state resources in development. García's promise to pursue a *concertación*—an ongoing dialogue with peak organizations and political forces—was reminiscent of the efforts of Argentina's Juan Perón to link the state, industrial elites, and labor in an antioligarchic coalition that pursued national development and glory in harmonious fashion. In his July 28 inaugural address, García attacked the IMF and its monetarist policies as imperialistic and announced a unilateral cap on debt service payments to 10 percent of Peru's export earnings. García also promised to address to Shining Path insurgency by implementing extensive social and economic reforms and to curb rights violations by the military and the police.

García named as his key economic advisors a group of economists rooted in the Latin American structuralist tradition who had criticized the IMF-style model as ineffectual and the cause of stagflation in the Peruvian context. Their plan to reverse the country's looming economic and social crisis was based first on anti-inflationary measures, to be followed by a reactivation of the domestic economy.[12] This heterodox economic model hinged on two key sectors: domestic entrepreneurs and the marginalized poor. To ensure that domestic entrepreneurs invested locally and did not take their capital outside the country, the government froze the exchange rate to control import costs, lowered interest rates to reduce the costs of working capital, and cut the price of government-supplied inputs. Price freezes, wage increases, and job creation would give the urban and rural poor disposable income, thus stimulating demand and reactivating the economy (Pastor and Wise 1992). The other cornerstone of García's heterodox program was limiting debt service payments: by reducing the outflow of dollars, it was expected that the exchange rate and hence prices would stabilize, and the substitution of intermediate imports for debt payments would allow for economic reactivation.[13]

The heterodox plan was initially a great success. Inflation dropped from 163.4 percent in 1985 to 63 percent in 1986. The economy grew by 8.5 and 7 percent in 1985 and 1986, respectively. Manufacturing production increased, reserves were up, and as a result of temporary employment programs and other social policies, real wages increased by 30 percent in the countryside and 25 percent in the cities (Thorp 1987). Programs such as the Temporary Income Support Program (PAIT), which provide income support to the urban and rural poor; the Emergency Employment Program (PROEM), which encouraged businesses to hire new employees by exempting them from job stability stipulations enacted under the Velasco regime; and the Institute for the Development of the Informal Sector (IDESI), which provided credit to informal sector entrepreneurs, had the double effect of shoring up García's political base while spurring internal demand to reactivate the economy. In 1986, García's approval rating was a remarkable 90 percent, and in November that year, APRA swept the municipal elections. APRA took many districts in Lima and throughout the country, and Jorge del Castillo, a close personal friend of García, defeated the incumbent mayor of Lima and leader of the IU, Alfonso Barrantes.[14] This was the first time since Velasco that a president so forcefully argued on behalf of the urban and rural poor and set as a goal the incorporation of these sectors into the political system. Indeed, García set out to integrate society into the state through a vast network of social programs that, while vertical and often clientelistic in nature, held great appeal for the urban and rural poor.

García's heterodox model was built on tenuous ground, however. García's unilateral decision to limit debt payments and his anti-imperialist rhetoric led to the quick isolation of Peru from the so-called international financial community. In 1986, the IMF declared Peru an "ineligible borrower," effectively cutting off the flow of external credits to Peru. The García administration had no contingency plan for creating alternative sources of foreign exchange, such as export promotion and more efficient import substitution even though, as Pastor and Wise (1992) have pointed out, it should have expected this reaction. Flows from other multilateral agencies also fell steadily in this period. Rather than using debt service limits to preserve foreign exchange and buy time for a structural transformation that could have reduced external dependence, the government opted for a rapid expansion that depleted reserves, fed inflation, and ended in an economic crash, as jittery investors converted their savings into dollars. This was partly the result of the logic of García's populist program, in which political motives often superseded economic rationale in policy decision making. Indeed, while several of García's economic advisors had become aware of the problems in the external sector by late 1986, they were unable to persuade García to slow the politically popular reactivation (Pastor and Wise 1992; Graham 1992). In essence, the same structure of policymaking evident in the Belaúnde administration—the personalistic handling of economic policy, a weak bureaucratic apparatus to sustain coherent policymaking, and the insulated nature of the government's economic team—persisted under García. The state continued to be controlled by a handful of powerful individuals with little input from social groups or organized political parties.

The heterodox experiment hinged on a boom in private investment that would expand export capacity, relieving foreign exchange constraints and inflationary pressures. García's model left investment decisions in the hands of private investors, which assured initial support for his program, particularly after the failure of Belaúnde's free market policies and growing concern over more radical alternatives. A brief honeymoon between the government and business ensued, as García wooed business with policies designed to protect profit margins by offsetting real wage hikes with reductions in taxes and interest rates, and holding a series of personal meetings with representatives of the country's twelve largest business groups, known as the "twelve apostles." Yet much of the business sector remained wary of the APRA government and its promises to protect business profits while improving wages. Between 1985 and 1987, private investment increased only slightly, from 12 to 14 percent of GDP. Frustrated with the slow growth of investment (as well as falling export revenues, declining international reserves, and a growing trade deficit), García decided to nationalize the country's private banks in July 1987 as a way of gaining leverage over the "twelve apostles" and preventing capital flight through the banking system. His plans backfired, however, and cooperation between the government and the private sector turned into outright conflict (Durand 1997).

The bank nationalization announcement ignited immediate opposition to the regime. Novelist Mario Vargas Llosa, who led massive street demonstrations of Peru's middle- and upper-class sectors, warned that the nationalizations represented the first step down the path to "totalitarianism." The bank nationalization measure was defeated, and an isolated García now faced unrelenting hostility on the part of the private sector, and the Right—previously moribund—was reborn under Vargas Llosa's newly formed party, Libertad.[15] Some scholars have suggested that the bank nationalization scheme might have fared better had the regime's economic team sought support within the APRA party and among sectors of the opposition, such as the IU, that might have backed the plan (Graham 1992; Pastor and Wise 1992). Again the hyperautonomy of elite decision makers resulted in a policy decision that lacked a clear basis of support and was overturned after sustained societal resistance. The state-society stalemate continued.

The bank nationalizations soon came to symbolize the failure of García's heterodox experiment. While it had given Peru the fastest growth rate in Latin America in 1986 and inflation had been cut in half, by the end of 1987, inflation was back. In 1988, inflation soared to 1,722 percent and to 2,775 percent in 1989, while GDP fell by 8 percent in 1988 and an additional 11 percent in 1989 (Cáceres and Paredes 1991). Inflation severely eroded the real value tax revenues, driving the government to the point of near-bankruptcy.[16]

Just as in the Belaúnde administration, the delegative nature of Peruvian democracy fundamentally undercut policy implementation. In other words, the structures of decision making facilitated autocratic leadership styles, making it nearly impossible for any policy adjustments to take place. García was unwilling to sacrifice his politically popular reactivation program even as his advisors were warning him about the model's impending difficulties. And because of the insulated nature of the executive vis-à-vis congress particularly in terms of economic policymaking, the opposition had little leverage. In addition, his discourse about state-led development aside, García did little more than his neoliberal predecessors to strengthen state institutions; indeed, the emptying out of the fiscal coffers that resulted from this populist experiment gone awry began to undermine what little coherency existed in state institutions and agencies. Segments of the state bureaucracy were soon at odds with each other over economic policy, and the continued weakness of the state's administrative capacity further hampered the implementation of the heterodox economic model (Pastor and Wise 1992; Graham 1992).

Like Belaúnde before him, García exploited the weak mechanisms of accountability to concentrate economic policymaking in the hands of the executive. While it is feasible to imagine that García might have been reigned in by his party, Graham (1992) argues that this was nearly impossible given APRA's political culture, forged through years of repression and underground political activity, which made questioning the *jefe máximo* (supreme leader) nearly impossible. Party members could not openly challenge the policy decisions of García and his team of advisors. When some of García's advisors began questioning government policy and called for austerity-like measures, García—concerned with his popularity among the poorest—repeatedly vetoed such policies at the last moment, exacerbating the economic crisis and feeding hyperinflation (Graham 1992).

Another element that undermined the coherency of the state bureaucracy was an APRA campaign to benefit party members and supporters by appointing them to key state agencies as political favors (Pastor and Wise 1992). Evans (1992) has noted how such political appointments can undermine the technical capacity of bureaucracies in the Weberian sense, by overriding the merit-based system of appointment and the professional nature of state bureaucracies. This situation not only undermined the efficiency of state institutions, but also spawned interagency conflict. For example, Luis Alva Castro, considered the top leader of APRA after García and his likely presidential successor, controlled the Finance Ministry and supported heterodoxy, but resigned his post almost as soon as the economic situation soured in an attempt to protect his status as a contender in the 1990 presidential race. The conflict between the Central Bank and the Finance Ministry is another example. The director of the Central Bank, a García loyalist, often contradicted the Finance Ministry's calls for more conservative monetary policies. The National Planning Institute, torn apart by internal dissent over whether to support García's heterodox plan, became irrelevant and was soon gutted. These conflicts revealed the fundamental weakness of the state apparatus, which in the end increased the control of the president and his small group of advisors over economic policy (Graham 1992).

Further difficulties followed the collapse of the heterodox experiment. Tax revenues fell, dragging down government expenditures. As government salaries declined, so did the incentives for public sector employment. Hyperinflation also made planning extremely difficult. Several policy advisors left García's inner circle, leaving García further isolated. The result was a devastating policymaking paralysis for more than a year. Store owners, expecting price increases, began hoarding basic products, resulting in long lines for essential products such as bread and milk. Other materials, such as tires and cement, were hard to come by due to the growing balance of payments crisis. Government social programs collapsed, cutting off key resources for important segments of the urban and rural poor.

By late 1988, the García government backed away from its heterodox program, announcing an austerity package in September 1988 that included a sharp devaluation of the *inti*, public sector price hikes and several tax-raising measures. These measures failed utterly, however, revealing the depth of the crisis of confidence in the state as an architect of economic policy. Inflation hit 114 percent in September alone, while GDP fell 10 percent. Soon after, hyperinflation set in: monthly inflation averaged 35 percent from October 1988 through July 1990 (when a new president took power) (Pastor and Wise 1992). Output continued to fall: by April 1990 GDP was 15 percent below its July 1985 level (García's first month), and 30 percent below the December 1986 peak reached in the heyday of the heterodox experiment. Hyperinflation persisted through 1989 and 1990 in part because of the government's attempt to reactivate the economy just before the November 1989 municipal elections and the April 1990 presidential elections (Pastor and Wise 1992). The result of García's policy inconsistencies was "a default into an IMF-style policy of the worst kind—austerity-induced recession—without the IMF and the credit relief that it provides" (Graham 1992:110).

The delegative nature of Peruvian democracy thus reinforced the politicized nature of the state, perpetuating the weakness of state institutions and undermining coherent policy formulation and implementation. The state was seen as a source of patronage, undermining the technical capacity of the bureaucracy and increasing sectarianism within the civil service. Congress and the judiciary were largely emasculated from the decision-making process, and therefore had limited capacity to challenge state-based patronage both vis-à-vis the civil service and the popular sectors. The result was limited policymaking coherence and a severe undermining of public confidence in state institutions. The explosion of crime and political violence after 1988, and a number of corruption scandals involving top government authorities, exacerbated this dramatic decline in the public's confidence in the state's ability to regulate conflict, preserve order, and protect citizen rights. A crisis of regime was becoming a full-blown crisis of the state.

## Antipolitics and Austerity

By the time of the presidential elections in April 1990, the depth of the political and economic crisis bred growing disillusionment with APRA and with "traditional" political parties in general (Panfichi 1997; Tanaka 1998). The first indication of this trend came in 1989, with the election of television personality and political novice Ricardo Belmont as mayor of Lima, who ran as an independent. The following year, another "outsider" candidate, Alberto Fujimori, was elected to the presidency on the independent ticket, Cambio 90. The erosion of support for "traditional" political parties, and the resulting opportunities for so-called independent candidates, will be further analyzed in chapter four. The remainder of this chapter will analyze the impact of Fujimori's economic policies during the first two years of his government to illustrate how neoliberal austerity and the politics of antipolitics exacerbated the crisis of the state, and how this created the conditions for the continuing expansion of Shining Path, particularly in the marginal urban areas of Lima. Paradoxically, it was in this context of crisis that state managers were able to refashion economic policy, implementing a radical version of neoliberalism with little societal resistance. This will be analyzed later in the book, where the Fujimori regime's neoliberal authoritarianism is examined in greater detail.

Fujimori was elected on a "no shock" platform; without stating precisely what his economic program was, he promised not to implement economic austerity measures and to find a "gradual" solution to the economic imbalances that had come to a head under the García administration. But within 10 days of his inauguration, the government implemented a radical austerity program designed to rebalance the state's accounts and stop hyperinflation. These measures resulted in a doubling of the country's poverty levels virtually overnight: after Fujimori's shock program was implemented, the number of Peruvians living in poverty nearly doubled, from 6 to 11 million, half of the country's population.[17] The uncertainty these measures provoked—as prices jumped tenfold overnight, and real purchasing power was slashed to 1960 levels (Instituto Cuánto 1993)—heightened the sensation of economic and political instability in the country. In Metropolitan Lima, consumption expenditures, which had already dropped by 46 percent between 1986 and 1990, fell an additional 31 percent between June 1990 and October 1991, the period when Fujimori's shock program was implemented (FONCODES 1994). Social spending, which had been on the decline since 1986, was further slashed in the first two years of the Fujimori regime (Ministry of the Presidency 1993). Government cutbacks further decreased the state's ability to respond to growing popular demands and the crisis of internal order.

Economic adjustment imposed high social costs, but there was little protest—either of an organized or spontaneous nature—in Peru, particularly in comparison to other Latin American countries that adopted similar policies. Structural adjustment policies adopted in Venezuela in 1991 set off a storm of protests in which several hundred people were killed in clashes with police; this set off a cycle of instability marked by two coup attempts in 1992 and tumultuous changes in Venezuelan politics (Lopez Maya and Lander 2004). Similar waves of protest were evident in Argentina and Ecuador after austerity measures were imposed (Walton 1989).

In Peru, by contrast, social protest was quite muted. Unlike the Belaúnde years, when austerity measures were challenged in the streets by a wide array of social movements and organized groups, or during the García years, when community leaders organized massive street demonstrations to protests state cutbacks in welfare programs such as the glass of milk program, which provided free milk to children of low-income parents and lactating mothers, Lima was a virtual ghost town the day after the austerity measures were announced. Army troops were deployed to downtown Lima and to the shantytowns that ringed the city to prevent riots. In San Juan de Lurigancho, the largest and one of the poorest districts in Lima, which I visited the day after the shock measures were announced, residents lined up around the front gates of city hall to purchase stored cooking oil at preshock prices. When an official announced that there was no more oil left to sell, those remaining on line began to shout; within minutes an army truck of young recruits with black hoods over their faces and AK-47s arrived, dispersing the crowd and effectively preventing a riot. Some looting did occur, especially in farmland on the outskirts of the city and in some rural areas. Still, the relative quietude was remarkable, given that the social costs were so high and that no assistance program had been devised to help the country's poorest citizens cope with the massive price hikes. A mixture of fear, despair, and hope that something good might come of this terrible sacrifice dominated the scene.[18]

This was partly due to the fact that a vast network of local community organizations and NGDOs existed in poor areas in urban and rural Peru to help mitigate the crisis. In addition, the Catholic Church reluctantly agreed to lead a government assistance program, though it soon withdrew after the government repeatedly demonstrated its lack of commitment to the program. The Church continued, however, to provide ample private assistance to community organizations throughout the country, primarily through its charity organization, Caritas. Indeed, Caritas, other NGDOs operating throughout the country, and community kitchens provided a cushion that many poor and newly poor Peruvians could turn to. In Lima's community kitchens, the number of rations served daily doubled and even tripled in the months following the austerity measures, stretching their capacity to the limit.[19]

The subdued reaction cannot be fully understood, however, without reference to the pervasive fear that dominated the country in this period, as Shining Path began launching offensives in Lima, government repression continued, and political violence reached new heights. The combination of resignation over what was perceived as a lack of alternatives and the fear of being arrested or killed meant that popular organizations were not able to mount a challenge to the retreat of the state represented by Fujimori regime's neoliberal policies, as they had in the early 1980s during the Belaúnde administration or during the austerity phase of the García regime. The state-society impasse was now shifting in favor of the state.

The historical process of state formation in Peru culminated in a weak state that failed to integrate the nation and extend citizenship to all its members. Despite efforts to strengthen the state and create broader notions of national identity and citizenship in the 1960s and 1970s, the retreat of the state in the latter part of the 1970s and early 1980s undermined this state-building and nation-building project. As Peru made a transition to democracy in 1980, the state's incomplete control over the national territory, and uneven service provision created political opportunities for societal power contenders—in this case, a radical Maoist guerrilla movement—to contest state power at the local level. Insurgent action and the state's use of indiscriminate violence to contain the insurgent threat contributed to a further weakening of state power and authority at the local and eventually the national levels and contributed to the collapse of Peru's party system. These processes will be explored in the next three chapters, and form the backdrop to understanding the dramatic expansion of Shining Path in the late 1980s. In effect, the retreat of the state and of organized politics created new opportunities for Shining Path to expand its presence, most notably in the urban shantytowns that surround Lima, Peru's capital city and center of economic and political power. This will be the focus of the next section of the book, which examines how Shining Path—following similar methods deployed in rural areas in the early 1980s—advanced its presence and authority in society by fulfilling functions the state never provided or, in the context of the extreme crisis of the late 1980s, had ceased providing. The retreat of the state and the dramatic decline of the state's legitimacy as an arbiter of social conflict became the key to Shining Path's urban success.

CHAPTER TWO

# Social Consequences of State Breakdown

Neoliberal acolytes celebrated the breakdown of the state. In the prologue to a book outlining neoliberal policy prescriptions for Peru, Richard Webb (1991:1) argued that the collapse of the state—he called it the "de facto privatization" of the "predatory state"—was a positive development that reflected the degree to which a highly interventionist and overbearing state was being imperceptibly overthrown by its citizens. According to Webb, the state had become so onerous that social groups were taking matters into their own hands. He argued that Peruvian society was sidestepping cumbersome state regulations, leading to an explosion of the informal sector and shrinking the tax base of the state. State-owned enterprises were in a state of collapse, he noted, and the state was increasingly absent from structuring daily relations. For Webb and his colleagues, this breakdown of the state proved the veracity of free market tenets such as those espoused by Hernando de Soto in his famous tract *The Other Path* (1986).

From the left of the political spectrum, there was little clarity about how to assess the dramatic decline of public authority. For those on the Left who subscribed to the classic Marxist view of the state as the instrument of dominant elites, the crisis of the state was not necessarily a bad thing—a prelude, perhaps, to a revolutionary breakthrough. (This was not distant from the view adopted by Shining Path). In the face of expanding political violence, some sectors within this camp favored arming civil society to defend local communities against the rapacious behavior of insurgents and the state alike. Other sectors of the Left sought to bridge the gap between state and society by establishing closer links between state agencies, such as the police, and local populations. In urban areas, this proved short-lived, however; Shining Path threatened individuals involved in such efforts, and the 1992 coup caused leftist leaders to abandon their attempts to coordinate with police and other state agencies. In general, the Left promoted the notion that organized civil society would serve as a barrier to the expansion of Shining Path, failing to note that without guarantees and protection from state institutions, civil society would be emasculated as armed actors such as Shining Path sought to impose their will by force.

Both the neoliberal and leftist approaches to the state neglect the vital importance of strong—and democratic—state institutions to provide a basic framework for conflict resolution and to guarantee basic rights. While neoliberals tend to exalt the ability of the free market to resolve all problems, including social conflict, progressives in Peru have tended to emphasize the role of civil society. Both views neglect that only the state can provide the legal structure necessary to assure a basic normative framework by which the majority of social actors agree to abide so that daily life may unfold in relatively peaceful conditions. The neoliberal exaltation of the "de facto privatization" of the state neglected the wide-ranging and largely negative implications of state breakdown for both the political system and for civil society. The Left often romanticized civil society's potential to resist violent actors, discounting the possibility of civil society being swept into the conflict as another agent of violence as well as the extreme vulnerability of civil society actors in contexts of armed conflict.

The breakdown of the state, evident in extreme economic and social policy paralysis, economic collapse, and expanding violence, led to a dramatic decline in public confidence toward the state. This chapter offers a brief glimpse into social costs and consequences of the breakdown of public authority in the late 1980s. This exercise, while by no means exhaustive, is meant to provide the reader with a sense of the dramatic impact of the breakdown of the state in the late 1980s and early 1990s. It highlights the severe social costs to the Peruvian people in terms of declining wages, growing joblessness, and the massification of poverty. The chapter also describes the related problem of growing crime and lawlessness, and how the institutional breakdown of the state exacerbated the population's sense of personal and collective insecurity. This is of special importance to the analysis given that this insecurity fueled people's willingness to harbor extreme solutions to problems of crime, disorder, and economic uncertainty, including Shining Path violence and authoritarian solutions from above.

## The Social Costs

The economic collapse of the late 1980s had immediate and dramatic social costs. GDP per capita fell by an accumulated 20 percent in 1988 and 1989.[1] By 1989, real wages were half their 1979 value. Labor unrest exploded over the inflationary decimation of wages and food shortages. Hours lost in strikes increased tenfold, and a two-month strike in the mining sector, a key source of foreign exchange, aggravated the reserves crisis and further fed inflation. The percentage of people who were under- or unemployed jumped from 50 percent in 1985 to 75 percent by 1990. It is well known that hyperinflation is most burdensome for the poorest, who spend a large percentage of their income on food and are rarely protected by wage indexation. Household income fell 24 percent between 1975 and 1990, and poverty levels increased dramatically over the five years of the García administration, as noted in table 2.1. Nongovernmental agencies working in poor shantytowns in Lima reported worsening trends in nutritional levels, height-weight measures, and infant mortality indicators (*The Peru Report* 1990).

By 1990, per capita government spending had fallen to $178 —an 83 percent decline from the 1975 level of $1,059.[2] Tax revenues fell from $710 to $159 per capita in the same period. In this context, government programs to improve lower-class income either by providing temporary jobs or credits were shut down, and other programs to benefit local groups with state subsidies such as the Direct Assistance Program (PAD), which provided supplies for government-sponsored soup kitchens, were drastically cut back. Any gains made by the poorest from social programs such as the temporary job program, PAIT, were wiped away as these programs were disbanded and no other social programs were established in their place. Though such programs were primarily clientelistic in nature, they did represent an important link between state and society during the García regime. The retreat of the state in terms of social policy undermined the ability of the poorest to negotiate the crisis, and the retreat of the state from the social arena, particularly in the *barriadas* of Lima, at precisely this moment of crisis led to a dramatic loss of confidence in the state. The other main aspects of state social policy—health and education—also suffered severe cutbacks as a result of the mounting fiscal crisis. There was a continual decline in social spending after 1986 in real terms:[3] social spending dropped from 4.61 percent of GDP in 1980 to 1.78 in

**Table 2.1** Distribution of households according to levels of poverty and lack of basic necessities in Lima, comparison of period between July 1985–July 1986 and June–July 1990.

| *Definition of Household Poverty* | *July 1985–July 1986* | *June–July 1990* |
|---|---|---|
| Households below the poverty line[a] | 16.9 | 44.3 |
| Households below the poverty line, with at least one basic deficiency[b] | 20.2 | 30.3 |
| Households in critical poverty[c] | 5.0 | 19.6 |
| Households in recent poverty[d] | 11.9 | 24.7 |
| Households with inertial deficiencies[e] | 15.2 | 10.7 |
| Households in conditions of social integration[f] | 67.9 | 44.9 |

*Notes:*
[a] Measured by dividing household spending per capita on food by the value per capita of a basket of foods that cover minimal nutritional requirements (2,168 calories per day plus 62.8 grams of protein).
[b] Consumption under the poverty line and presence of at least one basic deficiency (health, measured by access to potable water; education, measured by whether adult head of household is literate; and housing, measured by whether roof is made of noble material).
[c] Consumption under the poverty line and presence of at least one basic deficiency.
[d] Consumption under the poverty line and absence of at least one basic deficiency.
[e] Consumption above the poverty line and presence of at least one basic deficiency.
[f] Consumption above the poverty line and absence of at least one basic deficiency.

*Source: Perú en Números, 1992* (Lima: Cuánto, 1993), p. 1050.

1991 (Fernández Baca and Seinfeld 1993). The value of spending in the education sector, for example, decreased by nearly 75 percent between 1986 and 1990, and the situation was similar in the health sector. A cholera outbreak in early 1991 killed over 2,300 Peruvians. Cholera is a wholly preventable disease; health officials consider its spread was the result of the drastic impoverishment that followed on the heels of hyperinflation and austerity measures (Cueto 1997). World Health Organization director Hiroshi Nakajima stated that the economic adjustment policies adopted in the first few months of the Fujimori regime aggravated already-strained health conditions in Peru, making the spread of previously nonexistent diseases such as cholera more likely.

## "How to Defend Yourself against the Police": Crime, Lawlessness, and Institutional Breakdown

By the late 1980s, the inability of the Peruvian state to provide security and public order had become increasingly evident. Urban violence was on the rise. The number of homicides not related to political violence was increasing, as were crimes against property, including assaults, robberies, kidnappings, and extortion. Organized crimes rings, often involving police officers or former members of the police force, were expanding their activities. Hard figures on the full extent of crime in Peru during this period are difficult to come by, as the Special Commission on the Senate on the Causes of Violence noted in an exhaustive report on violence published in 1989. The commission based its findings on the only figures available, from the Civil Guard, one of the three police units in operation at that time. This data does not represent the total number of reported crimes, but it does indicate general trends.[4] These figures, as presented in table 2.2, illustrate an upward trend not only in the number of reported violent crimes, but also in their proportion in terms of population growth: while there was a twofold increase in the population between 1963 and 1988, there was a fivefold increase in reported crimes. The crime explosion is primarily an urban phenomenon: crimes against property were committed three times more in urban areas than in rural areas, and crimes against life were twice as common in urban areas than rural areas.[5] The commission also noted that many Peruvians lack faith in the police and judicial institutions and therefore often do not report crimes to the authorities, a finding that has been confirmed in numerous public opinion polls conducted during the 1990s.[6]

The police as an institution was woefully inadequate to the task of combating this rising problem of urban crime and violence. In the first half of the decade, rivalries among the three main components of the police institution—the Civil Guard, the Republican Guard, and the Investigations Police (PIP)—often hindered effective police action. The García government, using decree powers ceded to the executive by congress, undertook

**Table 2.2**   Reported crimes per 1,000 inhabitants, select years.

| Year | Number of Reported Crimes | Population per 1,000 Inhabitants | Crimes per 1,000 Inhabitants |
| --- | --- | --- | --- |
| 1963 | 35,789 | 10,985.4 | 3.20 |
| 1974 | 48,494 | 14,836.5 | 3.27 |
| 1978 | 76,097 | 16,376.7 | 4.65 |
| 1979 | 88,784 | 16,786.1 | 5.29 |
| 1980 | 123,230 | 17,295.3 | 7.13 |
| 1981 | 117,383 | 17,762.2 | 6.61 |
| 1982 | 113,755 | 18,225.7 | 6.24 |
| 1983 | 118,529 | 18,707.0 | 6.34 |
| 1984 | 134,292 | 19,197.0 | 7.00 |
| 1985 | 152,561 | 19,697.6 | 7.75 |
| 1986 | 158,619 | 20,207.1 | 7.85 |
| 1987 | 156,060 | 20,727.1 | 7.63 |
| 1988 | 172,121 | 21,255.9 | 8.10 |

*Source*: Comisión Especial del Senado sobre las Causas de la Violencia y Alternativas de Pacificación en el Perú (1989:241).

an extensive reorganization process that unified the three police forces into a single institution and placed it under control of the Ministry of the Interior. While this process was touted as an attempt to professionalize the police force, in fact it permitted the government to remove personnel not linked to the ruling party and grant key positions to party activists and supporters. This reduced the institutional autonomy of the police and politicized the institution.[7] As then congressional deputy for the IU, Julio Castro, noted, "The APRA regime... considered the National Police as an instrument at the service of the government and of the ruling party. This was the guiding force behind the successive reorganizations and laws passed by the government after 1985."[8] The unification of the police did little to resolve the duplication of efforts and interinstitutional rivalries among the three police forces, which remained essentially intact under different names until 1991.

While corruption within the institution was common and problems existed in terms of operative capacity, the economic crisis of the late 1980s seriously undermined the capacity of the police to function on a day-to-day basis. Police forces were starved for funds. Police stations I visited in two shantytowns in 1989 lacked many basic amenities to perform their daily tasks: they had a few typewriters, many of which were broken down; there was no ink or paper; they had cars but no money budgeted for gasoline. Police salaries had been eroded by the effects of hyperinflation, fostering a dramatic increase in petty corruption among police officers as well as a deep-rooted demoralization.[9] In November 1991, a police officer earned 120 new *soles*, approximately $100 a month—hardly enough to feed a family of four.[10] Sometimes police officers were simply not paid due to lack of funds. This had obvious implications for the ability of police to combat crime as well as terrorism. In early 1991, for example, a period of growing Shining Path attacks in Lima, the police went on strike to protest their low wages. A security vacuum was avoided only when the government called in the military to maintain order, a situation that became increasingly common in the capital.[11]

Newspapers reported daily on the involvement of police officers in bribery, extortion, assaults, and robberies, as well as acts of violence committed by police against neighbors and family members.[12] During the government of Alan García, police officers committed a total of 537 reported crimes, including 188 homicides (not related to political violence), 55 cases of kidnapping and extortion, 36 of corruption, 18 of drug trafficking, and 10 of rape.[13] Between August 1990 and October 1991, there were 80 reported cases of police involvement in assaults, robberies, and homicides, 70 percent of which occurred in Metropolitan Lima.[14] In some cases, police violence against citizens was linked to frustrated robbery attempts. Indicative of the growing mistrust of the police on the part of the population, the Lima daily *La República* published a manual in 1991 entitled "How to Defend Yourself against the Police."

Corruption was a widespread problem; police officers would stop city buses on the highway and demand bribes from chauffeurs and passengers alike. There were numerous reports of police officers detaining interprovincial buses outside the capital to rob passengers. In another notable illustration of the severe erosion of the institution, several officers were caught selling entrance exams to the police academy.[15] In drug trafficking regions in the Peruvian jungle, police and military officials were increasingly involved in drug-related corruption.

Due to the lack of resources as well as growing demoralization, the police as an institution—in terms of its capacity to police, protect the community, and help deter crime—was sharply deteriorating. Public confidence in the national police, never very high, was further eroded. In the annual public opinion surveys of Instituto APOYO, an independent think tank based in Lima, between 1987 and 1994, the police were consistently ranked as one of the most ineffective government institutions.[16] In a 1989 poll, 60 percent of those surveyed stated that they did not trust the police, and 43 percent said that they felt fear—as opposed to security—when they saw a police officer (Bedoya 1989). In some shantytowns, there was little police presence to begin with. In others, the problems described above sharpened the feelings of mistrust with which shantytowns residents regarded the police (it was often the police who were sent to remove urban squatters, which often involved the use of force).

Demoralization within the ranks of the police force was further exacerbated by the growing number of deaths of police officers at the hands of insurgents. In 1989, subversive groups killed 178 police officers; in the first 15 months of the Fujimori government (August 1990–October 1991), 275 police officers were killed.[17] The vulnerability of police officers to guerrilla attacks undermined morale and began to affect discipline within the institution: in 1991, it was reported that 3,000 out of 5,000 police officers had abandoned their posts.[18]

In this context, the Fujimori government passed a law reorganizing the police, placing it under the effective control of the armed forces.[19] This militarization of the police, presumably to improve its ability to combat guerrilla movements, made the use of excessive violence on the part of police officers more common. The police were increasingly involved in the torture and murder of suspects, for example. A few high profile cases are illustrative of this trend. Witnesses saw police detain Catholic University student Ernesto Castillo from Villa El Salvador in October 1990; he was never seen again.[20] In June 1991, numerous witnesses, including members of the press, witnessed the police arrest three students in Callao. Shortly thereafter the students were found murdered. In another incident, in July 1991, the police arrested a 24-year-old student, which was captured on video. Hours later, the student was found dead in the local morgue. These incidents generated a great deal of fear of state security forces, and further undermined popular confidence in the police as purveyors of safety and security for ordinary citizens.

## The Privatization of Violence

In the context of the institutional disintegration of the police and the widespread mistrust of the judicial system, the privatization of conflict and violence expanded dramatically. The state's inability to retain its monopoly on the use of violence and control over the national territory had become widely evident by 1988, as guerrilla movements spread throughout the country and drug traffickers colonized coca-growing regions in the central jungle areas. By the end of the decade, the Shining Path insurgency had expanded outward from its original stronghold in the south-central Andean highlands, and by 1989 was carrying out activities in 22 of 24 departments.[21]

In the face of the state's inability to protect citizens from growing crime and violence, private efforts to address these problems began to emerge, as ordinary citizens began to seek out various alternative ways to protect themselves from growing crime. In wealthy districts of Lima, residents built elaborate security systems and hired private guards to protect themselves and their property. Middle-class municipal governments began organizing private security systems, known as *serenazgo*, to mitigate the ineffectiveness of the police, deter crime and improve security. In poorer districts, which lacked the resources to establish such programs, neighbors took turns participating in all-night watch patrols to prevent robberies and assaults, while spontaneous lynchings of thieves caught in the act became increasingly commonplace after 1988. A review of newspaper reports reveals 30 reported lynchings between 1990 and 1996, 19 of which culminated in the death of the alleged criminal.[22] The majority were assault and robbery cases; one case in 1995 and two in 1996 involved attempted rape.

Moreover, social conflicts—ranging from domestic squabbles to land disputes—were increasingly resolved through the use of violence (Comisión Especial de Investigación y Estudio sobre la Violencia y Alternativas de Pacificación 1989). A few examples will illustrate the way violence became an increasingly common mode of resolving disputes among individuals and communities. In the working-class district of Ate-Vitarte, to the east of central Lima, a dispute arose between two families over a small plot of land. They resorted to physical violence, as one of the families, led by an off-duty policy officer, used physical force and the officer's weapon to force the rival group off the land. The group then set fire to the precarious houses of the rival group of squatters.[23] In another incident in the squatter settlement of "Manzanilla II," a local business owner hired a band of thugs to remove more than a hundred families squatting on a piece of land adjacent to his store. The hired gunmen opened fire on the squatters, killing one and severely wounding four others.[24] In another dispute over land in La Molina, rival groups resorted to violence, throwing sticks and stones; one student was killed in this incident.[25] What these cases all have in common is that they represent social forces engaged in disputes that lead to physical violence in which the state is completely absent as an agent of conflict resolution. The different groups involved neither sought out the intervention of the state nor did any individual or institution of the state intervene to diffuse tensions, which led to open physical violence and in some cases the deaths of some of those involved.

The privatization of violence also became evident in the state's counter-insurgency strategy. Paramilitary groups began operating in 1988 and continued to be active throughout the 1990s with direct logistical and financial support from the state. Scholars who have studied paramilitary organizations argue that such groups emerge when governments prove unable to combat subversive movements using legal means (Huggins 1991). Such organizations are often created by elements within state security forces in order to circumvent public controls on the use of violence and are intended to provide the state with a mechanism to engage in violence against opposition groups with little risk of being held publicly accountable for their misdeeds. This is yet another aspect of the privatization of violence that occurred in the context of Peru's political and economic crisis.

The first paramilitary group to emerge was the Rodrigo Franco Command (CRF), named for an APRA party member who was allegedly assassinated by Shining Path. The CRF reportedly was the creation of Alan García's minister of the interior, Agustín Mantilla, and operated in close collaboration with the police.[26] It carried out selective assassinations of regime opponents, such as the 1988 murder of Manuel Febres Flores, a lawyer for Osmán Morote, the second-ranking leader of Shining Path who had been arrested in Lima in 1987. The CRF is believed responsible for a number of attacks against suspected members of Shining Path and the Túpac Amaru Revolutionary Movement (MRTA), including a car bomb that destroyed the offices of *El Diario*, the Shining Path newspaper, and a letter bomb that killed Melissa Alfaro, a journalist at *Cambio*, a pro-MRTA weekly. It also engaged in a systematic campaign of threats and intimidation against members of the legal opposition. For example, the CRF is widely believed responsible for the killing of Saúl Cantoral, the head of Peru's mining confederation, in 1989. It also kidnapped and terrorized the daughter of Senator Manuel Piqueras, who was leading a parliamentary commission to investigate paramilitary groups, in a clear attempt to intimidate Piqueras and his colleagues from presenting their report.

While the Rodrigo Franco Command seemed to fade from view with the change in government in July 1990, other paramilitary units emerged under the new Fujimori government. This time, they were linked to National Intelligence Service (SIN), headed by Vladimiro Montesinos, a former army captain who became Fujimori's top advisor during the 1990 presidential campaign and became the regime's key architect of counterinsurgency policy. Like the CRF, these units continued to target presumed subversives as well as individuals linked to the opposition. In 1991, several migrants from Ayacucho were attending a barbecue in Barrios Altos, just a few blocks from the National Congress, when a band of heavily armed men entered the building shooting, killing more than a dozen people, including women and children, who were believed (mistakenly) to be Shining Path militants. This was the first death-squad-style execution in Lima and signaled a dramatic shift of the war to the capital city.

The unit responsible for this massacre, the Colina Group, was involved in a number of other ghastly crimes. In 1992, the Colina Group kidnapped nine students and a university professor from Cantuta University, also presumed to be Shining Path members.[27] The badly burned bodies of the victims were found a year later after an intelligence agent leaked a map of the clandestine grave to a local magazine. The Colina Group was responsible for numerous acts of violence and intimidation against opposition figures, independent journalists, and human rights groups, including a letter bomb mailed to the offices of the Human Rights Commission, which exploded and tore off the hand of human rights lawyer Augusto Zuñiga.

Another manifestation of the privatization of violence was the expansion of the civil defense patrols, also known as *rondas campesinas*, in the central Andes. *Rondas* first developed in northern Peru in the 1970s to protect peasant property and livestock from bandits; in the face of government inaction peasants decided to form patrols to protect and defend their communities (Starn 1992). The *rondas* in the central Andes followed a different path. While initial attempts by the army to force peasants into participation in civil defense units in the early 1980s failed, by the end of the decade peasants in many communities were organizing their own units to protect their ravaged communities from Shining Path violence (Degregori, Coronel, Del Pino, and Starn 1996; Del Pino 1992; Coronel and Loayza 1992; and Starn 1991). In its final year, the García government began handing out weapons to the *rondas*, a strategy that became official state policy under the Fujimori regime. Under Fujimori, the *rondas* were placed under the legal control of the army. Rondas have been implicated in numerous cases of extrajudicial executions against suspected subversives.[28]

## Citizenship and the (Un)Rule of Law

In this context of dramatic institutional breakdown, personal and collective insecurity, and privatization of violence, citizenship and the rule of law were swept by the wayside. Citizenship implies belonging to a defined political community in which equal rights are presupposed among all members of the community, and these rights are guaranteed by the rule of law. Only on the basis of universal citizenship can all members of the political community pursue their interests under equal terms. In Peru, while all Peruvians are formally "citizens" in that they are empowered to vote and participate in other aspects of political life, citizenship continues to be constrained by the long-standing ethnic and class-based divisions of Peruvian society.[29] Rather than promote democratic citizenship in Peru, the state has more often acted to reinforce the historic divisions of Peruvians into first- and second-class citizens. For example, during the height of the counterinsurgency war, to recruit soldiers, the military sent army trucks to shantytowns in Lima to forcibly recruit young men. This would have been unthinkable in middle- or upper-class districts in Lima; indeed, young men from these sectors often bribed their way out of military service.[30] The failure of the Peruvian state to provide institutional mechanisms to guarantee the rule of law further undermined the tenuous exercise of citizenship in Peru. For many Peruvians, their main contact with the state has been as a repressive force.

The rule of law has never been applied evenly in Peru; in more remote areas in the countryside and jungle, the institutions guaranteeing the rule of law have often been controlled by local elites, and access has been often mediated by money or personal contacts. For example, the courts were long used by elites to dispossess Andean peasants of their land (Flores Galindo 1988). This private use of public institutions reinforced popular views of the justice system as corrupt and as a tool for the powerful to preserve their privileges, rather than as a mechanism for conflict resolution or to seek redress in the face of an injustice. Like the police, the judicial system is one of the institutions most distrusted by ordinary Peruvian citizens.[31] The court system is seen as corrupt, ineffective, and inaccessible to poor people. In this context, lower-class Peruvians have often sought to organize their own solutions to social conflict. This has included village and town councils; the *rondas campesinas* created by local peasant communities in northern

Peru to protect their property and livelihood; the crime-watch patrols created in urban shantytowns; and the growing practice of lynching thieves caught *in flagrante delicto*. In these popular systems of justice, communities and residents impose sanctions on their own without relying on the court system or police intervention. While some of these practices can be interpreted as alternative models of social control and organization, and even as examples of civil society responses to a negligent state, others are deeply problematic. Lynching is the most obviously problematic of these, as it violates democratic guarantees such as due process. However, as social phenomena, these practices are rooted in specific historic formations of state and society.[32]

This chapter has analyzed briefly some of the most notable social consequences of declining public authority and state legitimacy in Peru in the late 1980s and early 1990s. It outlines the economic and social consequences of the state's growing inability to devise coherent economic and social policies, maintain macroeconomic stability, and promote programs to alleviate poverty in times of economic recession and hyperinflation. It has explored the institutional breakdown that followed on the heels of economic collapse, emphasizing growing lawlessness, criminality, and public insecurity. The economic impact of the crises tended to breed corruption and demoralization within state security forces, which came to be seen by the citizenry as not the guarantors of order but as abusive and parasitic institutions. The privatization of violence that resulted was perhaps a logical consequence of this institutional breakdown. Though this scenario was applauded by neoliberal acolytes as the inevitable collapse of a naturally parasitic state, as noted at the outset of this chapter, this view neglects the devastating impact of the breakdown of the rule of law and the privatization of violence. The breakdown of law and order exacerbated Peru's security crisis and created ideal conditions for Shining Path to extend its presence in marginalized rural and urban areas, and to carry out functions the state was increasingly no longer providing. The Left similarly exalted civil society initiatives in response to the crisis of the state, seeing in them the seeds of progressive social change but failing to note that without the rule of law and a context of security, such actors are likely to be subsumed as violence expands and deepens. As we shall see, this is precisely what occurred in Peru in the late 1980s and into the 1990s. Civil society became the terrain upon which violent actors sought to impose their will. As the public sphere shrank and political violence expanded, fear and insecurity came to dominate social life and undermine civil society's capacity to participate in political life.

# CHAPTER THREE

## Terror versus Terror

On March 27, 1989, a group of some 300 Shining Path guerrillas attacked a police post in Uchiza, a small town located in northeastern Peru on the edge of the vast Amazon jungle. Most of the residents in the surrounding areas were small farmers who had turned to the illegal cultivation of coca, the primary ingredient in cocaine. Coca cultivation spread like wildfire in this part of Peru particularly in the late 1980s as the economic crisis worsened, and the expansion of drug trafficking networks was another indicator of the Peruvian state's inability to regulate and control activities occurring within its borders. Shining Path had established its presence in coca-growing areas by providing protection to coca growers from Colombian drug lords and the Peruvian police who, prodded by Washington, engaged in forced eradication of coca in an effort to make cocaine more expensive and less available in the streets and neighborhoods of the United States.

Guerrilla fighters laid siege to the police post, and they exchanged fire with the police for several hours. Police munitions eventually ran out, and the guerrillas overran the police post. Shining Path fighters killed ten policemen, including three high-ranking officials; they spared the lives of lower officials. In the following days, it became public knowledge that Prime Minister Armando Villanueva had personally promised reinforcements by radio to the police commanders, but military troops at a nearby base had refused to assist their besieged comrades.[1] The minister was forced to resign his post, provoking a severe political crisis for the García government.

The Uchiza debacle came to signify a decade of failed counterinsurgency policy. Years of repression failed to contain Shining Path, whose activities were growing in intensity and scope. The state also failed in its basic duty to protect Peruvian citizens from guerrilla attacks. Perhaps most dangerously from the perspective of maintaining state unity and cohesion, Uchiza highlighted the government's inability to protect those working for the state from attack. Indeed, expanding political violence, growing public insecurity, and the ensuing vacuum of power in many parts of the country indicated a dramatic breakdown in state authority and capacity throughout the country.

Throughout the 1980s counterinsurgency policy was marked by inconsistencies and sharp disagreement over how to confront the Shining Path. As the Uchiza debacle so starkly revealed, there was a fundamental lack of coordination and support among state institutions charged with providing security. There were also sharp divisions over strategy and tactics. Within the armed forces, some sectors favored a hard line, "dirty war" approach to combating the insurgency, while others advocated a more integral approach that linked counterinsurgency operations with development initiatives aimed at addressing the root causes of the insurgency. Party leaders also disagreed on the best way to fight Shining Path: while more conservative groups favored a hard-line approach, seeing the Maoists as a foreign conspiracy that had to be mercilessly extirpated from the body politic, progressive sectors believed that the Shining Path was the manifestation of years of poverty and marginalization, and that profound social and economic reforms were necessary to address the underlying causes of the insurgency. Finally, there were sharp conflicts between civilian-led governments and the armed forces: the latter sharply resented the fact that the former called on them to combat the insurgency but failed to defend them when criticized for their methods. Civilian leaders mistrusted the armed forces, given the long history of intervention in political life, yet made little effort to find other ways of engaging the military to fight the insurgency other than handing the generals a virtual blank check to "resolve" the problem. These were some of the key problems that underlie the ineffective counterinsurgency measures adopted by state elites in the 1980s, and that led to a policy of fighting insurgent terror with state terror. It proved to be a fundamentally ineffective model, however. It failed to counter insurgent violence and may in fact have fueled support for Shining Path. It also undermined popular confidence in the state both as a provider of security and a guarantor of public order.

## Incomplete Transition[2]

When the Shining Path launched its revolutionary war against the Peruvian state in 1980, the new civilian regime was at first wary of entrusting the battle against the insurgency to the armed forces. But as the firepower of the insurgents grew, the military was increasingly drawn into the conflict. The new democratic government failed to develop mechanisms of civilian control and oversight over the military's behavior, allowing for virtually complete military autonomy over counterinsurgency matters. Tensions arose as civilian and military leaders sought to deflect responsibility for the failure to deter political violence and for mounting human rights abuses committed by the armed forces. To understand this conflict and how it shaped counterinsurgency policy in the 1980s, let us briefly examine the transition period of 1978–1979.

The transition to civilian rule was a process carefully controlled by the military to ensure that their prerogatives remained intact and that civilians friendly to their interests would be elected (Lynch 1992; Mauceri 1997). In the final years of military rule, the generals cultivated a relationship with the two parties least likely to challenge military privileges— APRA and the PPC—and favored the historic leader of APRA, Víctor Raúl Haya de la Torre, as president. The constituent assembly, which was controlled by an APRA-PPC alliance, hardly touched military power and made no real effort to redefine civil-military relations. To avoid future military coups, the members of the assembly included stipulations that the armed forces were "nondeliberative," a rhetorical right of popular revolt in the case of a military takeover, and a prohibition on members of the armed forces from voting. But they did not attempt to alter a series of military prerogatives in areas such as the budget, arms acquisitions, and ascensions (Mauceri 1997), nor did they establish civilian oversight over the armed forces. As Stepan (1988) has noted, this was a common problem in Latin America's transitions to democracy. Civilians had little knowledge of the inner workings of military institutions, nor did they seem to perceive the importance of reorganizing the armed forces or redefining its institutional mission during the transition period. Meanwhile, the Peruvian armed forces actively sought to preserve its prerogatives. For example, the new constitution established a National Defense System to design and adopt mechanisms to guarantee national sovereignty. Before handing power to civilians, the military passed legislation governing this body, granting itself de facto control over its operations that was left unquestioned after the transition. Through this and other mechanisms the armed forces retained significant military privileges (Degregori and Rivera 1993).

The sudden death of Haya de la Torre opened the way for the election of Fernando Belaúnde, who had been removed from power by the military in 1968. Belaúnde made much of his refusal to participate in the constituent assembly to avoid bestowing legitimacy on the military regime, but he did not challenge the continued prerogatives of the armed forces, as indicated by his decision to retain all high-ranking military officials after the transfer to civilian rule had been completed (Mauceri 1997). This was an ominous indicator of what was to come in the following years, as the Shining Path threat loomed over Peru's nascent democratic regime.

## From Disregard to Atrocity: The Belaúnde Years

The Shining Path launched its "prolonged popular war" against the Peruvian state in a remote village in Ayacucho on the very day that

Peruvians were voting for a new president for the first time in 17 years. In the beginning, Belaúnde grossly underestimated the threat posed by the insurgents, dismissing them as a band of "common delinquents" financed by "foreign elements" that would be easily destroyed.[3] Moreover, Belaúnde wanted neither to challenge the military, nor was he interested in providing them with the means to further increase their power by sending them to combat the Maoist insurgents. He decided instead to send an elite police unit, the Sinchis, to the south-central Andean regions where Shining Path was most active.

The decision to launch its revolutionary war just as the country was moving toward civilian rule was a strategic move on the part of Shining Path. Abimael Guzmán, Shining Path's chief ideologue and strategist, noted in a 1988 interview that he had calculated that the new civilian government would be reluctant, after 12 years of military rule, to send in the armed forces to combat an incipient insurgency, which would give the guerrilla movement crucial space to mature as a political and military force. While some analysts have sharply criticized the Belaúnde regime for failing to immediately send in the armed forces to quell the Shining Path insurgency,[4] such arguments decontextualize the context in which that decision was taken, neglecting both the contradictions of the transition process and the extreme fragility of civil-military relations during the first years of the new transitional government that informed Belaúnde's decisions.

Police action proved ineffective at stemming guerrilla activity. Spectacular guerrilla operations such as a breakout from an Ayacucho prison in which numerous Shining Path inmates escaped made it increasingly evident that Shining Path was a force to be reckoned with. Pressure mounted on the Belaúnde government to take more decisive action. In December 1982, an exasperated Belaúnde turned to the armed forces. He declared martial law in several provinces in the departments of Ayacucho, Apurímac and Huancavelica. A constitutional provision allowed the president to declare areas in conflict as "emergency zones," and to establish "Political-Military Commands" to oversee all aspects of governance. Administrative control over key conflict areas thus passed to the hands of the armed forces with little or no civilian oversight. Under a state of emergency, individual rights are suspended, including the right to public assembly and free movement as well as *habeas corpus*. Security forces are empowered to enter homes and make arrests without warrants. With the declaration of martial law, political violence increased dramatically, as indicated in tables 3.1 and 3.2. Entire communities were massacred, thousands were arbitrarily arrested and forcibly "disappeared," summary executions were increasingly common, and torture and sexual violence were routinely used against detainees. According to the CVR, 1984 marked the year of most intense violence, with over 4,000 murders and forced disappearances (see table 3.3).

**Table 3.1**  Deaths due to political violence during the Belaúnde administration, 1980–1985 categorized by victims.

|  | 1980 | 1981 | 1982 | 1983 | 1984 | July 1985* |
|---|---|---|---|---|---|---|
| Security forces | 1 | 2 | 39 | 92 | 99 | 65 |
| Civilians | 2 | 2 | 87 | 749 | 1,758 | 410 |
| Presumed Subversives | 0 | 0 | 44 | 1,966 | 2,462 | 884 |
| Total | 3 | 4 | 170 | 2,807 | 4,319 | 1,359 |

*Note*:
*Belaunde relinquished power in July 1985.

*Source*: Comisión Especial de Investigación y Estudio sobre la Violencia y Alternativas de Pacificación (1989:375).

**Table 3.2**  Number of persons detained and forcibly disappeared by security forces, 1983–1985.

| Year | Number |
|---|---|
| 1983 | 696 |
| 1984 | 574 |
| 1985 | 253 |
| Total | 1,523 |

*Source*: Comisión de Derechos Humanos, Lima, Peru.

**Table 3.3**  Number of deaths and forced disappearances reported to the CVR according to year in which the reported events occurred, 1980–2000.

| Year | Deaths/Disappearances |
|---|---|
| 1980 | 23 |
| 1981 | 49 |
| 1982 | 576 |
| 1983 | 2256 |
| 1984 | 4086 |
| 1985 | 1397 |
| 1986 | 920 |
| 1987 | 1135 |
| 1988 | 1470 |
| 1989 | 2400 |
| 1990 | 2327 |
| 1991 | 1837 |
| 1992 | 1771 |
| 1993 | 1016 |
| 1994 | 411 |
| 1995 | 290 |
| 1996 | 177 |
| 1997 | 140 |
| 1998 | 105 |
| 1999 | 86 |
| 2000 | 35 |
| Total | 22507 |

*Source*: CVR (2003, Anexo 4:84).

In effect, through the establishment of Political-Military Commands in the emergency zones, Belaúnde had ceded control over counterinsurgency policy to the Joint Command of the Armed Forces. Civilian authorities were sidelined, and no other mechanisms were established to provide civilian control over the military commanders who now held political authority in the emergency zones. This militarization of counterinsurgency was aptly described by Americas Watch in a 1984 report as an "abdication of democratic authority." In fact, the armed forces sent a proposal to the president requesting a specific mandate for their actions in the emergency zones, including "maximum freedom of action." Belaúnde never signed the proposal, but nor did he design a coherent policy of his own, instead leaving each military commander in the emergency zones to define counterinsurgency policy.

There were, at the same time, sharp divisions within the armed forces over how to confront Shining Path, resulting in inconsistent—and often counterproductive—policies with each new commander. The policy of rotating commanders yearly, designed to prevent any single officer from accruing too much personal power, tended to exacerbate this situation, undermining coherent policy formation within the armed forces and increasing the likelihood of internal conflict over policy choices within the armed forces (Mauceri 1996). In 1983, General Clemente Noel became the first military commander of the Political-Military Command in Ayacucho. He pursued a typical "dirty war" strategy based on national security doctrine in seeking to combat Shining Path. In the countryside, everyone was a suspected subversive; defeating the guerrillas meant depriving them of political and logistical support of the population by applying greater coercion and terror over that population. General Luis Cisneros Vizquerra, who was minister of war at the time, stated:

> In order for the security forces to be successful, they will have to begin to kill Senderistas and non-Senderistas alike.... They will kill 60 people and maybe 3 will be Senderistas, but they will say that all 60 were Senderistas.[5]

Nearly 7,000 civilians (including presumed subversives) were killed between 1983 and 1984, and over 1,500 disappeared, leading the armed forces to be seen by the local population as a force of occupation.[6]

The Belaúnde government viewed Shining Path as part of a vast international communist conspiracy. Mirroring the counterinsurgency doctrines adopted by military dictatorships in Latin America's Southern Cone in the 1960s and 1970s, the "internal enemy" was broadly defined to include not only armed fighters but also any individual or group who had or who advocated subversive "ideas." Based on this logic, the armed forces were locked in a total war with not only Shining Path, but also against the parties of the Left that participated in electoral politics as well as trade unionists, teachers, students, peasant leaders, and community activists who were active in movements demanding social and economic change.[7] This view was also shared by conservative civilian sectors, as evident in this editorial published in the Lima daily *Expreso* in 1984:

> The communist offensive in Peru is not only a military question. Shining Path is only the armed wing. This offensive has other wings. These include the Communist Party and organizations led and financed from abroad, the remnants of pro-Castro Velasco supporters…and trade unions controlled by the reds.[8]

This conceptualization of the nature of the insurgent threat contributed to the high number of victims during this and subsequent periods in Peru's internal conflict.

There was an ethnic element to this dramatic display of state violence: the officers and soldiers comprising the armed forces were primarily recruits from Lima and other coastal cities who had inherited Peru's longstanding disdain for Andean peasants, and cultural and linguistic differences exacerbated this sensation of an occupying army. In fact, the army, presumably fearing Shining Path infiltration, proscribed local residents from being recruited into units operating in the emergency zones.

A film made in the 1988 by Peruvian director Francisco Lombardi, *Lion's Den*, depicts the sharp cultural conflict that underlie Peru's internal conflict. Army and police officials, more concerned with their personal careers and with obtaining immediate results they could demonstrate to their superiors, treated local officials with disdain and displayed outright racism toward the Andean peasants of the region, be they communal elders or young women, who were often the victims of sexual violence. The film, which is based on the massacre that occurred in Socos in 1983, depicts the events leading up to the murder of 32 Andean peasants. A soldier, angered when rebuffed by locals from joining in their prewedding festivities, misleads his commanding officer into believing that the partygoers were members of Shining Path. The army officer leads a unit to investigate, and brutal interrogations of the male assistants ensue. The viewer of the film immediately perceives the cultural chasm that prevents the army officers from realizing that the men are native Quechua speakers who do not speak Spanish and therefore do not understand the officers' questions. When one of the men dies after repeated torture, the army officer orders his men to round up all members of the party. They are summarily executed, their bodies thrown by the mountainside and destroyed with hand grenades. One woman miraculously survived the Socos massacre, and later provided investigators with a firsthand account of the terrifying succession of events.[9]

The new military commander of Ayacucho, General Adrián Huamán—originally from the Andean department of Apurímac and a Quechua speaker—adopted a more "developmentalist" strategy to combat the insurgency. This "hearts-and-minds" approach, which sought to address the insurgency by attacking the socioeconomic roots of violence, had roots in the developmentalist theories that influenced Velasco's reformist government and formed an important current of thinking within the Peruvian military. Though Huamán sought develop closer ties with the local population through such measures, military repression continued unabated. Huamán's public statements criticizing the government's disinterest in pursuing development measures as a means of combating the insurgency led to his dismissal in August 1984. Interestingly, Huamán's remarks highlight the failure of the government's militarized counterinsurgency strategy, but little heed was paid to this view at the time. He is reported as saying:

> The solution is not military, because if it were military I would resolve it in a question of minutes. If it were just a question of killing, Ayacucho would cease to exist in half an hour and so would Huancavelica.... But this is not the solution. The problem is that we are talking about human beings, of forgotten communities that have protested for 160 years and no one has paid attention to their demands, and we are now facing the outcome of this situation.[10]

Counterinsurgency policy reverted to the hard-line policies of the Noel period, but these hard-line tactics did not quell the insurgency. On the contrary, most analysts agree that the scorched-earth policies used by the armed forces bolstered support for the insurgents at least in the short term. In Ayacucho, Shining Path had a visible presence in 26 districts in 1982; by November 1983, it had presence in 64 districts (Tapia 1997). In effect, the organization had survived the worst of the repression and had managed to obtain enough of a social base to replace lost cadre relatively quickly (Manrique 1989). Moreover, the Shining Path was able to expand from its initial base of Ayacucho into other areas of the country, primarily Junín, located in the strategic center of the country, the Huallaga Valley deep in jungle country—which was crucial in providing the organization with an endless source of funds through taxes imposed on drug traffickers and coca growers it "protected"—and, by the late 1980s, in the heart of political and economic life in Peru, the capital city of Lima.

As the government proclaimed ever-increasing areas of the country as emergency zones, the military's direct control over the lives of a significant number of Peruvians citizens swelled. Though the Belaúnde government managed to fulfill one requirement of consolidating democratic institutions—the peaceful transfer of power from one elected government to another in 1985—it had failed to meet the growing insurgent threat using democratic means. In its final hours, in fact, the outgoing government actually handed the military greater powers to control civilian life in the emergency zones. Law 24150, promulgated by Belaúnde in 1985, granted political-military commanders full administrative authority over political officials in the emergency zones. It also gave the military governing authority over the public and prive sectors and the power to formulate policy proposals directly to the executive.[11] This effectively legalized the growing autonomy and power of the armed forces in conflict areas, broadened the scope of military intervention in policymaking, and further militarized the conflict. The law also ensured military immunity from prosecution for human rights crimes by mandating that members of the security forces operating in emergency zones could only be tried in military tribunals.

By the end of Belaúnde period, criticism of the government's counter-insurgency policy was deafening. The weekly *Caretas* wrote:

> Something has gone terribly wrong in the antisubversive war...[I]f we do not stop it now the country will go over the edge.... The abyss of the [government's] indiscriminate violence will destroy the constitutional regime... Shining Path is today the first enemy of the country.... But let us not lose sight of the absolute necessity that Peruvian democracy cling to the ideals of justice and civilization in its battle against subversion.... The President of the Republic should stop the genocidal orientation the counterinsurgency war will assume if the current course continues.[12]

Despite massive militarization of the conflict, the state had lost control over large parts of the national territory. State authority was under assault by an armed group that managed to survive a period of brutal state-sponsored terror. The dominant strategy adopted by the military during the Belaúnde period—the use of state terror to combat insurgent terror—certainly did motivate many to abandon whatever support they may have initially displayed toward Shining Path, and tens of thousands of people, feeling trapped between two armies, opted to leave the countryside for the relative safety of urban areas (Kirk 1991). But it also motivated many others to turn to Shining Path in the face of what they perceived as the gross injustices inflicted upon their families, neighbors, and communities by state security forces. Most importantly, it failed in its principal mission: to detain the advance of Shining Path.

### Promises and Repression: The García Period

The election of Alan García in 1985 seemed to augur a change in counterinsurgency policy. García harshly criticized the massive use of violence by state security forces and, echoing the earlier critiques of General Huamán, argued that the military strategy was fundamentally flawed. García advocated a political strategy based on respect for human rights and emphasized the need to address the roots of violence by focusing on the socioeconomic causes of the insurgency. He reiterated this commitment in his inaugural address:

> We cannot accept that the democratic system use death as an instrument. Our presence here [in the National Congress] and our

commitment to struggle on behalf of the people and the Law is proof that social justice can be achieved in democracy. The law will [be] applied with severity for those who violate or have violated human rights through murder, extrajudicial executions, torture, and abuse of authority, since in a struggle against barbarity it is a mistake to fall into barbarity.[13]

As part of his new approach to combating Shining Path, García ordered the reorganization of the police force, established a pluralistic peace commission to promote human rights, and launched a development program for the southern Andean region known as the "Andean Trapeze" that included interest-free credits to campesinos and the promotion of public forums, known as Rimanacuy, in which campesinos could transmit their demands to the government.

The first test of García's new policy came just a month after his inauguration, in August 1985, when witnesses reported a massacre of some 70 campesinos, including women and children, by government forces in Accomarca, a remote village in the department of Ayacucho. García demanded a report from the Joint Command of the Armed Forces, which maintained that no such massacre had occurred. In the face of overwhelming evidence to the contrary, García ordered an investigation. After confirming reports that the army indeed murdered dozens of peasants, and that its highest commanders had sought to cover it up, García fired several high-ranking military leaders, including the president of the Joint Command of the Armed Forces, the chief military commander of Ayacucho, and the chief of the Second Military Region. This was unprecedented in Peru, where military power had far outstripped civilian control in matters relating to the counterinsurgency war.

Days after the dismissals, García sought to defend his position. In a speech before the UN, he stated:

We will combat subversion with unstoppable firmness, but with respect for the law and human rights.... [S]ubversion has flourished in the exasperated misery in which millions of our abandoned compatriots find themselves....Nothing justifies the use of torture, [forced] disappearance, or summary execution. Barbarity cannot be combated with barbarity.[14]

Human rights observers were cautiously optimistic that García's bold move against the military and his assertion of a democratic counterinsurgency policy might mark the beginning of greater civilian oversight over the counterinsurgency—and over the armed forces—as well as an end to state-sponsored human rights violations.

It would prove to be a Pyrrhic victory. The power of the armed forces had remained unchallenged since the return to civilian rule, and the direct intervention of the military in the counterinsurgency gave military commanders a higher stake than ever in assuring their power to direct the war against Shining Path—as well as to ensure impunity for military officials who engaged in human rights abuses during the course of the counterinsurgency. In what amounted to an effective boycott of García's new policies, the armed forces refused to engage in operations in the southern Andes for more than nine months, giving Shining Path an opportunity to reenter an area from which it had been largely expelled.[15] The military's effective boycott of the García regime also allowed the insurgency to expand and eventually consolidate its presence in other regions of the country, including the strategically important central department of Junín, considered to be the breadbasket of Lima; the Huallaga Valley in the central jungle, a key point of operations for the drug trade that would become a key source of financing for Shining Path; the southern Andean department of Puno and the departments of La Libertad and Ancash in the north; and the all-important department of Lima, home to the capital city of the same name and over one-third of the country's population.

Within a year, the military had demonstrated that in a head-on confrontation with the civilian government, it had sufficient autonomy and power to impose its rules of the game. The bloody aftermath of the 1986 prison uprisings revealed the degree to which García had abandoned his original plans, and the military's approach to counterinsurgency had prevailed. In June 1986, Shining Path political prisoners led simultaneous uprisings in three Lima prison facilities. The armed forces led an all-out assault on the prisons, resulting in more than 200 dead. Reports, later confirmed, that most of the inmates were killed after having already surrendered, and that the site of the killings was bombarded to destroy evidence, prompted an uproar in Peru and internationally.[16] In the wake of widespread protests against the massacre, García promised to prosecute those officers responsible for summary executions—"They will go, or I will go," he famously promised. A handful of mid-ranking officials were tried in military court, but the intellectual authors of the extrajudicial execution of nearly 200 inmates have not been prosecuted.[17] This, critics charged, revealed the limits of civilian authority over the armed forces that García found himself forced to accept. It also deepened the military leadership's suspicion of civilian elites, who they perceived as hypocrites for charging the armed forces with combating the insurgency but then questioning their tactics and blaming them for abuses they viewed as inevitable "collateral damage" of such conflicts.

By late 1987, government counterinsurgency policy reverted to the hard-line approach predominant in 1983 and 1984. Human rights abuses increased sharply (see tables 3.4 and 3.5). Civilian access to emergency zones was severely restricted: journalists were prohibited from entering these areas, and several relief agencies, including the Red Cross, were expelled from the Ayacucho region in 1988. Human rights activists were harassed and prevented from investigating reports of abuses in the central-southern Andes. Evidence of the military's outright refusal to accept

**Table 3.4**  Deaths due to political violence during the García administration, 1986–1990, categorized by victims.

|                      | 1986  | 1987   | 1988  | 1989  | 1990* |
|----------------------|-------|--------|-------|-------|-------|
| Security forces      | 136   | 126    | 289   | 348   | 258   |
| Civilians            | 510   | 388    | 1,030 | 1,450 | 1,584 |
| Presumed Subversives | 622   | 183    | 667   | 1,251 | 1,542 |
| Total                | 1,268 | 697**  | 1,986 | 3,049 | 3,384 |

*Notes*:
* García relinquished power in July 1990.
** DESCO, a Lima-based research center, estimates the 1987 total at 1,136.

*Source*: Figures for 1986–1988: Comisión Especial de Investigación y Estudio sobre la Violencia y Alternativas de Pacificación (1989:375); for 1998–1990: Comisión Especial de Investigación y Estudio sobre la Violencia y Alternativas de Pacificación (1992:84).

**Table 3.5**  Number of persons detained and forcibly disappeared by security forces, 1986–1990.

| Year  | Number |
|-------|--------|
| 1986  | 214    |
| 1987  | 69     |
| 1988  | 293    |
| 1989  | 308    |
| 1990  | 302    |
| Total | 1,186  |

*Source*: Comisión de Derechos Humanos, Lima, Peru.

civilian oversight—and the APRA regime's growing collusion with the military—came with the Cayara massacre. On May 14, 1988, soldiers massacred 29 campesinos from Cayara, presumably in retaliation for a Shining Path ambush of an army patrol the day before. The armed forces denied that a massacre had occurred, and military and APRA officials repeatedly obstructed the investigations being led by Attorney General Carlos Escobar.[18] A parliamentary commission of inquiry sent to Ayacucho to collect testimonies was also prevented from carrying out its mandate. Meanwhile, a presidential commission dominated by the ruling APRA party upheld the military's contention that no massacre had occurred. At least eight witnesses were reported killed or disappeared in the weeks following the Cayara massacre.[19] After enduring numerous death threats and near-attempts on his life, Escobar was forced to leave the country and obtained political asylum in the United States.[20]

Other government decisions had the effect of exacerbating tensions within the armed forces and undermining coherent policy formation. In 1987, the government fused the Ministries of War, Navy, and Air Force into a single unit, the Ministry of Defense. This was designed to increase civilian control over the armed forces, but as García's government began to lose legitimacy, it served only to increase tensions between the different

**Figure 3.1**  Terror versus Terror: Soldier and Shining Path Graffiti

A soldier stands guard at the National University of the Center (UNCP) in Junin. The wall behind him is covered with Shining Path posters and graffiti that read, "Long Live President Gonzalo!!" (the nom de guerre of Abimael Guzmán). The UNCP was the site of intense recruitment efforts on the part of Shining Path, which later came to dominate the university. In its effort to reassert state control, the armed forces resorted to extreme forms of violence; over 100 UNCP students were forcibly disappeared or executed by state security agents between 1989 and 1993.

*Source*: Photograph by Vera Lentz.

branches of the armed forces, which had long been at odds.[21] The measure resulted in a bureaucratic but not an operative unification of the three ministries (Degregori and Rivera 1993). At the same time, García sought to co-opt key figures within the armed forces to stave off incessant rumors of an impending coup d'état. At the same time, he sought to beef up the power of the Ministry of the Interior, which oversaw the national police, by placing APRA loyalist Agustín Mantilla as minister. This, along with several campaigns to "reorganize" the police, was seen as an attempt on the part of APRA to extend its control over the state bureaucracy and, more specifically in this instance, to control the police and use it as its private guard in the armed conflict. This tended to exacerbate long-standing tensions between the armed forces and the national police. It must be noted that as political violence began to intensify after 1987, APRA officials at all levels were increasingly targeted by Shining Path: some 800 members of APRA were killed during the García period (Tapia 1997).

A paramilitary organization, the self-denominated Rodrigo Franco Command, emerged in 1988. It was widely believed that the CRF was led by Mantilla from the Ministry of the Interior.[22] This fueled the perception that the APRA regime was seeking to involve the police in paramilitary activities to protect is party members. This further intensified interinstitutional conflict, and exacerbated one of the key problems of Peru's counterinsurgency: the basic lack of coordination between different government agencies, principally the police and armed forces. This came into sharp focus after the 1989 assault on the police station by a Shining Path column in the jungle town of Uchiza, when commanders in charge of a nearby military base refused to respond to a direct order by the prime minister to assist their besieged comrades. Such interinstitutional conflict and failure to coordinate operational movements between the state security forces displayed deep rifts within the state, which Shining Path exploited to its decisive advantage.

Other political decisions on the part of the García government exacerbated civil-military relations as well.[23] It is important to recall the deepseated historical rivalries between APRA and the armed forces dating back to the 1930s and 1940s when the military was often used as an instrument of the oligarchy to suppress APRA (as in the massacre of over one thousand Apristas in Chan Chan, Trujillo in 1932, or the military coups intended to keep APRA out of the presidential palace[24]). Aside from García's anti-imperialist discourse, which unsettled many military officers, a number of other gestures troubled the generals. For example, García received a delegation of the Farabundo Martí National Liberation Front (FMLN), which was still waging a guerrilla war against the Salvadoran government, at the National Palace. Prime Minister Armando Villanueva visited top MRTA leader Victor Polay in prison days after his capture, a gesture the military feared would bestow legitimacy on the guerrilla movement. The incident that caused the most uproar was a 1989 speech made by García to the Aprista Youth in Ayacucho that was later published in *El Comercio*, in which he praised Shining Path for its commitment and sacrifice, urging young Apristas to learn from their "mysticism."[25] While largely symbolic, such gestures reflected the chasm between the García government and the military top brass. Combined with the autonomy over counterinsurgency the military had secured early on in the García administration, this made it nearly impossible for García to realize his initial promise of developing a counterinsurgency program that both respected human rights and promoted socioeconomic development. In addition to the policy inconsistencies and the interinstitutional conflicts, after 1988 the economic crisis began to affect the military institution. Hyperinflation undercut the military's budget as well as wages paid to officials, prompting numerous officials to request retirement and fueling corruption within the institution. For example, a division general earned $210 in 1991, far below the average salaries paid in neighboring countries (Ecuador $558; Bolivia $910; Colombia $915; Brazil $3,700) (Degregori and Rivera 1993). Drug-related corruption in particular had begun to erode military discipline. In this policy abyss, Shining Path advanced relentlessly.

**Table 3.6**  Terrorist attacks, 1980–1991.

| 1980 | 1981 | 1982 | 1983 | 1984 | 1985 | 1986 | 1987 | 1988 | 1989 | 1990 | 1991 |
|------|------|------|------|------|------|------|------|------|------|------|------|
| 219 | 715 | 891 | 1,123 | 1,760 | 2,050 | 2,549 | 2,489 | 2,802 | 2,117 | 2,049 | 1,656 |

*Source*: Figures from 1980 to 1988: DESCO (1989a); figures from 1989 to 1991: Comisión Especial de Investigación y Estudio sobre la Violencia y Alternativas de Pacificación (1992:57).

By 1990, 32 percent of the territory and 49 percent of the population was under military control.[26] Despite the expansion of military control over much of the country, Shining Path had spread and increased its operations. By the late 1980s, the scope and intensity of the group's activities were on the rise. Shining Path had established a presence in the majority of Peru's 24 departments, and the number of terrorist attacks carried out in 1988 and 1989 were nearly 3 times higher than in 1981 and 1982 (see table 3.6). The group also became more aggressive in its strategy, as it perceived the growing weakness of the state. In 1988, Guzmán announced his intention to prepare the terrain for the popular insurrection, including the seizure of the cities. In 1991, Shining Path announced that it had advanced to a new stage of its revolutionary war, "strategic equilibrium," an intermediate stage between strategic defense and the strategic offensive, which would lead to the inevitable revolutionary triumph. With this declaration, Shining Path claimed it was now on an equal footing with the armed forces in terms of fighting capability (though not necessarily manpower).

The number of politically motivated deaths increased dramatically in the second half of the García administration, from 2 per day in 1987 to 5.4 per day in 1988, and then to 8.8 and 9.4 per day in 1989 and 1990 respectively.[27] Despite the fact that by the late 1980s over one-third of the national territory had been declared emergency zones, giving the armed forces control over half the Peruvian population, increasing swaths of territory were no longer controlled by the state. This situation grew worse as Shining Path launched an all-out campaign to boycott the municipal elections scheduled for November 1989. In the weeks before the elections, Shining Path assassinated dozens of local elected officials, and each killing prompted waves of resignations by officials and candidates in surrounding areas. In Huancayo, an area technically under the control of the armed forces, Shining Path declared 15 of 36 districts "liberated zones," prompting mayors from 26 districts to resign their posts.[28] By early July, 656 mayors and town council members had been killed, had resigned, or abandoned their posts throughout the country.[29]

State terror proved an ineffective remedy to Shining Path's terror. The democratic counterinsurgency program promised by Alan García never took hold. The military effectively resisted García's efforts to establish a counterinsurgency policy based on human rights and civilian control. García found himself accommodating the military's demands for autonomy and control over counterinsurgency, leading to a return to the counterinsurgency policies of the Belaúnda era. The return to state terror only exacerbated the situation of political violence, further alienated citizens at large from the state, and contributed to the growing crisis of public authority. With the failure of a democratic counterinsurgency, nondemocratic strategies emerged within the armed forces to deal with the growing crisis of the state and of public security. Chapter eight will examine the emergence of a group within the military that, alarmed by this situation, began to rethink the nature of Peru's counterinsurgency strategy, and began to prioritize intelligence work over more militaristic policies. As reported by Rospigliosi (1996), other sectors began conspiring to carry out a coup d'état in order to launch an all-out war against Shining Path and all opposition movements. In neither case did these sectors prioritize a democratic counterinsurgency policy such as that outlined and then abandoned by García.

But in the meantime, the immediate beneficiary of this dramatic failure of state counterinsurgency policy was Shining Path itself.

CHAPTER FOUR

# The Crisis of Organized Politics

Modern democratic theory posits the relationship between citizen and state as one of positive interaction in which the citizen feels himself or herself represented in the decisions taken at the state level (Dahl 1971). Political parties hold a central place in democratic theory in terms of facilitating this interaction (Lipset and Rokkan 1967; Sartori 1976). With a few exceptions, however, political parties in Latin America have rarely performed this essential function. As a result, the state has often taken the lead in forging mediations from above, either in the form of state corporatism, or via clientelism and patronage polices.[1] Though the early transitions literature tended to underemphasize the importance of political parties as mediating mechanisms between state and society (viewing them instead as mechanisms of social control to moderate social demands during delicate transition processes; O'Donnell and Schmitter 1986), recent literature has emphasized the difficulties of strengthening democratic governance in societies where political parties remain weak and fragmented (Mainwaring and Scully 1996; Mainwaring and Hagopian 2005). Indeed, establishing effective mediating mechanisms is essential to democratic governance, since it is through such linkages that the state accrues legitimacy and provides a basis for governing.

As Peru made its transition from authoritarianism to civilian rule in 1980, a plethora of new political parties emerged that structured political life and seemed to offer the promise of establishing new modes of linking state and society at the local, regional, and national level. In particular, the populist APRA party and the IU coalition, which came to dominate politics in the 1980s, seemed to offer the hope that these parties would help bridge the historic gap between state and society. Indeed, it was argued that APRA and IU represented a new "democratic consensus" around the center-left in Peru (Sanborn 1991). In the case of APRA, the election of Alan García to the presidency in 1985 elicited great expectations. The historical exclusion of APRA from formal politics, its history as Peru's oldest mass-based party, and García's promises to improve the lot of the poor majority, all seemed to indicate a new period of popular incorporation into the political system. The IU, while never in power at the national level, was active in congress and in municipal and regional governments throughout Peru in the 1980s. Its discourse of social change and popular participation—as well as its historic links with a variety of social movements dating back to the struggle against the Morales Bermúdez regime— also inspired hope in the possibility of forging new forms of popular representation and strengthening democratic rule. In particular, the Left's links with social movements and organizations in Lima's *barriadas* and in the countryside were, some argued, creating new, more democratic modes of political participation that stood in sharp contrast to the clientelism that traditionally dominated state-society relations.

The growing economic crisis and the subsequent collapse of the state in the final years of the García regime described in earlier chapters crippled APRA's ability to represent popular interests. On the one hand, the party lost all credibility in the face of its inability to revert the political and economic crisis and massive corruption scandals involving high-ranking party members; on the other, the fiscal crisis of the state undermined the social programs it had been implementing to reach out to social groups, particularly in the *barriadas* of Lima. The IU suffered a similar crisis of confidence, partly because it was never able to move beyond its opposition stance to develop concrete alternatives to the APRA regime and the looming crisis, and partly because of the growing internal conflicts that in 1989 tore the electoral coalition apart. The crucial links between state and society began falling apart, and with them popular confidence in democratic institutions and in the state itself.

This chapter will briefly analyze the evolution of Peru's political party system from the transition in 1980 to its virtual collapse in the early 1990s. It will examine the way in which these two political groupings structured society, how these interactions undermined autonomous action on the part of civil society, and how these relationships were affected by the economic and political crisis that set in after 1987. The inability of the political parties to devise concrete and viable alternatives to the economic crisis, the growing political violence, and the disintegration of the state fundamentally undermined popular confidence in elected representatives.

The ramifications of the collapse of political parties in Peru are numerous; for the purposes of this analysis, two stand out. First, the collapse of the party system destroyed one of the principal bridges between state and society in Peru in the 1980s. Despite the fact, as will be suggested later in this chapter, that those linkages often resembled the old-style clientelism of the past more than modern exchanges between parties and constituents, APRA and IU raised widespread hopes among the urban and rural poor that their needs and interests would finally be taken into account by politicians and, by extension, the state. With the collapse of these two parties (and of the Right, which despite a brief resurrection after the 1987 bank nationalizations, was already severely discredited), the gap between state and society became a gaping chasm.

Second, the collapse of the parties contributed to a retreat of organized politics. Social movements once linked to the IU or APRA now found themselves without political interlocutors. Often, these organizations turned inward, focusing on survival strategies and obviating more political forms of struggle, a process exacerbated by the economic crisis. In some instances, more radical elements linked to these parties looked to organized insurgent movements to channel their energies and demands.

This collapse of organized politics fundamentally imperiled Peruvian democracy. New actors sought to fill the resulting political vacuum, actors whose attachment to democratic rules and procedures was questionable and in many cases nonexistent. In the no-man's land left in the wake of the collapse of the party system, "independent" politicians were elected into office, first in the 1989 municipal elections and then in the 1990 presidential elections, who often acted in ways counter to the democratic rules of the game. At the local level, where political parties retreated from their earlier organizing activities, Shining Path exploited this vacuum, challenging state authority and building local support for its revolutionary war against the state.

## Clientelism to Corporatism and Back Again

Parties in Peru have historically played a weak role in organizing public space. The oligarchy systematically repressed attempts by APRA, Peru's historic mass-based party, to make inroads into the political system (Bonilla and Drake 1989). As a result, the state played a preponderant role in organizing social life, primarily using clientelism and repression to keep social unrest at bay (Cotler 1978a). The breakdown of these traditional mechanisms of domination were increasingly evident by the mid-1960s, as a series of rising protests, particularly in the countryside, fed elite fears of revolution from below.

This was the impetus behind the military intervention in 1968, an effort to head off any revolutionary alternative by implementing reforms from above and establishing a more solid basis of state authority in Peru. The failure of the corporatist experiment of General Velasco and the groundswell of popular mobilization demanding democratization and economic reform during the second phase of the military government in the late 1970s seemed to provide further evidence of the erosion of such traditional modes of domination. Rather than safely channeling popular unrest into state-chartered organizations, Velasco's reforms instead provided a broad basis for organizational autonomy for the labor movement, neighborhood and peasant organizations, and left-wing political parties (Tovar 1985; Stokes 1995). The convergence between the new unionism—with its militant ideology of *clasismo* (classism)—and an increasingly combative urban popular movement, coupled with the growth of the

New Left parties and progressive segments of the Catholic Church, seemed to be laying the ground for a counterhegemonic project to the old oligarchic state and to the military's corporatist experiment based on democratic modes of grassroots organization (Stokes 1995). The vast and growing grassroots organization of late 1970s and early 1980s captured the imagination of many observers, who saw in these movements a new way of "doing politics" (Ballón 1986). The practices of these new movements, it was argued, challenged the authoritarianism and elitism of traditional politics in Peru and would promote the democratization of society and politics. For example, Degregori et al. (1986) suggested that the emergence of neighborhood organizations, community kitchens, mothers' groups, and other local associational networks in Lima's *barriadas*, combined with the growing electoral presence of the IU in the early 1980s, was creating horizontal links between and among social groups and their political representatives that would undermine the "baseless triangle" that typified the segmented incorporation of Peruvian society by the state described by Cotler (1978a).

But by end of the decade Peru had witnessed a dramatic reduction of the public sphere. Expanding political violence and the collapse of the economy fueled the breakdown of state authority and further widened the gap between state and society. Political representation in such circumstances is difficult if not impossible: the growing chasm between state and society undermines any sense of political community and hence adherence to concept of citizenship, which democratic theorists view as essential to democracy (Dahl 1971, 1990).

Moreover, the parties that dominated the political scene in the 1980s continued to be structured along authoritarian lines, undermining their ability to democratically represent social interests. After Peru's transition, democratic leaders did not implement legislation to promote greater internal democracy and transparency within political parties. APRA, a populist and "catch-all" party, continued to be organized around the predominant role of the "*jefe máximo*" or "maximum leader." The same was true for the most part with the multiple parties in the IU coalition, which was based on the vertical and vanguardist principles of Leninism in which the intellectual-leader "knows best." Despite their ideological and organizational differences, in practice, both APRA and IU tended to rely on clientelism and patronage to build support within society (Cotler 1988). Other state reforms were also not forthcoming, such that access to state power, be it local or national, continued to provide party leaders with access to largesse to build the party faithful and, sometimes, for private enrichment. In such politicized states, the stakes for control of public office are extremely high, as party leaders view state monies and government positions as favors to be dispensed to party loyalists and as a way to attract new constituencies. Such practices, which often result in the creation of patronage and clientelistic networks, do not support a politics based on negotiation and consensus building, but rather reinforce mistrust among political parties and undermine chances for the consolidation of the party system (Chalmers 1977). The political culture of the politicized state hence impedes the creation of a public sphere, which is essential to democratic politics and the consolidation of citizenship.

The weakness of social groups meant that there was little pressure from below to demand greater responsiveness on the part of political parties and other institutions to social demands (Grompone 1991). It would be a mistake to ignore the demands from the rank and file of the parties for greater internal democracy and participation, as Pásara (1988) notes, but in general, demands from below were weak and poorly articulated, generally insufficient to prompt any real process of democratization of political structures. The image is one of parties floating above a weak civil society, with a number of top-down but ultimately weak linkages based primarily on clientelistic ties. This contributed to factionalism within local communities, as groups competed among themselves to obtain access to scarce resources, and as parties vied with one another to obtain control over different social groups by providing them with material assistance that would assure their loyalty. In a recursive cycle, hierarchical parties sought to organize society according to their own needs, further exacerbating the weakness of civil society and bolstering what Grompone (1991) refers to as the "hyperautonomy" of political society. This makes representation and interest mediation extremely difficult, and as a result political parties are seen as increasingly ineffective in resolving the daily problems of the population. As key mediators between state and society, the growing disdain for political parties would reinforce and exacerbate the growing crisis of the state.

## The Rise and Fall of Populism

In the context of declining living standards, growing popular unrest, and a general sense of governmental incompetence during the Belaúnde administration, Alan García, a young and charismatic APRA leader, was elected president in 1985. García had assiduously constructed his leadership within APRA by distancing himself from the old guard leadership and seeking to represent a broad-based alliance that would for the first time bring Peru's oldest mass-based party to power. García articulated a new vision of the party in which the business elite, the military, and technocrats would join forces to carry out important reforms. He appealed to the business elite by promising economic reactivation, while appealing to Peru's poorest sectors by promising a reduction in debt payments in order free government money to improve living conditions. Society, in his view, was disorganized and disarticulated; the "disposable masses" could be easily brought into a ruling coalition by offering them concrete material benefits and symbolic gestures of appeal (García 1989). García won with 53 percent of the vote, compared to 25 percent won by Alfonso

Barrantes, the IU mayor of Lima. Belaúnde's AP won 7 percent of the vote (Tuesta 1994).

García's personal charisma was central to his electoral victory and the immense popularity he enjoyed during his first few years in office. His weekly speeches from the balcony of the Government Palace were gestures that sought to directly link the popular masses to his personae as the ultimate representative of the nation-state (Cotler 1988; Grompone 1991). A constitutional clause permitting congress to delegate legislative faculties to the president allowed García to concentrate power in the hands of the executive, a hallmark of delegative democracy (O'Donnell 1994). García had a highly personalistic leadership style, relying on the advice of a few loyalists rather than the party apparatus, which generated tensions within APRA that would come back to haunt García.

García believed that to create a more stable and enduring political coalition, APRA had to renovate its alliance with the popular sectors, and that he as leader was more suited to the task than the party apparatus. García thus sought to develop a direct relationship with the masses, bypassing the party and preexisting organizations altogether. This also created tensions within APRA, since it undermined the ability of local bosses and power holders to develop their support networks (Grompone 1991).

García's ideas regarding the popular sectors were rooted in the fact that APRA had few direct links with the urban social struggles of the late 1970s and early 1980s. APRA's influence in the trade union movement had waned as the CGTP, loosely affiliated with the Moscow-line Peruvian Communist Party (PC-Unity), became the dominant labor federation, as the APRA-affiliated labor organization, the Confederation of Peruvian Workers (CTP), dwindled in importance.[2] This helps explain García's focus on the unorganized masses both as a political subject and as the main beneficiary of state programs. He believed that there were greater opportunities for building the party's influence among these sectors than in the urban social movements and the trade unions that had become linked with the parties of the New Left in the late 1970s in the context of the struggle against military rule. But García also observed that the organized movement itself was limited to a small portion of the working classes and the urban poor. Only 17 percent of the economically active population belonged to a trade union, and only 44 percent of active workers received a fixed salary. The vast majority of workers did not belong to a union, and well over half of all workers were informal workers—and they were not integrated into any political coalition, grassroots organization, or political party. These were groups that did not organize or that participated in social organizations only marginally, and on a strictly instrumental basis. In García's view, in the heterogeneous world of Peru's popular sectors, there were no consolidated identities, and therefore no defined political alternatives; only a charismatic leader could reach these groups by providing tangible material benefits and symbolic gestures.

Poor women and migrants were defined as the main social groups that would become the targets of the state's social policy. Through extensive clientelistic networks, the state could bring these sectors into the ruling coalition and assure enduring popular support and loyalty. For poor urban women, the García government formed mothers' clubs; for informal sector workers, it offered low-interest credit; for the unemployed, especially women, it offered temporary work programs (Graham 1992). As Grompone (1991) points out, García's populism sought to base itself on those excluded sectors that had a limited capacity to move from dependency on government handouts to new forms of organizational autonomy. In the logic of the politicized state, those in power provide gifts, not recognition of rights (Chalmers 1977). This would avoid the mistake made by the Velasco regime, which ultimately failed to control the popular support it was mobilizing via corporatist networks and, in fact, had provided social groups with the tools to organize against military domination. Such programs also created government jobs that could be dispensed to party loyalists—which led to a bloating of the state sector and contributed to the fiscal crisis of the state that came to a head in the late 1980s. The temporary job program (PAIT) employed some 4,000 government workers, most of whom were card-carrying members of APRA (Graham 1991). Social policy thus became a means of building support by expanding the party's social base and deepening party loyalties through state patronage (Grompone 1991).

These programs also became useful electoral tools for APRA: assignments and work positions were increased or decreased according to the political necessities of the moment. The PAIT program expanded dramatically, for instance, in the months preceding the 1986 municipal elections that, not surprisingly, were swept by APRA.[3] There was a definitive correlation, moreover, between the number of votes obtained by the IU and the number of PAIT jobs distributed in a given district (Paredes 1988). In other words, the program was more extensive in areas where voting support for the IU was high—a clear effort to win over support from IU to APRA (Graham 1991; Grompone 1991). In Villa El Salvador, for example, tensions between the IU and APRA ran high, as the latter was perceived as using government largesse to buy support and undermine the IU's hold on the district. There was also a sense among IU municipalities that these programs were attempting to address issues better left to local government. Tensions also emerged because these programs tended to disregard or bypass existing social organizations, making them "an affront to the autonomy of the existing kitchens and mothers' clubs" (Graham 1991:99). In Villa El Salvador, open conflicts emerged between autonomous community kitchens linked to the Popular Women's Federation (FEPOMUVES), which was loosely allied with IU in the 1980s, and the mothers' clubs affiliated with the government-funded PAD program. Many preexisting organizations complained that the PAIT disrupted their ability to function by drawing away members.[4] Graham (1991) reports that of the approximately 50 percent of her 23 interviewees who had participated in a mothers' club, the glass of milk program, or a community kitchen, half had ceased to participate after entering the PAIT. One of Graham's informants described that women in the community kitchens who had not entered the PAIT were resentful of those who had joined PAIT and shirked their duties within the community kitchen as a result; declining participation, she said, reduced the effectiveness of the kitchens and disrupted community unity. In effect, the bitter competition for support at the grassroots created antagonisms and divisions within local communities and inhibited more broad-based collective action.

Indeed, competition between APRA and IU undermined the possibilities of building a "democratic consensus" in the mid-1980s. APRA's unceasing efforts to directly compete for popular support in IU strongholds created resentment among many IU activists and local leaders. Though García sought to woo the support of Alfonso Barrantes, the IU mayor of Lima between 1983 and 1986, this only antagonized more radical groups within the IU coalition and undermined support for Barrantes. Both, in effect, reproduced the traditional political *jefe* (chief) model described by Cotler (1988), and though there were counterweights in society, this style of political leadership continued to dominate within APRA as well as IU. García's *concertación* with the so-called twelve apostles—the key business leaders in the country—rather than involving organized labor in tripartite discussions over economic policy also irked the Left. Mistrust of García deepened after the June 1986 prison massacres, in which over 200 Shining Path prisoners who participated in simultaneous uprisings in three Lima prisons were killed by security forces, many after having surrendered (Amnesty International 1987). Combined with what many IU leaders saw as fraudulent municipal elections in 1986, this heightened calls on the part of IU leaders for Barrantes to cease his negotiations with García.

With the failure of García's bank nationalization proposal in 1987, and the onset of hyperinflation and severe fiscal imbalances in 1988, APRA's ability to use state largesse to finance its activities declined dramatically. In September 1988, the government imposed austerity measures in a bet to hedge rapidly growing inflation, marking the end of its heterodox economic program. Efforts to incorporate excluded social groups through social programs and other clientelistic practices were greatly curtailed. The drying up of credit and employment programs—the key linkages between APRA and the popular sectors at this time—meant that thousands of poor women, microenterprise owners, and other beneficiaries of state programs saw their income-earning capacity decline sharply at a time when prices were skyrocketing. This caused deep discontent toward the García regime and APRA in general, particularly given the growing perception of massive government corruption.

In summary, the efforts on the part of the García government to forge direct links between the state and the most marginalized and underpoliticized sectors of the urban and rural poor provided short-term benefits for these sectors while providing popular and electoral support for APRA. These efforts did not incorporate these sectors of society into the governing coalition or a coherent political project, and when state largesse dried up, these linkages dissipated. Because they deliberately bypassed existing neighborhood and community organizations, these government programs generated resentment and competition in low-income districts. As in old-fashioned clientelism, there were no lasting benefits of García's programs: the income gains of 1985 were quickly eroded by the hyperinflation of the 1988–1990 period; many community kitchens and women's clubs that were largely created to receive state benefits dismantled once such benefits were no longer forthcoming, while the autonomous and church-run community kitchens that continued to organize faced the problem of dwindling resources; and those who depended on PAIT for income were left with nothing once the program was virtually eliminated in 1988. Those sectors of the marginalized poor who once found themselves being courted by APRA with a plethora of social programs and opportunities to work, obtain credit, or participate in rallies and other government-sponsored events were left suddenly on their own to negotiate the economic crisis.

### The New Left: The Paradoxes of Success

One of the most notable changes in Peruvian politics in the 1980s was the consolidation of the Peruvian Left as a national political force. The Communist Party was active in Peruvian politics dating back to the 1930s, but its dogmatism and its inability to successfully compete on organizational terms with APRA made it a marginal force in the decades that followed (Cotler 1978a). New groups began to emerge within the Left in the 1960s as a result of the influence of the Sino-Soviet split and the Cuban Revolution. While their development was temporarily stalled with the installation of the Velasco military regime in 1968, the reforms of this period facilitated the emergence of New Left parties by providing organizational opportunities to trade unions and urban social movements (Nieto 1983). While the PC-Unity supported Velasco's reformist efforts, the New Left parties were more skeptical of the military's top-down attempts at creating social organizations to build political support for its reforms.[5] Indeed, most observers agree that the resistance of social groups to Velasco's corporatist intentions—and the rise of increasingly autonomous and radical forms of social mobilization—was one of the principal factors in the ultimate demise of the so-called first phase of the military regime.[6]

As the military retreated from supporting social movements after 1975, the New Left parties, which were active in the trade unions, peasant communities, and Lima's *barriadas*, were well poised to fill the gap. Indeed, these parties became closely involved in the grassroots mobilizations and struggles against economic austerity and increasing government repression that characterized the Morales Bermúdez regime. While the New Left in fact comprised an amalgam of small parties with different and often diverging ideological tendencies, they played an important role in the organization of a series of general strikes and popular protests between 1977 and 1979, which played an important role in prompting the armed forces to turn power over to a civilian government (Tovar 1985; Stokes 1995).

The New Left parties initially believed that these mobilizations would usher in a period of revolutionary change. In fact, the military retained tight control over the transition process to assure that the return to democratic rule would occur in an orderly manner and without upsetting the entrenched prerogatives of the armed forces (Lynch 1992; Mauceri 1997). Popular discontent was largely channeled into an institutional context with the regime's call for elections for a constituent assembly in 1978 and presidential and parliamentary elections in 1980. Despite their ambivalence toward representative democracy, most left-wing groups, sensing the popular mood in favor of elections, decided to participate in the electoral process, but they primarily saw this as a tactical resource to improve their position vis-à-vis other groups[7] (Nieto 1983). The Left parties made a distinction between "formal" democracy (i.e., elections) and social or "real" democracy, a distinction that would shape the Left's ambivalent relationship to political democracy in the course of the 1980s.[8] Their ambivalence notwithstanding, the Left emerged as a significant force in Peruvian politics, winning a stunning combined 30 percent of the vote in the 1978 constitutional assembly elections.[9] Trotskyist Hugo Blanco was the third-most voted candidate in the constitutional assembly.

As the 1980 presidential elections drew near, attempts to unify the Left so as to improve its electoral chances collapsed. The fragmentation of the Left proved disastrous: the combined vote for the Left parties was a meager 14 percent. This fueled renewed efforts to build an electoral coalition for the November 1980 municipal elections, leading to the formation of the IU under the leadership of a lawyer from Cajamarca, Alfonso Barrantes. The IU showing improved in the municipal elections—the first held in the country's history thanks to reforms introduced by the new Belaúnde government. In Lima, the IU won 28.3 percent of the valid vote, second to AP's 34.7 percent, and far ahead of the PPC's 20.6 percent and APRA's 16.4 percent, winning a total of 5 of 39 districts.[10] Nationally, the IU held its second-place position at 23.3 percent, compared to 35.8 percent for AP, 22.5 percent for APRA, and 11.1 percent for the PPC.[11] The Left's strong showing convinced its member parties of the utility of continuing to participate in electoral politics, though many retained an ambiguous view of democracy, as we shall see below.

In 1983, in the context of the economic crisis and perceived ineptitude of the Belaúnde regime, the IU swept the municipal elections in Lima. Barrantes was elected mayor of Lima, and the coalition won 20 of 41 districts in Lima.[12] In the 1985 presidential elections, Barrantes came in second to Alan García, consolidating the IU as the second-most important electoral force in the country.[13] The IU lost ground to APRA in the 1986 municipal elections, losing 11 municipalities, in part because of the enormous popularity of Alan García, but it remained a significant electoral and political force.[14] As the García regime saw its popularity decline precipitously with the onset of an economic recession and hyperinflation, the IU became the early front-runner for the 1990 elections. Voting patterns in Peru tended to follow class cleavages, and the trend of popular sector voting from 1980 to 1986 for IU and APRA seemed to signal a shift in Peruvian politics toward a center-left democratic consensus (Sanborn 1991). But what seemed like the forging of enduring political identities along the center-left of the political spectrum would prove to be an ephemeral phenomenon by the end of the decade. The following section will examine the factors that help explain the dramatic demise of one of the strongest Left movements in Latin America.

### Social Movements, Popular Participation, and the United Left

In its claim to represent Peru's popular sectors, the IU proposed a vaguely defined model of popular participation as a grassroots democratic alternative to more traditional clientelistic and corporatist modes of social and political organization. The two constituent elements of the Left's vision were participation in local self-government—and not just in elections every few years—and cogovernment between local government and popular organizations. Yet the Left's ability to forge radically alternative modes of representing its constituents did not vary that much from the traditional style of clientelism that has dominated modern Peruvian politics. While there were some interesting experiments in popular participation—most notably the self-managing district of Villa El Salvador, which will be examined in chapter seven—in general, the Left's relationship to social organizations remained tenuous and instrumental. The Left faced a series of challenges as it became an active participant in Peruvian democracy that help explain this difficulty in realizing its alternative model of representation and interaction with the popular sectors.[15]

One of the defining characteristics of the Left's participation in democratic institutions in the posttransition period was a marked ambiguity toward democracy itself. As Rochabrún (1988) has noted, the Left did not "conquer" democracy, in the sense that democracy was not the primary goal or objective of the Left in the transition period. Long wary of parliamentary forms as a tool used by elites to ensure their hold on power, the Peruvian Left believed that revolution was the only way to implant "true"—that is, social—democracy in Peru. During the period of popular protests against the Morales Bermúdez regime, it was the Right that made the first call for elections—a move that the Left interpreted as a tactical maneuver on the part of the country's elites to retain power at the expense of the masses (Nieto 1983). The PC-Unity, for example, criticized the call for elections as reactionary—the "siren's song" of the Right[16]—preferring instead to maintain and deepen the revolutionary process initiated by Velasco. While the New Left parties—the Revolutionary Communist Party (PCR), Revolutionary Vanguard (VR), Red Fatherland, and the Revolutionary Left Movement (MIR)—were opposed to the military regime, they did not posit democracy as an alternative because they saw in the growing radicalism of the masses the possibility of a "true" revolutionary transformation under their tutelage.[17] The path was thus open for the Right to lead the struggle against the military and to guide the transition to civilian rule (Nieto 1983).

The military's proposal to hold elections for a constitutional assembly in 1978 to initiate the transition process forced the Left to confront whether it should participate. Sensing the mood in favor of elections, the majority of New Left parties decided to do so, but this decision was not based on a programmatic belief in the importance of democratic institutions; rather, the Left approached the elections in an instrumental manner. Participating in the elections was a tactical maneuver for the Left to better position itself for the return to civilian rule and to gain a piece of the electoral pie. The Left remained critical of political, or "formal," democracy, which was counterposed to social, or "real," democracy[18] (Nieto 1983; Pásara 1988).

The Left's electoral success in the 1980 general elections and the 1981 and 1983 municipal elections made it a significant actor in Peruvian democracy. Participation in democratic institutions faced the Peruvian Left with many challenges in terms of its political practices and beliefs. The parties within the IU, which had little tradition of cooperative interaction, were obliged to negotiate with each other over decisions in congress and in local government. How leftist parties interacted with their constituents also began to change. During military rule, the measure of a party's "representativeness," and hence its strength, vis-à-vis other parties was intimately linked to which and how many trade unions or social movements it controlled (Grompone 1991). Under democratic rule, representation became a question of how the Left responded to its constituents' basic needs and demands, particularly at the municipal level. This process led many sectors of the IU to embrace democratic institutions and to believe in the possibility of reforms and social change within the framework of democratic institutions. Alfonso Barrantes, the architect of the IU, headed this sector. Barrantes lacked organizational backing of his own—part of the reason it was he who was able to bring the different leftist parties together in the IU coalition in the first place. Nevertheless he was a favorite among the important and growing group of independents, who were affiliated to the IU but were not members of a specific political party. He also had broad popular appeal among the urban poor, which helped him win the 1983 mayoral elections in Lima.

More radical groups within the front, however, maintained a more ambiguous attitude toward democracy. This was most evident within the United Mariateguista Party (PUM) and the Maoist alliance National

Union of the Revolutionary Left (UNIR), the two parties with the strongest links to urban and rural popular movements. PUM and UNIR tended to adopt an instrumental approach to participation in Peru's nascent democratic institutions, although there were sharp discrepancies within these parties over this conceptualization of democracy and other related issues.[19] In general, however, these parties saw democracy in instrumental terms. It provided opportunities to strengthen their own organizations and to build up their popular support base toward what they believed would be an eventual process of revolutionary transformation (Pásara 1989, 1990; Roberts 1999).

With its growing popularity at the polls, the IU's social base grew rapidly, surpassing the narrow arenas of influence of each of its member parties. Those who were not active members of the IU parties or as independents within the coalition but who consistently voted for the IU in the 1980s were attracted by the Left's defense of a project based on a commitment to social change and popular participation, but they were also seeking out political allies who would serve as intermediaries between them and the state to obtain a variety of goods and services (Grompone 1991). Some members of the IU responded to such demands by becoming actively involved in providing such services to their constituents. Such practices often came under fire by the more radical sectors of the IU, who charged that such behavior was a form of clientelism or populism that ultimately favored an individual leader's career over the growth of the IU itself. This tension between pragmatism and radicalism within the front revealed profound discrepancies over what kind of relationship the Left should be trying to build with the popular sectors and for what purpose. Such tensions are common in parties that are primarily structured around ideology (Pizzorno 1981). Such parties do not just seek to process and channel social demands, but see themselves as engaged in a process of building socialism, which is the measure of all political actions. This was one of the central tensions at the heart of the IU: some groups were moving away from such a model by embracing democratic institutions and practices, while others believed that such basic tenets were nonnegotiable. This contradiction remained unsolved and would ultimately lead to the division of the front in 1989.

These tensions, which were superimposed on the logic of electoral competition and the existence of personal differences among party elites, would deepen and grow as the economic and political crisis worsened after 1988, with the onset of recession, hyperinflation, and the dramatic expansion of Shining Path and military violence. There were sharp disagreements between the moderate and radical sectors of the IU, for example, over the degree of support the Left should offer the populist government of Alan García. Barrantes, who had been a member of APRA in his youth, had forged a close personal relationship with García that was regarded as near treasonous by the more radical segments of the IU. These disagreements would sharpen as the García regime, departing from its electoral promises to deal with guerrilla movements by attacking the social roots of violence and by respecting human rights, began to rely increasingly on repression to deal with the Shining Path and the MRTA. This was patently notable after the June 1986 prison massacres. As the human rights situation began to deteriorate, it also seemed to confirm the historic mistrust of the state as little more than a repressive agent acting on behalf of the country's elites held by many Left activists (Abugattás 1990). The deepening political and economic crisis that characterized the last half of the García administration led the more radical sectors of the IU to believe that their participation in a decaying regime was a mistake that betrayed the most sacred principles of the Left. For organizations like PUM, the only solution was to construct popular power at the grassroots level, the building blocks of the revolutionary alternative to both representative democracy and the sectarian violence of Shining Path (Roberts 1999).

The organizational structure of the IU exacerbated these tensions. Each party maintained its own internal structure, leadership, and ideological principles, while the coalition was governed by a central committee composed of the secretaries general of each of the member parties. Decision-making capacity remained within each party, not in the front, undermining the possibility for the IU to develop coherent policy initiatives as well as its ability to build social support for the front per se rather than for each member party. As Grompone (1991) suggests, the overwhelming tendency was for the parties to see the front as a means to broadening the Left's social base, but not as an end in itself. This was partly the result of the underlying sectarianism of the Left and the resulting fear on the part of each party that it would lose influence and the ability to retain the support of their party cadre if the IU were to become stronger organizationally. As a result, the constituent members prioritized strengthening their own party organizations at the expense of the front. This meant that the IU would never be anything more than an electoral front, despite the fact that its popularity was such that it could have developed into a more organic organization unto itself. While the member parties of the IU coalition agreed that unity was beneficial in terms of winning elections, building consensus on other more complex matters of policy and interaction with social groups proved much more complex. The way the IU was structured not only made it difficult for the front to consolidate a coherent identity and program, but also fomented nondemocratic practices that ultimately undermined the alliance's links with social movements, contributing to its eclipse as a major political force in Peruvian politics by the early 1990s.

Related to this was the fact that under the cover of the IU electoral alliance, many of the IU's member parties continued to operate along the same Leninist theories of organization and vanguardism that structured their activisim during military rule. While such modes of organization may be well-suited for operating in an authoritarian regime that suppresses the right to association and dissent, they were problematic in a democracy

(Rospigliosi 1988). The clandestine tradition of party organization fomented the rise and persistence of caudillo-style leadership within the Left, a grave problem that impeded party unity and fed the logic of inter-party competition that was already built into the front. This excessive van-guardism had the paradoxical effect of reinforcing the caudillo tradition at a time when the Left was avidly promoting "popular participation" as its principal model of alternative government.[20] The vanguardist tradition permitted greater party cohesion and helped consolidate a cadre of party elite, but this emphasis on individual party organization came at the expense of building the Left's representation at a broader and more inclu-sive level. The resulting distance between the diverse leftist parties and the people prevented the IU from evolving from an organization of party cad-res to a broader-based party with solid roots in society (Rospigliosi 1988; Grompone 1991).

The structure of the IU, then, not only exacerbated interparty compe-tition within the front, but also reinforced the existence of undemocratic modes of interest intermediation. Grompone (1991:180) describes the ten-sion in this way:

> Radicalism helped maintain the cohesion of the party apparatuses, strengthen solidarity among party activists, gave a sense of continuity to the tasks of governing in a moment in which events occur quickly, and finally, it facilitated control over leaders who assumed political responsibilities. However, this maximalist discourse did not permit the left to respond to the aspirations of those sectors of the popular classes that sought alternatives that could be applied in the short term and that had limited political and social costs.

In the logic of trying to solidify political influence with specific groups or organizations, competing left-wing parties sought to monopolize "representation" by creating exclusive links with such organizations, reproducing a style of interaction with the grassroots that had its roots in the Left's Leninist style of organization and that often devolved into old-fashioned clientelism. Because of the weak nature of the political leadership of the front, parties tried to assert their hegemony within the front by demonstrating the strength of their position, which derived from their "representation" of particular organized interests. This fomented intense interparty competition at the grassroots level, leading parties to impose their own logic on social organizations and distorting their natural development (Calderón and Valdeavellano 1991; Grompone 1991). This control for "hegemony" was widespread: the PC-Unity controlled the CGTP, the country's largest labor federation; Red Fatherland controlled the Peruvian Education Workers' Union (SUTEP) and sectors of the student movement, while the different New Left organizations (most notably PUM and UNIR) controlled various trade unions, neighborhood organizations, and peasant associations.

**Figure 4.1**   Police Repress University Student Protest

Police use tear gas to repress a student protest at the National University of San Marcos (1988). Shining Path maintained an active presence in Peru's national universities, as the graffiti on the Law School building in the background attests.

*Source*: Caretas Archive.

Rather than seek broader representation among the totality of workers, peasants, students, or shantytown dwellers, the leftist parties rarely sought to move beyond their traditional small areas of influence (Grompone 1991). Moreover, the fact that some leftist groups controlled state resources through the municipal governments meant they were able to use these resources to their benefit, leading other groups to try to leverage other resources to counter their rivals (Calderón and Valdeavellano 1991). This was the dynamic feeding the growing clientelism and partisan rivalries within the IU—rivalries that often split social movements along party lines and segmented the Left rather than accumulating its forces.[21] In effect, this reproduced the kind of hierarchical segmentation that characterizes Peru's overall political system as described by Cotler (1978a), suggesting the degree to which the Left, rather than develop alternative social and political practices, often reproduced the authoritarian practices of the dominant political system.[22]

The weakness of civil society was also a key factor in the Left's difficulties in expanding its representation of diverse social groups. First, the organizations the IU considered its main interlocutors in civil society—trade unions, neighborhood organizations, peasant associations—were being weakened organizationally due to structural changes in the economy. The persistent economic crisis and the growing informalization of the economy undermined the organizational basis of class-based identities and mobilization (Cameron 1994). The once-militant labor movement had been placed on the defensive with the neoliberal reforms of the Belaúnde period, which cut into worker solidarity, and by the economic crisis in general, which made organizing more difficult (Parodi 1986; Balbi 1997). And while the economic crisis spurred the formation of a vast network of grassroots organizations to cope with the crisis, including community kitchens, mothers' clubs, and neighborhood associations, by the late 1980s a general sense of malaise was setting in, linked to the exhaustion of group members who had been involved for more than a decade in organizing efforts that were supposed to be temporary solutions to economic crisis and unemployment (Burt and Espejo 1995). Paradoxically, then, as the Left's electoral presence was expanding, its social base was disappearing, undermining the ability of such groups to make sustained demands on their political representatives in the Left. The Left became, to paraphrase Grompone (1991), stronger politically but less representative socially as the number of militants grew, but its social influence did not expand with the same level of intensity.

If the autonomous development of civil society is necessary to push political parties to expand their capacity to represent diverse social groups, then movements and organizations that are subject to party directives are likely not to develop autonomously; this in turn makes it unlikely that they will be able to affect changes in the nature of the party structures (Grompone 1991). The weakness of Peruvian civil society in this sense meant that there were few pressures from below encouraging the Left parties to alter their sectarian and elitist practices, as Grompone has noted, though the decision on the part of many grassroots activists to steer clear of party politics, despite their electoral support for the IU, was in part a reaction to the closed and self-absorbed nature of the left-wing parties. This was exacerbated by the Left's vanguardism, which put the parties at the center of politics and underemphasized the importance of social representation (Grompone 1991).

### Division and the Eclipse of the Left

The tensions within the Left had come to a head by 1988. The IU's first congress was to be held that year, but a series of complications delayed its realization until January 1989. The García regime was in a complete state of disarray; incoherent policy initiatives had set off a hyperinflationary spiral that was cutting into living standards, while the Shining Path viewed the growing chaos as a unique opportunity to expand its power to the capital city, Lima. This scenario faced the Left with a difficult situation. The moderate factions within the IU believed that the only response was to buttress the democratic regime through a national accord that addressed the multiple political, economic, and social crises facing the country. The radical sectors, including an important sector of PUM, interpreted the deepening crisis as evidence of the failure of the democratic regime and argued that attempts to salvage it or seek power within it were doomed to failure (Roberts 1999). The polarizing effect of the Shining Path in this process is often underappreciated by analysts of the Peruvian Left.[23] More moderate sectors moved to the political center in an effort to distinguish themselves from Shining Path, while the presence of the Maoists in base-level organizations exerted a radicalizing effect on groups such as PUM. This was evident in written documents by the more radical groups in the IU coalition, their public discourse, and some of their political practices (Pásara 1990, Roberts 1999).

Another critical dimension of the IU's internal divisions centered on the question of whether to support Alfonso Barrantes as the coalition's presidential candidate in the 1990 elections. For moderates, a Barrantes candidacy would attract support amongst centrist and independent voters and carry the IU to the presidential palace. Radical parties within the IU had long-standing qualms about Barrantes' centrism, and they specifically opposed his proposal of a broad-based front to save Peru's fledgling democratic institutions from the onslaught of the economic crisis and Shining Path's violence. Other more long-standing conflicts underlie the split, however, including personal rivalries, different visions of political democracy, strategies for achieving social change, and attitudes vis-à-vis Shining Path (Pásara 1989).

The IU's first congress was inaugurated with much fanfare in January 1989. Its objective was to democratize the front and address some of the problems outlined above, particularly the division among the different parties and leaders. Over 400 district and provincial elected representatives participated in the congress, under the motto of "one militant, one vote" to promote the democratic election of leaders (Pease 1994). But the persisting division over moderates and radicals finally tore the front apart in the aftermath of the congress, as a group of moderates formally abandoned the IU and formed the Socialist Left (IS), headed by Barrantes. This did not, however, resolve the polarization within the front, largely because the IU's most important party, PUM, was increasingly wracked with internal differences. The split between moderates (*Zorros*) and radicals (*Libios*) within PUM, which largely followed similar divisions within the IU between moderates and radicals, continued to exert a polarizing effect on the front.

The division of the Left deeply affected the social legitimacy of both groups, which were badly defeated in the November 1989 municipal elections and the 1990 presidential elections. An independent outsider, media personality Ricardo Belmont, won the mayorship of Lima, and the number of IU-held municipalities dropped to an all-time low: from a high of 20 in 1983 to 9 in 1986, and 7 in 1989. This was a foreshadowing of the trends to come: in 1990, an independent and relatively unknown engineer, Alberto Fujimori, won the presidential elections, and membership in a political party became the biggest liability to getting elected to public office in Peru. In 1993, for example, Obras, Belmont's independent "party," won 22 districts, while other independent candidates won 13 districts. IU did not win a single district in Lima, and neither did APRA; of the other parties, PPC won five and AP won three.[24] The Left's combined showing in the presidential elections was 11 percent—far below the 25–30 percent of the vote it had obtained throughout the 1980s.[25] These inroads by independents reflect the growing distance between political parties and the daily problems of declining incomes, insecurity, and scarcity facing society. Socialist intellectual Alberto Flores Galindo (1989), in a scathing critique of the behavior of the leftist parties, called attention to the Left's widespread mistaken belief that it had a captive voting bloc in the rural and urban poor. Unless the Left truly represented the interests of these sectors, he argued, it would continue to suffer electoral defeat. Unfortunately, the Left seemed immobilized and unable to learn from its past mistakes. It has since ceased to be a relevant political force in Peruvian politics.

By 1990, Peru was on the verge of collapse, with political parties on the run and civil society severely fragmented. In the wake of the collapse of organized politics and the dramatic decline of public authority, two deeply authoritarian political projects flourished: the Shining Path guerrilla movement and the neoliberal authoritarianism of Alberto Fujimori. The next section of the book explores the ways in which Shining Path exploited the crisis of public authority and organized politics by examining the insurgent group's dramatic expansion in Lima. The final section of the book will examine how this process facilitated the emergence and consolidation of the Fujimori regime in the 1990s.

# PART 2

# Gray Zones and Guerrillas: Shining Path and the Battle of Lima

# CHAPTER FIVE

## *The Iron Belts of Misery*

*Lima and the surrounding* barriadas *[shantytowns] are the scenario in which the final battle of the popular war will be defined.*

El Diario, July 1992

One summer morning in early 1988, several hundred workers gathered in Lima's Plaza Dos de Mayo to participate in a national strike called by Peru's largest trade union federation, the CGTP, to protest government austerity programs and spiraling inflation.[1] The political impact of the strike was minimal, especially in comparison to the dramatic national strikes that a decade ago helped bring down the military regime of General Francisco Morales Bermúdez; after several years of economic recession, factory closings and antilabor legislation, trade unionism in Peru had lost much of its political clout.[2] It was the presence of several dozen members of the Maoist guerrilla organization, the Communist Party of Peru (PCP-SL), better known as Shining Path, at the CGTP strike, and their attempts to radicalize the protest, that made this strike remarkable. Shining Path activists disrupted the gathering with shouts of "Long live the popular war!" and "Long live President Gonzalo!" (President Gonzalo is the nom de guerre of Shining Path leader Abimael Guzmán). They launched harsh criticisms of the CGTP and their allies in the IU electoral coalition for their "revisionist" politics. Later in the day, they tossed a handful of dynamite sticks at the CGTP locale, creating panic amongst the protesters and causing the crowd to disperse.

This marked the first time since the Maoist guerrillas declared their "revolutionary" war on the Peruvian state in 1980 that they made a public appearance at a national strike called by the CGTP.[3] In fact, Shining Path had consistently denounced such measures as instances of "trade union consciousness" and openly refused to participate in the eight national strikes called by the CGTP since the late 1970s. Participation in the 1988 strike marked an even more significant turning point in Shining Path's overall strategy for seizing state power. Since it declared its "prolonged popular war" against the Peruvian state in 1980, the Maoist organization had focused its military and political activities in Peru's rural hinterlands.

But in a 1988 interview Abimael Guzmán noted the strategic importance of the capital city for Shining Path's ultimate objective of seizing state power (Guzmán 1988).

Few observers thought Shining Path would fare well in the capital city, since the movement originated and thrived in areas remote from the centers of power. By 1990 and 1991, it was evident that Shining Path had established a significant presence in Lima, particularly in the immense *barriadas*,[4] or urban shantytowns, that encircle the city. How then did Shining Path make inroads into Lima? What role did the collapse of public authority in the late 1980s play in this process? What was the impact of this expansion of the insurgency into Lima for civil society? This section of the book will explore these questions with the objective of better understanding the microfoundations of political violence in urban Peru. This chapter examines the process of urbanization in Peru and the growing importance of the city in the national imaginary. It then explores the Shining Path's urban strategy, and the specific role of Lima's *barriadas* in Shining Path's larger revolutionary strategy, to better understand the contentious process of struggle for control of Lima and the poor *barriadas* surrounding the city.

Chapter six describes the methods deployed by Shining Path to develop its presence in Lima's *barriadas*. The Shining Path's use of intimidation and violence against its opponents, and as a means to establish control over given areas, has been well documented. Less attention has been paid to the Shining Path's efforts to construct grassroots political support, particularly in urban areas, which the data suggest were not insignificant. Drawing on ethnographic research in Lima's *barriadas* as well as archival research, this chapter documents the specific mechanisms Shining Path deployed to cultivate popular support in urban Peru. I explore the context in which these mechanisms were deployed—the retreat of the state and the crisis of organized politics, which structured political opportunities for Shining Path to build local bases of support—as well as the specific strategies used by Shining Path to build popular support in the city.

In Chapter seven, I engage these issues in greater depth through an ethnographic case study of Shining Path activity in one *barriada*, Villa El Salvador. For Shining Path, Villa El Salvador was an important area to control not only because of its geopolitical importance, but also because it represented a model of peaceful social change championed by the democratic Left, and as such represented an obstacle to the development of Shining Path's project of violent revolution. The fact that Shining Path made significant inroads into Villa El Salvador is significant precisely for this reason. The chapter documents Shining Path's political activities in the district as well as its use of violence to advance its presence and eliminate rivals. It also explores the valiant efforts of local community organizers and municipal authorities to resist Shining Path's incursions, which often had fatal consequences.

## Urbanization and the Growth of the *Barriadas*

Sixty years ago, Peru was a predominantly agrarian society. While in 1940, only 3 in 10 Peruvians lived in urban areas, by 1980, 7 in 10 Peruvians were urban dwellers. The process of modernization and capitalist development, coupled with the decline of rural society, induced a long-term pattern of rural-to-urban migration in the late 1940s that has converted Peru into an eminently urban society and Lima into an immense metropolis. Other factors contributed to the process of urbanization, including the perception of declining opportunities, both in terms of access to basic services and overall life chances, in the countryside, and perceived growing opportunities in the city. A city of 500,000 in 1940, by 1961 Lima had 1,846,000 inhabitants, reflecting a 5 percent annual growth rate. In the early 1990s Lima was estimated to have 6 million inhabitants, roughly a third of Peru's total population.[5] In the 1980s, political violence was also an important factor fueling migration from rural to urban areas, as families and sometimes entire communities sought to escape the ravages of violence for the relative safety of the city (Kirk 1991).

This explosive growth rate in Peru's capital meant an increased demand for housing. Initially, migrants moved into existing popular districts in central Lima. These areas, which became known as *tugurios* (inner city slums), were quickly and densely urbanized, and landlords had little incentive to improve the rapidly deteriorating conditions of these run-down buildings. The doubling of family units placed additional pressure on these areas, creating demand for new forms of housing. This gave rise to the first wave of land invasions in the late 1940s, primarily in the eastern part of Lima, strategically located near the Distributors' Market, the center of commercial activity, and the expanding industrial belt along Avenida Argentina (Driant 1991).

A true demographic explosion occurred in the 1960s, with Lima doubling in size between 1961 and 1972 from 1.8 to 3.3 million inhabitants.[6] With housing in the central areas no longer adequate to meet growing demand, land invasions began to spill over the traditional demarcations of Lima into the vast unoccupied desert to the north and south of the city (Riofrío 1978). This second stage of the growth of the *barriadas* was marked by massive and organized invasions by city slum dwellers, including migrants from the countryside and Limeños.[7] These invasions usually took place on state-owned land, though these lands were usually peripheral to the urbanized center of Lima and were far from any locus of economy activity. Because of the massiveness of the invasions, and the government's lack of an alternative solution to rapidly increasing housing demands, the state often had little choice but to allow the squatters to stay, although invasions of private land were usually violently repressed.[8] Squatters were then left on their own to build their own homes, and had to organize residents and mobilize protests to obtain basic services like water and electricity. The state's laissez-faire policy toward the invasions allowed it to channel popular discontent while exonerating it from forging a coherent urban housing policy[9] (Driant 1991). Squatters also provided state elites with an opportunity to secure votes through clientelistic arrangements, such as the promise of land titles or other needed goods.

These areas—known traditionally as *barriadas* and more recently as *pueblos jóvenes* (young towns)—generally lack basic infrastructure (water, electricity, sewage, public transport, health and educational facilities, etc.), and community residents have alternatively mobilized to demand basis services from the government, and pooled local resources to provide some services themselves on a self-help basis. The growth of Lima's *barriadas* has been dramatic over the past 25 years. In 1961, some 316,000 people lived in the *barriadas*, about 17 percent of the overall population. By 1981, 1.5 million people, nearly a third of Lima's population, lived in Lima's *barriadas*. A decade later 3–3.5 million Limeños—about half of the capital's total population—lived in *barriadas*.[10]

## Lima: The Final Battleground

For Shining Path, this large—and growing—population of urban poor concentrated in Lima's *barriadas* was fertile terrain to build a support base for its revolution. In a 1988 interview, Shining Path's principal leader, Abimael Guzmán, signaled that the time had come for the Maoist organization to increase its presence in Lima, the capital of Peru and home to a third of the country's inhabitants. The development of the "prolonged popular war" in the countryside, he reasoned, had progressed to the point that it was time to prepare the ground for the urban insurrection that would lead to Shining Path's seizure of state power. Key to establishing a foothold in Lima was gaining control over the enormous *barriadas* that ringed the city and housed nearly half of the capital's population, forming what Guzmán called the "iron belts of misery" from which the poor would rise up against their "bureaucratic-capitalist oppressors" (Guzmán 1988). As Shining Path's newspaper, *El Diario*, noted in July 1992, "Lima and the surrounding shantytowns are the scenario in which the final battle of the popular war will be defined."

Lima's *barriadas* were thus central to Shining Path's overall revolutionary strategy in geopolitical terms. While Shining Path had adopted Maoist principles of rural guerrilla warfare, Guzmán argued that decades of urbanization required a modification of Mao's strategy of encircling the city from the countryside. For Guzmán, the dense concentration of population in the capital city gave it greater importance in the intermediate and final stages of the seizure of state power. In Guzmán's conceptualization of the "prolonged popular war," guerrilla forces would encircle the capital from a series of concentric circles emanating from the countryside; the *barriadas* were key in this regard, as they were strategically positioned around the very heart of Lima (Guzmán 1988). Thus the original Maoist strategy of rural-based warfare must incorporate the city as an equal strategic component.[11]

Since the mid-1980s, Shining Path had been building up its presence in the departments surrounding Lima, including Junín to the east, and the Norte Chico and the Sur Chico regions to the north and south of the capital within the department of Lima (McCormick 1992). Controlling Lima's *barriadas* was the next crucial step to encircling Lima. The transition to "strategic equilibrium"—the crucial stage before the final strategic offensive, which would presumably lead to the final offensive and the seizure of state power—required political, if not territorial, control over key populations in Lima, particularly the *barriadas*. Control over these areas would give Shining Path control over travel routes to the north and south via the Pan-American Highway, and to the east along the Central Highway, the main route to Lima's breadbasket and the center of hydraulic and energy resources as well as crucial export earnings, principally mining. With control over the the immense ring of shantytowns surrounding Lima, Shining Path would be positioned to isolate the capital city from the rest of the country. In Shining Path's view, the situation of economic deprivation and social marginalization of *barriada* residents made them natural allies in the revolutionary struggle to overthrow the bureaucratic-capitalist state. If *barriada* residents did not support the popular war, it was, according to Shining Path, because they had been duped by government promises or by the revisionism of the legal Left. In time this would put the Maoists on a direct collision course with grassroots organizations in Lima's *barriadas* as well as the leftist parties of the IU.

### State Retreat and the Maoist Push into Lima

Until 1988, Shining Path's visible activities in Lima were limited to armed attacks primarily directed against government officials and members of the security forces, and sabotage of economic infrastructure and symbols of government authority. There were, however, important levels of underground organizing going on, especially in public universities (McCormick 1992). The first important increase in Shining Path military activity in Lima occurred between 1984 and 1986, when their actions in the capital nearly doubled. The number of actions dropped for the next two years, probably as a result of the prison massacres in June 1986 in which over 200 Shining Path cadre were killed, most after having already surrendered to security forces. Guerrilla attacks in Lima began to pick up again in 1989 and 1990, and nearly doubled between 1990 and 1991, while armed actions in the rest of the country diminished only slightly. In 1990, Shining Path carried out 903 armed attacks in rural areas and 395 in Lima, while in 1991 it carried out 826 and 789 attacks respectively.[12]

The CGTP strike in 1988 was one of the first examples of open activity by Shining Path in Lima. It also marked the first time that the Maoists supported a national strike called by the CGTP and attempted to influence its outcome, indicating what would later become an open push to radicalize the labor movement and other popular struggles as part of their logic of furthering the cause of the "popular war." The 1988 launching of *El Diario*, a weekly newspaper, was a key element of this strategy. The paper, professing an openly pro–Shining Path line, began to appear in kiosks on the streets of Lima, covering labor disputes and events in Lima's *barriadas*. *El Diario* printed harsh invectives against Shining Path's enemies, ranging from the "fascistoide" government and the "genocidal" armed forces to the "parliamentary cretins" of the IU. More importantly, the newspaper began to openly champion popular causes such as land invasions and protest marches, claiming that the growing "combativity" of "the masses" reflected the "advancement" of the revolutionary cause. More often than not, however, these protests responded to local conditions and were neither controlled nor directed by Shining Path.

Subsequent incursions by Shining Path into other organized protests in Lima in the months following the CGTP strike revealed the organization's new emphasis on urban politics. Following a strategy developed in the countryside over the previous decade, Shining Path sought to generate chaos and provoke state repression in order to "deepen the contradictions" of the capitalist state and hasten the final revolutionary moment that Shining Path strategists considered was clearly in the making. For example, just a few weeks after the CGTP strike, Shining Path members infiltrated a student protest marking the first anniversary of state intervention in the previously autonomous national universities, provoking confrontations with police and resulting in the death of one student. A few days later, the Maoists infiltrated a protest march by residents of Huaycán, a poor shantytown in the district of Ate-Vitarte, who were demanding basic services from the government. The detonation of two sticks of dynamite created panic and chaos. In the confusion, a police tank ran over two Huaycán residents, one of whom died as a result.[13]

It was not coincidental that Shining Path began to focus on organizing in Lima at this precise moment. The year 1988 marked a period of intense labor agitation and political instability, as described in previous chapters. The collapse of the García government's heterodox economic program plunged the economy into a prolonged recession and spiraling hyperinflation that drastically cut living standards. The severe fiscal crisis, coupled with growing government corruption and ineptitude, led to a severe weakening of the regime's legitimacy and fueled widespread popular unrest. The retreat of state and the consequent decline in public services and the drying up of social programs caused major discontent. Shining Path's decision to step up its urban activities reflected the Maoists' belief that the growing regime crisis could turn into a full-blown crisis of the entire political system, and that it was necessary to prepare the terrain for that inevitable moment, when the masses would follow the Shining Path leadership and rise up against their "bureaucratic-capitalist oppressors."

In early 1991, Shining Path's Central Committee met to evaluate the development of the popular war. The leadership confirmed that the "open popular committees" in the countryside—the foundation upon which the "People's Republic of Peru" would be erected—were now consolidated. The committee declared that after a decade of military struggle Shining Path had maintained the military and political initiative, and that the enemy was increasingly on the defensive. The party was now ready to move from the initial phase of the prolonged popular war ("strategic defense") to the second crucial phase—strategic equilibrium. In May 1991, *El Diario* affirmed publicly that Shining Path had achieved strategic equilibrium.

Strategic equilibrium ostensibly meant that Shining Path now had the capacity to fight on more or less equal terms with state security forces despite the state's superior man- and firepower. Strategic parity was the linchpin to the third and final phase of urban insurrection, the "strategic counteroffensive," which would bring ultimate victory. To reach "strategic equilibrium," it was necessary to consolidate political, if not territorial, control over key populations, primarily the vast *barriadas* that ring

**Figure 5.1**   Aftermath of a Shining Path Car Bomb in Lima

Police inspect the aftermath of a Shining Path car bomb in the commercial and residential district of San Isidro in 1992. Selective assassinations and bombings in Lima became a central feature of daily life in the capital after 1991, when Shining Path declared it had achieved "strategic equilibrium" with government forces.

*Source*: Caretas Archive.

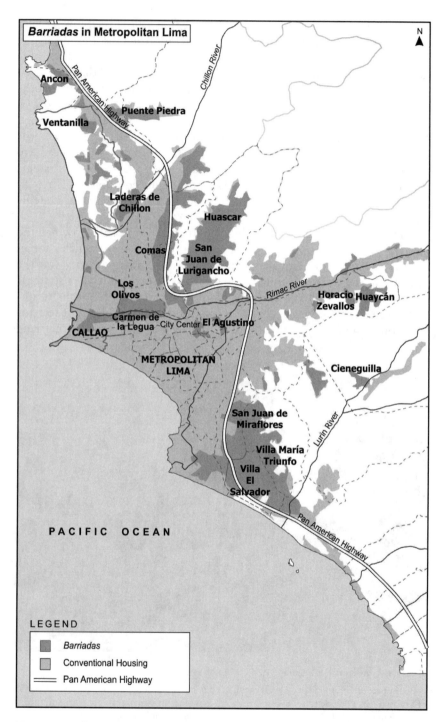

**Barriadas in Metropolitan Lima**

N

Ancon

Puente Piedra

Ventanilla

Chillon River

Pan American Highway

Laderas de
Chillon

Huascar

Comas

San
Juan de
Lurigancho

Los
Olivos

Rimac River

Horacio Huaycán
Zevallos

Carmen de
la Legua     City Center    El Agustino

CALLAO

METROPOLITAN
LIMA

Cieneguilla

San Juan de
Miraflores

Lurin River

Villa María
Triunfo

Villa
El
Salvador

PACIFIC OCEAN

Pan American Highway

LEGEND

Barriadas

Conventional Housing

Pan American Highway

Map courtesy of www.mapsofworld.com.

*Source*: Gustavo Riofrío, Programa Urbano/DESCO.

the city. As *El Diario* noted in January 1992, it was in Lima's *barriadas* that the "decisive battle" would be fought. This kind of all-out political and military struggle for political and territorial control over civilian populations was unprecedented in Latin America, and certainly there were no comparable guerrilla organizations that acted with the brutality of the Shining Path.[14] Indeed, alone among Latin American insurgent movements, Shining Path has been held responsible for 54 percent of all deaths during the period of internal conflict (1980–2000), while government forces have been held responsible for just over one-third of all deaths (CVR 2003).

## Reactions

Few observers considered that Shining Path posed a serious threat in Lima. State security forces vastly outgunned the insurgency. But more importantly, it was argued, Shining Path's efforts to extend their influence would not go unchallenged. Shining Path had developed in extremely poor and historically marginalized regions of the country like Ayacucho, where the state's reach was tenuous, where political parties were largely absent, and civil society was weak. Scholars of the early development of Shining Path in rural areas found that Shining Path's authoritarian leadership flourished in regions where democratic social organizations were weakly developed or absent (Degregori 1986). In contrast, it was argued, Shining Path would encounter serious obstacles in other parts of the country where democratic social organizations had developed and would serve as a kind of social bulwark against Shining Path's organizing efforts.[15] As events unfolded in the mid- and late 1980s, examples such as Puno, where the organized peasant movement and its political allies within the Left and progressive sectors of the Catholic Church did in fact challenge Shining Path's attempts to radicalize their struggle for land, seemed to confirm this argument. It became conventional wisdom, and was increasingly adopted by left-wing scholars and activists alike (Smith 1992).

The "social bulwark" theory seemed particularly valid for Lima. Lima was not only the center of government; its political space was also populated by a broad spectrum of political and social groups. Political parties, including the center-right AP and PPC, the populist APRA party, and the left-wing coalition IU, were active in the city, and especially in the case of APRA and IU, in the *barriadas* of Lima. Grassroots organizations, which had been mobilizing since the late 1970s to demand government services, challenge antipopular economic and social policies, and resolve local problems on a self-help basis, were also very active in the *barriadas*. The result was the emergence of a vast network of social organizations, including neighborhood associations, community kitchens, women's clubs, church, and youth groups, many of which received technical training and financial and other assistance from progressive sectors of the Catholic Church and NGDOs. Progressive scholars and left-wing activists alike pointed to the link between these social organizations and the IU, forged during the struggle against military rule in the late 1970s, and consolidated during the 1980s, when the Left won municipal elections in numerous popular districts in Lima. In contrast to places such as Ayacucho where organizational alternatives were weak, it was argued, the IU represented a viable alternative for democratic and nonviolent social change that provided poor people with an alternative to the desperation and frustration that underlie Shining Path's political violence.

Yet, by 1991, when *El Diario* announced that Shining Path had achieved "strategic equilibrium," the Maoists had made important inroads in Lima, both in terms of its growing organizational influence in specific districts in the city and its growing military presence. By late 1991 and the first half of 1992, Lima was a city under siege. Successive Shining Path offensives rocked the capital during this period, and the scope and intensity of Shining Path's military operations increased dramatically. By then familiar acts of sabotage against banks, government buildings, and basic infrastructure were overwhelmed by potent car-bombs, "armed strikes," and political assassinations.

But these armed actions were only the most visible manifestations of the Shining Path's urban presence. There was also growing evidence of Shining Path inroads into Lima's immense *barriadas*. Observers noted that these incursions were not only military in nature; Shining Path was also successfully constructing support among the urban poor of Lima:

> Shining Path has grown in the popular *barriadas* of Lima not only in relation to the number of attacks and armed actions; they have also managed to construct a vast social base. The [neoliberal] economic policies that have pushed a high percentage of the families that live in the shantytowns into a situation of extreme misery have helped Shining Path's plans. (IDL 1992:211)

Though little data existed at the time about popular responses to Shining Path's incursions into the *barriadas*, the publication of the results of a public opinion poll conducted in Metropolitan Lima in June 1991 revealed that Shining Path was commanding a not insignificant amount of grassroots support. According to the poll, 17 percent considered subversion to be "justified." When asked their response to a terrorist attack, 11 percent said they would "understand" while 16 percent said they would be "indifferent." The poll was met with surprise in intellectual circles, where it was almost an article of faith that Shining Path could not obtain significant levels of support among the urban and rural poor. More startling was the clearly class-based nature of the responses: while only 2 percent of those from the highest socioeconomic level (A) considered subversion justified, 23 percent considered it so within the lowest socioeconomic level (D); and while none within level A held a favorable opinion of Abimael Guzmán, 17 percent within level D openly expressed a favorable opinion of the Shining Path leader.[16]

Even more surprising was Shining Path's growing influence in *barriadas* such as Villa El Salvador, where the IU-popular organization matrix was most developed, and where vast organizational networks brought community residents together to resolve their common problems of land tenure, infrastructure development, joblessness, and hunger. Shining Path specifically sought to penetrate areas such as Villa El Salvador that symbolized the "revisionism" of the mainstream Left parties. Gaining influence in these areas would permit Shining Path to "unmask" the "revisionism" of the IU and prove that it offered the only truly "revolutionary" alternative for social change.

By early 1992, observers alarmingly noted that Shining Path appeared to be on the verge of taking state power. After winning the presidential elections in 1990, Alberto Fujimori could boast important achievements on the economic front by taming hyperinflation and gaining renewed access to international credits. However, he had little success on the counterinsurgency front. Indeed, as the quote above suggests, the immediate effect of Fujimori's neoliberal economic policies was to deepen the crisis of the state, exacerbate poverty, and further undermine the institutions capable of mediating the crisis. The rhythm of Shining Path's advance in the city seemed unstoppable, and government forces seemed paralyzed to respond. The growing possibility of a Shining Path victory provoked great consternation in the United States: at a U.S. congressional hearing on the impending crisis in Peru in March 1992, then assistant secretary of state for Inter-American Affairs Bernard Aronson warned congressional leaders that the U.S. must be prepared to take decisive action in Peru to prevent Shining Path's rise to power, which he argued would result in the twentieth century's "third genocide."[17]

Not even President Fujimori's dissolution of congress and suspension of the constitution in April of that year seemed to detain Shining Path's relentless advance. A wave of bombings in Lima in the months after the coup culminated in an "armed strike" that virtually paralyzed Lima. It is illustrating to cite an editorial from *Expreso*, an important conservative newspaper from this period. After extolling Fujimori's attempts to regain state control over Shining Path's strongholds in the universities, the prisons, and key rural areas in the aftermath of the April 5 coup, the editorial goes on to criticize his failure to address Shining Path's growth in the *barriadas*:

But there is a fourth front that Fujimori does not mention frequently: that of the *barriadas*, where Shining Path's advance is consistent and the government has done very little to support the population in order to oppose this advance. We worry more about the armed attacks that the subversives carry out in the commercial and financial centers of the city, in San Isidro. But that is the spectacular part, the psychological terror. What is truly worrisome is the organizing activity, which is daily and subterranean, that the Shining Path subversives carry out in the peripheral squatter settlements of Lima.[18]

Chapter six describes these organizing activities in the gray zones of Lima and the responses of the urban poor to them.

# In the Gray Zones: States of Shining Path

As Shining Path began to focus its organizing efforts on Lima after 1988, Peru's overall political, social, and economic situation was deteriorating dramatically. Though García's heterodox economic experiment was an initial success, by 1988 it had collapsed under the weight of foreign exchange constraints and looming government deficits. Spiraling hyper-inflation—1,722 percent in 1988 and 2,775 percent in 1989—forced a sharp decline in real wages and a 25 percent contraction of the economy between 1988 and 1990 (Pastor and Wise 1992). This provoked massive labor unrest and seriously weakened the government's fledgling legitimacy. The process of state decomposition that followed the economic fiasco, and the consequent decline of public services, the drying up of social programs and the disengagement of the state from society, caused major discontent. Political violence was growing and expanding into new areas, adding to the sensation of a situation gone out of control.

Popular support for APRA eroded quickly. For a short time, it seemed possible that the IU—APRA's principal competitor for support among the lower classes—would pick up votes from disaffected Apristas in the 1989 municipal elections and presidential elections the following year. But in early 1989, long-standing tensions between moderates and radicals within the coalition culminated in the division of the IU in early 1989, deflating the Left's electoral chances. The division of the Left fed the growing perception that representative institutions were incapable of resolving the political and economic crisis. Political parties across the ideological spectrum became increasingly seen as vehicles of personalistic power and patronage, and parliament became seen as an ineffective body that spent hours debating irrelevant points while the country veered toward instability and chaos. The political expression of this growing disaffection was the election of independent candidates who played up their status as "outsiders": Ricardo Belmont, a popular TV show host, won the 1989 municipal elections, while Alberto Fujimori, an agronomist and rector of a local university, defeated novelist Mario Vargas Llosa for president in 1990.

This combination of a devastating economic crisis, the retreat of the state, and the collapse of traditional mediating mechanisms between state and society were the background against which Shining Path stepped up its organizing activities in Lima after 1988. The exacerbation of the economic crisis fed feelings of frustration and desperation among important segments of the urban poor. Hyperinflation was especially devastating to the poor, who often had few available cushions in times of crisis. The growing incapacity of the state to mediate popular demands, and to provide even basic public services left the poor with few resources to negotiate the crisis. This was particularly true for newer migrants. Whereas governments from the time of Odría sought to obtain the support of the urban poor via specific social programs and clientelistic handouts (Collier 1976), the fiscal crisis after 1988 eroded the government's capacity to maintain clientelistic networks. Nor was the state capable of responding to new demands for housing and infrastructure such as electricity, water, sewerage, and transportation (Driant 1991). The collapse of traditional mechanisms of interest representation such as political parties and trade unions meant that poor people had fewer options to seek redress for their grievances. The growing frustration and discontent among important sectors of Lima's urban population gave Shining Path a crucial window of opportunity to organize in the *barriadas*. Shining Path also proved extremely adept at exploiting the growing social conflicts that began to unfold in Lima as these multidimensional crises deepened, and the state seemed paralyzed to respond. These combined factors are important contextual variables that help explain why Shining Path's push into the cities was more successful than originally predicted.

This chapter documents how Shining Path manipulated the structural conditions of personal and collective insecurity in Lima's *barriadas* in the late 1980s and early 1990s, which was rooted in the combined effect of the retreat of the state and of organized politics and the devastating economic crisis. By examining the relationship between these changing structural conditions and Shining Path's efforts to develop a social base in Lima's *barriadas*, the chapter contributes to the ongoing debates about revolutionary movements and in particular to what Eric Selbin (1999) refers to as the "fourth generation" of scholarship of revolutionary movements. This scholarship represents a synthesis and a challenge to what Goldstone (1980) once termed the "third generation" of revolution studies, which were historically grounded and focused on the state as the main variable in explaining revolutionary outcomes (Theda Skocpol's *States and Social Revolutions* being the field-defining text). The first generation, between 1900 and 1940, lacked a theoretical framework; while the second, which dominated the social sciences between 1940 and 1975, drew on psychological explanations to explain revolutions (Davies' frustration–aggression hypothesis) or drew on pluralist traditions and saw revolutions as the outcome of conflict between competing interest groups. The "fourth generation" scholarship challenges the notion that structural factors or political agency can be singled out as primary explanatory variables of revolution, prioritizing instead analysis of the dynamic interplay between structure and agency to explain the advance (or failure) of revolutionary movements. This is indicative of a broader trend in social science scholarship away from state-centric analyses toward more nuanced explorations of the dynamic and relational interactions between state and society to understand political outcomes.

A central concern of this and the following chapter is to understand how political organizations structure, negotiate, and recreate their relationships with potential constituent groups, and how these groups respond to these overtures. Though insurgent movements may mobilize grassroots support and even recruit members through moralistic and ideological appeals to notions such as justice and equality (Wood 2003), the data in the case of Shining Path points to the crucial importance of exchange relationships to understand the growing appeal of insurgents in Lima's shantytowns. Migdal (1974) defines exchange relationships between insurgent groups and constituents as interactions based on the provision of concrete good and services by the former to the latter in an effort to construct local support for insurgent activities. Understanding these exchange relationships is crucial to understanding the evolution of insurgent movements. To construct a social base, guerrilla groups seek to mobilize support through a variety of mechanisms, including providing specific goods or benefits to local populations.[1] In the context of such pragmatic exchange relationships, local populations offer or withdraw support according to rational calculations of their own interests (Migdal 1974; Popkin 1979). From a comparative perspective, Shining Path's focus on the pragmatic concerns of potential constituents mirrors efforts of like-minded groups that seek to articulate local needs into broader and more sustained support of their organizational goals and objectives. Groups ranging from the Revolutionary Armed Forces of Colombia (FARC) to Hamas in the Palestinian Territories have pursued similar strategies designed to build support networks by meeting the needs of disadvantages and marginalized groups in society.[2]

At the same time, the historical context in which these political processes unfold is also important. Subaltern patterns of accommodation and resistance to authority are the result of historical processes that shape political attitudes and behavior (Scott 1985, 1990; Stern 1987; Mallon 1995). In this sense, understanding the way the crisis of the state and the growing sense of personal and collective insecurity shaped the attitudes and behavior of the residents of Lima's *barriadas* is crucial to understand popular attitudes toward Shining Path. In other words, Shining Path was able to develop exchange relationships with the urban poor in the context of the retreat of the state and of organized politics, and the dramatic decline in economic and human security that this implied.

## Imposing Order

The fiscal and administrative crisis of the Peruvian state after 1988 had direct consequences for residents of Lima's *barriadas*. In addition to the precipitous decline in living standards due to economic recession and hyperinflation, benefits, and resources from the state were largely cut off as social programs were shut down and clientelistic networks faltered. Public order also became a growing problem in the *barriadas*. In part because of growing poverty, crime and delinquency rose dramatically in Lima's *barriadas*; it is often easier for thieves to operate in poor communities than in wealthy areas, where residents have the resources to pay for private guards and high electric fences.[3] Drug addiction has also become a growing problem in Lima's *barriadas*, especially among young people. The state security apparatus grew increasingly ineffective in protecting citizens. More alarming, however, was the growing involvement of police officers in criminal activity, including assaults and robberies, exacerbating the population's traditional mistrust of the police. Corruption was a common practice among the police forces, but this more violent and criminal activity was qualitatively different. In 1994, for example, a violent criminal gang known as *Los Destructores* (The Destroyers) was involved in numerous cases of kidnapping, extortion, and murder. When the group was finally disbanded, it was revealed that its members were primarily active and retired members of the national police (Leger 1994).

In wealthier districts in Lima, municipal governments had the resources to create *serenazgo*, a local anticrime force, in the face of the inability of the national police to provide protection and security. Municipalities in poorer neighborhoods lacked the resources to implement such local forces, and sometimes the residents themselves established local anticrime patrols, known as *rondas*, to dissuade criminals and thieves.[4] However, as crime became more pervasive and violent, these unarmed patrols were inadequate to the task.

Regarding this growing situation of crime and insecurity, *barriada* residents I interviewed between 1990 and 1995 expressed a common sentiment: the police are ineffective in dealing with crime, and in many instances are allied with the criminals. This sentiment has been widely corroborated in numerous public opinion polls. In the annual polls carried out by APOYO, the two principal institutions in charge of providing justice and order—the judicial system and the police—have received consistently low ratings in terms of their efficacy since 1987.[5] In a 1989 poll, 60 percent stated that they did not trust the police, and 43 percent said that they felt fear (as opposed to security) when they saw a police officer; 49 percent said that if they had the resources they would purchase a weapon for self-defense (Bedoya 1989). An August 1993 poll showed that 45 percent of respondents had been the victims of a robbery in the previous 12 months. Only 39 percent of the victims denounced the crime to the police. Of the 59 percent of respondents who said they did not report the crime, 40 percent said that they did not go to the police because they "don't do anything"; another 16 percent said it would be "a waste of time."[6]

The crisis of public security provided opportunities for Shining Path to operate as purveyors of public order in Lima's *barriadas*. This affirmation is based on extensive research and interviews carried out in four districts in Lima in which Shining Path had developed an extensive presence: San Juan de Lurigancho, Ate-Vitarte, El Augustino, and Villa El Salvador. In response to the growing sense of personal and collective insecurity in the context of expanding violence and crime—and the perception that state institutions were ineffective or indifferent to these problems in the *barriadas*—Shining Path became a de facto purveyor of protection and security to the urban poor. Shining Path adopted a series of measures— ranging from warnings to extrajudicial executions—to punish thieves and other criminals, reduce crime and reestablish a sense of public security. Numerous interviewees reported that Shining Path had a "three strikes" policy. Thieves and delinquents first received a warning to change their ways. If they failed to heed the warnings, they were physically beaten and punished. Those who refused to reform were often killed as a final resort. Interviewees also reported that Shining Path publicly berated and some- times physically punished wife beaters, and adulterers were also publicly scorned. In some *barriadas*, Shining Path sought to head off efforts to cre- ate local crime-watch patrols (*rondas urbanas*) to dissuade criminal activity. In the case of Villa El Salvador, local residents reported that they were visited by local Shining Path members who told them to stop participating in the patrols because Shining Path would be controlling the crime prob- lem. A couple that I interviewed who participated in the *rondas* reported that most people felt relief, because crime would be stopped and they would not have to maintain their all-night watch.[7]

The majority of my interviewees expressed varying degrees of sympa- thy with Shining Path's punishment and even physical elimination of thieves, delinquents, and drug addicts, who were widely considered "social deviants" and threats to the larger community. One resident of a *barriada* in San Juan de Lurigancho expressed the reasons she approved of Shining Path's policy of punishing thieves in her neighborhood:

> I think it's a good thing, because it helps get rid of the thieves and the drug addicts, who harm the community.[8]

Another resident of San Juan de Lurigancho, who lived in a *barriada* on the dusty, hilly slopes at the outer edges of the district, noted that state author- ities neglected to visit these more remote areas and could not be trusted to provide protection as an explanation for people's acceptance of Shining Path's vigilantism:

> The [police] don't even come around here, and even if you go to them to report a robbery, they won't come up this far.[9]

A woman from another remote area within San Juan de Lurigancho who expressed her approval of Shining Path's vigilante-like activities conveyed similar reasoning:

> We are completely unprotected here, you see, the nearest police station is far away [a 15 minute bus ride]. People do whatever they want here…with [Shining Path] crime has gone down, they [the criminals] leave us alone now.[10]

One community activist noted a dramatic rise in crime and delinquency in his neighborhood in Ate-Vitarte, including robberies, assaults, and rape, after 1993, when Shining Path was forced to retreat after the capture of Guzmán, resulting in a significant decrease in Shining Path's vigilante activity in Lima's *barriadas*.

> Shining Path combated [crime]. They definitely killed several delinquents. They were a kind of counterweight to [criminal] activity.…In one way or another, they stopped these criminal activities from manifesting themselves so aggressively, as they do today.[11]

My interviews established that by threatening and sometimes killing delinquents, Shining Path imposed social order at the micro level. For the urban poor, particularly in the more remote areas where state presence had always been weak or absent, this provided them with a greater sense of security and generated sympathy for Shining Path. I conducted a survey in January 1994 that broadly confirmed these findings. In the survey, which was administered to 300 residents each in San Juan de Lurigancho and Villa El Salvador, a surprising number of residents openly affirmed their approval or comprehension of Shining Path's punishment and even killing of corrupt or abusive people and delinquents [see table 6.1]. Support for such vigilante activities is particularly notable when compared to other insurgent activities, such as blackouts or the killing of innocent people, which were widely repudiated, and armed strikes, which were also largely rejected.[12] For example, in San Juan de Lurigancho, 25.7 percent expressed "approval" or "comprehension" of Shining Path's punishment of "abusive people"; 26.3 expressed "approval" or "comprehension" of Shining Path's punishment of "criminals." In Villa El Salvador, the numbers were slightly higher: 33.6 expressed "approval" or "comprehension" in both instances. In both districts, between 18 and 25 percent responded that they were "indifferent" to such acts, which given the context of fear and insecurity, might be interpreted as passive acceptance of such actions. About one-third expressed "rejection" of such actions in both cases.

As noted, Shining Path also killed corrupt leaders, criminals, and drug addicts in Lima's *barriadas*. Drawing from the same 1994 survey, the percentages expressing support for such actions is small but significant: in San

**Table 6.1**  Popular attitudes toward Shining Path activities in two Lima shantytowns, 1994.

Question: How would you describe your reaction when Shining Path...

|  | Rejection | Indifference | Approval | Comprehension | No Response |
|---|---|---|---|---|---|
| *Villa El Salvador (n = 312)* | | | | | |
| ...Caused blackouts? | 93.6 | 4.5 | – | 0.3 | 1.6 |
| ...Killed innocent people? | 89.1 | 6.4 | – | 0.3 | 4.2 |
| ...Called an armed strike? | 73.7 | 20.5 | – | 1.3 | 4.5 |
| ...Killed a corrupt person? | 48.1 | 24.7 | 13.8 | 9.0 | 4.4 |
| ...Killed delinquents/drug addicts? | 43.3 | 18.6 | 15.1 | 12.5 | 10.5 |
| ...Punished abusive people? | 33.3 | 21.8 | 18.9 | 14.7 | 11.3 |
| ...Punished criminals? | 31.7 | 25.3 | 17.6 | 16.0 | 9.4 |
| *San Juan de Lurigancho (n = 304)* | | | | | |
| ...Caused blackouts? | 82.9 | 10.9 | 0.3 | 0.3 | 4.6 |
| ...Killed innocent people? | 82.2 | 7.2 | – | 3.3 | 7.3 |
| ...Called an armed strike? | 70.1 | 18.4 | 0.3 | 3.3 | 7.9 |
| ...Killed a corrupt person? | 50.1 | 23.4 | 5.3 | 10.9 | 10.4 |
| ...Killed delinquents/drug addicts? | 43.1 | 18.4 | 9.9 | 13.8 | 14.8 |
| ...Punished abusive people? | 40.1 | 20.1 | 10.9 | 14.8 | 14.1 |
| ...Punished criminals? | 39.1 | 18.4 | 12.2 | 14.1 | 16.2 |

*Source*: Survey designed by author in collaboration with IMASEN, S.A., and carried out in January 1994.

Juan de Lurigancho, 16.2 percent expressed "approval" or "comprehension" if Shining Path killed a corrupt person, while 23.7 percent expressed this reaction when insurgents killed criminals or drug addicts; in Villa El Salvador, the respective numbers are 22.8 and 27.6 percent. Indifference to such killings was 18.4 percent and 23.4 percent in San Juan de Lurigancho and 18.6 percent and 24.7 percent in Villa El Salvador. Rejection of such killings was higher than of "punishments": between 43 and 50 percent in both districts expressed outright rejection of this extreme use of physical violence on the part of Shining Path, but it is notable that rejection of other Shining Path practices was much higher: for example, 83–94 percent rejected blackouts caused when insurgent blew up electricity pylons, and 82–89 percent repudiated the killing of "innocent people." This would seem to reflect greater (though certainly not unanimous) tolerance for the use of physical punishment and even extrajudicial killings when individuals were perceived to have engaged in some activity, be it crime or corruption, that was perceived as harmful to the local community.

Shining Path thus seized upon the situation of insecurity and social disintegration that emerged as public authority collapsed in the late 1980s and early 1990s. By punishing and sometimes killing perceived wrongdoers, it intimidated potential criminals and thus provided many local residents with a greater sense of security and social order at a time when they perceived that the state was incapable of fulfilling this essential role. It was evident through my interviews that the democratic mechanisms that are supposed to ensure order and provide justice were viewed almost universally as dysfunctional. The police did not protect citizens or provide order, and were more often seen as delinquents themselves. The court system was seen as riddled with corruption and inaccessible to poor people. These views were widely confirmed in my surveys of residents of San Juan de Lurigancho and Villa El Salvador. The police and the judiciary—the principal state institutions charged with maintaining public order and guaranteeing the rule of law—were seen as the most corrupt institutions in the country. In my survey of Villa El Salvador residents, for example, 85 percent said that they did not believe that there was equal access to justice in Peru; 75 percent said money was the principal factor in obtaining access to justice. In this context, popular notions of justice, in which residents impose sanctions on their own without relying on the court system or police intervention, have flourished. This has been the case in the countryside as well, notably in the north, where peasants have organized patrols, or *rondas campesinas*, to protect their communities from cattle thieves and other related problems (Starn 1991). As Starn has noted, these *rondas* are effective in providing security to the community, but they sometimes resort to physical beatings, and occasionally lynchings, to punish thieves and teach a lesson to other potential transgressors.

Support for Shining Path's aggressive imposition of order might be better understood if placed in a broader comparative context. Since the late 1980s, lynchings of criminals, rapists, and other alleged wrongdoers have become increasingly common in poor urban and rural communities throughout Peru—and indeed in many parts of Latin America. Researchers have documented lynchings in several countries in the region, including El Salvador, Guatemala, Brazil, Venezuela, and Mexico. While some suggest that the phenomenon of lynchings has arisen in the context of massive state repression and impunity (Godoy 2006), the Venezuela and Mexico cases, where lynchings are also frequent, would seem to offer evidence to suggest that other factors are also at play.[13] This seems to be a growing phenomenon that has arisen in the context of weak state presence and functionality particularly in urban shantytowns and some rural areas in parts of Latin America.[14] Nor is this a problem unique to Latin America; in postapartheid South Africa lynchings have risen dramatically.[15]

One of the first lynchings documented in Lima's shantytowns took place in Pamplona Alta, in the district of San Juan de Miraflores, in 1989. I interviewed several members of the community where the lynching took place the following year. Interviewees universally pointed to the failure of state institutions to protect their communities from criminal activity and to adequately punish those responsible for criminal acts. As one interviewee stated,

We once caught a thief in the act and handed him over to the police. The next day he was set free. How? We do not know, maybe he paid off the police, or maybe the police officer was working with him. But after that we decided that we would have to take matters into our own hands.[16]

Citizens thus perceived that the state had failed to provide a safe environment, nor had it created mechanisms to deter future crimes through effective punishment. In this context, the *barriada* residents reasoned, it was up to the members of the community themselves to deal with the problem of crime. Meting out harsh punishment or even killing those caught stealing or engaged in some other violation of community norms was seen as a deterrent. Lynchings are thus not simply a manifestation of an angry and desperate mob in response to a criminal act. It is, rather, a calculated response to a very real problem in poor urban communities where state institutions failed to provide minimum security and justice. In some ways, this is an extension of the self-help logic that predominates in the *barriadas*, in which the failure of the state to provide basic needs—including order and security—led local residents to organize to find solutions to common problems.

Given the dramatic collapse of state institutions in the late 1980s and early 1990s, it is not surprising then to find that Shining Path's use of similar mechanisms to deter crime met with high approval ratings. Independent public opinion polls confirm these findings. A 1993 poll found that nearly half the population in Lima—and over 60 percent amongst the poorest—approved of lynchings.[17] Lynchings are seen as a way of punishing wrongdoers and symbolically dissuading future thieves with the threat of physical punishment, and possibly death, if they are caught in the act. A follow-up poll carried out in December 1994 by the same polling firm revealed nearly identical findings.[18]

The data gleaned from my interviews and research suggests that it is this context of personal and collective insecurity that fuels support for lynchings, whether committed by members of the local community or by outside groups, such as Shining Path, seeking to exploit the situation of insecurity to build support for their political projects. In many of Lima's *barriadas*, marked by extreme poverty, weak state institutions, and growing crime and insecurity, Shining Path sought to establish its authority at the microlevel by performing the functions of a state: punishing accused wrongdoers and thus establishing a system of justice that it enforced through the threat of physical punishment and death. It is not surprising that such activities created levels of sympathy for Shining Path's presence in urban communities.

## Shining Path and Grassroots Organizations

Lima's *barriadas* were, as described in numerous studies, the center of intense organizing activities by left-wing party activists and local community leaders in the late 1970s and the 1980s (Degregori, Blondet and

Lynch 1986; Ballón 1986, 1990; Blondet 1986; Stokes 1995). Many of the social organizations active in *barriada* life, such as neighborhood associations, community kitchens, women's clubs, glass of milk committees, and youth groups, emerged as collective efforts to meet the concrete needs of the local population. Neighborhood associations usually formed during the initial period of preparing a land invasion and continued to be active after securing the land by promoting community improvement projects and pressuring the government and cajoling state bureaucrats for basic services. Community kitchens began to form in the late 1970s due to the growing economic crisis and the inability of some families to meet their basic nutritional needs; Catholic Church activists were key in bringing families together and helping provide them with organization tools as well as basic supplies.[19] The municipal administration of IU leader Alfonso Barrantes created the glass of milk program, which actively promoted the formation of grassroots organizations to distribute milk at the community level. Lima's *barriadas* became the site of some fascinating experiments in grassroots and community organizing, and many people benefited materially as well as personally—in terms of greater participation, gaining organizing, leadership and administrative skills, etc.—from their participation in these movements.

While community kitchens and local milk committees proliferated as the economic crisis worsened after 1988, the neighborhood councils tended to dissipate once initial goals (obtaining land titles, water, electricity) were realized. As older sectors of the original *barriada* are consolidated, new squatter settlements emerge in peripheral areas of the district. These new settlements, particularly those that emerged in the late 1980s, encountered a much more difficult context for local organizing. Given the growing crisis of the state, organizing to demand services from the state seemed futile. Municipal governments, also suffering a budget crunch, were unable to fill the gap. Moreover, the deepening economic crisis after 1988 and Fujimori's structural-adjustment measures in 1990 undermined the resource base of many organizations, especially the community kitchens, deepening their dependency on external donations and exhausting their members. According to one leader who has been active in the community kitchens since 1979,

> The enthusiasm that existed before is no longer the same. It is necessity that forces us to participate... It used to be like a service to the community... [but now] there is much sadness, resentment and bitterness.[20]

And while the community kitchens provided important benefits for some families, many others could not afford the minimal fees charged for a daily ration.[21]

This growing context of deprivation exacerbated the tensions and conflicts that were part and parcel of these social organizations. Scholars and activists alike often understated these more complex and difficult aspects of community-based organizations, instead emphasizing their positive features: they fomented grassroots participation (Tovar 1986); they encouraged women's participation in the public sphere (Blondet 1986); they represented a democratizing potential at the grassroots (Ballón 1986). More critical researchers uncovered evidence of problems of authoritarian leadership (*caudillismo*), ideological and partisan differences, and power struggles, as well as over the distribution and control of resources (Delpino 1991). Corruption was a real and growing problem in organizations like the community kitchens and the milk committees, which received donations from NGOs, religious organizations, and especially in the case of the milk committees, the government. The fragile institutionality of these organizations meant that few mechanisms existed to resolve conflicts, including arbitrary decision making, caudillismo, and petty corruption (Delpino 1991). These tensions grew as resources became scarcer. The drying up of government benefits and patronage to the popular sectors, particularly in the last years of the García administration and the first two years of the Fujimori administration, further undermined the capacity of grassroots leaders to deliver desired goods to the rank and file. Leaders were often judged by the rank and file according to their ability to obtain needed resources; as resources dried up, the legitimacy of these leaders came under question (Parodi and Twanama 1993; López Ricci 1993). This undermined the very notion of exercising leadership of a social organization, as the rank and file held a skeptical view of community leaders. This was revealed in both my interviews with *barriada* residents as well as my survey. A significant majority—64 percent in Villa El Salvador and 54 percent in San Juan de Lurigancho—affirmed the view that most individuals seek out leadership positions in order to benefit personally from such a position, rather than from any intrinsic desire to help the community.

The closing of government and other channels as means of obtaining resources and other desired goods, and the resulting challenges this presented to local community leaders, played into Shining Path's hands. An extensive quote from Luis, a community leader from El Agustino, is worth highlighting. First, he notes that pro–Shining Path leaders challenged the utility of peaceful forms of organizing in a public community meeting:

> We were organizing a protest march to the government palace to demand solutions to a series of problems in the *barriadas*, including land titles, legal recognition of new squatter settlements, problems of water, electricity... We were in Bocanegra, discussing the plans with the local organizations... Then some leaders linked to Shining Path intervened, publicly saying that a peaceful march would not get us anywhere, that it wouldn't resolve any problems, and that if we did organize a march it should be confrontational. They said the kind of protest march that we were trying to organize—a peaceful march,

where the leaders try to talk to the mayor of Lima, to give him our list of demands, or to go to the government palace—was futile.

He then explains that he and other leaders argued against this position, and the march was eventually carried out. The failure of the march to achieve its objectives, however, seemed to reinforce Shining Path's arguments, according to Luis:

We mobilized a mass protest in downtown Lima, we put together delegations to go the government palace, but no one would receive us. We wanted to give them our list of demands, but in the municipality of Lima, [mayor] Belmont refused to see us...It was difficult for the leaders to return [to the community]...we had to tell them that nothing had happened....

Luis is quite conscious of the consequences of the failure to achieve any concrete results for his organization and its strategy of pursuing peaceful methods of social change. Most importantly, he notes that it is the state's unwillingness to address the concerns of its citizens that creates the opportunities for Shining Path to advance its logic of confrontation and violence:

The spaces of democratic struggle for our demands were closing up...This hurt the possibilities of maintaining the organizations... in the end, the organizations are [seen as] useless because they don't resolve the problems [of the community]....I think there has been a systematic shutting out of the people's organizations [by the government], though there are some vices to be criticized in these organizations.[22]

Tensions of this nature within community-based organizations provided Shining Path with additional opportunities to challenge incumbent leaders, many of whom were associated with the left-wing parties that formed the IU coalition—for Shining Path, the "revisionist Left" that had to be eliminated to facilitate its path to revolution. The division of the IU in 1989 facilitated Shining Path's activities in Lima's *barriadas*, as the splintering of the Left into several smaller parties undermined popular confidence in the Left parties as well as in the local community activists affiliated with them. It also exacerbated the partisan and personal differences among left-wing activists at the local level. Shining Path initiated intense propaganda campaigns in *El Diario* and within the *barriadas,* accusing left-wing grassroots leaders of corruption and selling out the "revolution" in an attempt to deepen the growing wedge between leaders and the rank and file. The intention was to "deepen the contradictions" within the *barriadas*, thus allowing Shining Path to advance and establish control in these strategic areas. Shining Path sought to manipulate popular sentiments of mistrust and anger over corruption, playing on rank-and-file suspicions of leaders who—by virtue of their very positions as leaders—were perceived as likely to engage in some form of corruption; "everybody does it," from government officials to grassroots leaders—had become popular wisdom. Shining Path thus pursued a strategy designed to simultaneously discredit the local IU leadership while also establishing control over local organizations in Lima's *barriadas*.

Between 1989 and 1992, Shining Path killed over one hundred community leaders and local political activists, including about two dozen women from the community kitchens and milk committees, and hundreds others received death threats.[23] This assassination of unarmed civilians was deplored by many Peruvians from different social sectors and internationally, especially in the case of Maria Elena Moyano, a well-known community activist and the left-wing lieutenant mayor of Villa El Salvador who became a vociferous critic of Shining Path.[24] Part of Shining Path's goals in killing Moyano and leaders like her was eliminate local left-wing leaders and neutralize any attempts at resistance, in order to facilitate their control over key *barriadas* in Lima. Accusations of corruption were a way to justify the killings to the population at large. Some of my interviewees expressed their repudiation of this kind of "sanction," but many others had much more ambiguous attitudes. *"Por algo será"* (they must have done something to deserve it) was a phrase that was often repeated in my interviews when discussing these cases. As one of Moyano's close friends told me,

> In these trying times, people believe that everyone steals—everyone, including grassroots leaders like Maria Elena.[25]

Popular acceptance of Shining Path's sanctions against community leaders suspected or accused of engaging in corruption was evident in my interviews and focus groups of *barriada* residents from four popular districts of Lima. Ana, a member of a milk committee in a poor shantytown in San Juan de Lurigancho, recalled that Shining Path had killed a leader of the milk program in her neighborhood in 1991. When asked her opinion, she said that the killing was justified, since it was well known that the woman was hoarding some of the milk and reselling it for profit. Lourdes, a community kitchen leader in Villa El Salvador, stated that she believed that Shining Path attacked the FEPOMUVES because they stored their food supplies in warehouses, which inherently gives rise to suspicion that the food was being resold for profit. She was referring to the September 11, 1991 bombing of a warehouse administered by the FEPOMUVES. Indeed, rumors circulated in Villa that some of the leaders responsible for the warehouse that was bombed were involved in petty corruption, trading food donated to the soup kitchens for other-goods or for cash. Lourdes noted that Shining Path did not interfere with the church-run soup kitchens in which she participated because they do not store their food.

> Our food supplies are immediately handed out to the members [of the soup kitchen], we don't store them. . . . That is why we haven't had any problems [with Shining Path]. There are other organizations that sell their food donations, and Shining Path is against that.[26]

The implication is that Shining Path has local knowledge of which individuals are engaged in petty corruption and acts as local sheriffs by punishing their misdeeds. This view of Shining Path was significant among the urban poor and even middle-class Peruvians. According to a public opinion poll carried out in 1992, a significant percentage of the urban poor stated that in their view, Shining Path punished corrupt leaders[27] (see table 6.2). In times of scarcity, such petty corruption is viewed harshly by local community members, and for some, such punishments were often viewed as desirable.

Indeed, at the *barriada* level, many accepted the accusations of corruption as true, whether or not proof existed, and viewed these assassinations as the "just desserts" of individuals who had presumably used their positions of leadership to enrich themselves. Interviews with informed observers who worked in the shantytowns corroborated the prevalence of this attitude among many *barriada* residents. It was also notable that many of the community organizations leaders I interviewed said that they had made efforts to demonstrate to the rank and file that they were honest administrators of their organizations' resources. This reflects the degree to which Shining Path's efforts to establish itself as the local arbiter of behavior among grassroots organizations through its "exemplary punishments" of allegedly corrupt leaders were successful.

While it is difficult if not impossible to prove or disprove the allegations of corruption in specific cases, in the context of scarcity of resources in the late 1980s and early 1990s, the fact that there were some instances of corruption among some leaders led to a growing perception that all

**Table 6.2**  Popular attitudes toward Shining Path actions in Lima according to social class, 1992.

Question: In your opinion, does Shining Path punish corrupt leaders?

|  | Total (all responses) | According to social class | | |
|---|---|---|---|---|
|  |  | lower class | lower-middle class | middle and upper class |
| Yes | 29.1 | 32.5 | 33.6 | 19.1 |
| No | 47.5 | 41.7 | 47.1 | 55.7 |
| No response | 23.4 | 25.8 | 19.3 | 25.2 |

*Source*: IMASEN, S.A., as reported in *Caretas* (October 1, 1992), p. 15.

leaders with access to resources would seek some personal benefit. Shining Path sought to reproduce this perception, accusing certain leaders of corruption in its newspaper, in hand-delivered flyers, and through the rumor mill. In a context of extreme poverty that feeds mistrust and suspicion of leaders and those with access to benefits and power, rumors of corruption often became the equivalent of proof of corruption. As economic conditions worsen, tolerance for corruption seems to decline, and drastic measures are often seen as justified. The actual reality of corruption mattered less than people's perception that anyone with access to resources is more likely than not to engage in acts of corruption. As in the case of criminal activity, with no state institutions to control such behavior—or even to investigate it—it was relatively easy for Shining Path to establish itself as the judge and jury of alleged corruption. While many repudiated Shining Path's "exemplary punishments," others thought such tactics were acceptable, in that they punished perceived wrongdoings and served as a preventive measure so that other community leaders would behave more appropriately. My data reveals that in some cases, leaders killed by Shining Path were a posteriori accused of corruption, leading many to perceive the "sanction" as therefore "justified." This was a convenient tactic for Shining Path, who eliminated several left-wing leaders in this way.

While Shining Path's anticorruption activities were most extensive at the local level, it occasionally targeted national figures who were engaged in corruption and who were widely unpopular. Such was the case of Felipe Salaverry, head of the Social Security Institute (IPSS) under the García administration, who was killed by Shining Path in 1989. Most of my interviewees expressed repudiation of Salaverry for his involvement in corruption at the expense of ordinary Peruvians, and their sympathy with Shining Path's sanction. The following is quite illustrative both of the ambiguous nature of popular attitudes toward violence, and of the popular rage against corruption that Shining Path's actions were able to channel:

> There are innocent [people] who die and that is very bad, but there are also people who deserve to die and that is the truth. One reaches the point of recognizing this. Look at what happened to the man who was president of the Social Security Office [Felipe Salaverry]. [Shining Path] killed him and everybody said he deserved it (*está bien muerto*) because he was an undesirable man who closed the doors to everyone, and President [García] supported him. In my opinion, he reaped what he sowed.[28]

## Providing Other "Public Goods"

Greater public security and punishing and inhibiting corruption were not the only "goods" that Shining Path sought to provide to *barriada* residents. Informants also attested to Shining Path's attempts in some shantytowns to assure fair market prices and prohibit speculation and hoarding—widespread practices in light of the economic maladies of the late 1980s and early 1990s. Not all my interviewees were aware of this kind of activity in their neighborhoods, but those that were held a generally favorable attitude. María described Shining Path's efforts to assure fair market prices in San Juan de Lurigancho. Shining Path cadre visited a local merchant who was overcharging for her products:

> [Shining Path] took some of her merchandise, and warned her to lower her prices, that it wasn't fair to the poor people in the neighborhood to charge such high prices. Everybody was glad, because that woman was really abusive with her prices.[29]

As with its punishments of criminals and other delinquents, Shining Path seemed to operate by first warning the alleged infractor to change his or her practices. Failure to heed such warnings might lead to physical punishment or death. As with other killings of this nature, these "exemplary punishments" were meant to have dissuasive value, as noted by a Catholic priest who worked in San Juan de Lurigancho:

> [Shining Path] has a policy of controlling the prices of the vendors, who sometimes can be abusive or speculative. For example, there were a number of assassinations of people who had stalls in the Sarita Colonia marketplace in Bayóvar. The news spread quickly: they kill one vendor, then everybody in Canto Grande knows about it. It acts as a kind of a warning.[30]

Again the context of scarcity in poor urban shantytowns is crucial for understanding Shining Path's actions as attempts to construct its image as local arbiters of morality and justice. Particularly in very poor communities, local merchants who charged inflated prices for essential goods were viewed as abusive and selfish. Recognizing people's sense of injustice over such practices, Shining Path's enforcement of price controls generated a great deal of sympathy for the Maoists, particularly in the poorest neighborhoods where state presence was most negligible.

Shining Path sought to agitate around other unpopular measures at the local level in Lima's *barriadas*. In Villa El Salvador, for example, Shining Path led a campaign with its allies in the district's centralized neighborhood organization, the Self-Managing Urban Community of Villa El Salvador (CUAVES), against the municipal property tax in 1991. The tax was a heavy burden for most of the district's residents, whose real incomes had been decimated as a result of the combined effects of hyperinflation and neoliberal austerity. As a result, the campaign against the tax (which is described in greater detail in chapter seven) was viewed sympathetically by many of the *barriada's* residents. This caused a dramatic impact on public opinion in Peru, since CUAVES was a key symbol of the popular movement and of left-wing organizing in the *barriadas*.

Shining Path also sought to mobilize support around the contentious issue of land tenure. While residents in the more consolidated areas of Lima's *barriadas* may have acquired legal title to their land, each year new squatter settlements emerge in the outlying areas of popular districts such as Ate-Vitarte, Villa El Salvador, and San Juan de Lurigancho. The squatters seek to establish their right to the land, but often they are forcibly evicted. Shining Path seized on this problem as a way to organize squatters against the government and to build local support. The most prominent case was that of Raucana, a settlement in Ate-Vitarte that began as a land invasion in July 1990. Police initially evicted the squatters, resulting in the death of one man. After the police retreated, the squatters resettled on the land. Shortly thereafter Shining Path began intensive political work in the settlement. When police returned a year later with a judicial order to evict the squatters, they were met with violent resistance. Observers remarked that the hand of Shining Path was visible in this confrontational response, a view that was reinforced a few days later, when the owner of the land, a private businessman, received death threats and a car bomb exploded in front of one of his factories. The landowner withdrew his claim to the land and the squatters were left alone.

Shining Path also exploited conflicts over land tenure in Pachacamac, a rapidly growing urbanization within Villa El Salvador. In 1987 and 1988, hundreds of young people had invaded unoccupied houses that had been constructed during the Belaúnde government. The squatters were lobbying the municipal government of Villa El Salvador to obtain legal titles to the houses, but bureaucratic hold-ups in the Ministry of Housing prevented any quick resolution. After two years of failed attempts to obtain legal titles, the squatters were growing increasingly impatient with the municipal government. Shining Path, which had been organizing in Pachacamac, saw an opportunity to both build support within the community and create problems for the municipal government of Villa, which was run by a mayor from the IU. When the armed forces established a military base in front of Pachacamac (shortly after the assassination of the district's lieutenant mayor, Maria Elena Moyano, by Shining Path), Shining Path activists had little trouble convincing the squatters that the municipal government had called the army in to have them evicted. Pachacamac residents participated in rallies mobilized by Shining Path activists against the municipal government, creating dramatic scenes of insurgent activism in the district. Both Raucana and Pachacamac served as examples Shining Path could point to in order to illustrate the futility of peaceful mechanisms to obtain local demands and the necessity of more combative social action.

It is important to note, however, that in many cases Shining Path's championing of such local causes was quite utilitarian. In the case of Raucana, there is little doubt that Shining Path's leadership helped the squatters establish their settlement in the face of government repression. But Shining Path was also aware that its open activity in Raucana and its incitement of the squatters to confront the police would provoke a response from the government. In fact, in Shining Path's logic of all-out confrontation, it was expecting that response to be violent and repressive: provoking the security forces would "deepen the contradictions" and hasten the "revolutionary moment," just as it had done in the highlands in the early 1980s. It expected the armed forces to react as it did in the highlands: trying to destroy Shining Path through brutal and indiscriminate displays of violence against the local population. By 1991, however, the state had refined its counterinsurgency strategy. The army occupied Raucana and raided every home in the settlement, but rather than engaging in indiscriminate repression, it identified suspected terrorists and arrested them, and then began to hand out food and medicines. This new civic-action approach, a classic counterinsurgency strategy designed to win the hearts and minds of the local population, was increasingly deployed in Lima's *barriadas,* and became a growing counterweight to Shining Path's presence in the *barriadas*, especially when the organization was forced to retreat after the September 1992 capture of Guzmán.

**Figure 6.1**    Soldiers Direct Civic-Action Campaign in Lima Shantytown

Soldiers hand out food and cooking oil to residents of Huaycán, a poor community in eastern Lima, as part of the state's counterinsurgency strategy to win the "hearts and minds" of the urban poor. Shining Path maintained an active presence in Huaycán and other *barriadas* in Lima.

*Source*: El Peruano Archive (February 12, 1992).

## Contingent Support and Shifting Allegiances

In poor shantytowns, marked by the absence of state services, extreme poverty, growing crime and insecurity, and weak local institutions to mediate conflict, Shining Path's use of intimidation and violence came to be seen as an effective means of restoring social order and imparting justice. The failure of the police and justice system to protect poor Peruvian citizens and provide for their material security provided the Shining Path an opportunity to build currents of sympathy and support within poor urban communities by imposing social order and punishing wrongdoers. Such activities garnered local sympathy when they were perceived as contributing to a larger, socially desired good. As institutional mechanisms of providing order and justice waned, popular codes of justice and morality became more widespread. Authoritarian methods and even physical violence were not unilaterally rejected by the urban poor, but evaluated according to the target, the motive, and the social desirability—and utility—of the act. Did it achieve a specific—if not necessarily tangible—social good? Did it punish someone who "deserved" to be punished for transgressing group norms or because of some real or imputed wrongdoing? Did it serve to inhibit future instances of such wrongdoing? Subaltern groups were not inherently disposed to accept violence, as some have suggested (Manrique 1989), but nor were they completely opposed to violent acts, as others have claimed (Degregori 1991a). It depended on who the victim was and the reasons for the killing.

The data suggests that Shining Path attempted to build local structures of authority by exploiting the local effects of a weak and ineffectual state. In effect, Shining Path sought to create its own microlevel order. Shining Path's microstate was based on the perceived need for order, security, and mechanisms of control in a context of personal and collective insecurity and profound economic scarcity. In areas where state authorities did exist, Shining Path sought to discredit them and to eliminate them to generate a power vacuum that they would then fill. These findings substantiate those of earlier studies examining local support for Shining Path's rural activities. Scholars have documented how Shining Path initially generated a great deal of sympathy and some passive support in rural areas by killing hated landowners and merchants, distributing goods like cattle, sheep, and land, rallying against state-run cooperatives that had become widely repudiated by peasants, and punishing cattle thieves (Berg 1986/1987, 1992; Isbell 1992; Manrique 1989). In his discussion of Shining Path's activities in Andahuaylas, Berg (1992) argues that peasants were generally sympathetic to Shining Path's assassinations of wealthy peasants, abusive merchants, and cooperative functionaries. These individuals were seen as having distanced themselves from a moral economy based on reciprocity and mutual obligations, and they had become widely viewed as abusive. Such sympathy did not become revolutionary sentiment or active support for Shining Path or its war. It did, however, allow the Maoists important room to maneuver in the countryside. Sympathy often became de facto passive support. The peasants' long-standing mistrust of the police and army also worked in Shining Path's favor. In Lima, Shining Path was similarly able to marshal important levels of sympathy among the urban poor by playing on popular resentment against abusive authorities and real or perceived corruption, by providing greater levels of security, and in some cases by championing local popular causes.

Scholars of Shining Path's rural activities also note that support for Shining Path decreased when it failed to protect its peasant allies from military repression in 1983–1984, and when it attempted to close down local and regional markets, which are crucial to peasant subsistence (Degregori 1986; Berg 1986/1987; Isbell 1992). Manrique's study (1989) of the central Andean department of Junín reveals a similar phenomenon. After the initial "honeymoon" between Shining Path and local peasant communities, when the former was widely applauded for attacking hated landowners and state-run cooperatives, distributing land and punishing thieves, concrete divergences began to appear between Shining Path's objectives and those of the local peasants. In some communities, this eventually gave rise to the formation of *rondas campesinas*, or civil defense patrols, in which local communities organized to protect themselves against Shining Path's incursions (Starn 1991; Degregori 1996).

These shifting attitudes reflect an ongoing and dynamic reappraisal on the part of the rural poor to Shining Path and its repertoire of actions. The data collected in Lima's *barriadas* reflects a similar process of examination and reappraisal of Shining Path's activities. It also helps explain ambiguous attitudes vis-à-vis Shining Path among *barriada* residents, who accept or are sympathetic toward certain attitudes and actions carried out by Shining Path but not others. In other words, popular support or sympathy for a given group hinges on ongoing appraisals of that group's capacity to deliver certain desired goods. When that group delivers, sympathy is forthcoming. Diverging from local concerns and interests may result in the undermining of that support, and may become, as was the case in many parts of the countryside, active resistance.

What this ultimately suggests is that Shining Path's success in organizing among the urban poor hinged on its delivery of socially desired goods, which reflects a complex and dynamic pattern of political behavior among Peru's subaltern groups. It highlights a pragmatic understanding of politics, which focuses on constantly negotiating the terrain of politics with external actors, whether they are left-wing groups like Shining Path, right-wing populists, or state agencies seeking to co-opt the urban poor. Subaltern groups in Peru are not the simple recipients of clientelist or populist—or guerrilla—actions. Rather, they are constantly negotiating and renegotiating the terms of their relationships with outside actors. This was true not only for Shining Path, but also for popular relations with the García administration, with the IU, and later with the Fujimori regime. Clientelism—the predominant mode of state organization of society in much of Peruvian history—has created a political culture in which the rural and urban poor seek to negotiate with more powerful actors to obtain whatever benefits possible at the least possible cost to local autonomy. What Stern (1987) has termed "adaptive resistance" seems a particularly useful concept in this regard, as it recognizes the ongoing struggle at the grassroots level to negotiate goods and services that outside actors offer without glossing over the attempts to keep those actors at arms' length and preserve local spaces for action and decision making.

This chapter highlights the patterns of activity uncovered during my interviews and discussions with *barriada* residents that generated currents of sympathy for Shining Path activity in Lima's shantytowns. These elements are crucial for understanding Shining Path's ability to operate in Lima's shantytowns between 1989 and 1992, the height of the insurgent group's urban activity. At the same time, this examination of Shining Path's exchange relationships with the urban poor also highlights the limits of Shining Path's organizing abilities in the shantytowns. Generating sympathy was not as difficult as building longer-term bases of support. Shining Path eschewed the latter—in part because of its dogmatic belief in the ability of its "self-generated" organisms and the "contamination" of those grassroots groups that participated in the electoral process and sought change through local organizing. This was an inherent limitation to Shining Path's capacity to develop more sustained levels of popular support.

After Guzmán's arrest, the military regained the tactical initiative and the government sought to reassert state presence in the *barriadas*. Military bases were erected in several *barriadas* throughout Lima, and the army launched civic-action campaigns to win the hearts and minds of the urban poor. The civic-action campaigns typically began early in the morning. After door-to-door searches and the arrest of suspected subversives, the army delivered food and medicine to local residents in an effort to win local sympathy. The performative nature of the civic-action campaigns were often captured on local TV stations: poor chola women would gratefully accept sacks of rice and cans of milk, or happily submit their young children to haircuts by army personnel. On some occasions President Fujimori would make an appearance and dance with chola women to the music performed by a military band. In effect, the state was reasserting its presence in the *barriadas*, sending signals to residents that the authorities were now sensitive to their needs as long as they steered clear of trouble.

The civic-action campaigns were followed by massive state intervention in the *barriadas*. Government programs were launched to provide electricity and potable water. New schools were built and other infrastructure projects begun. The new state-created development agency, the Fund for Development and Social Compensation (FONCODES), began funding locally designed projects. This was one aspect of the reconstitution of the state under the Fujimori, and will be examined in greater detail in subsequent chapters. These efforts were also accompanied by stiff punishment of anyone suspected of sympathizing or collaborating with Shining Path. The result was hundreds if not thousands of innocents arrested under the draconian antiterrorist legislation put in place after the 1992 *autogolpe*. In several cases, community kitchen activists who had been forced to feed Shining Path militants were arrested as collaborators and given harsh prison sentences (Burt 1994). Such harsh punishment effectively undermined local tolerance for Shining Path activities, and proved to be a fundamental element in the shift toward support for the government and the armed forces by 1993.

Historian Steve Stern (1998) has noted that one of the fundamental paradoxes of Shining Path was its penetrating insight into the nature of local conflicts and its ability to exploit them to its advantage, even as it failed to understand that its authoritarianism and violence was destroying its ability to build long-term support. In the case of Lima's *barriadas*, Shining Path did create microlevel states where it became the local authority, providing and dispensing judgment and punishment in cases of corruption and crime. These types of activities created important currents of support and sympathy for Shining Path among the urban poor. However, Shining Path did not channel this into any structured mechanism to build longer-term support for its revolutionary project. Clearly, the group's authoritarian and dogmatic logic prevented it from conceiving of the importance of such long-term support. The states of Shining Path were thus premised on extremely fragile foundations. This helps to explain why the sympathy that Shining Path had generated in Lima's *barriadas* dissipated so quickly after the capture of Guzmán. As the Shining Path was forced to retreat and its capacity to deliver desired goods waned, so did its image as a powerful alternative purveyor of order and security—and the local support networks it had so carefully constructed in the *barriadas* of Lima.

# CHAPTER SEVEN

# The Battle of Villa El Salvador

In a context of relentless insurgent attacks and car bombs in Lima, Shining Path declared an armed strike in the capital for February 14, 1992. María Elena Moyano, a prominent Afro-Peruvian community leader who grew up and lived in Villa El Salvador, decided that the time had come to challenge Shining Path. The insurgent group had been gaining ground in Villa El Salvador, particularly among the rank and file of the different women's organizations in the district, including the community kitchens. Moyano, co-founder and former head of the FEPOMUVES, was elected deputy mayor of the district in 1989. She and several local IU leaders were mercilessly fustigated in Shining Path's newspaper *El Diario*.[1]

Moyano organized a march for peace on the day of Shining Path's declared armed strike. She sought to mobilize broad support from different political parties and social organizations. However, only about 50 people participated in the march, a small number compared to past mobilizations in the district. The recent history of division of the Left, and the pervasive fear that gripped Lima's residents in the context of the ongoing violence, meant few people were willing to challenge Shining Path in a head-on confrontation such as Moyano was proposing.

The day after the armed strike, while visiting a community barbeque, Moyano was ambushed by a Shining Path hit squad. She stood before her would-be assassins, telling her two children to turn the other way so they would not see what she knew was going to be her murder. After the assassins shot her, they placed sticks of dynamite on her body, physically obliterating her in a brutal display of violence.

The murder of Moyano shocked Peru. She was one of the few grassroots leaders who had become a public figure due to her outspoken defiance of Shining Path. She was celebrated by the local press, and was often invited to give interviews. In late 1991, invoking the name of a play by Bertolt Brecht, the weekly *Caretas* referred to her as "Mother Courage" for her defense of the poor in the face of hunger and political violence; the daily *La República* named her "person of the year." But Moyano was very much alone in her determined, if quixotic, campaign to challenge political violence on the part of both Shining Path and the armed forces.

Neither the state that lionized Moyano after her death, nor the insurgents who demonized her to justify her murder, cared much to recall Moyano's rejection of insurgent *and* state violence. Each actor sought to cast an image of her that best suited their own political purposes: for the state, she became a community leader who stood up to the brutality of Shining Path, proof positive that the insurgents were repudiated by the people and justifying state actions to crush them using all means at hand. For Shining Path, Moyano was a state collaborator *and* a member of the revisionist Left the Maoists considered their principal enemy—a double betrayal of the revolution that must be paid in blood.

Moyano's life and struggle were far more complex, as was the situation in *barriadas* like Villa El Salvador, where unarmed men and women struggling to survive in a poor country made poorer by foreign indebtedness, economic crisis, political violence, and harsh austerity measures, now found themselves facing pressure from different armed groups to collaborate or

**Figure 7.1**    María Elena Moyano Leads Protest against Hunger and Violence

Community leader Maria Elena Moyano leads a march protesting political violence by the Shining Path and state security forces, as well as government economic policies that perpetuate hunger and poverty. Moyano became a visible symbol of civil society resistance to political violence. On February 15, 1992, she was murdered by Shining Path in her hometown of Villa El Salvador.

*Source:* Caretas Archive.

participate in their struggles. This is not to suggest that Shining Path was an external actor that preyed upon local community organizations; this too is a simplistic view of a very complex reality. On the contrary, many young people were attracted to Shining Path's cause and became active recruits. Nor should it be forgotten that Moyano was an active member of the legal Left who was defending not only community organizations, but also a political project that was very different from Shining Path's popular war.

Villa El Salvador was of particular importance to Shining Path precisely because of the alternative model of state-society relations that the IU was attempting to construct there. Shining Path had begun organizing in the district in the early 1980s, trying to win recruits and gaining intimate knowledge of the political and social terrain of the district. In the late 1980s, *El Diario,* Shining Path's weekly newspaper, began publishing vociferous critiques of local leaders, including Moyano as well as Villa El Salvador's former mayor, Michel Azcueta, and current mayor Johny Rodríguez, each of whom had led a number of local initiatives to resist Shining Path's advance in the district. A series of attacks made it evident by the early 1990s that Shining Path was making a stand in Villa, seeking to decapitate the IU leadership, take over the district's key organizations, and extend its presence at the grassroots.[2] Those viewed as obstacles to Shining Path's revolutionary project—local authorities, political leaders, and community activists—were the object of systematic intimidation and often physical attack. In this lethal mix of politics and terror, and in the context of the division of the Left, a deepening economic crisis, and state retreat, Shining Path advanced steadily in Villa El Salvador. By the early 1990s it had infiltrated many of the district's key organizations, placed allies in leadership positions in organizations such as CUAVES, the Industrial Park and the FEPOMUVES, and created a climate of fear that inhibited opposition and further weakened local forms of organization.

The Peruvian state's failure to provide a local context of security for citizens and local authorities contributed to this sensation of fear. Its counterinsurgency strategy, which sought to establish an alliance between the armed forces and popular leaders and local authorities already under threat by Shining Path, made the situation all the more complicated and difficult for local leaders. For example, some moderates within IU had sought to build bridges with local police forces to defend the district from Shining Path, an effort that collapsed after the 1992 *autogolpe* and the implementation of a more aggressive counterinsurgency strategy. Moreover, insurgent and state violence and intimidation reduced public space and made social organization and action virtually impossible. Shining Path's brutal murder of María Elena Moyano brought this point home to many activists. Moyano's death symbolizes not only Shining Path's extreme authoritarianism and willingness to use violence to eliminate its rivals; it also underscores the extreme dispersion of the Left and its paralysis in the face of the dramatic challenge Shining Path represented to its political project as well as to the physical integrity of its members (Burt 1997b). It also revealed the state's incapacity—or perhaps its unwillingness—to protect governing authorities and citizens like Moyano who challenged violence on the part of *both* Shining Path and the state.[3]

By exploring the history of Villa El Salvador, its changing status in the political imagination of Peru first as a symbol of the reformist military regime's commitment to the poor, then as a model of grassroots organization and popular power championed by the democratic Left, and then as a battleground as Shining Path sought to extend its control over the district, this chapter provides insight into the complex and contentious political processes that came to the fore in Villa El Salvador, as elsewhere in Peru, in the 1990s. The chapter explores the diverse strategies adopted by Shining Path in the district; the varied responses of the immediate and wider civil society to these incursions; and the specific impact of political violence on the community.

## Villa El Salvador, Model District

At the time of Shining Path's move into Lima, Villa El Salvador was home to 260,000 inhabitants and was perhaps the most important symbol of left-wing organization and community development in Peru.[4] A settlement originally designed as the urban showcase of General Juan Velasco's reformist military government (1968–1975), Villa El Salvador became a center of left-wing organizing and grassroots mobilization against the more conservative Morales Bermúdez regime (1975–1980). The self-help efforts to develop the community fostered under the Velasco regime continued despite the withdrawal of state support, giving rise to a vast network of grassroots, community-based organizations. After Velasco's ouster in 1975, the state withdrew its support from Villa, and left-wing parties played an important role in supporting local grassroots efforts. After Peru's return to democratic rule in 1980, the IU won successive municipal elections in Villa throughout the 1980s. Considered to be the Left's most advanced model of popular participation and self-management (*autogestión*), Villa El Salvador was touted as a model of local organizing and a viable alternative to a neglectful state. Its model of urban planning and community participation was replicated in other *barriadas* in Lima, and its achievements were celebrated nationally and even internationally. As Shining Path sought to extend its presence beyond its initial base in the south-central Andes, Villa El Salvador was held up as an important example of a well-organized community based on solidarity and democratic participation that was virtually impenetrable to an authoritarian organization like Shining Path. Yet Shining Path continued to advance its presence in Lima. Perhaps most surprisingly, the Maoists also advanced relentlessly in popular *barriadas* such as Villa El Salvador, demonstrating important levels of influence in specific geographic areas as well as in the very social organizations that would presumably comprise a "social bulwark" against Shining Path.

Villa El Salvador is an illustrative case study of how Shining Path was able to extend its reach into the *barriadas* of Lima by exploiting the "gray areas" abandoned by the retreating state and the crisis of organized politics. As in other *barriadas*, Shining Path sought to extend its influence and authority in Villa El Salvador by fulfilling functions the retreating state was no longer fulfilling, or perhaps had never fulfilled. It sought to provide basic levels of security and order by punishing and sometimes assassinating perceived "wrongdoers" and "deviants" deemed dangerous to the community, such as drug addicts, drug dealers, thieves, and the like, and those violating basic norms of the community, such as wife beaters, adulterers, and corrupt leaders. In the context of the inability of state or other institutions to mediate local conflict, the group also sought to act as an arbiter of social conflict by imposing its own version of justice in case of perceived wrongdoings. Finally, as social organizations became seen as increasingly ineffective in obtaining goods from an increasingly disengaged and unresponsive state, Shining Path sought to demonstrate the superiority of its method of struggle—violence—compared to peaceful protest and social organization.

Villa El Salvador was an important objective for Shining Path for strategic and geopolitical reasons. As the largest popular district in Lima's southern cone, Villa El Salvador was a strategic area to control for Shining Path's larger plan of encircling Lima. In geopolitical terms, on one side Villa borders the Pan-American Highway, Lima's main link to southern Peru; on the other, across the foothills of the Andes, it links up to other shantytowns that surround Lima, forming part of the "iron belt of misery" that Guzmán said would encircle and strangle the capital city. Aside from these strategic considerations, Villa El Salvador was also an important political objective for Shining Path. Its status as "model district" for important sectors of the Left made it a dangerous symbol for Shining Path. Peaceful organizing was not part of Shining Path's agenda; only violent revolution could produce "real" changes in Peru. In fact, an important part of Shining Path's ideological battles were fought not only against the state or the right, but against Peru's legal Left and the organizations that had become associated with it. The legal Left participated in elections, had members in congress, and ran local municipal governments. For Shining Path, this "revisionism" meant that the Left had been "contaminated" by the "putrid old order" that they sought to destroy by force. The real battle, Guzmán is reported as saying, was against this "revisionist Left"—its principal competitor for popular support. Villa El Salvador— the Left's showpiece of grassroots organizing and local participatory government—was a key symbol of the legal Left that Shining Path was bent on obliterating. By gaining influence in precisely those areas that, like Villa El Salvador, were such crucial symbols of the mainstream Left, Shining Path could "unmask" the "revisionism" of the IU and prove that it offered the only truly "revolutionary" alternative for social change.[5] As one of my interviewees stated when asked why Shining Path wanted to control Villa El Salvador, "Shining Path knows that if they can control Villa, they can control anything."[6]

Based on extensive ethnographic research carried out in the mid and late 1990s in Villa El Salvador, this chapter provides additional evidence of how Shining Path exploited the retreat of the state and the crisis of organized politics to expand its presence in marginal urban communities. It also examines in greater detail how Shining Path sought to challenge the crisis of organized politics to its advantage by reconstructing the evolution of Shining Path activities in the district and analyzing on the ways it sought to challenge the dominance of the IU, which was increasingly divided, in the district. Shining Path also sought out individual leaders and groups who were disgruntled from the IU leadership and its affiliated organizations in the district for a variety of reasons. Maoist strategies of revolutionary action maintain that insurgents must identify the "principal contradiction" in each site of struggle and act upon those contradictions to further the revolutionary cause (Mao 1937). Shining Path identified the main sources of strife or conflict in a given area, which it then deliberately tried to exacerbate and manipulate to its advantage. In its logic of confrontation politics, Shining Path identified local popular demands and struggles that were not being addressed and sought to radicalize them to win popular sympathy while at the same time discrediting local and national authorities. It also played on existing conflicts within and among local organizations and left-wing parties in the district as a way of discrediting grassroots leaders affiliated with the IU—which, as discussed previously, the organization had long considered the principal enemy of its revolution—as well as building up its local influence.

Finally, the chapter explores the responses of civil society to Shining Path's incursions into Villa El Salvador. Many left-wing grassroots activists and local organizations tried to contest Shining Path's attempts to control Villa El Salvador and its organizations. In response to these resistance efforts, the Maoists did not hesitate to use coercion, threats, and assassination. The case of María Elena Moyano is just one example of Shining Path's willingness to use terrorist tactics to eliminate rivals, decapitate local organizations, and destroy alternative political projects.

Shining Path thus engaged in a complex and deadly mix of politics and terror. Shining Path's ability to negotiate the complex terrain of urban politics was fatally underestimated by politicians, scholars, and local activists alike. A detailed examination of Shining Path's activities in Villa El Salvador, the response by local civil society to its presence, and the nature of popular attitudes and responses toward Shining Path will highlight some of the key aspects that permitted Shining Path to gain a significant foothold in this popular district as well as in other *barriadas* in Lima. It will also provide a more contextualized understanding of grassroots attempts to resist Shining Path's overtures, and the debilitating impact of the Shining Path's campaign of intimidation and violence on civil society.

## Urban Utopia

Villa El Salvador was founded in 1971 by the populist military regime of General Juan Velasco Alvarado in response to a land invasion organized by poor migrants and slum dwellers. Some 200 families organized the original land invasion, but within a few days over 9,000 families had joined the invasion, which spilled over onto privately owned land. After a brief but tense stand-off between police and the squatters, in which one squatter was killed and several were arrested, the Velasco regime—under pressure to prove its commitment to the poor Peruvians that its "revolutionary" experiment promised to benefit—decided to relocate the invaders to an extensive piece of barren desert land 18 miles south of Lima. Thousands of poor families were given land by the Velasco government in this new settlement, which residents called Villa El Salvador, and which would become the urban showcase of Velasco's "revolution." State planners were charged with turning this spontaneous invasion into Peru's first planned urban community, simultaneously resolving the pent-up housing crisis and obtaining popular support for the military regime. This was a marked departure from the traditional laissez-faire attitude that characterized the state's approach to the development of Lima's *barriadas* since the 1940s.

Another novel feature of the state's involvement in Villa El Salvador was the organizing principle of *autogestión* that guided the project. Through the *autogestión* model, which encouraged local residents to organize and mobilize to develop the community and participate in local decision making, the state would assist Villa El Salvador in establishing community-owned enterprises that would lay the foundation for the settlement's autonomous and socialist development. This was part of Velasco's larger reformist experiment in social property, designed to increase worker participation and benefits in local enterprise.[7] Villa quickly became the urban showpiece of Velasco's "revolution."

The community's structure was laid out block by block, in grid fashion. Every block was composed of 24 family lots, and 16 blocks constituted a residential group. Each residential group had an area demarcated as communal land for the future development of community projects such as preschools, meeting houses, community kitchens and soccer fields. Today, these residential groups are assembled into 10 large sectors.[8] Each block elected 3 representatives, and of the 48 chosen from each residential group, 8 were selected as the main group leaders. This territorial division was designed not only to rationalize the urbanization process, but also to facilitate local organizing as well as state control over the mobilization process.

State planners created a centralized governing body, the CUAVES, that would oversee the development of the community and represent it before the government and other outside agencies. The rank and file of the CUAVES was made up of the leaders of the residential groups, from which a ten-member executive council was elected. Areas were also slated for the future development of an Industrial Park and an agricultural zone as part of Velasco's design to make Villa El Salvador a self-sustaining and self-managing community.

The first convention of the CUAVES was held in 1973. The following year, the Velasco government financed the formation of several community enterprises, including a credit union (*caja comunal*), a cooperative bakery, hardware store, and kerosene store, which were to be administered by the community represented by the CUAVES. Through the credit union, social property enterprises would be financed with government assistance, generating local employment in the Industrial Park. CUAVES was to oversee community participation and negotiate and plan with the appropriate government agencies. Housing construction, however, was to be undertaken by each individual family, though neighbors often helped each other construct their homes.

Villa's first years were marked by intensive organizing by the newly settled inhabitants. Community involvement spread over a broad range of self-help activities, and even today Villa's first residents recall the enthusiasm and commitment with which they participated in different community improvement projects. Some of these collective efforts were carried out under the guise of state agencies and planners, including the group provision of manual labor in infrastructure development (digging holes to install water and sewage pipes, or leveling the sand dunes for road construction). Other activities evolved from the community's own initiatives: perhaps the first true community effort was the construction of several classrooms, built and financed by donations from the community members themselves. The community often had to pay teachers' salaries as well. At the block level, women organized "clean-up committees" to deal with the lack of garbage collection, and "tree committees" were created to beautify VES and populate the desert with trees and gardens.[9] Nursery school teachers, called "animators," were chosen by the members of each community block to work with preschool children. Local neighborhood watch groups helped prevent crime and punish wrongdoers.

The regime created the National System of Social Mobilization (SINAMOS) in 1972 to channel urban support for the military regime. In Villa El Salvador, SINAMOS was charged with overseeing CUAVES and work with it to implement the regime's vision of social property and self-management. The government provided direct support to the settlement, including food handouts, public lighting, and water transported in large cisterns. But the corporatist model that the regime sought to impose soon came up against the resistance of local organizers. Many of these were activists linked to the New Left parties that, unlike the pro–Moscow

PC-Unity, repudiated the military regime and agitated for a popular revolutionary alternative. These activists sought to exploit the contradictions within the regime over the nature of its support for the *barriada*. Growing dissatisfaction with the scope and pace of government support, and conflicts with SINAMOS planners as CUAVES sought to expand its margins of autonomy, led to a more critical approach to the regime. These conflicts grew more intense after the ouster of Velasco in 1975, as government support for the district gave way to government austerity, and as co-optation as a mode of social control gave way to outright repression.

The palace coup led by Francisco Morales Bermúdez in 1975 marked the hardening of the military regime's posture toward Peru's popular sectors. Not only did the central government abandon its assistance program to Villa El Salvador, but it also stepped up its repression against popular protests, which picked up in the aftermath of the regime's implementation of harsh austerity measures. Villa El Salvador reflected the changing balance of forces in Peruvian politics. Once a pet project of the military government and a bastion of pro-Velasco sentiment, it swiftly became a center of left-wing organizing and community development independent, and often in confrontation with, the central government. One protest, called by the CUAVES in coordination with the SUTEP and local parent-teacher associations in March 1976, brought 30,000 together demanding local improvements an end to austerity measures; the government responded with repression. Villa and its organizations became the vanguard of the *barriada* protest movement against the military regime, and the emerging parties of the New Left jockeyed to gain influence in the settlement.

The increasingly antipopular stance of the military regime opened up important political spaces in places like Villa El Salvador. The New Left parties saw in the spontaneous popular mobilizations of the poor and working classes the seed for a true revolutionary change in Peruvian society (Nieto 1983). Organized labor, shantytown organizations, and the New Left groups joined forces to challenge the military regime and its policies on the streets. Three successful national strikes between 1977 and 1979 against the regime's economic policies, and against military rule in general, helped push the military toward a return to civilian rule. Although the New Left parties initially hoped to see this mobilization turn to more radical directions, most of them agreed to participate in the constituent assembly called by the military to lead the transition process to democratic rule, though in many cases this was more of a tactical move designed to gain and maintain local support rather than a normative acceptance of democracy as the "only game in town" (Nieto 1983).[10] In the 1978 constituent assembly elections, the New Left parties emerged as a significant force in Peruvian politics, winning a combined 30 percent of the vote.[11] Yet the Left continued to distinguish between "formal" electoral democracy and "real" social democracy, a distinction that would shape the Left's ambivalence vis-à-vis Shining Path during the course of the 1980s.

Moving to the forefront of the opposition against the military carried its costs. As state resources dried up, Villa El Salvador was left on its own to meet the challenges of providing basic infrastructure to its growing population, which increased from 105,000 residents in 1973 to 168,000 in 1984. Villa El Salvador depended administratively on the municipal government of neighboring Villa María del Triunfo, but little assistance was forthcoming to help the settlement resolve its problems. Little changed with the new democratic government of Fernando Belaúnde Terry (1980–1985); austerity measures fueled the economic crisis, and the Belaúnde administration displayed little concern with improving the lot of poor residents of Lima's *barriadas*. In Villa El Salvador, members of the community began to mobilize collectively to address poverty and hunger. Women, for example, began organizing after 1979 to meet their families' basic nutrition needs by forming community kitchens, often with the assistance of the Catholic Church and other development agencies. The CUAVES, however, had lost its principal resource base with the retreat of government support and many of its projects faltered, generating mistrust among the population (Burt and Espejo 1995). This was the case, for example, of the credit union, which collapsed after government support was withdrawn. Many families lost their savings, and charges of corruption in the management of these enterprises further undermined confidence in the CUAVES and its leaders. Partisan infighting among the left-wing parties in the CUAVES also undermined the organization's image. The district seemed increasingly adrift. But the combination of municipal neglect and the collapse of the CUAVES fueled a growing movement among local residents to establish Villa El Salvador as an independent municipality. In 1983, congress approved the creation of Villa El Salvador as an independent municipal district, and elections were held the following year.

## The Democratic Left and
## Popular Power

Michel Azcueta, a Spaniard by birth and a teacher at *Fe y Alegría*, a well-known experimental high school, was elected mayor of Villa El Salvador for two consecutive terms in 1983 and 1986 on the IU ticket. Azcueta, the principal architect of the movement to make Villa an independent municipal district, proposed an ambitious project of promoting grassroots participation and community development through local government. Azcueta hoped to reactivate the CUAVES and the block-level organizations, and new elections were held for the executive council of the CUAVES. Some old-time CUAVES leaders were nervous about—and some outright opposed to—the creation of the municipal government, fearing that it would usurp the traditional role of the CUAVES. To allay such fears, Azcueta's first act as mayor was to formally recognize the

CUAVES as the central representative organization of the community, and he promised to respect its organizational autonomy. Azcueta's proposal was to create a partnership between the municipal government and the CUAVES to develop a coherent development plan for the district. In Azcueta's retooling of the model of self-management, the municipal government would provide institutional support to the community organizations, using state resources to decentralize government and devolve power to the community organizations. The Left helped promote the formation of new organizations in Villa El Salvador, including the FEPOMUVES and the Association of Small Entrepreneurs of Villa El Salvador (APEMIVES). The latter would become a key protagonist of the Industrial Park, which Azcueta helped get off the ground with assistance from the central government and international donations. The Industrial Park was crucial to the self-management model because support for local industry would help promote local business initiatives and stimulate the district's economy.

From its position in the municipal government, the Left promoted grassroots organizing and participation in local decision making, in some cases devolving control of municipal-run programs to the community organizations. This was the case, for example, with the glass of milk program, initiated by Lima mayor Alfonso Barrantes, architect of the IU coalition, in 1984, in which the municipal government provided a glass of milk each day to children and pregnant women in Lima's shantytowns, and women organized local committees to distribute the milk. Azcueta signed an agreement devolving control of the milk program to the FEPOMUVES, which continues to run the program. This was part of the left-wing project of building "popular power."

After Alan García was elected president in 1985, intensified party competition imposed its own dynamic on local social movements. In an effort to broaden its social base among the urban poor, the APRA government developed extensive social programs, including a temporary work program, though these were often criticized for being highly clientelistic in nature (Graham 1992). Rather than channel food aid to existing community kitchens—many of which received funds from NGDOs and the Catholic Church and were viewed therefore as the constituents of the IU—the government used public funds to create new social organizations that were dependent on state funds, such as mothers' clubs, in Villa El Salvador and other *barriadas* throughout Lima. These new groups competed with other established organizations for scarce resources and for social recognition, and fueled partisan competition. Despite APRA's inroads in Villa El Salvador, the IU dominated local politics in the district during the 1980s. Nevertheless, the competition between the two groups, as described in greater detail in chapter four, often divided social movements and inhibited efforts at common action. Interparty conflict within the IU itself would also prove to undermine the Left's stated goal of building grassroots unity.

In particular, the way the IU was structured would prove to have dire consequences for left-wing organizing in Villa El Salvador and elsewhere in Peru. The coalition was based on a loose structure of affiliation with no strong central leadership. This flexibility permitted each party to retain its own sense of identity while being able to participate in the IU coalition. What worked in terms of national-level politics, however, often had negative consequences at the grassroots. In effect, rivalries emerged among the different parties in the search to control social organizations and establish hegemony vis-à-vis other left-wing parties. As one left-wing activist and former member of the IU said, "relations between the different parties in Villa were cordial and fraternal, but they were also very complicated. It was difficult to figure out who was working for the front [the IU] and who was working for his or her political party."[12] These rivalries would grow and fester, with important repercussions both for the future of the IU and for the district as a whole, as we shall see.

Villa El Salvador won international recognition for its accomplishments, including Spain's Prince of Asturias Award in 1987 and the title "City Messenger of Peace" by the UN in 1985.[13] Social scientists and radical political activists alike considered Villa El Salvador to be a paradigmatic case of the *"barriada* movement," noteworthy for its dense network of grassroots organizations and the affirmation of a new identity based on membership in the community (*vecino* [neighbor]) (Tovar 1986). Scholars contrasted the democratic and participatory nature of these organizations with the elitism and authoritarianism of national politics (Ballón 1986). As Shining Path sought to develop its presence in Lima, these positive elements of Villa El Salvador's development were highlighted as factors that would block Shining Path's incursions. A city constructed by poor people through organization and sacrifice would not succumb to the authoritarian dictates of the Maoist insurgents.

Events would demonstrate that things were much more complex. Shining Path came to exercise significant levels of influence in organizations like CUAVES, the FEPOMUVES, and the small industrialists' association that constituted the key pillars of the district's unique and widely heralded model of self-management. Shining Path was particularly adept at identifying individuals and groups that felt excluded or marginalized from the dominant influence of the IU in Villa El Salvador, and sought to channel this discontent into its own struggle to discredit the Left and its political project. Shining Path tried to demonstrate the futility of peaceful strategies for social change in an attempt both to discredit the left-wing parties that continued to organize and that were its chief rival on the ground and to radicalize popular struggles in its logic of confrontation with the state.

Shining Path also sought, often successfully, to build sympathy among local populations by championing popular causes. This was especially the case in more recently established settlements in Villa El Salvador, where there was little or no state presence, few if any NGOs, political parties, or even parishes. Shining Path was able to mobilize sympathy among local populations in such areas by becoming purveyors of goods and services local communities desperately wanted and needed. As in other *barriadas*, Shining Path played upon the state's incapacity to provide basic security to its citizens, and its clean-up campaigns to rid the community of thieves, drug addicts, and other delinquents, won it a great deal of sympathy. At the local level, Shining Path attempted to construct an image of itself as a harsh but fair imparter of justice in a country in which justice was routinely bought and sold, and where conflict resolution mechanisms at the grassroots were sorely lacking. It "punished" local authorities, vendors, and community leaders who it claimed were corrupt, and in many instances successfully manipulated popular outrage at such petty acts of corruption in its favor.

Underlying all of these political strategies was the Shining Path's campaign of terror in Villa El Salvador. In 1991 Shining Path began a campaign to eliminate local authorities, including the assassination of some and threats against others. This mirrored Shining Path's strategy in the countryside in the early 1980s, where it sought to eliminate representatives of the "old state" and build its own local organizations and political authority. Shining Path also engaged in selective assassinations against community leaders and others it charged with corruption or other misdeeds. Whether these charges were real or not, many members of the community perceived Shining Path's action to be part of a moralizing campaign of sorts. Corruption was widespread, and often a simple accusation was enough to confirm suspicions of wrong-doing. Thus Shining Path often simply accused someone it sought to eliminate with corruption to justify its actions. Before exploring Shining Path's lethal mix of politics and terror in Villa El Salvador, a brief overview of Shining Path's development in the district is necessary.

### Laying the Groundwork

In order to understand how Shining Path gained a foothold in Villa El Salvador and challenged its most important institutions and organizations in 1991 and 1992, it is important to look back to Shining Path's previous clandestine and subterranean organizing activities in Villa since the early 1980s.[14] During these initial years of the war, Shining Path's public presence in Lima was minimal. It mainly engaged in armed attacks against the state security apparatus, government agencies, economic infrastructure, and centers of economic activity as a way of disrupting normal activity and demonstrating its presence. Since armed attacks in Lima were more likely to be covered by the press both nationally and internationally, these acts of sabotage had significant symbolic and propaganda value (McCormick 1992). In Villa El Salvador, a relatively small number of armed attacks were carried out between 1981 and 1986 against government agencies, the district's only police station, and economic infrastructure such as banks and electricity pylons, which had the dramatic effect of submerging the city in darkness. Occasional agit-prop activities were also carried out in Villa El Salvador, including huge bonfires outlining a hammer and sickle on the hills surrounding the district. But for most of the residents of Villa El Salvador, Shining Path was a movement in far-off Ayacucho that rarely impinged on their daily lives.

Several reports indicate that there was low-level organizing activity going on in many Lima shantytowns as well as public universities and trade unions (especially SUTEP) in this early period. Analysts—focusing on the war raging in the countryside, where Shining Path armed activity was strongest and military counterinsurgency harshest—paid little attention to Shining Path's clandestine organizing in Lima. Radical student groups at different national universities in Lima—particularly San Marcos University, Enrique Guzmán y Valle (La Cantuta) University, and the National University of Engineering—organized small cells that later galvanized student support for Shining Path's insurgency. A small nuclei of students from San Marcos organized study groups in Villa El Salvador (and other shantytowns) to recruit new members.[15] Public universities were privileged sites of recruitment for Shining Path; indeed, studies have demonstrated that the majority of Shining Path recruits have some degree of higher education (Chavez de Paz 1989). High schools were also important recruitment sites. In Villa El Salvador, Nelly Evans, a former nun and member of a prominent Lima family, was a professor during the late 1970s and early 1980s at Fe y Alegría, one of the district's most important high schools. A high-ranking member of Shining Path who was arrested in the late 1980s, Evans reportedly promoted study groups of the literary works of Peruvian novelist José María Arguedas to recruit young students to the "revolutionary cause."[16]

By 1987, Shining Path's intention to establish a more organic presence in Villa became evident. While sabotage activities continued, there were signs of more grassroots political activism. According to several interviewees, Shining Path members created new discussion groups and cultural associations to recruit followers, as well as technical academies, where many high-school graduates with scant chance of entering the university sought training for—or at least to delay their entrance to—an otherwise unpromising job market. After 1988–1989, Shining Path's agit-prop activities became more visible. For example, small Shining Path contingents participated in activities and protest marches organized by legal left-wing groups, often directed against government economic measures or human rights violations committed by the military, but raising the banner of violent revolution as the only solution to Peru's political, economic, and social problems.

Many local left-wing activists considered Shining Path to be misguided in its use of violence. There was, however, an important element of ambiguity in the Left's perception of Shining Path, rooted in a common ideological legacy that saw armed struggle as both legitimate and necessary to bring about structural change.[17] This was not only the case in Lima's *barriadas*, but in the trade union movement as well, which had a long trajectory of combating the military regime and was struggling to cope with economic austerity and new antilabor legislation (Sulmont et al. 1989; Balbi 1992, 1997). The government's poor human rights record—including the arbitrary detention of hundreds of left-wing activists not affiliated to Shining Path, massacres, and forced disappearances—made it difficult for mainstream Left activists to challenge Shining Path's characterization of the regime as repressive.

This ambiguity at the grassroots level reflected divided opinions within the IU coalition toward Shining Path and its struggle. While moderate elements distanced themselves from Shining Path in the early 1980s, more radical groups within the IU maintained a more permissive attitude. Although critical of Shining Path's terrorist methods, they noted the "popular extraction" of Shining Path's militants, their moral commitment to realizing the march toward socialism, and the confluence of positions between the Left and Shining Path against a common enemy—the capitalist state.[18] In 1987, Jorge del Prado, general secretary of PC-Unity, said that Shining Path was a "revolutionary force" and that they should not be "excommunicated" from the rest of the Left. As one national leader of the IU stated, "These more radical elements in the IU did not see Shining Path as an enemy that had to be defeated."[19]

An important segment of Peru's mainstream Left came to value the political and civic liberties guaranteed at least in principle by a democratic system, and tried to defend Peru's democracy while challenging the violence unleashed by both Shining Path and government forces. However, controversy was intense within this sector over *how* to relate to both the state and to Shining Path. Some within the Left reached the conclusion that Shining Path was the principal enemy of the Left and began to advocate active collaboration with the state in order to defeat Shining Path.[20] For others, however, the massive human rights violations committed by the armed forces throughout the 1980s and into the 1990s reinforced their vision of the state as an essentially repressive and antipopular entity (Abugattás 1990). As another IU leader stated, "Supporting or collaborating with the armed forces was a hard pill to swallow. For some, it amounted to treason."[21] Within this group, the meager results of a decade of left-wing participation in democratic government fueled disillusionment with the possibility of peaceful social change. Many of these individuals eventually left the IU to join MRTA or Shining Path, particularly after the IU split in 1989.

Over the course of the 1980s, the *barriada* population grew dramatically, from 1.5 million to an estimated 3–3.5 million in the early 1990s. Continued rural migration to Lima—now increasingly fueled by the state and insurgent violence—was one factor in fueling this rapid growth, but it was also largely due to population growth within existing *barriadas*.

Second- and third-generation *barriada* residents were now seeking to create their own households, but the absence of viable housing led them to follow in the footsteps of their parents, organizing small invasions on the outskirts of existing *barriadas* (Driant 1991). Villa El Salvador was no exception. Between 1984 and 1993, the population had grown from 168,000 to 260,000, a 5 percent annual growth rate. According to the 1984 census carried out by CUAVES, new invasions made up 27 percent of Villa's overall population, consisting mainly of young couples with smaller families and lower incomes who lived in precarious houses of cane matting (CUAVES/CIDIAG 1984). More recent data is not available, but new invasions have continued in the late 1980s and early 1990s, expanding Villa El Salvador's original six sectors to ten. Most of these families lacked land titles, although the municipal government usually adopted a permissive attitude toward squatters. According to 1993 census, one-third of Villa residents lacked piped water, while 24 percent lacked electricity (INEI 1994). With the fiscal crisis, the central government was unable to provide these new settlements with basic infrastructure (piped water, sewerage, electricity) that older, more established parts of the district had obtained in the 1970s and early 1980s. This process of internal diversification created tensions within the district, as many households in the older, more established parts of the district had housing and basic infrastructure, while a significant and growing sector had fewer personal resources as well as less access to outside assistance to improve their local living conditions.[22]

Shining Path's organizing efforts focused especially in these parts of Villa El Salvador. Local observers say that after 1989 they began to note the presence of Shining Path cadre in newly formed settlements such as Pachacamac, which had grown dramatically. It was relatively easy for Shining Path members to join a land invasion and become part of the local community. Many became active in the local neighborhood councils that formed the rank and file of the CUAVES, the centralized community organization in the district. Squatters organized these councils to improve conditions in the community and petition the government for infrastructure. Shining Path sought to win local sympathy by taking up the demands of the local population. For example, Shining Path took up the banner of land tenure for squatters in Pachacamac. Some local leaders in these areas became sympathetic to Shining Path's cause, especially as the economic crisis deepened and state resources dried up, demanding services from the government seemed increasingly futile. Shining Path actively sought to encourage this perception, often challenging IU leaders at the local level over their proposals to organize protest marches and petition the authorities. By radicalizing popular struggles, Shining Path believed it would reveal the state's unwillingness to respond to the local population's demands and the need for more drastic alternatives.

Little attention was paid to Shining Path's subterranean organizing efforts in shantytowns such as Villa El Salvador. Some of the group's activities were so unobtrusive that they were difficult to perceive except to the most informed local observers, and by the early 1990s, Shining Path activists and new recruits worked side by side with their unwitting neighbors at the local level, forming water and electricity committees and seeking to gain positions of influence in local community councils linked to the CUAVES. Other more open organizing efforts were tolerated, in part out of fear—"snitches" were sure targets for Shining Path reprisals—but also because of the continuing assumptions among segments of the legal Left that despite Shining Path's misguided methods, they were ultimately fighting the same enemy: a corrupt and increasingly delegitimized state. Coupled with long-standing mistrust of the police and the military, this prompted many local activists with knowledge of Shining Path activity to simply stay quiet. As Shining Path's intentions of destroying the project of Villa El Salvador became increasingly apparent, many activists who strongly identified themselves with Villa El Salvador and the larger project of self-management and popular participation it represented began to directly challenge the Maoists in the district. But this initial permissiveness allowed Shining Path a crucial space to organize, collect information, and establish a local network of sympathizers and activists that was central to its campaign of direct confrontation in the early 1990s. The problem of how to confront an armed movement willing to use violence would also create conflict within the Left in Villa El Salvador.

### Destroying the Myth: The
### Politics of Confrontation

After 1991, as part of its larger plan of upping the ante of the war in Lima, Shining Path began to engage in openly confrontational politics in Villa El Salvador. Guzmán's announcement in May 1991 that the organization had reached "strategic equilibrium" meant launching more aggressive campaigns on all fronts, especially in the strategically important *barriadas*, where the "decisive battle" would be fought.[23] Gaining influence in a left-wing stronghold like Villa El Salvador would not only promote Shining Path's strategic objectives of strengthening its hold on Lima's *barriada* districts; it would also have significant political impact by demonstrating that the organization was in fact capable of maneuvering in the more complex terrain of urban politics.

Shining Path's clandestine organizing and recruitment activity laid the groundwork for its more direct confrontational politics by permitting the organization to elaborate an exhaustive diagnostic of the political and social situation in Villa El Salvador. Operating on the Maoist maxim of the "principal contradiction," Shining Path sought to identify the central sources of strife or conflict in a given area, which it then deliberately tried to exacerbate in its logic of confrontation politics. Shining Path identified local popular demands and struggles that were not being addressed and sought to radicalize them to win popular sympathy and discredit local and national authorities. At the same time, it played on existing conflicts within and among local organizations as a way of discrediting the Left leadership, enhancing its own status, and polarizing local society.

Based on this logic of the "principal contradiction," Shining Path engaged in a head-on confrontation against the IU leadership in Villa El Salvador. The Left was targeted not only because Shining Path considered it revisionist and the principal "enemy" of its "revolution." In addition, after nearly a decade in formal, institutional power in Villa El Salvador, the mainstream Left had become part of the local power structure around which a series of conflicts—some recent, some more long-standing—had emerged. Shining Path identified conflicts such as that between the IU municipal leadership and the CUAVES as the focal point to mobilize disgruntled individuals and groups, discredit the IU leadership, create the social space for its own organizing and propaganda activities, and demonstrate the futility of peaceful organizing and the necessity of revolutionary armed action. Pinpointing local conflicts and seeking to exacerbate them would help undermine the legal Left and its project of self-management while permitting the Maoists to build up their local presence by exploiting local grievances. By radicalizing popular struggles and exacerbating conflict between different actors in the district, Shining Path sought to provoke military repression, which it believed would ultimately favor its cause. This not only had importance for Shining Path's designs in Villa itself, but also had repercussions at the national level given the symbolic significance of Villa El Salvador and its central organizations such as the CUAVES.

Since its formation in 1980, the IU was the central political actor in Villa El Salvador. Michel Azcueta led the campaign to establish Villa as an independent municipality in 1983, and he was elected mayor on the IU ticket for two consecutive terms between 1983 and 1989. His administration could point to several achievements. Starting from scratch, he got the municipal government working by mobilizing volunteer support. Committed to the Left's model of popular participation, Azcueta not only promoted the formation of new organizations like the small industrialists' association, APEMIVES, and an association of street vendors, FUCOMIVES, but also devolved control of municipal programs to community organizations. For example, with the direct support of the mayor, FEPOMUVES assumed administrative control of the glass of milk program. Azcueta was also able to muster international support for various local development projects, and progress could be counted in the number of paved roads, streetlights, and municipal garbage trucks that kept the district clean. In conjunction with local NGDOs that were active in Villa El Salvador—many of which promoted small workshops and lent assistance to popular organizations such as the community kitchens and the milk committees—the municipal government devised an Integral Development Plan, which laid out a series of proposals for the district in different policy arenas such as housing.[24] The mayor also obtained government and international assistance to implement the Industrial Park, where nearly 200 small business owners had set up workshops or factories by 1990. Villa El Salvador became a model of popular participation and grassroots decision making, which was held up by the Left as an example of its capacity to govern and offer concrete solutions to Peru's structural problems of poverty and unemployment. This was a crucial experiment for the Left, which was a serious contender for the presidential elections in 1990.

The IU easily won the 1989 municipal elections in Villa El Salvador. Johny Rodríguez was elected mayor, and María Elena Moyano, former president of the FEPOMUVES, was elected deputy mayor. The Rodríguez–Moyano administration faced more difficult times. In Peru's highly centralized political system, municipal governments in Peru have always operated under serious budget constraints, especially in poorer districts. But the ravaging effects of hyperinflation decimated the municipal government's budget. And as Villa El Salvador grew and became more internally diverse and heterogeneous, the problems that community organizations helped resolve in an earlier epoch became more complex. The district's more established areas experienced a general demobilization of the neighborhood councils as communities obtained basic infrastructure. New squatters, meanwhile, turned to the municipal government to resolve their problems of infrastructure and land tenure, but it had few resources available to meet the growing demand.

Azcueta, Rodríguez, and Moyano all belonged to the PUM, one of the best-organized parties in the IU coalition, until the party split in 1989. The party's division was due in part to growing discrepancies over conceptions of armed struggle and the role of the Left in supporting Peru's fledgling democracy. The radicals within the PUM, known as *Libios*, maintained that armed struggle was still valid and necessary, but that their participation in the state was justified as a tactical movement, as it was an important space in which to wage the political struggle for social change. This ambivalence vis-à-vis democratic rule made a clear split with Shining Path difficult. The moderates, known as *Zorros*, reiterated their commitment to strengthening Peru's democracy and condemned Shining Path, although there was still controversy over the degree to which the Left should collaborate with the state in the struggle against Shining Path. Along with an important block of followers in Villa El Salvador, Azcueta and Rodríguez joined the newly formed Revolutionary Mariateguista Party (PMR), while Moyano later joined the newly created Movement of Socialist Affirmation (MAS), which was linked to progressive Catholic activists. Both groups remained in the IU coalition, but tensions with the more radical sectors remained. With the approaching 1990 presidential elections, these tensions, coupled with conflicts within the IU over leadership and the apportionment of electoral seats, led to a split in the coalition. Alfonso Barrantes, the ex-mayor of Lima, was selected as presidential candidate for the more moderate IS, while the IU chose sociologist Henry Pease as its candidate. On the ground, however, the IU coalition was dead letter. Each political party focused on defining its own political profile and popular support base, exacerbating an existing trend in which each party sought to obtain "hegemony" over particular social groups and organizations. As Shining Path sought to up the ante in Lima's "iron belts of misery," this would have grave ramifications in *barriadas* such as Villa El Salvador.

The division of the IU led to the surfacing of the underlying tensions that had existed within the left-wing coalition on the ground well before the formal split in 1989. While Azcueta was able to mobilize important levels of support for his project in Villa El Salvador, there were nonetheless important levels of jockeying for grassroots support among the different IU parties, and partisan rivalries were often intense. The fact that Azcueta's project was dominant did not mean that it was uncontested. While PUM had gained prominence in many of Villa's key organizations, other IU parties were also seeking to establish their own influence, reflecting the gravest weakness of the IU coalition. The fact that the electoral coalition permitted each organization to maintain its own party structure and goals often translated into intense struggles to establish "hegemony" within local contexts. As one PUM activist noted in 1994 during a workshop to discuss the impact of political violence on the district, "this struggle for hegemony dominated the Left's actions in Villa, and led to divisions within the organizations, which all the different parties tried to control."[25] This partisan jockeying intensified after the 1988 split of PUM, making united action among the Left in Villa El Salvador far more difficult. The divisions between small radical left-wing groups within the CUAVES that remained marginalized from the IU coalition throughout the 1980s was also a significant source of conflict within the district, as we shall see later.

By 1991, Shining Path's presence in Villa El Salvador had become decidedly more aggressive and high profile. The Maoists had launched an open campaign to intimidate and eliminate local authorities, just as it had in the countryside. In June, Shining Path killed the governor of Villa, Alejandro Magno Gómez, who was affiliated with the governing party, Cambio 90.[26] Between 1989 and 1992, Shining Path's newspaper, *El Diario*, frequently and vociferously criticized Villa El Salvador and its principal leaders. Azcueta and Moyano were singled out as "opportunists" and revisionists, and the Left's experiment of self-management in Villa El Salvador was sharply attacked as a sham designed "to castrate the combativeness and the revolutionary potential of the masses."[27] Moyano, along with other left-wing mayors and vice-mayors of *barriada* districts in Lima, was accused of corruption and "working against the Maoist revolution" in *El Diario* in 1991.[28] Rodríguez and Azcueta began receiving repeated death threats from the Maoist organization, and between 1991 and 1993 both survived unsuccessful assassination attempts.

As Shining Path began to target the local leadership, and its intention of expanding its influence in key community organizations within Villa El Salvador became clear, local authorities began to actively denounce Guzmán and his followers. Azcueta, Rodríguez, and Moyano were at the forefront of these efforts. They helped mobilize a core group of local left-wing activists linked to the PMR and the MAS, who began to react to what they increasingly perceived not only as attacks against the project they had dedicated their lives to building, but also to their very lives. As one grassroots activist who was a member of PMR stated,

> Before we weren't so clear as to what Shining Path wanted in Villa. We thought we could coexist in a way. But soon we started to realize that they didn't want to coexist with us; they wanted to get rid of us, they wanted to get rid of Villa.[29]

As some members of the Left sharpened their critique of Shining Path, however, others retained a more ambiguous stance.

In September 1991, a bomb exploded and destroyed one of the central warehouses where the FEPOMUVES stored donated foodstuffs that were used by the community kitchens in their daily cooking. Moyano accused Shining Path of the attack, and she became an open and unrelenting critic of the Maoist organization.[30] Moyano admitted in an interview shortly after the bombing that her criticism of the Shining Path had been muted until they began attacking the FEPOMUVES:

> Until some time ago I thought that Shining Path was a group that committed errors, but that, in some way, they were trying to fight to obtain justice. But when they killed labor leader Enrique Castilla [in October 1989], I repudiated them. However, I didn't dare condemn Shining Path's terrorist attitude. But now they have attacked the grassroots organizations, where the poorest organize... They are trying to undermine these organizations... I no longer consider Shining Path a revolutionary group.[31]

Moyano was especially critical of the leaders of the IU for permitting the coalition to split. This division, she said, caused many people to feel disenchanted with the Left, leaving them few alternatives. As a result, she said,

> Some people from the popular *barriadas* look at Shining Path from afar, they see them as almost mystical, and they say that they fight for justice.... And the most radical sectors of the Left did not distance themselves from Shining Path when it was opportune to do so. And now, what left-wing party has made a statement about what is happening in Villa El Salvador? Not one, no political leader has come to see what is happening here.[32]

In a workshop of over 40 grassroots leaders from several popular districts in Lima that I observed in October 1993, a leader of the milk program made a more biting critique of the Left:

> The Left is the only party that is concerned with the people, but they are selfish. They are concerned with their partisan interests and not those of all the people. Too often they talk from above but they don't live among us. They do not experience the lack of water, electricity, or mothers who go to the market and cannot afford to buy food for her children.

In the same 1991 interview, Moyano said that the women's organizations in Villa would resist Shining Path, and that she would promote the creation of autonomous neighborhood defense groups (*rondas vecinales*) to combat Shining Path.[33] Subsequent attempts to organize urban *rondas* were quickly disbanded after Shining Path visited the homes of the *ronda* organizers, one by one, warning them of their fate should they attempt such an endeavor. Nevertheless, Moyano became something of a local celebrity for her outspoken criticism of Shining Path, and she was featured on the news and in Lima's newspapers and weekly magazines as an example of how to combat Shining Path. The division of the IU and the subsequent weakening of the Left as a political force meant that grassroots leaders like Moyano were increasingly, and dangerously, on their own.

As mayor, Rodríguez tried to use the institutional clout of the municipal government to create a front against Shining Path in the district. In late 1991, he announced the formation of the Peace and Development Forum, a broad-based coalition uniting the Catholic Church, local human rights groups, popular organizations, and the municipal government.[34] The objective of the Peace Forum was to develop alternative strategies to respond to Villa's social problems and to check Shining Path's growing influence in the community. One of the Peace Forum's member groups, the Youth Coordinating Committee, was one of the most active and daring. For example, the Youth Committee mobilized groups of young people to paint over Shining Path graffiti in the district.

While these attempts at building unity continued, Shining Path was penetrating into the heart of the district. On February 9, 1992, Máximo Huarcaya, a small business owner who had a small factory in the Industrial Park, was elected president of the APEMIVES, with the open support of Shining Path. Activists of the Peace Forum attempted to preempt Huarcaya's victory by convincing the different left-wing parties to back a single candidate in the elections. The recent history of divisions had sharply marked the Left in Villa, however, and there was no agreement on a consensus candidate. With the Left ticket split, Huarcaya won the election.

APEMIVES was one of the members of the Autonomous Authority (AA), the governing body of the Industrial Park. Other members of the AA included the mayor of the district, the president of the CUAVES, and representatives from the central government and the local business community. Conflict had been brewing within the Industrial Park over several aspects of the Park's administration. One of the most conflictive issues was the use of the land plots that were loaned to the small industrialists, who had the obligation of constructing locales on the plots and transferring their workshops to them. Many industrialists, hard hit by the economic crisis, lacked sufficient resources to build on their plots, and reacted negatively to the AA's assertion that they would have to give them up if they did not develop the plots as agreed. Shining Path activists took up their cause, with Huarcaya at the head, demanding that no industrialist be evicted from the park. They accused the AA of using its power to assign plots in favor of small industrialists linked to Azcueta and the PMR. Another controversial issue was the AA's administration of international donations and a loan program for industrialists set up with international funding. The AA maintained that the books were in order and open for all to see, but other informed observers suggested that there was a problem of corruption within the AA. In any case, Shining Path and Huarcaya played on this issue and demanded that control of the resources be transferred to the APEMIVES alone. After all, they reasoned, the donations were a "gift" for the "poor"; therefore they alone should administer them. They also argued that they should not have to pay back the loans. This discourse became increasingly common after the onset of the economic recession. Another factor that complicated the situation was the failure of NGDOs to be more transparent about their sources and administration of funding, which often raised suspicion on the part of beneficiary groups (SASE-Instituto APOYO 1993). Shining Path played on this sentiment in Lima's shantytowns and in rural areas where NGDOs had been active for over two decades, playing on long-standing resentments and promising to return control of the money to "the people."[35]

Four days after Huarcaya's victory, a meeting was held in the Industrial Park to discuss the gravity of the situation. Moyano urged Huarcaya and Filadelfo Roa, president of the CUAVES, who supported Huarcaya's candidacy, to sign a document stating their opposition to Shining Path, but both refused. Moyano decided that a test of wills was in order. The following day, Shining Path declared an armed strike in Lima, and Moyano argued that Villa and its organizations should protest the strike in a public demonstration against Shining Path. Many activists declined to participate out of fear—Shining Path's penchant for killing those who openly opposed it was well known. Other left-wing groups who were active in Villa also refused to participate, citing the need to maintain their own "profiles," reflecting the context of division within former IU coalition partners that mitigated against the formation of a united front against Shining Path. In a public letter to the leaders of the other left-wing parties,

Miguel Azcueta of the PMR wrote,

> For more than a week, María Elena, Johny Rodríguez, José Polo and
> I have been clearly denouncing Shining Path's intentions in Villa El
> Salvador and about the continuous threats—now confirmed—against
> our lives. No one said a word. One the contrary... María Elena asked
> PUM to support an act of unity in the Industrial Park... What was
> PUM's response? "No, we have to strengthen our own profile." That
> was their literal answer to María Elena.... We now see the results.
> Neither PUM, nor the Communist Party, the Democratic Popular
> Union (UDP) or the Popular Front supported the peace march.[36]

Only about 50 people participated in the march, carrying white banners
to symbolize peace.

Shining Path immediately punished Moyano's defiance: the following
day, she was killed by a Shining Path hit squad. In *El Diario* and in flyers
that circulated throughout the district in the following days, Shining Path
accused her of corruption and favoritism, and said that she was a *soplón*
(informant) who deserved punishment. A massive funeral procession was
held for Moyano, in which dozens of prominent politicians, including
former president Belaúnde, participated. Yet observers noted that local
participation was minimal, and that Shining Path's intended objective—to
inculcate fear and inhibit any further efforts at resistance in Villa El
Salvador—had largely succeeded.

In the immediate aftermath of Moyano's assassination, FEPOMUVES
leaders noted their indignation over the brutal murder of their former
leader and their determination to resist Shining Path.[37] But Shining Path
continued to pressure and intimidate the top leaders of the FEPOMUVES.
Shortly after Moyano's assassination, Ester Flores, the president of the
FEPOMUVES, who had received numerous threats from Shining Path,
left the country. Flores said that she also felt pressure because the military
parked an armed tank by her house, presumably to protect her. Given
Shining Path's disposition to attack community leaders who collaborated
with the state, she felt that this exposed her unduly to charges of being a
"traitor" and a "collaborator."[38] The media added to the tension, Flores
reports, printing sensationalistic headlines suggesting that she would be
Shining Path's next victim.[39] Many other leaders quit their positions,
while some continued to work but avoided a political discourse. This is
one example of how Shining Path's policy of selective assassinations generated a culture of fear and undermined civil society organization. With
Flores gone, the vice-president of FEPOMUVES, Pilar Anchita, assumed
control of the organization. Anchita was from Ayacucho, and her brother
was allegedly a member of Shining Path. Her own inclinations in favor of
Shining Path became increasingly evident.

A notable shift in Shining Path's discourse vis-à-vis grassroots
organizations such as the community kitchens appeared around this time.

In the late 1980s, *El Diario* severely criticized the community kitchens and the milk program as the "shock absorbers" of the dominant system that inhibited the poor's "revolutionary consciousness."

> The objective of the so-called "self-management" model is to ensure that the masses do not combat this bureaucratic, oligarchic state, and that they content themselves with palliatives within the system so that they can ostensibly resolve their problems... The same thing happens with the community kitchens and the milk committees, that is, making the masses, with their unpaid labor, conform themselves with receiving charity from the NGOs, so they won't fight for their rights.[40]

In a 1988 interview, Guzmán himself charged these organizations with "selling out the revolution for a plate of beans" (Guzmán 1988). Just a few years later, however, as Shining Path was seeking to establish its authority and control in Lima's *barriadas*, its discourse shifted. Now, the Maoists claimed that they were not opposed to these organizations per se, but to the presumably corrupt leaders who betrayed them:

> The PCP is not against the community kitchens, the milk program, or the mothers' clubs... But we are against those counterrevolutionaries who defend the old State and its rule of exploitation and oppression... We are against those who traffic with the popular sectors' demands... We are against those who want to make us eternally poor, to eternally receive "charity," "pity," "assistance," or "philanthropy" from the rich of our country and abroad via NGOs.[41]

This shift in discourse reflected Shining Path's new concern with winning sympathy among the rank and file of grassroots organizations such as the FEPOMUVES. As in the Industrial Park, Shining Path played on controversial issues like authoritarian leadership within the organization, the lack of transparency and mishandling of the organization's resources and donations, and political favoritism. In particular, it played on the issue of corruption, a particularly sensitive issue for organizations like the FEPOMUVES that often had weak mechanisms for administering and accounting for donated resources and dealing with conflicts over resource administration—a problem that gave rise to suspicion among the rank and file that the organization's leaders were using their positions of leadership for personal benefit.[42] This was undoubtedly exacerbated by the context of economic deprivation, which heightened suspicions of those with access to resources and power at all levels of society.

In the aftermath of Moyano's murder, the Peace and Development Forum disbanded. Rodríguez and his allies continued to denounce Shining Path and groups within Villa El Salvador who had allied themselves with Shining Path, particularly the CUAVES leadership. Roa, the

CUAVES president, refused to sign a document condemning Shining Path for the murder of Moyano, and later emitted a document that blamed Michel Azcueta for her death.[43]

In this context CUAVES adopted an openly critical stance against the leftist leadership of the municipal government using terms very similar to those used by Shining Path. Radical groups within CUAVES had in effect entered into a tactical alliance with Shining Path against what they perceived to be their "common enemy." This was another critical blow to the Left in Villa. Though CUAVES had lost much of its political clout, it still remained *the* central community organization uniting the entire district, and epitomized the model of self-management. Shining Path was adept at manipulating the resentment of disgruntled groups such as those in the CUAVES against the municipal leadership, and its pragmatism permitted it to establish tactical alliances with diverse groups as long as it furthered its longer-term goals. Roa was likely not a Shining Path activist, as some accused him of being, but it seems evident that he willingly forged an alliance with the Maoists in order to undermine and discredit the left-wing leadership in the municipal government.

This alliance manifested itself soon after Moyano's death. In March, the executive committee of the CUAVES and the "District Committee of Struggle"—a Shining Path front group—mobilized hundreds of protesters in two protest marches, the first demanding the impeachment of Mayor Rodríguez "for promoting the militarization of Villa El Salvador" and the second to declare Michel Azcueta persona non grata in the district. The largest contingent on both occasions was from Pachacamac, a sector within Villa El Salvador in which hundreds of squatters had invaded an abandoned urban housing project in 1989. The residents had requested the municipal government's assistance in obtaining land titles from the central government, but the government's inaction created a situation of hostility and tension between the squatters and the municipal government. Shining Path had been active in Pachacamac since these land invasions began, playing on the institutional voids in this newer and less developed *barriada* to win sympathy and establish a beachhead in the district.[44] As the situation over the land titles deteriorated, Shining Path manipulated a local grievance into a larger issue of confrontation against the left-wing municipal leadership. When the army set up a military base in Pachacamac just after Moyano's death, Shining Path activists convinced residents that Rodríguez had brought the army in to force them off the land. This fueled popular resistance to the municipality and the "militarization" of Villa El Salvador.[45] The sensation of Shining Path spreading its tentacles throughout Villa El Salvador had an impact not only within the district. Given the place Villa El Salvador held in the public imagination as a popular district with a vibrant, democratic civil society, the expansion of Shining Path was noted with alarm by politicians and the national press.[46]

In this context, many grassroots activists began staying home and avoiding participation in any activities that might compromise them. At the same time, a core group of activists strongly identified with the left-wing project of Villa El Salvador continued to mobilize to defend the project that they had helped to build. In the aftermath of Moyano's murder and growing evidence of extensive Shining Path influence in Villa El Salvador, a handful of these activists, leaving aside their historic mistrust of the police forces, sought to build closer ties with the local police force to rout out Shining Path. Activists who at one point did not consider Shining Path an enemy to be confronted now believed not only that it was important for the Left to fight Shining Path head-on, but that the old fears about collaborating with the state had to be put aside given Shining Path's intention of completely wiping them—and the project they had dedicated their lives to—off the map. Some even began carrying weapons for self-defense. As one prominent local activist of the PMR stated,

> We finally realized that Shining Path was more than willing to use violence against us, and you can't fight politically against someone who is pointing a gun at you.[47]

These initial discussions about how to best combat the Maoists on the ground were disrupted in the aftermath of Fujimori's April 5, 1992 *autogolpe*. Local efforts to build bridges with the state crumbled as the coup ignited old fears about the repressive nature of the state and the security forces.

Days after the coup, Shining Path launched an all-out offensive in Lima. In Villa El Salvador, the Maoists attacked the municipality with a massive bus bomb that destroyed part of the municipal building, the police station, the Center for Popular Communication (an NGO founded by Azcueta), and several dozen nearby homes. One police official was killed in the attack and several others wounded.

As local efforts at resistance faltered in the face of growing authoritarianism and political violence, Shining Path continued to pursue a strategy of infiltrating local organizations in order to establish its leadership and control. Shining Path won an important symbolic victory in August 1992 when its proposals were adopted by majority vote in the VI convention of the CUAVES. Shining Path's influence in the CUAVES was evident to informed observers by 1991, when radical groups within the organization forged a tactical alliance with pro–Shining Path members of CUAVES to oust the elected president Roque Quispe. A militant of the UNIR, Quispe won the presidency of the CUAVES with the support of the PMR, the party holding power in the municipality. At a CUAVES meeting, the municipal government put forth a motion asking CUAVES to propose ideas to determine spending priorities for the municipal property taxes that were to be collected later that year. Radical CUAVES groups, in alliance with pro–Shining Path members, put forth a motion that said that given the economic situation, the municipal government should not collect the property tax. Although the tax was progressively scaled according to the type of housing construction, the proposal to eliminate the property tax became widely popular among the CUAVES rank and file and the motion was approved. After meeting with the mayor, Quispe agreed to resubmit the municipal government's request to the CUAVES assembly. In this meeting, the prior motion was rejected, and a new payment scale was proposed. A week later, the radical sector, led by under secretary general of the CUAVES Filadelfo Roa, called another meeting, which resulted in Quispe's impeachment. Roa—whose alliance with Shining Path came to light the following year, after he refused to denounce Moyano's murder—became the secretary general of the CUAVES.

Radical elements within the CUAVES—part of the Marxist Left but not linked to the IU and known as the "Cuavista current"—had long resented Azcueta, who was the impetus behind the municipalization of Villa El Salvador, and his political allies in the IU.[48] The Cuavistas feared that the municipal government would impinge on the CUAVES's autonomy and its role as the central organization of the district. To allay these fears, Azcueta signed a compromise deal with the CUAVES upon assuming the mayorship, promising to respect the CUAVES' autonomy. But as the municipal government expanded its influence, helped develop new organizations such as APEMIVES, and obtained international resources to develop projects in the district, CUAVES felt its institutional feet were being stepped on. Conflicts began to emerge between the CUAVES leadership and IU leaders in the municipality over issues of power, political rivalry, social legitimacy, and control over resources. When Shining Path sought to extend its influence in Villa El Salvador, it ably exploited these tensions, seeking out alliances with disgruntled sectors within the CUAVES against a common enemy—the revisionists in the municipality—in order to "deepen the contradictions" within the district, delegitimize the IU, and destroy the self-management model that Villa El Salvador represented.

The final document of the VI convention openly attacked the municipality as part of the "old, rotten, and extinct state" and called for its deactivation; it also called for the removal of the army base from the district, the disbanding of the urban *rondas*, the expulsion of all NGOs and some private enterprises, and an end to the municipal property tax. It also demanded that all international technical and financial support be channeled through CUAVES. The original proposal included several names of leaders to be "liquidated," though this list was not included in the final document.[49] This was an important symbolic victory for Shining Path, not only within Villa El Salvador but also at the national level, as it demonstrated the insurgents' ability to penetrate into the very heart of "Left revisionism."

Shining Path's victory was only partial, however. Less than half of the usual 500 delegates participated in the convention. Some delegates did not participate out of fear, while others, particularly those linked to the PMR, MAS, and PUM, refused to participate so as not to legitimize the convention. These leaders argued that Shining Path was manipulating the voting process, and that the Pachacamac delegates were being duped by the

Maoists into believing that the municipality was preparing to evict them. Immediately after the convention, the municipal government publicly denounced the CUAVES leadership for its conciliation with Shining Path and stated it would not recognize the legitimacy of the VI convention or the CUAVES leadership.[50] Some 40 grassroots CUAVES members issued a joint statement that also repudiated the CUAVES leadership.

But the damage was done. Shining Path infiltrated CUAVES and decisively influenced the outcome of the VI convention. Though residents continued to recognize CUAVES as a "historic" organization of Villa El Salvador, it lost the standing it once had as the central organization of the district. Shining Path achieved an important goal: it had driven out the revisionists and dealt a stinging blow to a key element of the self-management model. This paralleled the outcome of Shining Path's ascendancy in the Industrial Park as well. Shortly after Huarcaya became president of APEMIVES, international donors cut off assistance to the Industrial Park. The government also withdrew, leaving the entire project to flounder. In both cases, Shining Path's goal was not to take over the CUAVES or the APEMIVES and lead these organizations, but destroy them and the experience of self-management they embodied, extend their own influence in the district, and provoke military repression. In Shining Path's logic of "deepening the contradictions," fomenting conflict and greater polarization would hasten the "revolutionary victory."

### The Limits of Confrontation Politics

Shining Path's strategy of undermining alternative projects for change, radicalizing popular demands, and provoking military repression might have panned out had Shining Path been able to culminate its offensive in Lima through 1992 and into 1993.[51] By March 1992, it had advanced to the point that the U.S. State Department began to urge more decisive U.S. action to prevent Shining Path from seizing state control.[52] Since the early 1980s, Shining Path's logic of confrontation—along with the state's virulent, often brutal response—had been pushing the country toward greater levels of polarization and political violence, as Fujimori's *autogolpe* of April 5, 1992 revealed. Many observers feared that increasing military control would play into Shining Path's hands and strengthen their possibilities of victory.

Terror was a crucial element of Shining Path's ability to extend its influence in Lima's *barriadas*. Through its campaigns of intimidation and selective assassination, Shining Path effectively eliminated rivals, neutralized opposition, and generated a climate of fear that made resistance increasingly difficult, particularly in the context of government repression and the historic gap between state and society in Peru. At the same time, Shining Path was far more astute at operating at a political level than observers imagined possible. Ultimately, Shining Path's urban strategy was intimately linked to what its leaders perceived as the imminent collapse of the capitalist state and its overall strategy of confrontation to hasten that moment and, presumably, ultimate victory.

Shining Path's seemingly inexorable path to victory was cut short on September 12, 1992, when Abimael Guzmán was arrested by a special police intelligence unit, the National Directorate Against Terrorism (DINCOTE). The surprise capture of Guzmán led to a radical change in the balance of forces, which shifted—for the first time in a decade of political violence—in favor of the state and the armed forces. While Shining Path continued to carry out significant military campaigns in the months after Guzmán's capture, by mid-1993 its operational capacity had declined precipitously. The future of Shining Path's insurgency was further called into question in late 1993, when Guzmán wrote a letter from prison requesting peace talks with the government. This provoked a sharp confrontation within the group's imprisoned leadership, who rallied behind Guzmán's peace proposal, and the leadership that remained at large, led by Oscar Ramírez Durand (alias "Comrade Feliciano"), who argued for the continuation of the "popular war."[53]

In this new context, the tentative nature of Shining Path's political alliances at the local level became increasingly evident. By focusing their political mediations with the local population on radicalizing popular grievances and promoting confrontation and polarization, Shining Path was able to advance at the local level by locating the weak points in specific local contexts and exploiting them to their advantage. Shining Path was able to obtain sympathy by acting as a local vigilante, punishing thieves and corrupt leaders, but they rarely sought to consolidate their popular appeal by offering people viable alternatives to other local problems. In fact, the Maoists were not concerned with building a mass popular movement, or leading local organizations. They were operating on their own political and military logic, which calculated that the crisis of the capitalist state—and ergo their victory—was at hand, and that provoking confrontation and polarization would hasten that moment. This failure to build more enduring bases of support meant that as its power and authority declined within Villa El Salvador after Guzmán's capture and the withdrawal of many of its activists from the district, local groups became emboldened to challenge Shining Path. For example, in October 1993, the FEPOMUVES held its yearly convention in the midst of great tension and fear, with activists from the Youth Committee providing security and support. A number of leaders publicly criticized Pilar Anchita for her conciliation with Shining Path and her current dealings with Villa's new mayor, Jorge Vásquez, an independent who did not actually live in the district, who was seeking to withdraw the FEPOMUVES's control of the milk program.[54] The assembly voted to oust Anchita and chose a new leader. This was a tentative but hopeful sign of new times in Villa El Salvador.

Yet, Shining Path's ability to expand in Villa El Salvador—a prominent symbol of community organizing and leftist politics—remains a disturbing paradox. A district celebrated for its democratic and participatory politics and community organizations, Villa El Salvador also became a terrain of effective Shining Path political organizing. Changing structural conditions favored Shining Path's expansion in Villa El Salvador: the deepening of the economic crisis after 1988 and the disengagement of the state from its most critical public functions as a result of the fiscal crisis led to popular frustration and anger that provided Shining Path with plenty of raw material to exploit to their advantage in *barriadas* such as Villa. The gray zones provided fertile terrain for Shining Path's relentless advance in Lima. Engaging local issues that affected people's daily life, and for which neither the state nor political parties were providing solutions, also allowed Shining Path to navigate within the local body politic, challenging the leadership of existing organizations and building local support networks. While some groups in civil society organized to detain Shining Path's advance in Villa, the Maoists' use of violence and intimidation paralyzed such efforts, particularly after the murder of María Elena Moyano. Though groups in civil society sought valiantly to defend their community from the effects of Peru's internal conflict, in the end the logic of violence imposed itself. In the resulting culture of fear, civil society leaders left the public square for the safety of their homes, in search of—as one community leader noted—"refuge in silence."

PART 3

State Making against Democracy

CHAPTER EIGHT
_____

# The Authoritarian Reconstitution
# of the State

At 10:30 p.m. on the evening of April 5, 1992, as Peruvians were watching the Sunday evening news, the program was interrupted. President Alberto Fujimori appeared on the screen, and in a grave and serious tone, announced that his government was adopting emergency measures to address the problems of guerrilla violence, drug trafficking, and corruption in the judiciary. He announced the dissolution of congress, the suspension of the 1979 constitution, and the reorganization of the judicial branch. In effect, the president dissolved existing democratic institutions and assumed dictatorial powers. Immediately following the broadcast, Commander in Chief of the Armed Forces General Nicolás Hermoza Ríos announced the military's firm support of President Fujimori and the so-called *autogolpe*.[1]

Shortly before the coup was announced, military units were dispatched to key locations throughout Lima, including the congress building. Armed units occupied newspaper offices, printing presses, and radio and television stations, establishing military control over the flow of information. Twenty-two journalists were arrested, including Gustavo Gorriti, a journalist for the weekly *Caretas* who had written extensively on Shining Path and who more recently published several highly critical articles about Vladimiro Montesinos, Fujimori's principal advisor. Soldiers were also dispatched to arrest top APRA leaders, including former president Alan García, who had become the principal critic of Fujimori's neoliberal program. García hid in the water tank on the roof of his home and later sought refuge in the Colombian embassy, and from there, to exile in Bogotá and later Paris.

The coup d'état was perhaps the most dramatic aspect of the reassertion of state authority that occurred under the Fujimori regime. It made evident the regime's intention of concentrating power in the hands of the executive branch in an effort to restore the power of the state over society. The vast web of corruption that came to characterize the Fujimori government—and that led ultimately to its implosion in 2000—has left the impression that this was little more than a kleptocracy whose sole purpose was to enrich a small circle of friends and allies of President Fujimori and Montesinos. In fact, in its early years the Fujimori regime had embarked on a political project that involved reconstituting state authority and restructuring the economy and state-society relations following the basic contours of the neoliberal model of free market capitalism and limited state involvement in the economy and social welfare provision. The regime's political project was also fundamentally an authoritarian one, in that it proposed to achieve its objectives through nondemocratic means.

In other words, the Fujimori regime had embarked on a project of state building in which the dominant objective was to rebuild state structures and institutions and reestablish state control over society. As scholars of state formation have noted, the process of state making, which is designed to create and support centralized state institutions and authority, is often bloody and violent (Tilly 1978). Drawing on this framework, this chapter analyzes the Fujimori regime's effort to remake the state in Peru. The central argument is that the social conflicts of the 1980s and the near-collapse of state institutions created the impetus as well as the opportunity for state makers to reassert state authority, while the crisis of organized politics and the debilitation of civil society meant that few social obstacles existed to challenge the authoritarian and often repressive methods deployed by the regime in this process. The chapter explores the three phases of state reconstitution under the Fujimori regime, examining each in detail and explaining how these state-making efforts reinforced authoritarian rather than democratic outcomes.

## Reasserting the Power of the State

The first stage of reconstituting the state focused on restoring confidence in Peru's economy through radical austerity measures, neoliberal restructuring, and "reinsertion" into the international economy. The Fujimori regime laid the foundation for state reconstitution by marshaling international financial support to stabilize Peru's economy, which in turn helped create support for the state and for a new social and political project, neoliberalism, both among the business class and average citizens. This so-called reinsertion into the international financial community permitted international loans and foreign capital to enter the country, funds that were desperately needed given the deep fiscal crisis and administrative disarray that characterized Peru in the late 1980s. This flow of international funds provided crucial resources to reorganize key state agencies, on the one hand and, on the other, for the state to rebuild clientelistic links with society and thereby obtain a modicum of support and legitimacy. It also led to the incorporation of the Peruvian bourgeoisie, which was initially very wary of Fujimori, into the ruling coalition.

The second dimension of state reconstitution emphasized the reorganization of state power by centralizing decision-making power in the hands of the executive and the armed forces. This process was in the making from the outset of the Fujimori regime, culminating in the *autogolpe* of April 5, 1992, which gave Fujimori and his military allies almost exclusive power over economic and political decision making. This reorganization of state power and the removal of democratic checks and balances in congress and the judiciary permitted the regime to concentrate power and sidestep democratic accountability to pursue its authoritarian political project, which consisted of a militarized counterinsurgency policy and a radical neoliberal program whose ultimate goal was not only to restructure the economy and reduce the role of the state, but also to fundamentally recast state-society relations. Despite the return to constitutional rule by the end of 1993, the postcoup reordering of power remained largely intact. Democratic institutions created the illusion of democracy; yet power was exercised in a fundamentally authoritarian manner, as we shall see. Congress became little more than an appendage of the executive branch, and other democratic institutions, from the judiciary to independent agencies such as the constitutional tribunal, were systematically subverted to bend to the regime's political will.

The third dimension of state reconstitution was the containment of the Shining Path insurgency, which began with the capture of the insurgency's top leader, Abimael Guzmán, in September 1992, just six months after the *autogolpe*. While it may reasonably be argued that the *autogolpe* and the subsequent hardening of the regime's policies had little if anything to do with Guzmán's arrest, as will be suggested below, the regime frequently asserted that the arrest was due primarily to the new efficacy in governing since the *autogolpe*. The arrest was crucial in rebuilding public confidence in the Peruvian state and its ability to restore order and some modicum of normalcy to daily life, providing the regime with significant political capital to pursue a wide range of policies aimed at reconstituting the Peruvian state along neoliberal and authoritarian lines. With Shining Path under control, the state—primarily via the armed forces—sought to project its power into poor urban and rural communities to reestablish territorial control of the nation as well as its rule-making capacity within that territory.

These three elements—economic stabilization; the concentration of power; and the containment of Shining Path—were the foundations of state reconstitution under the Fujimori regime. However, as I shall argue in the concluding section of this chapter, the reconstitution of the state under Fujimori took place along authoritarian lines, reinforcing praetorianism and undermining the possibilities for rebuilding democracy and expanding citizenship in Peru. The trend toward the expansion of military power that began in late 1982, when Belaúnde sent military troops to Ayacucho to quell the Shining Path insurgency, was taken to its logical extreme under the postcoup regime. There was, moreover, a deliberate effort to undermine democratic actors and institutions. In effect, the Fujimori regime took advantage of the same conditions of deinstitution-alization and political and social disintegration that nourished Shining Path at the local level to carry out the *autogolpe* and consolidate power. Remaking the state came at the expense of Peru's fledgling democracy, as the regime systematically sought to prevent any kind of reinstitutionaliza-tion within political and civil society through a variety of mechanisms, ranging from old-fashioned clientelism to more nefarious kinds of surveillance and intimidation of the opposition to outright repression. Preventing new institutions and political and social actors from develop-ing was key for the Fujimori regime to retain its hold on power, and undermined the possibilities for reconstructing democratic governance in Peru, as the key actors who would theoretically have an autonomous basis for action and could press for democratizing reforms remained debilitated and fragmented. By maintaining its absolutist chokehold on the state, the Fujimori regime eviscerated democratic institutions and reinforced old patterns of political behavior, including a highly personalistic form of autocratic rule and old-fashioned top-down clientelism.

### Getting Peru's Economic House in Order

Within 10 days of assuming the presidency, Fujimori announced harsh austerity measures as a means of restoring stability to Peru's erratic econ-omy. Though he had campaigned on a "no shock" platform, in the month between the second round of elections and his swearing in, Fujimori adopted the very neoliberal shock program advocated by his defeated rival, novelist Mario Vargas Llosa. Orthodox monetary policies were adopted to bring down inflation, close the fiscal deficit, and enhance the state's financial reserves. Though the measures had a high social cost (as described in chapter two), the new government deemed them necessary to address Peru's macroeconomic imbalances. But perhaps most importantly, these measures were viewed as essential by the international financial institutions (IFIs) whose approval was necessary to restore Peru's credit rating and achieve its "reinsertion" into the international financial community.

Fujimori's turnaround on economic policy was facilitated by the fact that he was elected without the backing of a well-established political party, and was beholden to no formal coalition.[2] The organization that helped him win office, Cambio 90, was little more than a personal elec-toral vehicle that lost its significance after Fujimori became president. While the Left and APRA had urged their supporters to vote for Fujimori in the second round vote in order to defeat the conservative Vargas Llosa, no formal pacts had been made between the presidential candidate and these parties. Moreover, with the debacle of organized politics, neither the Left nor APRA had the capacity to call Fujimori to account once in power.

Upon assuming office, Fujimori faced an incredibly difficult situation. While in some respects his lack of a party apparatus gave him great freedom to make policy choices, it was extremely problematic in terms of devising a concrete plan of how to govern and staff a country on the edge of chaos. During the two-month period between the first elections in April 1990 and the run-off elections in June, the business elite and the armed forces made no bones about their preference for Vargas Llosa. Rumors of a coup in case of a Fujimori victory were rampant. A visceral and markedly racist campaign was launched aimed at discrediting Fujimori's candidacy by suggesting that because he was a descendant of Japanese parents, he was not a "real" Peruvian. (In retrospect, this campaign actually improved Fujimori's appeal to a majority of indigenous and *mestizo*, or mixed race, voters, who were increasingly unwilling to vote for the small white minority that had dominated the country for centuries [Degregori and Grompone 1991; Oliart 1998].)

Fujimori had very little room to maneuver: he had no party to help him design and implement policy; he faced a hostile bourgeoisie and an extremely uneasy military, both of whom had firmly supported a Vargas Llosa candidacy; and his "no shock" economic policy was unlikely to be well received by the international financial community, which was advocating the orthodox recipes of the Washington Consensus as a precondition to renewing the flow of international credits, which had been cut off after García's unilateral reduction of debt payments. To survive politically, Fujimori would have to negotiate with these powerful actors to ensure that they would back his regime—or at least not destabilize it—revealing the dependence of Peru's economy on external factors, the weakness of Peru's democracy vis-à-vis the armed forces, and the veto power of the bourgeoisie (Mauceri 1995). Revealing Fujimori's remarkable political skills, he was able to forge a coalition that incorporated each of these actors.

Civilian technocrats who supported a neoliberal solution to the crisis of the Peruvian state and economy became key policy advisors to the Fujimori regime. For example, Hernando de Soto, director of the neoliberal think tank Liberty and Democracy Institute (ILD), became Fujimori's primary interlocutor with international lenders to renegotiate Peru's foreign debt. As he began to devise his economic program, Fujimori quickly realized that his alternatives were limited by the demands imposed by international financial agencies for renewing funds. These agencies, including the IMF and the World Bank, were enthusiastically promoting the neoliberal agenda of orthodox monetary policies, privatization, and a drastic reduction of the role of the state in the economy throughout Latin America. This policy agenda had become hegemonic by the late 1980s in the region, due to the perceived failures of populist experiments like that of García; the collapse of socialism; and the purported success stories of neoliberal economies like that of Chile in sustaining growth and combating poverty. Technocrats like de Soto enthusiastically supported these free market policies, as they were convinced that the heavy involvement of the state in the economy was to blame for economic stagnation, as it stifled entrepreneurial initiative by imposing too many regulations on business.[3] The domestic bourgeoisie also favored the overall neoliberal agenda and compliance with the demands of the IMF. With a few exceptions—most notably the small manufacturing sector that subsisted on government subsidies—the domestic bourgeoisie supported liberalization and privatization, believing that the statist reforms enacted under Velasco hampered free enterprise. The business elite's initial reticence toward Fujimori quickly gave way to enthusiastic support once his commitment to neoliberal policies became evident (Durand 1997).

The first phase of the adjustment program implemented in August 1990 managed to stem the inflationary tide and rebalance Peru's fiscal accounts. Inflation dropped dramatically from over 7,000 percent in 1990 to just over 50 percent in 1992, and to just 10 percent by 1995 (see table 8.1). More importantly, the adjustment measures put Peru back into the good graces of the so-called international financial community, and credits and loans began to pour into Peru, providing sorely needed resources for the Peruvian state to launch a more extensive reform effort. As Mauceri (1995) notes, given the deterioration of the state's extractive apparatus, obtaining new credit was critical for the Peruvian state to gain access to funds that could underwrite the rebuilding of key state agencies and deteriorated infrastructure. International resources were also crucial to the reorganization of key state agencies, primarily the National Tax Collection Agency (SUNAT), the National Social Security Institute (IPSS), and the National Customs Agency (SUNAD). These reforms were crucial in terms of providing state managers with a functioning apparatus to extract resources from society in order to rebuild the state's administrative and coercive presence in society, giving the state greater tax resources to carry out administrative functions, as seen in table 8.1. Tight fiscal policy kept public sector spending in line with tax collection, while the fiscal deficit was financed almost entirely through external credit.[4] The combined

**Table 8.1**  Macroeconomic Indicators, 1990–1995.

| Year | Inflation[a] | Tax Revenues as Percentage of GDP[b] |
|------|------------|--------------------------------------|
| 1990 | 7,649.7 | 9.5 |
| 1991 | 139.2 | 9.5 |
| 1992 | 56.7 | 11.4 |
| 1993 | 39.5 | 11.3 |
| 1994 | 15.4 | 13.2 |
| 1995 | 10.0 | 13.9 |

*Source:*

[a] Figures from 1990 to 1994: Wise (1997); 1995: World Bank Group: http://www.cdinet. com/DEC/wdi98/new/countrydata/aag/per_aag.pdf.

[b] *ideéle,* Nos. 93–94 (December 1996), p. 132.

public sector deficit fell from 6.5 percent of GDP in 1990 to about 3 percent of GDP between 1991 and 1994. Privatization, which expanded dramatically in 1993, also became an important source of financing for the state (from 0.5 percent of GDP in 1993 to 4.5 percent in 1994), and helped bolster foreign exchange reserves.[5] Further neoliberal restructuring would follow these initial reforms, including trade liberalization measures, further curtailment of labor rights, and the privatization of social security.

This process—Peru's "reinsertion" into the international financial system, the reorganization of key state agencies, and the consolidation of a supportive ruling coalition—was the first key element to reconstituting the state. Fujimori's technocrat advisors, the business elite, and the multilateral financial institutions agreed that Peru's "reinsertion" into the international financial system was key to rebuilding the state, reestablishing its administrative capacity and presence in society, and refurbishing its tattered social legitimacy. Key to the reorganization of the state was reestablishing equilibrium in Peru's fiscal management, improving tax and revenue collection, and restoring public order (Mauceri 1996). The armed forces, which early on became the most important coalition partner of the Fujimori regime (a process that will be analyzed in further detail below), agreed to support the neoliberal reordering of the state in exchange for greater freedom in the counterinsurgency war. A new ruling coalition was thus established, highlighting the way periods of economic crisis and dislocation may produce radical shifts in policymaking (Grindle 1996). Fujimori's early economic successes fortified the ruling coalition, setting the stage for the next phase of state reconstruction: the centralization of power and the reassertion of state authority over society.

### Centralizing State Power

President Fujimori's April 1992 *autogolpe* launched a fundamental reorganization of state power. Congress and the judiciary were plagued with inefficiency, corruption, and political cronyism, he asserted, making them incapable of resolving the country's long-standing economic crisis and addressing the growing threat posed by the Shining Path and MRTA insurgencies. He proclaimed the creation of a "Government of Emergency and National Reconstruction" to end corruption and rid the country of Shining Path. This concentration of power in the executive gave Fujimori the ability to dictate wide-ranging economic reforms as well as political measures granting greater power to the armed forces in the counterinsurgency war. Fujimori's announcement was immediately backed by the high command of the Peruvian Armed Forces.

This was a decisive moment in the reconstitution of the Peruvian state, as it signified a break with the previous constitutional order and a process of reorganization that resulted in the centralization of power in the hands of the executive branch. The argument developed here differs from existing analyses of the Fujimori regime on two counts. First, I argue that the coup marked a fundamental reordering of political power in which the centralization of power in the hands of the executive and the armed forces that followed the coup became a permanent feature of the political system even as the regime—under intense international pressure—acceded to reestablishing democratic institutions. New congressional elections were held and a new constitution was put in place; this did not signify, however, a transition to democracy but rather a tactical retreat designed to preserve the new power structure in which the executive exercised virtually total control over decision making. The other branches of government were made subservient to the will of the executive (and its military allies), and, when necessary, the regime broke the law and violated its own constitution (put in place in 1993) to beat back challenges to its power. Democratic institutions thus became mere window dressing for an authoritarian regime that wielded power in an arbitrary fashion.[6]

Second, I suggest that the *autogolpe* was neither inevitable nor was it the result of institutional gridlock (as some have suggested). Rather, it was the result of concrete political and social conditions—the extreme weakness of democratic forces, which proved incapable of devising peaceful and democratic solutions to Peru's multiple crises—and of the political will of state makers who embarked on a project to reassert state power over society that they believed could be achieved only through authoritarian means, and who managed to construct a broad-based coalition to support this authoritarian political project. This suggests that though the Peruvian case was one in which an authoritarian outcome to rebuilding the state and restoring stability was more likely, given the extreme weakness of social forces, it was not preordained. A different leadership could potentially have led to a distinct outcome.

The cornerstone of the coalition supporting the Fujimori regime was the armed forces.[7] The military, strapped economically, demoralized by its failures in the war against Shining Path, and under attack for its systematic abuse of human rights, was searching for a president who would support an increased and more autonomous role for the military in the counterinsurgency war while providing desperately needed resources. Given his outsider status, coupled with persistent coup rumors immediately before the second round election, Fujimori was highly vulnerable, making it imperative for him to seek out allies within the armed forces.

This alliance was facilitated by Vladimiro Montesinos, a former army captain who was cashiered from the army in 1976 for reportedly selling state secrets to the CIA (Central Intelligence Agency) (for which he spent a year in jail) but who had retained close ties with the army, and during the final years of the García administration had begun working with the SIN.[8] While in prison, Montesinos studied law, and after his release became a full-fledged lawyer. Many of his clients were reputed drug traffickers, and he had developed extensive contacts within the judiciary and the police, becoming a key player in a wide-ranging drug mafia within the state apparatus (Gorriti 1994). During the run-off campaign with Vargas Llosa, Montesinos offered to help Fujimori by using his connections in the judiciary to get charges of fraudulent real-estate dealings against him dropped.[9] He did so, and gained Fujimori's confidence. Montesinos would soon become the president's principal adviser and his key link to the armed forces.

Evidence of Fujimori's budding relationship with the armed forces came almost immediately after he won the presidency. He established an office not in the presidential palace, but in the Círculo Militar, a military social club in Lima. He named an active army general minister of the interior, placing the police under the direct control of the armed forces. Then, under the guidance of Montesinos, Fujimori passed a decree law giving the president the power to promote and retire military officers. Previously, promotions and retirements were decided by the high command itself, leading some analysts to view this as a positive move toward establishing greater civilian control over the military. In fact it gave Fujimori and Montesinos the power to promote loyal officers to high-ranking positions while forcing officers whose loyalty to the president was suspect into early retirement[10] (Obando 1998). Massive purges within the police and armed forces followed. As Montesinos maneuvered to promote sympathetic officers to key posts, such as General Hermoza, who was named head of the army and commander in chief of the armed forces in December 1991.[11] General Hermoza retained this position until August 1998, which was unprecedented: typically commanders in chief held their post for one year and then retired. Maintaining Hermoza as head of the armed forces was crucial for assuring continuous military support for the regime. The quid pro quo of military support for Fujimori was a blank check to wage the counterinsurgency war. Some observers cite these the early purges and promotions as evidence that Montesinos and Fujimori had designed the coup plan well before carrying it out in April 1992 (Gorriti 1994; Rospigliosi 1996). Certainly, the dismissal of presumably uncooperative officers and institutionalists within the armed forces, and the promotion of officials sympathetic to the regime, helped guarantee institutional military support for a coup. It also, however, deeply politicized the armed forces. Dissident groups comprised primarily of mid-ranking officers came to the fore in 1993 with sharp criticisms of the military high command and charging Fujimori with manipulating the armed forces. Such dissidence was swiftly punished, however, with demotions and soon extensive surveillance by the SIN curtailed open dissent within the armed forces.[12]

Montesinos also oversaw the revamping of the judiciary that took place following the *autogolpe*. As with the armed forces, on the pretext of weeding out corrupt judges linked to APRA, many honest judges were removed and replaced with Montesinos loyalists. One judge, Guillermo Cabala, told the *Miami Herald* that he had been fired due to a "personal vendetta" Montesinos held against him for remaining independent. Cabala is reported as saying to the *Herald*: "After this purge the judicial branch will be completely subordinate to the executive, and that means to Vladimiro Montesinos" (Gorriti 1994). Judges who were given provisional positions remained beholden to the regime for their jobs and hence were easily manipulated. This set the groundwork for one of the key elements of the postcoup power arrangement: a judiciary beholden to the executive, easily manipulated and unwilling to challenge executive decisions.[13] It was also a means of ensuring impunity—for Montesinos himself, for other military and police officers linked to drug trafficking, and for Fujimori and his family—as Montesinos arranged for the disappearances of hundreds of judicial archives in the days immediately following the *autogolpe*.[14]

Some analysts maintain that the *autogolpe* was the result of an institutional deadlock between the executive and legislative branches (Kenney 1996, 2004). In late 1991, after the executive passed an avalanche of 126 decree laws, opposition leaders in congress began to work together to overturn what they viewed to be the most abusive decrees, particularly those granting a blank check to the military in the counterinsurgency war. Fujimori's coup announcement came the day before congress was scheduled to reconvene to continue debating the decree laws. This congressional action represented an intolerable constraint on the executive's policymaking abilities, hence the coup was an effort to get around these constraints. It is true that Fujimori lacked a legislative majority in congress, and the nature of the presidential system in Peru is such that it does not promote legislative cooperation among different parties.

Yet this explanation for the *autogolpe* is unsatisfying on several levels. First, the Fujimori government was granted special decree powers by congress to implement its reform measures. This gave the president a great deal of freedom to legislate economic as well as internal security policies without the alleged congressional interference. It is true that congress did seek to limit some of those decree measures. Indeed, in a rare show of unity, members of congress from all sides of the political spectrum joined forces in overturning or modifying those decree laws they considered egregious violations of the constitution. Some of these laws, they argued, amounted to a "white coup"—a de facto coup d'état within formal democratic structures.[15] Congress was exercising its democratic role by checking the abuse of power by the executive.

The abuse of power was evident both in the way the decree laws were emitted and in their content. On June 17, 1991, congress granted Fujimori a period of 150 days to legislate in 3 policy arenas: promoting investment, fostering employment, and pacification strategies.[16] Just as the period granting Fujimori the power to legislate by passing decree laws was about to end, the executive brought forth an avalanche of 126 decree laws with broad-ranging consequences: a rapid liberalization of the economy on the one hand, and total control over counterinsurgency policy to the armed forces on the other.[17] The new laws, for example, gave the military control over all aspects of civilian governance in the emergency zones, which amounted to full authority over a third of the national territory and one-half of the population. This eliminated congressional oversight on military affairs and activities, while sharply reducing civil and political rights in the emergency zones. Opposition groups in congress, arguing that Fujimori had overstepped the boundaries of his decree powers, joined forces to modify or overturn decree laws they considered egregious violations of the constitution in a special session in early 1992 (Vidal 1993). The opposition's plan to continue its review of Fujimori's decree laws on April 6 was cut short with the announcement of the *autogolpe* on the evening of April 5.

This suggests more than just a legislative impasse: it suggests an authoritarian intention on the part of Fujimori and his allies to remove all constraints inherent within a democratic system of checks and balances in order to permit the centralization of power and decision making in the hands of the executive (Burt 1992; see also Gorriti 1994; Rospigliosi 1996; and McClintock 1996). While the executive bristled at the congress's review of its 126 decree laws, in general, rather than conflict between congress and the executive, there was a broad process of dialogue between the two institutions led by Prime Minister Alfonso de los Heroes. There was broad agreement among opposition leaders that certain economic reforms, as well as a complete redesign of counterinsurgency policy, were necessary. The one point on which the opposition would not negotiate was permitting Fujimori an opportunity to run for reelection. Some observers suggest this was the real motive behind the *autogolpe*. This view does not contradict the more conspiratorial view that the *autogolpe* was the result of careful planning by military officers. Gorriti (1994) and Rospigliosi (1996) make a convincing case that plans for a coup were in the works since the late 1980s. A group of military officers authored the Plan Verde in 1989, which delineates a plan for a military coup and justifies the need for a military-led government for 20–30 years in order to reorganize state power and reassert state authority over society (Rospigliosi 1996). Adjustments to this plan were presumably made after Fujimori was elected and his willingness (indeed, his need) to collaborate with the armed forces became evident, making it unnecessary to dissolve the executive as in a traditional coup d'état. Montesinos, according to Rospigliosi, was the main conspirator behind the new version of the coup plan, linking Fujimori with those elements within the armed forces that devised the initial coup plot in the late 1980s.

Initial reactions to the coup were varied. On the ground, many Peruvian citizens, weary of economic and political chaos that set in at the end of the García administration, supported Fujimori's "get tough" stance. Public opinion polls revealed that 80 percent of Peruvians approved of the coup, a figure Fujimori repeatedly invoked to claim legitimacy for the *autogolpe* and the de facto regime now in place. This "authoritarian consensus" will be examined in greater detail in chapter nine. Peru's political class opposed the *autogolpe*—having the most to lose as they were shut out of participation in the political process—but found little support in society. This reflected the dramatic decline of popular support for Peru's "traditional" parties, as described in previous chapters. On the domestic front, then, there appeared to be few obstacles to consolidating the regime's authoritarian project.

However, the international community—principally the U.S. government and the regional governments represented in the Organization of American States (OAS)—immediately criticized the *autogolpe*. Fujimori and his military allies were confident that Washington would understand Peru's mitigating circumstances, given the imminent threat posed by the Shining Path insurgency, and support the coup. Indeed, even as the *autogolpe* was underway, the U.S. Congress was debating whether, in light of the dramatic expansion of Shining Path, to increase military aid to Peru, or whether to consider other possibilities, such as a U.S.-led intervention force.[18] But in the post–cold war era, Washington had articulated a new policy under the rubric of free elections and free trade that barred support for military regimes. International factors also came into play in the U.S. stance against the coup. Just a few months earlier, in February 1992, a coup attempt in Venezuela was barely averted, and Haiti saw a successful military takeover in September 1991. The U.S. government feared that anything less than outright criticism of Fujimori's *autogolpe* would appear tantamount to tacit support, giving a green light to restless militaries throughout the region. The Bush administration suspended military aid and most economic assistance to Peru, though it continued humanitarian aid and part of its counter-narcotics program. The U.S. government also urged the OAS to exert pressure on Fujimori to encourage him to return to constitutional rule.[19]

An interruption of international assistance would wreak havoc on Peru's fledgling economy. Fujimori thus was forced to shift tactics. In an effort to appease his international critics, Fujimori made a surprise appearance at an OAS meeting called to discuss the situation in Haiti, in which he announced that he would hold new congressional elections in late 1992. This was enough for Washington to give the green light to the World Bank and the Inter-American Development Bank to approve loans to Peru, though the U.S. Congress refused to approve military assistance funds in FY1993 due to ongoing human rights concerns.

The retreat was a tactical one only. Fujimori and his allies calculated that they could sufficiently control the process they had, under international pressure, now set in motion. And so it was. The *autogolpe* had created a new scenario on the ground: the congress elected in 1990, dominated by opposition parties, was now disbanded; the regime could construct a new legislature that it could control more closely. The 1979 constitution, with its ban on immediate presidential secession, could be replaced with a new document hand-tailored to meet the needs of the regime's authoritarian and neoliberal political project, including allowing for reelection to assure the regime's continuity in power while addressing the international imperative of free elections. In effect the *autogolpe* had cleared the way for the construction of a new structure of power in which the president and his military allies would govern without the horizontal accountability so essential to a democracy (O'Donnell 1998). Democratic institutions would be reinstated, but they would be recrafted in such a way as to make them utterly dependent upon and subordinate to the executive. Challenges to the new power structure would be met with whatever means necessary. The military, Fujimori's erstwhile allies in this endeavor, would be granted full control over counterinsurgency, and impunity for military personnel involved in human rights abuses or acts of corruption would be guaranteed.

The first step was congressional elections in November 1992. Fujimori insisted that the new legislature should be unicameral, which he argued would be more representative and more efficient than the previous two-chamber legislature. This new body, which was given the name the Constituent Democratic Congress (CCD), would serve as the legislative body until the next electoral process in 1995 and was charged with drafting a new constitution. Several of the main opposition parties, including AP, APRA, and IU, refused to participate, arguing that with Fujimori as president there were no guarantees of a free and fair election. They also criticized the proposed unicameral congress, charging that it would be easy for the executive to manipulate—precisely the reason most democratic systems have two congressional chambers. The newly formed official alliance, Change 90-New Majority, won a majority in the CCD, and Jaime Yoshiyama, a key Fujimori ally, was elected as its president. Revealing the extent to which this new congress was intended to institutionalize the postcoup order, the new CCD legalized all the decree laws issues by the executive branch after the *autogolpe*, and ratified Fujimori as the "constitutional head of state."

The following year, the CCD drafted a new constitution. The new document gave the executive complete control over promotions in the armed forces, eliminating congressional oversight, and expanded military powers. It consolidated the model of a unicameral legislature with rules designed to limit debate and push through measures quickly. The new document also eliminated many of the social protections for workers and peasants enshrined in the 1979 constitution and set the stage for the expansion of neoliberal reforms. It established the death penalty in cases of terrorism and treason. Perhaps the most controversial clause was the one that allowed for immediate presidential reelection. The progovernment majority steam-rolled the process, limiting debate time allotted to the opposition, and approved the final document when opposition members were absent.

In July 1993, opposition mayors and congressional leaders, as well as intellectuals, church groups and trade unions, launched a campaign to defeat the constitution. One of their key demands was a vote on the entire constitution rather than on only partial measures the regime might pick and choose that were more likely to be approved. The CCD majority agreed, and a referendum was scheduled for October 31, 1993, in which citizens would cast a Yes or No vote on the entire constitution. The opposition did not unite, however, in its rejection of the proposed constitution, with PPC leaders opting to organize their own separate campaign. In the end, the constitution was approved, though not by the overwhelming numbers the regime's leaders expected. The opposition charged that the regime had fixed the vote count in some regions, but electoral authorities rejected the charges. The OAS mission paid little attention to the opposition's claims of fraud.

In effect, the international community accepted congressional elections and the approval of a new constitution as sufficient evidence of Peru's return to the democratic fold. While the Clinton administration initially adopted a harsh stance vis-à-vis the Fujimori regime—withholding, for example, U.S. support for a $2.1 billion IMF bridge loan until the Fujimori regime agreed to allow local and international human rights groups to operate without government interference—by 1993, encouraged by Fujimori's economic liberalization program as well as a string of positive developments in the counterinsurgency war, the administration sought to restore U.S. aid to Peru. Nonetheless, congress blocked the request on human rights grounds, and similar efforts to fully restore U.S. assistance to Peru were stymied in 1994 and 1995 also in response to new revelations of human rights abuses. Despite such aid restrictions, Peru in 1994 and 1995 was the largest recipient of U.S. aid in Latin America, as other forms of U.S. financial support to Peru continued, including development assistance, the Food for Peace program, and counternarcotics efforts. Funding for these programs reached $137 million in 1994 and $150 million in 1995 (Roberts and Peceny 1997).

The reordering of power that followed the 1992 coup installed an authoritarian regime. Though the legislature was restored later that year, both congress and the judiciary were routinely subjected to the intervention of the executive branch. Rather than a system of checks and balances—the foundation of horizontal accountability in presidential democracies—Peru's postcoup political system lacked checks on the power of the executive branch and means to counter the interference of the executive in the legislature, the judiciary, or other nominally autonomous institutions. Moreover, the progovernment majority in congress often used its power to interfere in other institutions, particularly the judiciary, to prevent challenges to the regime's authoritarian arrangements. Examples will be provided later in the chapter. Before that, it is necessary to analyze the third dimension of state reconstitution: the containment of the Shining Path insurgency.

### Checkmate Shining Path

On the evening of September 12, 1992, an elite police intelligence unit raided a two-story house in a well-off residential district in Lima. The police had the house and its occupants under surveillance for several weeks. Maritza Garrido Lecca ran a dancing studio on the second floor of the house. Police suspected her companion, Edmundo Cox Beauzeville, of being an important leader of Shining Path.

Several clues, culled from surveying visitors to the couple's home, their purchasing habits, and even their garbage, led the police to suspect that an important member of Shining Path was hiding out in the house, perhaps Guzmán himself. The couple purchased a large amount of food for just two people. On one occasion, Garrido Lecca reportedly purchased an extra-large pair of men's long underwear, much too large to fit her partner's small frame. Cartons of Winston cigarettes—the brand preferred by Guzmán—as well as discarded tubes of ointment to treat psoriasis, an illness Guzmán was believed to have suffered from, were found in the couple's garbage.

The elite police unit, known by its Spanish acronym, DINCOTE, decided to move on the house quickly, without reporting to the top military brass or to President Fujimori, in case it was in fact Guzmán who was hiding out in the dancer's home. On previous occasions, DINCOTE had come close to capturing Guzmán but inevitably missed the mark, the result of political interference or bureaucratic infighting from other security forces.[20] This time, when the police stormed inside the house, they came face to face with Abimael Guzmán, who was unarmed, and sitting, relaxed, watching television. Though several of Guzmán's closest aides moved immediately to his side to protect him, there was no resistance; not a shot was fired. The head of DINCOTE, Police General Antonio Ketín Vidal, said to Guzmán, "In life you must know when it is your turn to win and when it is your turn to lose." Guzmán responded stoically, "It was my turn to lose." He was led away and put in solitary confinement in a top-security prison in the naval base located on a small island just off the coast of Callao. Also arrested were Guzmán's second-in-command, Elena Iparraguirre, and two other high-ranking members of Shining Path's Central Committee.[21] After the capture of Guzmán, numerous other leaders were arrested, and several organizational structures, including the important Socorro Popular, which operated in Lima, were dismantled.[22]

President Fujimori was on a fishing trip in the Amazon the day Guzmán was arrested. He returned immediately to Lima to address the nation and to claim success in his mission to defeat subversion. While he was cautious in noting that Guzmán's arrest would probably not mean an immediate end to the violence, Fujimori glowingly affirmed that Guzmán's arrest was a decisive chapter in the effort to defeat subversion by the end of his presidential term in 1995. Three months earlier, Víctor Polay, the head of the MRTA insurgency, was arrested and jailed for the second time,[23] and with Guzmán's arrest, Fujimori asserted, he was fulfilling his promise to the Peruvian people to end the "terrorist scourge."

Without a doubt, the arrest of Guzmán and other top Shining Path leaders resulted in a significant shift in the balance of forces. It reversed

**Figure 8.1**    The Arrest of Abimael Guzmán

Abimael Guzmán, the top leader and ideologue of Shining Path, was arrested in Lima on September 12, 1992. The National Police presented him to the press on September 24, 1992. This was a key victory for the Fujimori regime.

*Source*: Caretas Archive.

the image that the state was losing the war against Shining Path, and thus helped restore legitimacy to the Peruvian state. It gave renewed confidence to the armed forces and to the police forces that were waging the battle against insurgent groups. It created crucial political capital for the Fujimori regime, whose popularity rating of 80 percent at the time of the April coup was now flagging to around 60–65 percent. After Guzmán's arrest, Fujimori's popularity soared again to 75 percent.[24] While many Peruvians remained fearful—and Shining Path's violent campaign continued to rage for many months following Guzmán's arrest—it also inspired hope in many that the violence might soon be brought under control and some normalcy returned to their daily lives.

Fujimori and his allies sought to capitalize on Guzmán's arrest to vindicate the coup and the repressive system that had been put in place in its aftermath. The coup, they claimed, had made Guzmán's arrest possible, an argument that allowed them to assert the efficacy of the coup and the concentration of power that followed it. As Fujimori stated at a meeting with international journalists in March 1993,

> It would have been irresponsible to not consummate the *autogolpe*, which permitted us to successfully address the struggle against terrorism, corruption within the judiciary and to deepen neoliberal reforms.[25]

Fujimori and his allies, especially the progovernment media such as the daily *Expreso*, repeatedly asserted the thesis of the efficacy of the postcoup order. They pointed to the arrest of Guzmán to highlight the necessity of a "firm hand" and contrasted the postcoup order to the inefficacy of civilian elites and of democratic rule itself, which were portrayed as fundamentally incapable of dealing with the economic and political crisis that had engulfed the country by the late 1980s. Establishing the efficacy of the coup was crucial to justifying the larger project of the civil-military government that had been put in place in April 1992. It permitted the regime to push through neoliberal reforms, including a rapid privatization program, with relative ease, and it legitimated the preponderant role of the military in politics, while at the same time permitting the extension of military control over society.

The argument that the arrest was due primarily to the concentration of power following the April 1992 coup is spurious at best. Guzmán's arrest was the result of significant shifts in counterinsurgency policy initiated in the late 1980s and that were continued under the Fujimori regime, primarily greater emphasis on intelligence gathering to identify the top leaders of the Shining Path and MRTA insurgencies. Guzmán was arrested not because of the curtailment of civil liberties, the concentration of power in the hands of the executive that followed the coup, or the blank check the military had been handed over the military to deal with the insurgency. On the contrary—and this is perhaps one of the central paradoxes of Peru's internal conflict—the decisive blow against subversion was carried out in a fundamentally democratic manner, following traditional detective work and extensive surveillance against an illegal and violent armed group. Nevertheless, the Fujimori regime constructed an elaborate discourse that sought to validate the coup by claiming it had laid the groundwork for the arrest of Guzmán and the containment of Shining Path.

## Militarization and Counterinsurgency

As noted in previous chapters, early counterinsurgency policy had been hampered by doctrinal incoherence and bureaucratic infighting. In addition, counterinsurgency operations emphasized immediate results, measured in the number of arrests and deaths of presumed insurgents. A decade of this approach failed to detain the advance of Shining Path. In the late 1980s, a group of strategic elites within the armed forces began to perceive the need to radically alter counterinsurgency policy.[26] New emphasis was placed on intelligence gathering and surveillance, resulting in greater success in identifying individuals who had some connection to insurgent group activity. Indiscriminate violence on the part of state actors declined, but human rights violations continued. Now, however, state actions were more targeted. Rather than large-scale massacres (as were common throughout the 1980s), state security forces targeted individuals believed to be involved in Shining Path or the MRTA through extrajudicial killings and forced disappearances.[27]

The coup provided the Fujimori government with the opportunity to restructure counterinsurgency policy with no public accountability. It launched a devastating strike against the Shining Path leadership just 48 hours after the *autogolpe* was announced. Military forces occupied the Miguel Castro Castro high-security prison where dozens of top-ranking Shining Path leaders were being held. Despite the fact that these were government facilities, Shining Path prisoners had established control over the pavilions where their members were held, and prison authorities rarely entered or interfered in the disciplined and orderly authority the group itself had imposed. In effect, prisons were privileged sites for reinforcing the commitment to the revolutionary cause and for recruiting and indoctrinating new members.[28] After several weeks of tension, on May 6, army troops launched an all-out assault on the Shining Path pavilion that lasted two days. Fifty-four Shining Path members were killed. Among those killed were all the high-ranking members of the organization with the sole exception of Osmán Morote; according to the Inter-American Human Rights Commission, they were summarily executed after having surrendered.[29]

Fujimori proceeded next to pass decree laws similar to those that had been overturned or modified by the congress in the months prior to the coup in an attempt to solidify a legal framework for the militarization of the counterinsurgency war. On May 5, Fujimori announced the promulgation of decree law 25475 on the crime of terrorism and related acts as well as new procedures for investigation and trial of terrorist suspects.[30] The law imposed harsh penalties on individuals convicted of membership in terrorist organizations, including life sentences for national leaders, as well as for collaborators. The definition of terrorism was broadened to include not only those responsible for carrying out acts of violence, as was the case in the previous legislation, but also those who "create a state of anxiety" by any means, including nonviolent ones, and sentences were set at a minimum of 20 years. This definition was widely criticized by national and international human rights organizations for being so broad it could encompass legitimate social activists, human rights leaders, or journalists.[31] The law established prison sentences of 6–12 years for anyone guilty of "apology for terrorism," which was left undefined. This similarly was criticized as a threat to freedom of expression and to the ongoing work of human rights groups, whom Fujimori has repeatedly accused of being "apologists" of terrorism. Other changes virtually eliminated due process for terrorism and treason suspects. For example, new legislation made it nearly impossible for suspects to obtain adequate representation: defense attorneys were restricted to representing one client at a time nationwide; suspects could be held for 15 days incommunicado, during which time they were not allowed to see a lawyer;[32] and perhaps most alarmingly, the regime established a system of faceless military courts that removed accountability from the entire trial process and fundamentally contradicted due process (Human Rights Watch 1992, 1993). Military trials are in effect summary trials, in which one of the parties to the conflict—the military—acts as judge and jury, denying defendants of their fundamental democratic right to an impartial trial. In practice, moreover, the defendant is presumed guilty and must prove his or her innocence.[33]

Hundreds if not thousands of Peruvian citizens who had no connection to guerrilla movements, or who may have collaborated unwittingly or under coercion with guerrilla groups, were arrested and sentenced to long prison terms under this new legal regime. This new legal framework thus created a new pattern of human rights violations in which hundreds of people were caught up in the draconian antiterrorist legal regime and convicted even though they were innocent of any real crime. In addition, many others who were convicted of a real crime, such as collaboration, received hugely disproportionate sentences. This was seen as particularly egregious in cases where collaboration was performed under duress or coercion. The new congress installed in December 1992 ratified this new legal framework, consolidating a draconian regime that eliminated key civil liberties and gave the state inordinate power to combat insurgent groups, and resulting in the arrest of hundreds if not thousands of *inocentes,* or innocents, as they were described by human rights organizations (de la Jara Basombrío 2001).

After the coup, the armed forces also moved to centralize decision making by creating a unified command structure. The police were placed under military control, effectively reducing rivalries between these two institutions but also subordinating police to the logic of the military. In particular after the arrest of Guzmán, counterinsurgency policy began to emphasize winning the support of the population—the battle for the hearts and minds of civilians central to modern warfare. In the countryside, for example, the armed forces modified its practices to a significant degree. Whole-scale massacres of peasant communities, common until 1989, became less frequent. A greater focus on intelligence work allowed army operatives to more selectively target presumed terrorists, which presumably reduced the need for indiscriminate killings. Abuses still occurred, but now the problem was an alarming rise in disappearances and rising incidence of arbitrary arrest and conviction under the vaguely worded antiterrorism laws.[34] In addition, the armed forces sought to develop links with peasant communities to win their support; this was partly accomplished through government and army support for the nascent *rondas campesinas,* or peasant self-defense patrols, that were organizing in many highland communities to ward off Shining Path violence.

Analysts have documented instances of peasant resistance to Shining Path in the early 1980s. Degregori (1998) has suggested that the military's use of indiscriminate violence during this period postponed the rupture between peasants and Shining Path. By the late 1980s, growing peasant unease with Shining Path spilled over into increasing displays of armed and unarmed resistance. In many parts of the Andean highlands, peasants began to organize *rondas campesinas* to challenge Shining Path. Though Shining Path had marshaled peasant support in the highlands in the early 1980s by attacking hated local figures, such as landlords and abusive merchants, peasant unease with Shining Path was increasingly evident in the second half of the 1980s. Shining Path's increasing demands on peasant communities—extracting more resources, recruiting more young people, forcing peasants to stay away from markets, imposing their hierarchy structures over communal traditions—began to generate resistance. At the same time, Shining Path's violent attacks on members of peasant communities were seen as violating essential notions of the Andean worldview, including the notion that transgressors may be punished but then reincorporated into the community to maintain equilibrium in a delicate and sometimes hostile ecosystem.[35]

The military's new emphasis on winning the population's support led to a policy of encouraging the formation of *rondas* and incorporating them into the counterinsurgency war. During the last year of the García regime, and then massively during the Fujimori regime, the state handed out weapons to the *rondas* and placed them under the legal control of the armed forces.[36] Experts estimate that 200,000 peasants belonged to these units by 1993 (Tapia 1997). At least nominally controlled by the armed forces, these units became crucial strategic weapons in the war against Shining Path. Not only did they provide manpower to patrol desolate areas and engage in combat with guerrilla columns; they also allowed the army to gain strategic control over populations—a key aspect of modern guerrilla warfare in which controlling populations is often the defining element of victory or defeat (Nordstrom 1992).

Also important was the fact that the armed forces began to allow locally recruited soldiers to operate in the highlands area. As noted in chapter three, a key problem during the 1980s was that the army, which was made up primarily of recruits from coastal areas who viewed indigenous peasants with disdain and often could not communicate with them, was widely perceived as an occupation force rather than an ally.[37] The incorporation of local recruits who better understood the local language and culture helped to reduce ethnic and class tensions between the military and the local population. This, coupled with growing coercion on the part of Shining Path, led many local communities to now see the armed forces as an ally. This was especially the case in communities where Shining Path, seeking to stem the rise of the *rondas campesinas*, brutally assassinated *ronda* members, accusing them of being "traitors" and "sellouts" to the revolution. The army also began civic-action campaigns throughout the countryside, providing food and medicine to poor communities as part of its campaign to win the hearts and minds of the local population. Since the arrest of Guzmán, the Shining Path's aura of invincibility—and the fear it inspired—had been broken, making action against the Maoists seem more viable.[38] *Ronda* members now felt emboldened to challenge suspected Shining Path members and to engage columns when they were detected.

A similar process of militarization was evident in the cities as well. The armed forces stepped up their civic-action campaigns in poor shantytowns throughout Lima. These would usually begin with early morning raids, in which soldiers would go door to door, searching homes for suspicious material and activities and then register all household members. "Suspicious" individuals—most often those lacking identity documents—were questioned and detained. This would be followed by measures designed to reestablish state presence and authority as well as win local support by providing concrete goods and services. Flag-raising ceremonies were held; food and medicine distributed; free treatments offered by physicians and pediatricians, dentists, and barbers. On occasion, army bands played highland music, and sometimes President Fujimori himself made an appearance and danced with local women to highland music.[39] Early morning raids and massive arrests were increasingly common in Lima's shantytowns, but prior to 1992, they were conducted almost clandestinely, with no prior notification or publicity. The civic-action component was added first in February 1992 in response to the formation of Shining Path's first "popular support base" in Lima in the squatter settlement of Raucana, in the popular district of Ate-Vitarte. This marked the first step in an increasingly concerted effort on the part of the armed forces to win the hearts and minds of shantytown residents by coupling coercive tactics with the provision of material goods and other services.[40]

After Guzmán's arrest, the civic-action dimension of the raids was stepped up considerably. Each adult member of a household who was registered by soldiers during raid was given a ticket to exchange for rations of food and medicine. These campaigns became increasingly common throughout Lima, and were now highly publicized, often accompanied by television reporters who filmed soldiers cutting young boys' hair and army commanders dancing with poor Andean women. Soldiers also handed out patriotic literature that presents the armed forces as a "friend" of the people and the promoters of national pride and development, suggesting a clear intention to use these programs to improve the army's—and by extension the state's—relationship with the urban poor. After 1993, the army began carrying out civic-action campaigns independently of the early morning raids, suggesting that their primary objective was to improve the military's image among the urban poor.[41] Notably, the same logic that gave rise to sympathy and support for Shining Path's provision of order and security in Lima's *barriadas* could be detected in the positive evaluation many shantytown residents offered of these programs. One *barriada* resident said of the civic-action programs: "It's good because there are not enough authorities around here." Another resident invoked the army's presence as an assurance of public security: "It's good that the [armed forces] are here because they get rid of the bad elements in the community."[42] Yet another viewed the army's presence as a necessary return of the state to Lima's poor *barriadas*, and considered the handouts and services provided as positive: "We need the authorities to pay attention to what is going on in these neighborhoods. These programs are helpful to the community."[43] Notably, young people—those most likely to be arrested during these raids—were the least enthusiastic (APRODEH 1994b).

In both the cities and the countryside, the army also became involved in local development projects, particularly infrastructure development. Soldiers began building roads, fixing potholes, constructing new schools, installing electricity grids. A massive propaganda campaign was evident in the shantytowns of Lima I visited between 1993 and 1995, as well as in rural areas, such as Ayacucho, which I visited in 1993, portraying the armed forces as the promoters of national "pacification" and development. On the Central Highway, just before arriving at the turn-off to enter Huaycán, in the district of Ate-Vitarte, a huge billboard with a picture of soldiers and local shantytown residents standing beside an army tank announced: "The Peruvian Armed Forces and the People Working Together to Forge National Pacification and Development!"

The armed forces and the civic-action campaigns thus became a key tool for the government to bridge the deep divide between state and society. Other programs were adopted to further bridge this gap, such as FONCODES, the poverty-alleviation program that was created in 1992 with the financial assistance of international lenders such as the IMF and the World Bank. FONCODES was billed as a way for social groups to organize grassroots improvement projects and obtain funding from the state to carry out those projects. In fact, the program became a massive machine to reestablish clientelistic networks at the local and regional level that were tightly controlled from the center.[44]

The regime also passed legislation allowing for reduced sentences for members of Shining Path who turned themselves in and/or who gave authorities information leading to the arrest of other Shining Path militants. With Guzmán in solitary confinement, hundreds of Shining Path activists—some long-time militants as well as less seasoned sympathizers and collaborators—decided to cut their losses and avail themselves of the Fujimori regime's repentance law. There are numerous reports of abuses involving this legislation. Many Shining Path militants, particularly those who had felt coerced into joining or supporting the insurgency, participated willingly in the provisions established by the repentance law. However, human rights groups documented numerous cases in which participation was coerced by government authorities (de la Jara Basombrío 2001). While some of those who repented revealed the names and locations of bona fide militants of Shining Path, others named low-ranking members of the organization or individuals who collaborated logistically, often under threat of coercion. The repentance law was significant in drawing out low-level collaborators with Shining Path, depriving the organization of key logistical support, and undermining its support base. It also created serious problems, however, including questions of due process; judicial backlog; and numerous instances of false accusations against individuals.[45]

## The New Authoritarianism

As political violence declined in the aftermath of the capture of the top leaders of the MRTA and Shining Path, one might have expected the opening of democratic spaces in Peru. This was not, however, the case. Even after Fujimori was reelected in 1995, which prompted some observers to argue that Peru had returned to the democratic fold, the postcoup reordering of power remained intact. Horizontal accountability was destroyed by the concentration of power in the executive branch and its manipulation of the legislature to do its dirty work when challenges to the regime's policies or power structure arose. In addition democratic institutions remained highly circumscribed by the power of nonelected officials, including the armed forces.[46] Civil and political rights were sharply curtailed, and freedom of the press was threatened, particularly as opposition groups became emboldened to challenge some of the regime's worst abuses. Peru under Fujimori was not a delegative or illiberal democracy, or even an expression of some form of neopopulism, as some have argued.[47] Rather, this was a type of authoritarianism—a civil-military regime—whose architects recognized the impossibility of a traditional military-led coup given the international (primarily U.S.) temperament in favor of democracy.[48] Formal democratic institutions such as congress, the judiciary, and the constitutional tribunal remained in place as long as they helped maintain the illusion—necessary for international purposes—that Peru was a democratic regime. But if such institutions dared challenge those in power or their designs to retain it, they were subordinated, subverted or eviscerated.

This section provides several examples that reveal the dynamics of political power in postcoup Peru to illustrate the authoritarian nature of the regime as well as the undue influence of the armed forces and other nonelected actors, despite its formal democratic structure. Perhaps the most infamous case demonstrating the absence of checks and balances, as well as the undue power of the armed forces in the political process, is the Cantuta case. On July 18, 1992, nine university students and a professor were kidnapped from the Enrique Valle y Guzmán University campus, also known as Cantuta. The students and professor were never seen from again. Suspicions that the abduction of the students and professor was the work of the Grupo Colina death squad, comprising members of the SIN and army intelligence (SIE), have since been confirmed. The case received little public attention as it took place in the midst of a dramatic Shining

Path offensive in Lima. But the case reemerged a year later—well after Guzmán's arrest—when a disgruntled group of military officers leaked a document to an opposition congressman indicating that the intelligence services were responsible for the Cantuta disappearances.[49] The military high command refused to cooperate with the subsequent congressional investigation into the case, and the head of the armed forces, General Hermoza, accused the investigating congressional leaders of acting "in collusion with the homicidal terrorists" (APRODEH 1994a). The following day, Lima awoke to a parade of army tanks and declarations by army generals backing Hermoza and accusing congress of engaging in a "systematic campaign orchestrated with the dark objective of undermining the prestige of the armed forces."[50]

Two weeks later, General Rodolfo Robles, the army's third highest-ranking officer, sought refuge in the U.S. Embassy, where he made a public statement accusing a death squad known as the Grupo Colina as responsible for the disappearances. He made public the names of the officers who were involved, and accused Montesinos and General Hermoza of giving the orders. Hermoza reacted immediately, saying Robles was a liar and a traitor.[51] On June 24, the Fujimori-controlled congress passed a minority report absolving the armed forces and the SIN of responsibility for the Cantuta crimes. But a few weeks later, on July 8, the charred bodies of the students from La Cantuta were found in Cieneguilla, just east of Lima, again thanks to information leaked from within the armed forces.[52] While the government tried desperately to present this as a set-up by Shining Path to discredit the armed forces,[53] another burial site was located in November in Huachipa, the original site of the murders of the professor and the nine students.[54]

It was at this point that the extent of the military's power and the subservience of the legislature became evident. As a civil court was reviewing the case, the military court announced it was carrying out its own investigation. In a clear contravention of its legislative powers, the majority in congress passed a bill in February 1994 that granted jurisdiction over the Cantuta case to the military courts—a decision that constitutionally was the purview of the Supreme Court. Despite the fact that the Supreme Court had generally ruled in favor of the military courts since the mid-1980s, the high command apparently was unwilling to risk it. Two weeks later, in secret military proceedings, a handful of military officers were found guilty of the Cantuta murders and sentenced to 20 years in prison. (It was later revealed that the officers never in fact went to prison nor were they ever relieved of their duty.)

Just over a year later, on the evening of June 13, 1995, progovernment congress members presented a bill that granted amnesty to all military and police officers, convicted or otherwise, who committed or were accused of committing crimes during the war against terrorism. The bill was passed in the early morning hours of June 14, signed by President Fujimori the same day, and published in the official gazette, *El Peruano,* the following day. The lack of public debate, the haste with which the law was passed, and the fact that it was passed during what amounted to a lame-duck congress, revealed again the way purportedly democratic institutions had been placed at the service of the regime's authoritarian project. All officials convicted in the Cantuta case were now cleared of any charges. Observers noted that the law was designed specifically to free the authors of the Cantuta murders, but it also granted a blanket amnesty to all military and police officials implicated in human rights crimes and is regarded as one of the most sweeping in a hemisphere known for very generous amnesty laws (Amnesty International 1996). The officers convicted for the Cantuta massacre reportedly threatened to reveal all they knew—including the involvement of General Hermoza and Montesinos in the Grupo Colina activities and the subsequent cover-ups—unless they were freed.

In the aftermath of the "reorganization" of the judiciary after the *autogolpe*, hundreds of judges were sacked and judicial appointments became temporary, making judges dependent for their positions on the executive. As a result, judges remained fearful of handing down sentences that may not be to the government's liking. In a display of bravery and judicial independence, one judge, Antonia Saquicuray, challenged the validity of the amnesty law, claiming that it did not apply to cases already under investigation. Saquicuray was investigating the Barrios Altos massacre, which had occurred in 1991, presumably also at the hands of the Grupo Colina. Paramilitary units stormed a multiple family home in the working-class neighborhood of Barrios Altos, and using high-powered weapons and silencers, shot at civilians attending a neighborhood barbeque. Fifteen people, including children, were killed. Saquicuray argued that the amnesty law could not be applied to investigations in progress, and stated that she would continue her inquiry into the Barrios Altos case. In response, the majority in congress passed a second law mandating the termination of the investigation and, once again completely overstepping its constitutional bounds, ordered the judiciary to implement the amnesty law.

The efforts to ensure Fujimori's ability to run for a third term in office similarly revealed the nature of power in the postcoup order. The 1993 constitution states that a president may be reelected to one consecutive term. In order to sidestep this limitation so as to permit Fujimori to be a candidate in 2000, the progovernment majority in congress passed the "Law of Authentic Interpretation" in mid-1996, which basically stated that since the 1993 constitution was not in force when Fujimori was first elected in 1990, his first term did not count, thus making him eligible to run for a third term. In 1997, the constitutional tribunal ruled that the law did "not apply" to Fujimori, thereby challenging the re-reelection project. In response, the majority in congress passed a law—that again violated the legislature's constitutional powers and the autonomy of the judiciary—dismissing the judges. Congress, clearly acting as the stand-in for the executive, thus arbitrarily and unconstitutionally eliminated the body charged with ruling on the constitutionality of legislation passed by the legislature and the executive, leaving citizens with no recourse to challenge existing and future unconstitutional laws.

Many of these abuses occurred in the context of high popularity ratings for President Fujimori, which seemed to give the regime a wide margin of maneuverability in terms of its efforts to retain its hold on power. In a trend evident by 1996, and which continued as the economic situation failed to improve significantly for a majority of Peruvians, Fujimori's popularity ratings began to drop dramatically—from an average of between 60 and 70 percent between the 1992 *autogolpe* and the end of 1995, to all-time lows of 30–40 percent in 1997 and 1998.[55] As opposition groups sought to exert pressure on the regime in the wake of these shifts in public opinion, the government's response was to harden its posture, using unconstitutional means to overturn opposition challenges and increasing its use of threats and intimidation against both opposition leaders and the independent press. This includes the torture and murder of regime operatives who were found to have leaked information to the press about death squad activities; clamp downs on the opposition; efforts to control the media, including as is now known thanks to hundreds of videos documenting the regime's corrupt dealings, the purchasing of the editorial lines of all the major electronic media and a substantial portion of the print press; and campaigns of surveillance and intimidation of the opposition. This process, and societal responses to it, will be explored further in the next two chapters.

These examples illustrate the way the executive and the ruling majority in congress manipulated democratic institutions to perpetuate the civil-military regime's power, assure impunity for the armed forces, and prevent any challenge to their power from emerging. As Karl and Schmitter (1996) have convincingly argued, a political system cannot be called democratic simply because it holds elections; this is the "fallacy of electoralism" in which democracy is equated with elections and no other conditions are required as necessary to qualify as a democracy. Schmitter and Karl argue that for a procedural democracy (or polyarchy, to use Dahl's term) to exist, elections must be free, fair, and competitive, suggesting that certain basic rights and civil liberties must be guaranteed for all citizens, and nonofficials may not exercise undue power, including constraining the behavior of elected officials. Throughout Fujimori's reign, the armed forces were deliberative and interventionist. They participated directly in the political process as the cogoverning allies of President Fujimori. They were his direct link to the urban and rural poor through civic-action campaigns and diverse other "development" initiatives, including the building of roads and other public works projects. They had become, as one observer noted, Fujimori's political party (Obando 1998). The armed forces also interfered as a matter of routine in the political system in order to preserve military privileges, prevent investigations into corruption or human rights abuses, and assure impunity. The inordinate power of other nonelected officials, primarily Vladimiro Montesinos, the de facto head of the SIN during the Fujimori decade, is also significant in this regard.

But the military's influence during the Fujimori decade transcended the political realm and penetrated into the very interstices of Peruvian society. Long after the threat of Shining Path receded, huge swaths of national territory continued to be declared in a state of emergency, giving the military ongoing de facto power. Through its control over the *rondas campesinas*, the self-defense units that organized throughout the countryside to combat Shining Path, the military also retained a significant presence in much of the central highlands. The military continued to interfere in the provision of due process by challenging the jurisdiction of the civil court system and pursuing parallel trials, and by the maintenance (until recently) of the faceless military court system. The military was also accused by domestic and international observers of facilitating and in some cases engaging directly in electoral fraud in diverse electoral processes, most famously the 2000 presidential elections.[56]

The *autogolpe* concentrated power in the hands of the executive and gave broad power to the military in the counterinsurgency war. While the coup was internationally criticized and the Fujimori regime was forced to modify its plans, acceding to holding congressional elections and restoring constitutional rule, the institutional reordering that took place in the aftermath of the coup did not restore democracy; it simply provided a window dressing to mask the regime's fundamental authoritarianism. In effect, the regime reinstated democratic institutions but employed a variety of mechanisms to control these institutions to retain its power over decision making. This resolved Peru's problems in terms of the international community, while permitting Fujimori and his cronies to continue to rule in near-dictatorial fashion.

### Political Order or Authoritarian Walkover?

The reconstitution of the Peruvian state under Fujimori was impressive and dramatic in many respects, but it also raises a number of disturbing questions, especially for those concerned not just with the restoration of order but also with the democratic process. The process by which the Peruvian state was reconstituted was fundamentally authoritarian. This raises the question of whether societies facing extreme situations of economic collapse, expanding political violence, and social malaise must resort to such heavy-handed measures to restore order and some degree of normalcy. This is precisely what authoritarian-minded leaders would have us believe. There is also a strand of thought in political science that would seem to support such a view, dating back to Samuel Huntington's concern with political order above demands for participation and democracy in his 1968 book *Political Order in Changing Societies*. This chapter suggests that authoritarianism was a contingent outcome based on a number of specific conditions. Thus rather than a preordained outcome, authoritarianism was the result of specific conditions and a specific set of decisions by state managers and other elite groups.

Reasserting state control over warring groups can be achieved through political negotiation or top-down efforts involving the centralization of state power and the repression of violent challengers. In the Peruvian case, a number of factors mitigated against the former path. The first of these is that the principal insurgent group, Shining Path, had long articulated its absolute unwillingness to negotiate under any circumstances. As Abimael Guzmán famously said in a 1988 interview, "Negotiation is the equivalent of capitulation." The second is that civil society was too weak and disarticulated to sustain demands for a peaceful, democratic solution to Peru's multiple crises. Legislators linked to the democratic Left as well as human rights organizations and social movement leaders promoted such initiatives, but they collapsed under the weight of the implosion of the Left, on the one hand, and the decimation of civil society on the other. After the IU split in 1989 and the punishing results of the 1990 elections for the Left, the IU ceased to be a significant actor in Peruvian political life. In the meantime, social fragmentation and the demobilizing effects of fear were undermining citizen participation in public life. The opportunities for peaceful conflict resolution were closing, which created greater opportunities for state makers to pursue other methods. This was facilitated by the fact that elites had come to power that had no ties to existing political parties, and thus had tremendous latitude to pursue objectives as they defined them. A group of strategic elites within the state apparatus—specifically, within the armed forces—saw the need for unifying the military command in order to devise a coherent counterinsurgency policy and overcome the debilitating interinstitutional rivalries that were hampering the state's actions vis-à-vis Shining Path. Power was increasingly centralized in the hands of the executive, culminating in the April 1992 *autogolpe*, which established the basis for an enduring reordering of political power. With a new congress and a new constitution in place by the end of 1993, it appeared that democratic institutions had been restored. In fact the regime remained an authoritarian one grounded in a civil-military alliance that utilized the institutionality of democracy to obscure its autocratic decision making, arbitrary use of power, and violations of human rights.

Given the disarticulation of social and political actors, newly assertive state leaders had little checks or control to their power. Moreover, as this new coalition achieved substantial policy successes—the taming of inflation, the resumption of macroeconomic growth, and the 1992 arrest of Abimael Guzmán and the subsequent containment of the Shining Path—this bestowed them with legitimacy and substantial political capital. In this context, Fujimori and his military allies were able to consolidate a highly authoritarian and personalistic form of rule in postwar Peru.

The lesson is one that democratic theorists would foresee. In the absence of a robust political and civil society, democratic routes of state reconstitution—a negotiated political solution, based on an attempt to bring all those political actors willing to participate in the political system together—becomes less likely. John Keane (1996) has noted that one of the central elements of democracy is what he calls "social obstacles"—civil and political society—to prevent autocratic-minded leaders from having their way.

Moreover, leaders who successfully concentrate power are then likely to seek to perpetuate the conditions that permitted this in the first instance. In the case of Peru, these conditions include social and political fragmentation and deinstitutionalization. One of the main tasks of an authoritarian regime is sustaining its own power base—and seeking to prevent any alternatives from emerging that could challenge its power. Hence such regimes are likely to adopt policies aimed at undermining the emergence of independent actors in political and civil society. This became one of the defining characteristics of the Fujimori regime: It systematically sought to keep political and civil society—already decimated by the impact of economic chaos and political violence—weak and disarticulated in order to prevent challenges to its autocratic concentration of power and privilege. For Fujimori and his allies, perpetuating the weakness of political and civil society was key to undermining potential challengers and maintaining the regime's hold on power. How it carried out this task, and its consequences for civil society and democracy, is examined in the next chapter.

# CHAPTER NINE

# Quien Habla es Terrorista: The Politics of Fear

*Cultures of terror are based on and nourished by silence.*
Michael Taussig (1984:469)

For nearly a decade, President Fujimori enjoyed high popularity ratings. It was not until 2000, in the midst of a tense electoral process and allegations of government fraud, that massive protests erupted against the regime. On July 27, 2000, the eve of Alberto Fujimori's swearing in as president of Peru for the third consecutive time, protestors from throughout the country converged on downtown Lima to challenge what they argued was an illegitimate electoral process. According to the 1993 constitution, which Fujimori and his allies in congress put in place after the infamous *autogolpe* of April 1992, a sitting president could be reelected only one consecutive time. This would be Fujimori's third term in office, made possible, critics charged, by the manipulation of the rules of the game on the one hand and outright intimidation of the opposition on the other. Indeed, the Fujimori regime seemed bent on assuring a third term in office for the president at any cost.[1]

In this context, social mobilization burst onto the scene to contest the legitimacy of the electoral process and of Fujimori's third term. From middle-class feminists to working-class moms, from community kitchen organizers to university students, from urban shantytown dwellers to peasant federation members, thousands of people took to the streets during the contested first and second round of elections in April and May 2000. Massive street protests on the three days preceding Fujimori's swearing-in ceremony on July 28 revealed widespread repudiation of the regime. These mobilizations were so remarkable precisely because for most of the previous decade, social protest had been scarce.

Why was civil society unable to articulate an effective opposition to the Fujimori regime until the very last years of his decade in power? The traditional answer to this question—that civil society and the political opposition remained weak and unable to articulate effective leadership—is unsatisfying. By locating the source of weakness in factors endogenous to the opposition, it fails to grapple with the complex interactions between the state, political society, and civil society that might provide a more complete understanding of the state of civil society in Peru in the 1990s. Other explanations for the weakness of civil society point to the economic crisis of the 1980s and the application of neoliberal reforms in the 1990s. While economic factors certainly played an important role in the demobilization of civil society, this does not account for the specifically political factors that undermined civil society organization. This chapter seeks to contribute to this discussion by examining the ways in which state power was deployed during the Fujimori regime to maintain civil society disorganized and hence unable to articulate an effective oppositional discourse and politics. One mechanism deployed by state elites to demobilize civil society was the widespread use of patronage, which has been widely analyzed in the literature (Roberts 1995; Schady 1997; Graham 1994). This chapter explores another means by which state elites demobilized civil society that has not been extensively examined: the instrumentalization of fear.

Analyzing the political use of fear during the Fujimori regime is important for a second reason. Much of the literature on this period in recent Peruvian history emphasizes the consensual dimension of politics under Fujimori, despite and notwithstanding his government's use of repression and authoritarian tactics. While scholars highlighted the existence of a culture of fear in Peru in the 1980s (Bourque and Warren 1989), few analysts paid attention to the ongoing effects of fear, particularly after the capture of the top leaders and "strategic defeat" of the Shining Path guerrilla movement. Scholarship focused on Fujimori's surprising success in achieving key policy objectives, and how these successes, particularly on the economic and security fronts, along with his "neopopulist" style of governing, helped him consolidate substantial popular support. Indeed, particularly after the 1992 *autogolpe*, when Fujimori and his military allies shut down congress, suspended the constitution, and centralized power in the hands of the executive, approval ratings for the president shot up to 70–80 percent and remained surprisingly high throughout the decade.[2]

The persistence of a culture of fear and its demobilizing effect on civil society came to my attention during interviews with community activists in low-income districts in Lima between 1992 and 1994. Activists often expressed their repudiation of the Fujimori regime's economic policies, its authoritarian practices and human rights abuses, and its manipulation of grassroots organizations, but they remained reluctant to contest the regime publicly. One community activist, when asked why she and others who shared her point of view did not engage in public protest against the regime, answered unequivocally: "*Quien habla es terrorista*" (Anyone who speaks out [in protest] is [considered to be] a terrorist).[3] This response and others like it went against the grain of much of the common understanding of the Fujimori regime, suggesting that there was something going on in society that was not being registered by the polls. A current of opposition existed, if in latent form, even during the regime's most popular moments, but that felt that it could not safely express itself in the public realm.

This chapter draws on the work of Antonio Gramsci (1987) to highlight the coercive dimension of power in Fujimori's Peru. In Gramsci's analysis of power, consensus and coercion exist in tandem; the former cannot be understood without also understanding the way the latter operates. Consensus is predicated not only upon a material basis; coercive power relations exist that will enforce authority with force should consensus break down. In Fujimori's Peru, alongside policies and political strategies designed to marshal popular support, state elites developed strategies to penetrate, control, and immobilize civil society. Clientelistic relationships were used to build regime support and simultaneously to undercut autonomous organizations and opposition groups. And the regime's use of fear and intimidation kept opposition groups disorganized and on the defensive, and hence incapable of mounting a challenge to the authoritarian practices of the Fujimori regime.

Drawing on ethnographic research, including interviews with grassroots activists, student leaders, and other opposition leaders carried out between 1992 and 2000, as well as discourse analysis, this chapter examines the practices of fear deployed by the Fujimori regime. It begins by briefly reviewing the period of political violence in the 1980s and its demobilizing effects on civil society. Fear was multidirectional, since violence was used strategically by the Peruvian state *and* by insurgent groups, especially Shining Path, to achieve political objectives and to deny support among the civilian population to enemy forces. Violence and the fear it engendered reordered political and social meanings in Peru, creating a "culture of fear" in which citizens willingly surrendered rights in exchange for the promise of order and stability. These new understandings were harnessed by the Fujimori regime into support for an authoritarian political project at the same time that coercive methods were used to keep opposition groups off-balance and unable to mobilize against the regime. Attention is focused on the discursive practices of the Fujimori regime and the actual deployment of state power to achieve these ends, not only in the latter years of the regime, when regime operatives engaged in a systematic campaign of intimidation to diffuse the opposition to Fujimori's reelection project, but also throughout its tenure in power. The next chapter analyzes the shifts that occurred in the latter half of the 1990s that contributed to a reactivation of civil society in the context of the 2000 electoral process and which contributed to the eventual collapse of the Fujimori regime.

## Civil Society in Peru

Civil society in Peru has long been characterized as "weak," but such categorization obscures important variations in civil society mobilization.[4]

Cycles of mobilization and demobilization are evident over the course of the past century, corresponding to changes in the political opportunity structure, the degree of political repression, the internal cohesion of social actors, and their ability to mobilize support and forge alliances with other groups in civil and political society.[5]

In the late 1970s, for example, trade unions, neighborhood associations, university students, peasant federations, and the emerging parties of the New Left mobilized massive strikes and street protests first in opposition to the military regime's economic austerity policies, its rollback of reforms, and later to demand the military's ouster (Nieto 1983). This represented an important shift from a corporatist model of social organization (under the Velasco regime, see Stepan 1978; McClintock and Lowenthal 1983) to the affirmation of a more independent civil society (Stokes 1995).

The transition to a democratic regime in 1980 opened up political space, creating new possibilities for civil society organization. In this context, alongside traditional movements such as trade unions, peasant federations, and student movements emerged "new" social movements, including women's organizations, communal soup kitchens, neighborhood associations, and other community-based organizations. Such organizations were viewed not only as valuable grassroots efforts to resolve concrete problems, but also positive contributions to the democratization of the country's rigid and hierarchical social and political structures (Ballón 1986; Degregori et al. 1986). The formation of a new alliance of left-wing parties, the IU, promised to represent the concerns of these and other groups, such as workers and campesinos, while constructing the basis for a more participatory and inclusive democracy (Stokes 1995; Schönwälder 2002).

At the same time, however, a number of factors worked against the consolidation of civil society in Peru. The power of organized labor was shattered by the military regime's dismissal of some 5,000 public sector workers, as well as by legislation that eroded workers rights to organize and negotiate with the state. The weakening of the industrial economy and the rise of the informal economy also weakened the power of labor (Parodi 1986; Cameron 1994). While "new" social movements represented vibrant and creative solutions to immediate problems of hunger and unemployment, the persistence of the economic crisis and the onset of hyperinflation in 1988 undermined their resource base and led many activists to opt out in favor of individual solutions to the crisis. Hyperinflation in particular undermined long-term perspectives and shifted peoples' focus on immediate issues of survival (as was the case of the community kitchens), but as short-term survival strategies became quasi-permanent "solutions" to endemic poverty and unemployment, people's willingness to work voluntarily grew thin. Leaders felt burnt out; rank-and-file members grew increasingly suspicious of those in leadership positions and charges of corruption became widespread; and free riding became increasingly common as people turned to individual survival strategies[6] (Burt and Espejo 1995). State-led clientelism also weakened social movements, offering people cash and other immediate benefits that often drew them away from participation in grassroots organizations (Graham 1992). By 1990, the collapse of the party system, and particularly the division of the IU and its eclipse as a major political force, further contributed to the fragmentation of civil society.

As Rochabrún (1988) has suggested, while leftist academics and intellectuals saw these movements as the harbingers of a "new social order," they were primarily defensive organizations—he called them "neomutualist associations"—created to weather the crisis and lacked a solid basis for autonomous action. This may be overstating the case to some degree, and it certainly overlooks the important political learning that took place within the context of these organizations, particularly among women who were previously marginalized from the public realm and whose participation in community-based organizations gave them the experience and skills to enter into positions of public authority (Barrig 1988). It also understates the degree of synergy that existed between new social movements and the IU, particularly in the mid-1980s, when municipal governments under IU control developed a range of social programs and initiatives that helped constitute civil society organization that, in turn, developed an impressive mobilizational capacity (Stokes 1995; Roberts 1999). Yet the ease with which many of these groups were later co-opted into vast patronage networks set up by the Fujimori regime in which material benefits were given (or withheld) in exchange for political support highlights the extreme vulnerability of such organizations to external forces, particularly the state.[7]

## The Demobilizing Effects of Political Violence

Political violence also contributed to the disarticulation of civil society organization in Peru in the 1980s. As John Keane (1996) has suggested, violence is the ultimate act against individual freedom. Keane argues that violence is not only incompatible with civil society "rules" of solidarity, liberty, and equality of citizens; by destroying the space for the practice of these rules, it makes solidarity and collective action impossible to sustain.[8] Violence, in other words, silences civil society, and destroys its ability to act in the public realm. It is important to clearly delineate how, in the Peruvian case, violence on the part of state *and* nonstate actors reduced the public space that is an essential condition for democratic political action, and thus contributed to the demobilization of civil society.

The recent report of the CVR testifies to the magnitude of the phenomenon of violence in Peru. Between 1980 and 2000, some 68,000 people were the victims of political violence, 54 percent at the hand of insurgent groups and about 40 percent at the hand of state security forces, paramilitary groups, and other "irregular forces" such as peasant defense patrols. Of these, some 12,000 were detained and "disappeared" by state security forces. Countless thousands more were detained without cause, tortured, and suffered long years of incarceration (CVR 2003).

Shining Path became notorious for its attacks against the civilian population.[9] Shining Path was a classic Leninist-style vanguard party, and its leader, Abimael Guzmán, had argued that only Shining Path's interpretation of the "correct thinking" was admissible in developing its strategic plan of action. Shining Path's organizational structure and its ideological extremism—including a belief that violence was both "purifying" and a historical necessity—led it to repudiate any organization that did not support its revolutionary war and to engage in brutal acts of violence against leaders and members of such organizations (Degregori 1989; CVR 2003). Shining Path considered the IU to be its greatest enemy: its participation in democratic government revealed its support for the bureaucratic-capitalist state, while its project of participatory, grassroots democracy stood as an alternative to Shining Path's violent project of social change.[10] Shining Path targeted scores of IU activists, particularly those involved in trade unions, peasant federations, neighborhood associations, and other community-based organizations. The murder of grassroots leaders who had ties with the IU such as María Elena Moyano (described in chapter seven) were "examplary punishments" that sent a message to activists throughout the country that resistance would not be tolerated (Burt 1998; CVR 2003).

Shining Path also relentlessly attacked peasants involved in the *rondas campesinas*, or peasant defense groups. While *rondas* often organized independently of the armed forces, the Fujimori regime incorporated them directly into its counterinsurgency strategy, placing them under the legal control of the armed forces and using them as frontline combatants in the war against Shining Path.[11] For Shining Path, any sort of collaboration with authorities was punishable by death, and thousands of peasants perished at the hands of the Maoists, often after mock trials conducted before forcibly assembled villagers. Like the murder of Moyano, such killings were designed to terrorize and intimidate the rural peasantry into submission to Shining Path's revolutionary project.

In the context of the counterinsurgency war against Shining Path, the state also engaged in acts of political violence that by design or default contributed to undermining the basis of civil society organization. The state's role in the demobilization of civil society must be examined at two levels: the actual use of violence, on the one hand, and the state's inability (or unwillingness?) to prevent nonstate actors such as Shining Path from exercising violence against Peruvian citizens.

The CVR (2003) notes that "in some places and at some times" the state security forces engaged in systematic human rights violations. In the countryside, the security forces engaged in classic counterinsurgency operations—draining the "sea" to catch the "fish," resulting in massacres, extrajudicial executions, and "disappearances." In the city, individuals suspected of terrorism were detained and sometimes "disappeared." One case in 1989 that was captured on video and replayed on the nightly news made this secretive practice of state terror chillingly real: police detained and beat two university students, then placed them in the trunk of their car; no record of their arrest was made, and, when they seemingly vanished, officials denied any knowledge of their whereabouts.

State security forces made little effort to distinguish Shining Path combatants from civilians. The IU was viewed by security forces as little more than the legal arm of Shining Path—despite overwhelming evidence to the contrary and the fact that Shining Path was also systematically attacking IU activists. As a result of the state's inability/unwillingness to distinguish between Shining Path activists and individuals engaged in legitimate forms of social protest and political activity, many of those victimized by state security forces were members of such civil society organizations who were wrongly suspected of involvement in terrorist activity.[12]

At the same time, the Peruvian state, as the entity charged with guaranteeing citizen security, rule of law, and civil and political liberties, failed to preserve these basic elements of a democratic polity, which are crucial to the ability of civil society to organize in the first instance. While institutions such as the police and judiciary have rarely been seen as acting on behalf of ordinary citizens, the lack of responsiveness on the part of these institutions to the growing violence and the resulting breakdown in civil order further eroded their credibility. The institutional structures that protect individual and civil rights—the sine qua non of civil society organization—disappeared in this context. Without state institutions to guarantee the rights to organize, to free speech, and to the inviolability of the person, civil society organization shriveled under the threat of state and insurgent violence. Thus as both an agent of violence and in its failure to prevent acts of violence by nonstate actors, the state contributed decisively to the disarticulation and fragmentation of civil society.

Political violence, while deployed against individual bodies, is also directed at the larger social body (Suárez-Orozco 2000). In the Peruvian case, both Shining Path and state security forces used violence as a means of invalidating individuals and groups who (presumably) opposed them, and to send a powerful message to the rest of the social body that resistance would not be tolerated. In the context of such polarizing conditions, solidarity and trust were destroyed, collective identities undermined, and social mobilization weakened. Groups such as trade unions, community kitchens and neighborhood associations were regarded suspiciously by the state, while these same groups were under assault by Shining Path if they failed to submit to their vision of revolutionary violence. This multidirectionality of violence meant that fear took on many forms. For civil society activists in particular the fear of being suspected of terrorism by the state, on the one hand, and of incurring Shining Path's wrath for not supporting its revolutionary war, on the other, forced many to abandon their role in the public sphere. As one community activist from Villa El Salvador stated,

> While [the state] threatened our leaders by detaining them and sending them to prison, [Shining Path] threatened them too, accusing them of being traitors and a series of other things. The leader-activist hid, avoiding positions of public responsibility, seeking refuge in silence.[13]

Fear became ingrained in the psyche of the Peruvian population. Fear—and suspicion of the "other," particularly acute given the strong social segmentation in Peru by social class and ethnic background—came to dominate social relations at all levels, to the point that even allies in the IU coalition began to suspect each other of belonging to Shining Path.[14] The Peruvian case was thus unique in comparison to the Southern Cone in two ways. In Peru, state terror was unleashed during nominally democratic governments (rather than military regimes), and, unlike the Southern Cone, where the state was the primary agent of violence, in Peru a combination of state and insurgent violence weakened collective identities and assaulted the material and moral bases of civil society organization.[15]

### Coercion and Consensus in Fujimori's Peru

While these factors help us explain the disarticulation of civil society in the 1980s, how can we understand the continued weakness of civil society in the 1990s—when state structures were rebuilt, the economy improved markedly, and political violence diminished significantly after the arrest of the top leaders of Shining Path (and the less significant MRTA) in 1992–1993? Focusing on the internal weakness of civil society itself is insufficient, for it neglects consideration of external factors that may continue to inhibit or undermine civil society formation. Examining such factors is consistent with social movement theory, which emphasizes the importance of political opportunity structures for the emergence of social movement activity (Tarrow 1994). Neoliberal restructuring certainly was one external factor contributing to the continued weakness of civil society. Less attention has been paid to specifically political factors in this process. This section thus focuses on the state and its instrumentalization of fear to create an "authoritarian consensus" within society, on the one hand, and to maintain civil society demobilized and unable to articulate its voice in the public realm, on the other.

The intense violence of the 1980s created a context in which many Peruvians were willing to cede citizenship and other rights to an extremely personalistic, authoritarian regime in exchange for order and stability. This reordering of social meanings was ably exploited by the Fujimori regime to generate consensus for its authoritarian state-building project. But even as the Fujimori regime was constructing this "authoritarian consensus," it also deployed a series of mechanisms designed to keep civil society fragmented and disorganized. Patronage was one of these mechanisms, and its use by the Fujimori regime has been widely documented (Roberts 1995; Schady 1997). Such clientelistic forms of domination and control helped to build support for the regime even as they marginalized those who refused to abide by the new rules of the game, contributing to the fragmentation of civil society. Another key mechanism of social control, which has not been widely analyzed, was the instrumentalization of fear, which had at least two dimensions. The regime was itself an agent of fear, deploying state power to silence and intimidate opponents. At the same time, it sought to exploit existing fears in society in order to maintain civil society disorganized and unable to articulate its voice.

### *The Reordering Effects of Violence on Peruvian Society: The Authoritarian Consensus*

Scholars of societies that have experienced prolonged and/or particularly intense periods of political violence have noted the ways in which violence reshapes or reorders political and social meanings (Corradi 1992; Coronil and Skurski 2004). As Lechner (1992) has noted, in contexts of extreme crisis, collective referents are lost, future horizons deconstructed, and the social criteria of "normalcy" are eroded. In such contexts, those in power play on the vital need for order, presenting themselves as the only solution to chaos. In other words, elites shape and mold these new social meanings to justify and legitimize their authoritarian projects. The bureaucratic authoritarian regimes of the Southern Cone, for example, built upon societal fears of violence and chaos to assert that politicians, political parties, and democracy were incompetent to deal with the crisis and that the armed forces were the only actor capable of stopping the downward spiral and restore "law and order" (Corradi 1992).

A similar process was evident in Peru during the late 1980s, when the country's democratic leaders seemed incapable of addressing the dramatic expansion of violence and economic free fall. This contributed to popular dissatisfaction with politicians of all ideological stripes, while also undermining confidence in democratic institutions and, indeed, in the state itself as an arbiter of social conflict. The violence thus directly contributed to a reordering of political and social meanings in Peru, fueling popular disillusionment with democratic norms and procedures and making authoritarian solutions appear more palatable. The result was a growing "common sense" favoring heavy handed and extralegal solutions to the problem of violence and economic chaos.

It is tempting to suggest that this "authoritarian consensus" represented little more than a reversion to Peru's long-standing authoritarian political culture (Atwood 2001). Yet such arguments do not take into account the nascent democratic practices being forged in Peru in the 1980s, or the specific effects of political violence in reshaping popular understandings of authority, governance, and order. Nor do they consider the way in which state elites sought to harness and encourage such notions to justify and sustain an authoritarian political project.

The 1980s witnessed a wide range of experiments in democratic forms of participation and citizenship, not only through the exercise of the vote, but also through broader forms of citizen participation such as community-based organizations and local and regional government. Political parties played a dynamic role in this process, seeking (not always successfully) to represent channel popular demands and operating within the context of democratic rules and procedures. At the same time, civil society was constructing a space for autonomous action (though this space was often ignored or trampled on by parties themselves through the use of clientelism and patronage).[16]

These nascent democratic modes of participation and governance were fundamentally challenged by the political violence that was engulfing the country by the end of the decade. Guerrilla violence created a crisis of public security and of public authority, to which the state reacted with either ineptitude or brutal repression, revealing its inability to respond to the guerrilla threat and also protect civil and political rights. As the crisis of public authority deepened, private solutions to public problems were increasingly advocated, from the organization of civil defense patrols to deal with urban and rural crime and violence to the widespread use of private security systems in more affluent areas. By the late 1980s, the state's inability to guarantee citizen security, control its territory, or administer justice contributed to growing rejection of the system itself: democratic institutions seemed incompetent, corrupt, and aloof from the problems assaulting ordinary Peruvians. Increasingly, the political and civil liberties essential to democracy were viewed as expendable, and heavy-handed solutions, from arbitrary arrest and detention to extralegal killings, were viewed as acceptable. As one human rights advocate noted, "Most people think that it is okay to kill a *senderista*."[17] Social conflict in the 1980s bolstered authoritarian understandings predicated on order, stability, and efficacy, over and above values such as human rights, democracy, and negotiation.

Fujimori and his allies ably harnessed such notions into support for an authoritarian political project. Fujimori frequently justified heavy-handed solutions to Peru's multiple crises as the "only" solution to Peru's problems, and repeatedly attacked politicians, trade unions, human rights groups—even democracy itself, which he resignified as "party-cracy" to imply it had been corrupted to its core by party elites and special interests. In this context, space for the defense of human rights and of basic democratic values (such as due process) was increasingly marginalized. Indeed, Fujimori often attacked those advocating such values as little more than the handmaidens of terrorism. State elites carefully constructed a discourse that played on peoples' fear and desire for normalcy and reiterated the claim that only heavy-handed solutions would revert the crisis and return order and stability to Peru. Thus when Fujimori and his allies in the military carried out the *autogolpe* in April 1992 promising to restore order, eliminate the guerrilla threat, and rout out corruption, it was widely applauded by Peruvian society.

The Fujimori regime used a variety of other methods to create and perpetuate this "authoritarian consensus." As Gramsci suggests, consensus is premised on a material basis, and Fujimori effectively delivered the goods: he stopped hyperinflation, he got the economy moving again, and with the capture of the top Shining Path and MRTA leaders in 1992, he had defeated (if not eliminated) the guerrilla movements. He also began a more aggressive plan of social spending, building schools, roads, bridges, and encouraging community-based groups to apply for funds for local development projects (though these were tightly controlled by the Ministry of the Presidency, which superseded traditional ministries, such as Health and Education, and came to resemble traditional forms of clientelism). This consensus-building aspect of the Fujimori regime has been widely studied (Roberts 1995; Weyland 1996; Panfichi 1997; Carrión 1999). Within this literature the term "neopopulism" has been widely used to describe the unmediated nature of the relationship Fujimori cultivated between himself and the masses, and to explain the surprising coupling of a populist leadership style with neoliberal economics (Roberts 1995; Weyland 1996). While such analyses recognize the authoritarian elements of the Fujimori regime, they do not adequately address the coercive dimensions of power, and in particular the way in which the state used its coercive power to demobilize political and civil society to prevent challenges to its rule from emerging.[18] Roberts (1995), for example, notes that the failure of representative institutions such as political parties, labor unions, and autonomous social organizations to mediate between citizens and the state makes possible the direct, unmediated mobilization of the masses by a personalistic leader. This is doubtless true, but it does not account for, nor does it problematize, the ways in which the state might use coercive methods to perpetuate the inability of these intermediate institutions to act in the public realm. In this sense, the instrumentalization of fear is a key aspect to understanding the continued demobilization of civil society in Fujimori's Peru. Only by grasping both dimensions of consensus and coercion—the basis of power as defined by Gramsci—can we understand how the Fujimori regime used state power to undermine these intermediate institutions and other civil society organizations as a way of maintaining its hold on political power.

### The Instrumentalization of Fear

As Lechner (1992:31) notes in his comparative study of the Southern Cone military regimes, the instrumentalization of fear does not require repression, only to reinforce the absence of alternatives: "It suffices to induce a sense of personal and collective inability to have any effective influence on the public realm." The only alternative for ordinary people in such situations is to seek refuge in private life, contributing to a process of atomization or anomie. The mechanisms employed by the Fujimori regime to keep civil society disorganized were not dissimilar to those used by the bureaucratic authoritarian regimes of the Southern Cone of South America, which exploited societal fears of a "return to the past" of violence and chaos to assert that politicians, political parties, and democracy itself were incompetent to deal with the situation and that the armed forces were the only actor that could preserve national unity, restore "law and order," and pursue the national interest (Garretón 1992; Lechner 1992). General Augusto Pinochet, for example, who ruled Chile with an iron fist between 1973 and 1990, frequently relied on such rhetorical manipulations of fear of the past—the economic debacle, food shortages, and political instability during the last year of Salvador Allende's socialist government—to shore up support for his authoritarian regime and question the credibility of those contesting his power (Martínez 1992). In Fujimori's Peru, fear was similarly instrumentalized by elites to undermine social mobilization and to keep civil society fragmented and disorganized. Fear was used both as a narrative discourse and as an instrument of power in Fujimori's Peru—not only in the latter years of the regime, when state violence sought to silence opposition to the regime's reelection project, but also throughout its tenure in power. The neoliberal economic model implemented by the Fujimori regime, which eschewed structural explanations of poverty and violence and instead emphasized individual responsibility, dovetailed with this process of atomization and reinforced it.

Foucaultian analyses suggest that discursive formations do not simply reflect power relations; they fundamentally constitute and reproduce relations of domination, power, and control. Through discursive formations, elites assert state power and control over social groups, and these relations of domination are reinforced by political and social practices that reiterated the claims embedded in elite discourse. The remainder of this chapter analyzes both the elite narratives and practices that sought to constitute and reproduce power relations in Fujimori's Peru.

*Narratives of Fear*

The Fujimori regime systematically manipulated fear of Shining Path and of the chaos of the 1980s to undermine social mobilization and keep civil society fragmented and disorganized. The regime developed a visceral antipolitics discourse that blamed political parties and politicians for the economic and political crises of the 1980s, extolled the success of its heavy-handed measures (including the 1992 *autogolpe* and the repressive measures that were put in place following the coup) in returning order and stability to the country, and warned—as Pinochet frequently did in the 1980s—of the certain descent into chaos should the politicians be allowed to return.[19]

Particularly after Guzmán's arrest, which occurred just five months after the *autogolpe*, Fujimori repeatedly asserted the efficacy of the heavy-handed measures his government had taken. Just a few months after Guzmán's arrest, for example, Fujimori stated,

> It would have been irresponsible to not consummate the *autogolpe* [since it] permitted us to successfully wage the battle against terrorism, combat corruption within the judiciary and deepen neoliberal reforms.[20]

This idea would be reiterated with frequency. Just after his reelection in 1995, Fujimori continued to cultivate an image of himself as a decisive leader and of his authoritarian practices as an historical necessity: "What Peru needed was order, discipline, the principle of authority, good management—and an iron fist against terrorism."[21] Fujimori juxtaposed his policy successes with the past failings of civilian politicians, and he frequently referred to the political system he inherited as a party-cracy to suggest that political parties ruled in their own self-interest rather than on behalf of those who elected them:

> My government is the product of rejection, of Peru's fatigue from frivolity, corruption and inefficiency of the traditional political class.... [T]he people who voted for me are tired and weary of this false Peru.[22]

By discursively locating himself as "part of the people" challenging the power and privilege of the *partidocracia* (party-cracy, a derogative term suggesting that parties put their particular interests above those of the nation), Fujimori created an "us versus them" framework that played on and stoked popular disgust with the failings of the political class to address Peru's multiple problems. He constantly played on peoples' fears by suggesting that without his heavy-handed approach, the chaos of the past would return. "Terrorism had infiltrated everything," said Fujimori, who described the self-coup as an act of "realism" that sought to reestablish "true" democracy in Peru.[23] A made-for-television documentary narrated by one of Fujimori's top legislative allies, Jaime Yoshiyama, and aired in November 1992, similarly portrayed the *autogolpe* as a historical necessity given the corruption and myopia of the traditional ruling class. The efficacy of the regime's authoritarian methods was thus constructed discursively, first in contrast to the *in*efficacy of civilian politicians, and second by affirming that such methods had borne fruit, evidenced by the arrest of Guzmán and the subsequent decline in political violence. Such discursive formations in turn helped constitute popular approval for Fujimori and his authoritarian methods.[24]

In the regime's Manichean discourse, regime opponents were categorically defined as illegitimate. For example, human rights organizations that denounced the regime's abuses were vilified as the "legal arms of terrorism." During a ceremony on armed forces' day on September 24, 1991, Fujimori stated,

> We know that the terrorists and their front organizations, or useful idiots, will not give up and will use all possible resources to harm the image of Peru by alleging that the Peruvian armed forces systematically violate human rights.[25]

Attacks such as these against groups questioning regime policies stoked fear among the opposition and effectively reinforced a sense of collective inability to challenge the regime's policies in the public realm. As the community activist quoted earlier stated, *quien habla es terrorista,* an ideological construct imposed by state elites to justify the criminalization of dissent and opposition activity and which left the individual so categorized devoid of rights and guarantees.

This discourse was deployed in the context of the radical militarization of society and politics, a process that intensified after the *autogolpe.* Civilian governments dating back to 1982 had ceded authority to the military to deal with Shining Path. Political-military commands were established in emergency zones, where constitutional guarantees were suspended and civilian authorities sidelined by military officials. Military power increased through a series of decree laws after the *autogolpe*—power that was not substantially altered when, under pressure from international criticism, a new congress was elected and a new constitution approved. The new legislature ceased to monitor the activities of the armed forces, which had acquired total control over counterinsurgency, and rather became a virtual rubber stamp of executive initiatives.

In this context, the militarization of social and political life expanded dramatically. The armed forces continued to rule directly in the emergency zones, which encompassed about one-half of the population. The proliferation of military bases in rural communities and urban shantytowns gave the military vast power to control the urban and rural poor. "Civic action" programs were deployed to win the hearts and minds of local populations while also allowing the armed forces to more easily monitor and control the movements of the civilian population. Public universities were occupied by the armed forces, violating constitutional guarantees of autonomy. The *rondas* were placed under the direct control of the armed forces. This process of militarization demonstrated to the population the newfound power of state authorities to survey, control, and repress undesired social behavior.

State and para-state institutions were given new, broad powers to penetrate, dominate, and control civil society. Of particular importance was the strengthening of the SIN and the deployment of the Colina Group, a paramilitary group that operated out of the SIN and the SIE. Under the guiding hand of Fujimori's chief advisor, Vladimiro Montesinos, the SIN became the regime's political police, and the Colina Group its instrument to intimidate and silence regime critics through often macabre spectacles of violence.

One of the most infamous cases of such state violence was the 1991 Barrios Altos massacre, the first death-squad-style mass execution to take place in Lima. A Colina Group unit was sent to assassinate presumed members of Shining Path, but the operatives went to the wrong floor, killing 15 people and severely wounding 4 others who had no political connections whatsoever. Another well-known case was the disappearance of nine students and one professor from Cantuta University in 1992. The fact that the armed forces had assumed direct control over the university campus left little doubt as to who was responsible. When the victims' charred remains were discovered a year later, prompting opposition congressional leaders to launch an investigation, the head of the armed forces accused them of acting "in collusion with the homicidal terrorists,"[26] and army tanks were paraded in front of congress to thwart further inquiry. As the case was being pursued in civil court, proregime legislators gutted the trial by passing a law relocating the case to military courts, a violation of judicial autonomy. When the military court convicted a few Colina Group operatives for the crimes, congress engineered an amnesty law in 1995 to free them.

**Figure 9.1** Remembering the Dead of La Cantuta

Family members of the nine students who were abducted from "La Cantuta" University on July 18, 1992 and later killed by the Colina Group death squad participate in a symbolic burial of their missing loved ones. The corpses of the students were found a year later after an intelligence agent leaked their location to the press.

*Source*: Photograph by Vera Lentz.

While the Barrios Altos and Cantuta murders were allegedly directed against presumed Senderistas, other cases reveal the state's use of its coercive power to silence legitimate opposition, and its justification of such abuses by equating opposition activity with terrorism. Such was the case of the assassination of the general secretary of the CGTP, Pedro Huilca, who was gunned down in December 1992 by the Colina Group. Huilca, a strong critic of Fujimori's neoliberal policies, was trying to mobilize social protest against the regime. Two weeks before his death, Fujimori publicly attacked Huilca after critical remarks he made at the Annual Conference of Entrepreneurs (CADE). According to a national media report,

> Fujimori said, reading from his notes, "we have been constructing a national consensus since 1990. Bit by bit the grand social structures of deep Peru are emerging." Then Fujimori looked up at the auditorium and stopped reading, saying, "This is no longer a country ruled by the bosses *[cúpula]* of the CGTP or SUTEP, or the hordes *[huestes]* of Shining Path and the MRTA, or the bosses of the traditional parties." The message was directed against Huilca, who was in the auditorium.[27]

Fujimori was discursively locating trade unionists (and "traditional" political party leaders) in the same category as the armed insurgencies of MRTA and Shining Path, despite the CGTP's long history of participation in democratic politics and the fact that Shining Path had targeted several of its leaders. Government investigators and the media initially blamed Shining Path for Huilca's murder, but Huilca's widow and CGTP leaders claimed that Fujimori and the government were responsible. The government's failure to investigate the murder of two other CGTP leaders suggested official complicity, and the administration's hostility to Huilca and the CGTP was evident in comments such as that by President Fujimori cited above, and by Finance Minister Carlos Boloña, who had earlier assured business leaders that "the top leadership *[cúpula]* of the CGTP will soon be destroyed" (CVR 2003). In 1993, a dissident army general accused the Colina Group of Huilca's murder, a charge confirmed a decade later by the Inter-American Court of Human Rights (IACHR 2005).

A second example illustrates the way state violence was deployed to suppress legitimate social movement activity. On May 2, 1992, nine campesinos disappeared from Santa, a village on the northern coast. They were protesting land-tenure arrangements against a local landlord, who called on powerful friends, including the brother of the head of the armed forces, to have the protest organizers identified as subversives and "eliminated." Days later, the Colina Group was deployed to Santa and, one by one, the peasant leaders were plucked from their homes and disappeared (CVR 2003). As in the Huilca case, the regime blamed Shining Path. Sowing confusion over authorship of such killings stoked fear of insurgent violence while also instilling fear of state repression in regime opponents.

*The Law as a Source of Fear: Legal Repression*

The state's failure to stem the Shining Path insurgency in the 1980s led to important shifts in counterinsurgency policy. Emphasis was placed on intelligence gathering and dismantling the organization's top leadership, which proved effective with the arrest of Shining Path's top leaders in 1992–1993. Civic-action campaigns to win the hearts and minds of the population were designed to undermine support for Shining Path. As a result of these shifts, there were fewer indiscriminate massacres, but extra-judicial executions and forced "disappearances" against more selective targets continued. And increasingly, the use of legal repression—through massive and often indiscriminate incarceration of suspected "subversives" using the antiterrorist legislation put in place after the 1992 *autogolpe*—became a centerpiece of the regime's efforts to eliminate Shining Path (Degregori and Rivera 1993; CVR 2003).

The antiterrorist legislation was widely criticized by international jurists and local human rights organizations for its negation of due process guarantees and for the anomaly of trying civilians in faceless military courts (ICJ 1993; Human Rights Watch 1995). It defined the crimes of terrorism and treason so broadly that individuals engaged in legitimate protest could be (and were) caught in its web. Indeed, under this legislation, hundreds if not thousands of individuals innocent of any crime were arrested and sentenced to long periods in prison. In other cases, individuals who were coerced into collaborating with Shining Path, such as community kitchen organizers who were forced to provide food to insurgents, were convicted of "terrorism" and given disproportionately long prison sentences (Burt 1994). Such harsh treatment was designed to destroy any logistical support for Shining Path. The fact that nearly 500 individuals were eventually found innocent of any wrongdoing and pardoned by Fujimori himself reveals the extent to which this mechanism was abused by the regime (de la Jara Basombrío 2001).

This use of legal repression exacerbated uncertainty and fear, especially among the rural and urban poor, who have a tenuous sense of rights and protection and who were the most likely victims of political violence. Interviews with community leaders in several Lima shantytowns in 1993 and 1994 revealed that such legal repression deepened fear among activists that their involvement in grassroots organizations might be construed as aiding terrorists, leading many to retreat into the private sphere. Participants in focus groups carried out with randomly selected residents of lower-income districts in Lima in 1995 clearly expressed that fear of being associated with terrorist activity inhibited participation in public forms of protest:

Q: Why don't people protest?
A1: Because they feel afraid. They fear that making demands could put them at risk.
Q: Put them at risk, how so?

*A1*: The police would arrest them.

*A2*: And so they don't participate in protest marches.

  *Q*: And why is there fear that you could be arrested, if you haven't done anything wrong?

*A1*: Because people are afraid the police will detain them for 15 days and there is nothing you can do; they are afraid of being arrested and put in jail.[28]

The reference to 15 days demonstrates a remarkable awareness of the broad powers possessed by authorities to question detainees without an arrest warrant, the period during which torture is most likely to occur. It also shows awareness of the absence of legal guarantees for detainees, and how this knowledge inhibited opposition activity. Challenging abuse by authorities was out of the question, given this reality of legal repression and the ease with which legitimate protest was equated with terrorism:

  *Q*: One can report police abuse, no?

*A1*: We have rights, yes we can.

*A2*: But they arrest us and accuse us of terrorism.

*A3*: It's not possible, they accuse us of different things.[29]

By equating opposition activity with terrorism, the regime discursively undermined the space for civil society activity. The deployment of selective killings and disappearances, and the application of antiterrorist legislation that failed to distinguish between legitimate opposition activity and terrorist activity, and that meted out harsh punishments, had a chilling effect on social mobilization. Regime opponents dared not voice their criticism publicly for fear of being labeled a "terrorist" and receiving the same treatment they receive—death, imprisonment, torture, silencing.

### Impunity

Scholars of political violence in Latin America have long noted the ways in which impunity contributes to a culture of fear by creating structures that prevent accountability for state-sponsored violence against citizens (McSherry 1992; Roht-Arriaza 1996; McSherry and Molina 1999). Since the start of Peru's internal conflict, few state agents were convicted of human rights violations, and impunity certainly contributed to the climate of fear that reigned in the 1980s and 1990s.[30] With the 1995 amnesty law, which was passed specifically to free members of the Colina Group who had been convicted by military courts for the Cantuta murders, impunity was institutionalized. State agents implicated in human rights violations were granted immunity from prosecution, and the few who had been convicted of such abuses were freed.

While the amnesty law was widely repudiated by public opinion—three quarters of those polled opposed the law and believed it should be revoked (Youngers 2003)—the testimonies of student and human rights activists reveal the way in which fear prevented opposition to amnesty from translating into broad-based mobilization. Though activists successfully organized a series of small-scale protests against the law, their efforts to launch a referendum to overturn it met with dismal failure. According to Susana Villarán, then president of the National Human Rights Coordinator, people were afraid to publicly sign a document of this nature that could identify them as opponents of the regime, which could lead to the suspension of material aid, incarceration, or worse.[31] In other words, the effort to overturn the widely unpopular law found little echo in society due to the prevailing climate of fear.

The testimony of a student activist from the Catholic University highlights the extent to which the population had internalized the regime's equation of opposition activity with terrorism. She is referring to a student protest against the 1995 amnesty law.

> We went to the center of Lima for the first time. It was the first time we found our public voice. But we saw the "other"—the student[s] from San Marcos [University], from La Cantuta [University]—not only as different from us, but also as dangerous. So what you had in the street protests, where everyone was scared to death...was the idea that we should not mingle with them. Our generation had lived and lived with a profound trauma, fear of Shining Path and of repression. There was a great deal of insecurity...which made people retreat in terms of demanding their fundamental rights.[32]

This testimony also reveals how the multidirectionality of fear reinforced existing class and ethnic cleavages in Peru, effectively undermining efforts on the part of university students from different socioeconomic and ethnic backgrounds to build more enduring bonds of trust and solidarity, the basis of collective action. Public universities such as San Marcos and La Cantuta, which were occupied by the armed forces and where student federations were not recognized by new state-appointed authorities, had become associated in the public mind with subversion; the poorer, darker-skinned Peruvians who studied there might have some connection to subversive groups, hence middle- and upper-class students from universities such as Catholic University would do best to avoid associating with them in order to avoid any problems with the authorities. Protest activity dissipated in the wake of such fears.

### Fanning the Flames of Fear

As political violence declined in the aftermath of the capture of the top leaders of the MRTA and Shining Path, one might have expected the opening of democratic spaces in Peru. But this was not the case. On the contrary, the regime tightened its stranglehold on power, and became even more systematic in its efforts to shut down any and all possible sources of opposition. Even as the threat posed by Shining Path had begun to recede, the regime continued to equate opposition activity with terrorism, so that fear of being associated with Shining Path either in thought or in deed, and of state repression, continued to inhibit civil society organization. This became particularly acute as the regime revealed its determination to assure a third term in office for Fujimori, which will be discussed briefly below.

In this context, the regime continued to fan the flames of fear by exploiting the latent threat of terrorism for political purposes. It would periodically warn of a "resurgence" of terrorist violence or exaggerate the terrorist threat as a way to remind Peruvians that its heavy-handed measures were still necessary. For example, in April 1994, the Fujimori government ordered the armed forces to launch a "final offensive" against Shining Path in the central jungle region of the country. In fact, Shining Path was not particularly well-entrenched in this region at this point, and the military had already established control of this area. The CVR notes that the government initiative, dubbed "Operation Aries," was more of a political show designed to remind Peruvians of the Fujimori regime's successes on the counterinsurgency front. The government exaggerated the real threat of Shining Path forces in the area, and the vast media coverage reinforced the idea that this was a propaganda campaign designed to portray President Fujimori as a determined leader who would spare no effort to deal Shining Path the final and ultimate blow in the context of the upcoming presidential elections.[33] According to the CVR (2003),

> Counterinsurgency operations ceased to be a means of capturing subversive leaders and concluding the war with the PCP-SL (Shining Path) and the MRTA, and became a means of propaganda for the government, in the best case, and a smokescreen, in the worst, to cover up the regime's crimes and excesses, which were being denounced with greater frequency. This was possible largely because of the progressive and almost total control the state had accumulated over the communications media, paid for with state moneys.

Similarly, the MRTA hostage crisis of late 1996 was also exploited by the regime to affirm its tough stance against terrorism. The hostage taking itself revealed a serious security breach: 500 diplomats and other dignitaries who were attending a cocktail party at the Japanese ambassador's residence were taken hostage by a small MRTA column. After four arduous months of negotiation, the government sent an elite army unit to retake the compound. All but one of the hostages survived, while each of the 14 rebels was killed, many after having surrendered. The hostage crisis occurred at a moment of growing crisis for the regime, but it provided an opportunity for the regime to highlight the ongoing threat of terrorism, justify its heavy-handed measures, and assert the need for continuity to avoid slipping back into the chaos of the past.

The regime also stoked societal fear of other types of violence, such as criminal and gang-related violence, which had risen significantly even as political violence was on the wane. Executive decrees defined criminal activities such as theft, robbery, kidnapping, assault, and gang activity as "aggravated terrorism," and many of the same harsh measures from the antiterrorist legislation were put in place. Opposition legislators and human rights activists complained that the vague definition of these crimes could result in legal repression against legitimate social protest.[34]

The regime also sought to reduce the space for independent media, particularly the electronic media (Conaghan 2002). Journalists who dared investigate the shady or criminal dealings of the regime were threatened and intimidated. In the meantime—as we know now thanks to the thousands of videotapes that document the regime's illegal dealings—the regime bought and extorted its way into controlling the rest of the principal media outlets, which gave it direct control over the scope and content of news coverage. Opposition views were rarely voiced, and the official version of events was the only story in town.[35]

The print and electronic media, increasingly controlled by Fujimori's inner circle, echoed the regime's discourse of fear. News programs reporting the day's events regularly portrayed opposition activity as inspired by terrorist groups. For example, in 1995 a human rights group sponsored an alternative rock concert in downtown Lima called *Olvidarte Nunca* (Never Forget You) that focused on the state practice of forced disappearances. The next evening, Channel 4 news (which was on the regime's payroll) broadcast a story alleging that alternative rock groups were infiltrated by Shining Path.[36] In the context of the 2000 electoral process, Channel 2 news (also on the payroll of the Fujimori regime) broadcast a program in 1999 menacingly titled "The Red Spider Web." The program documented the leftist affiliations of several individuals working in the Human Rights Ombudsman's Office in an effort to sully the public image of one of the few state institutions that was able to maintain its independence vis-à-vis the Fujimori regime. This occurred in the context of the Ombudsman's questioning of several of the regime's policies and practices, most significantly its unconstitutional bid for a third term for President Fujimori.

Swift punishment met those who challenged the regime's media monopoly, as evidenced in the Baruch Ivcher case. In 1997, Ivcher, owner of Frecuencia Latina, broadcasted a series of stories that revealed serious abuses by the regime, including a story about government espionage of opposition leaders and Montesinos' inexplicably high income. Another series of stories on the murder of a former army intelligence agent, Mariella Barreto, and the torture of another, Leonor La Rosa, who presumably leaked information about the Cantuta murders to the press, exposed serious abuses of state power. In retaliation, Ivcher, an Israeli by birth, was stripped of his Peruvian citizenship and control of his television station. The Ivcher case prompted much international attention and helped unmask the authoritarian underpinnings of the Fujimori regime. However, even as such abuses ignited the conscience of some and prompted them into opposition activity, it also evidenced the regime's willingness to go to any lengths, even murder, to silence those who challenged its power. These assaults sent a larger message to those within the regime and to society at large that dissent would not be tolerated. As opposition legislator Anel Townsend said at the time, "Fear became more palpable after Barreto. People think, 'if they [the SIN] do this to one of their own, what might they do to us?'"[37] A former human rights leader made a similar observation: "We care about human rights, but we don't want to happen to us what happened to Mariella Barreto."[38] This reflects the Foucaultian notion of how power reproduces itself even when it is under attack and its practices are coming under scrutiny.

## A License for Despotism

Social movement theory suggests that political opportunity structures create the context for social mobilization to occur (Tarrow 1994). The degree of repression, of the cohesiveness of state elites, and the existence of institutional guarantees for civil and political liberties, are all elements of political opportunity structures that might be considered in evaluating the likely emergence and the relative weakness or strength of social movement activity. In the case of Fujimori's Peru, it has been suggested that each of these elements contributed to maintaining civil society weak and on the defensive, and particular emphasis has been placed on the instrumentalization of fear by state elites as a mechanism of social control. It is certainly true that civil and political society had been severely weakened by the political violence and economic crisis of the 1980s. But as the threat of violence waned and the economic situation improved, the Fujimori regime deployed a variety of strategies to keep civil society weak and disarticulated. These included consensus-building measures, such as the extensive use of patronage. But it also included the authoritarian exercise of power and the instrumentalization of fear. Civil society remained weak in the 1990s not only because of the devastating crises of the 1980s, or because of neoliberal social and economic policies, but also because state power was deployed with the aim of keeping civil society disarticulated and fragmented. As Fujimori and his allies sought to consolidate an authoritarian political project and prevent challengers to it from emerging, this strategic use of consensus and coercion prevented what social theorist John Keane calls "political and social obstacles to state power" from developing. Such a situation—an increasingly assertive state in the hands of technocratic elites and supported by the domestic bourgeoisie and international capital, and a weak and fragmented political and civil society—is, according to Keane, "always hazardous and undesirable, a license for despotism" (1996:51).

CHAPTER TEN

# The Authoritarian State and the Resurgence of Civil Society

*Before oppression was stability for all. Today oppression is instability for all.*
University student leader, 2000

The collapse of the Fujimori government in November 2000 was surprising in many respects. Just a few months earlier, Fujimori had weathered massive street protests and international condemnation over the fraudulent electoral process that ultimately resulted in his securing a third term in office. International pressure initially prevented the Fujimori regime from securing electoral victory through fraudulent means in the April 2000 first round elections. But despite ongoing protests and the withdrawal of international election observers, who charged that there were insufficient guarantees for a free and fair electoral process, second round elections were held in May. Fujimori ran unopposed and, with 74 percent of the valid vote, was sworn in to a third term as president on July 28, 2000.

Opposition leaders and civil society groups continued to seek ways to challenge the regime. Alejandro Toledo, the leading opposition candidate who claimed he was denied victory in the first round and who withdrew from the second round in light of the regime's failure to guarantee the integrity of the elections, called for a "third round" of struggle against the regime through street protests and mobilizations. At the same time, the international community continued to intervene to push the regime toward reform. The OAS reviewed the opposition charges of electoral fraud at a June 2000 meeting in Windsor, Canada, and though it fell short of calling for new elections, as the opposition was demanding, it did require the Fujimori regime to accept its role in mediating a dialogue between the government and the opposition on a series of reforms. Yet, opposition protests and international condemnation notwithstanding, Fujimori had secured a third term in office.

Six weeks later, two scandals broke that triggered the collapse of the Fujimori government. The first revealed that Fujimori and his advisor,

Vladimiro Montesinos, were involved in a drugs-for-arms deal with the Revolutionary Armed Forces of Colombia (FARC). The second and more explosive scandal involved the public airing of a video footage showing Montesinos bribing Alberto Kouri, an opposition legislator, to join Fujimori's political party. Since the first round elections, the opposition had accused the regime of bribing opposition legislators—who were labeled *trásfugas* (turncoats)—to switch to the governing party in order to ensure a legislative majority in congress. The videotape not only provided incontrovertible evidence of the regime's fraudulent practices, but also bolstered the opposition's charges of government corruption of the broader electoral process. In effect, it cut to the heart of the regime's legitimacy, already severely under assault by civil society mobilization and contestation.

Much more was revealed in this videotape. It made clear that Montesinos, who had long been criticized by the opposition for his alleged role in human rights violations, drug trafficking, and influence peddling, was indeed involved in extensive corrupt dealings designed to control the outcome of the political process. The transaction between Montesinos and Kouri was taped in the security advisor's office in the SIN, suggesting that Montesinos was filming many of his clandestine dealings for the purpose of keeping his clients in line. This in turn revealed the impunity with which Montesinos operated and his certainty that he was untouchable— that these videotapes, which in the end also implicated him in illegal acts, would never be used against him. Finally, the public airing of the videotape revealed that the wall of silence that had protected Montesinos and his shady dealings for nearly a decade had collapsed, leaving Montesinos— and the regime—vulnerable and exposed. The fact that Montesinos fled Peru immediately after the videotapes were publicly broadcast suggests how damaging he realized they were. Fujimori attempted to manage the crisis in the following weeks, offering to hold new elections in a year's time. But just two months later he fled the country and faxed his resignation from Japan. The newly emboldened opposition in congress declared the presidency vacant and proceeded to elect Valentín Paniagua, from AP, interim president until a clean electoral process could be assured.

How did this dramatic shift occur, from the apparently triumphant consolidation of the Fujimori regime's power after the contested 2000 electoral process to the dizzyingly swift collapse of the regime between September and November of the same year? Some scholars emphasize the internal dynamics of the Fujimori regime as the key explanatory variable. Cameron (2006) prioritizes the internal rifts produced within the regime after the airing of the Montesinos-Kouri video. There is little doubt that the videotape was the catalyst of regime change, but this view assumes an insular, elite-controlled process unaffected by developments in society. Weyland (2006) emphasizes the instability inherent in "neopopulist" forms of rule and the erosion of support for Fujimori as his policy successes, initially central to establishing his legitimacy, were fewer and farther between, but this seems overly deterministic, as if it were merely a matter of time before the neopopulist model exhausted itself. My view coincides more with that laid out by Conaghan (2005) in her analysis of the 2000 electoral process. Conaghan argues that civil society played a central role in the regime's undoing, effectively challenging the regime's legitimacy and forcing it to engage in a series of actions that later proved fatal to its own survival. This chapter takes a similar relational approach to regime breakdown, and offers further evidence to support the idea that the resurgence of civil society played a central role in the demise of the Fujimori regime.

This chapter aims to contribute to our understanding of this contentious and extremely dynamic process by examining the process by which civil society began to regain its moorings and emerged to contest state power, and the impact this civil society mobilization had both on international support for the Fujimori regime and on the regime coalition itself. It first explores the roots of the civil society mobilization that burst onto the scene in the context of the 2000 elections in an effort to understand how, despite limited opportunities for opposition mobilization, key groups in civil society began to forge new understandings of the nature of the Fujimori regime and their role as protagonists struggling to restore Peruvian democracy. It then examines how civil society protests influenced the regime, leading it to adopt decisions and take actions intended to stop organized protests, but that in the end proved to be more damaging to the regime's image abroad and domestically. It explores how, through a learning process that included many setbacks, groups in civil society began to forge greater unity and redefine their struggle as a proactive one in favor of Peruvian democracy.

Thus, while the 2000 popular protests did not topple the regime, and Fujimori was indeed sworn in as president in July of that year—they contributed to several important processes that were central to the regime's ultimate collapse. First, by focusing on the flaws in the electoral process—a central theme in the democratization discourse of diverse international actors, from the U.S. government to the OAS to international election watchdog groups—the opposition effectively framed its critique of the Fujimori regime in a way that was compelling to the international community. The charges of fraud by groups such as Transparencia, an elections watchdog organization that documented the regime's fraudulent electoral practices, and of human rights organizations, which provided a broader critique of the corruption of the entire framework in which elections were taking place, including the use of state monies to buy votes and influence the outcome of the election process, became harder for the international community to ignore, contributing to the isolation of the Fujimori regime.[1] Civil society groups, including human rights groups, Democratic Forum, and others, had established a relationship early on with Eduardo Stein, the head of the OAS mission sent to observe Peru's elections. Stein took the concerns raised by these groups seriously, and the synergy between domestic prodemocracy groups and transnational actors such as the OAS was especially important in challenging the regime's claim to democratic legitimacy. In the end, both the OAS and the U.S. government declared that the electoral process was fundamentally flawed and did not pass basic tests of democratic legitimacy; the OAS pulled its observers from the second round elections due to these concerns. The result was a profound legitimacy deficit for the Fujimori regime that would later contribute to the regime's implosion.

Second, the opposition protests did more than highlight the flaws in the electoral process; they also opened political space for those opposing the regimes on other grounds. In poor urban and rural communities, where protest had been muted by a combination of fear, clientelism, and repression, the regime's inability to translate its macroeconomic achievements into gains for the poor strained the tenuous link Fujimori had constructed between the authoritarian state and civil society. The neoliberal model implemented by Fujimori addressed macroeconomic issues, effectively controlling hyperinflation, stabilizing the economy, and even producing growth through the mid-1990s. But the regime's approach to the social question (persistent poverty and growing inequalities) fell short. It gutted traditional ministries oriented toward addressing social issues (especially education, health, and housing), while emphasizing targeted social programs that were popular for the short-term benefits they offered but were not sustainable, either as new mechanisms for linking state and society or as means to effectively reduce poverty. As the economy began to stagnate in the late 1990s, growing discontent over these economic and social policies became more acute, as evidenced by Fujimori's declining popularity ratings after 1997. But it was not until the civil society protests surrounding the electoral process that this discontent was able to articulate itself in the public realm. Thus housewives, shantytown activists, community organizers, peasant leaders, teachers, and trade unionists joined university students, professionals, and human rights activists in opposition to the regime, adding their discontent over unemployment, low wages, weak protection for workers, and so on, to the growing public rejection of the Fujimori regime's electoral shenanigans and its authoritarian political project writ large.

Finally, the protests exacerbated growing rifts within the ruling coalition that compromised the regime's ability to manage and control the political process. These rifts were evident as early as 1996 but had been deftly managed by the regime in the context of limited public dissent, strong international support, and nearly absolute control over the electronic media. With growing international criticism; sustained grassroots protests; and increasing challenges to the regime's control over public discourse and information, the regime committed fatal errors that further fueled domestic and international protest, and ultimately exacerbated the regime's internal crisis to the breaking point. Civil society protests called into question the regime's claim to legitimate democratic authority, which had reverberations both domestically and internationally. In a global context favoring electoral democracies, the civil society protests of the regime's fraudulent practices helped strip away its legitimacy and led many who had previously supported the regime to become more questioning. At the same time, the civil society protests generated concern within the regime about its ability to retain control over the political process, leading it to engage in acts—from open fraud in the electoral process to murder—that further harmed its legitimacy and exacerbated already existing rifts within the regime itself.

Indeed, without the massive social protests that took place during and after the 2000 electoral process, which brought into question not only the electoral process, but also the fundamental legitimacy of Fujimori's third term in office, it is possible that the Montesinos-Kouri bribery scandal would have been managed, covered up, or otherwise handled so as to prevent a full-blown crisis of the regime. The sustained protests and criticisms of civil society groups pierced a hole at the heart of the regime's legitimacy, limited the regime's ability to maneuver when crisis hit, as it did just weeks after Fujimori's contested inauguration with the Montesinos-Kouri video. It is this complex and iterative dynamic between popular mobilization against a corrupt and authoritarian regime, the shifting terrain of international support of the regime, and the internal dynamics of the regime itself, that help explain the collapse of the Fujimori regime. The "vladivideo" was the catalyst of regime breakdown, but it was the broader process of societal contestation of state power that shifted the terrain, limiting the regime's ability to respond to the video scandal and contributing to its collapse in November 2000.

## Stirrings: Recovering Civil Society

The first major instance of opposition protest to the Fujimori regime occurred in mid-1997, when street protests emerged in response to congress's dissolution of the constitutional court. The row centered on a dubious law passed by congress in 1996, the so-called Law of Authentic Interpretation, which was meant to clear the way for Fujimori's bid for a third term in 2000. Proregime legislators had to find a formula to overcome the limitation imposed by the 1993 constitution, which allows for only one consecutive presidential reelection. Their formula was premised on the argument that Fujimori's first term, which began in 1990, did not count since the 1993 constitution was not yet in place, thus he was able to run for a third term in 2000. Opposition leaders condemned the legalistic double-speak and the intention of bypassing the constitution to clear the way for Fujimori's reelection bid, but at the time they were unable to galvanize public support.

Though legislators were unable to prevent the passage of the Law of Authentic Interpretation, other routes were still available to challenge its validity. The Lima Bar Association filed a case before the constitutional court challenging the legality of the law. The constitutional court was a relatively new body, created by the 1993 constitution to evaluate the constitutionality of laws and government decrees. Given its newness—and previous instances of government manipulation of the judiciary—few observers imagined the constitutional court would render a verdict contrary to the regime. Surprisingly, in January 1997 three of the court's judges issued a ruling declaring that the law was "inapplicable" to President Fujimori; two judges voted to uphold the law, while two, including the president of the court, abstained. The judges voting to invalidate the Law of Authentic Interpretation asserted that their verdict represented a majority opinion and therefore the definitive word on the issue. The direct challenge now being posed to the Fujimori regime's re-reelection project by the country's top judicial authority stunned regime operatives and opposition leaders alike. In response, the proregime majority in congress engineered a series of legal machinations, culminating in a late-night session of congress that ordered the dismissal of the three judges who had challenged the Law of Authentic Interpretation. This opened the way for congress to set aside the previous ruling; it also essentially gutted the constitutional court, which by law requires the vote of six of its seven members on constitutional issues.

The dismissal of the judges was a clear transgression of legislative powers. According to the 1993 constitution, the constitutional court is an autonomous body; congress has no powers to challenge its rulings or dismiss its judges. This congressional overstepping—and the clear intention it represented on the part of the regime to remove any obstacles to Fujimori's continuation in power—unleashed local and international condemnation. Significant street mobilizations occurred in response to the judges' dismissal, driven mainly by opposition legislators, university students, and human rights activists. The protests started in Lima and spread to several other major cities across the country, prompting international condemnation as well. The Inter-American Commission on Human Rights of the OAS expressed its concern over the judge's dismissal, as did U.S. Ambassador to Peru Dennis Jett.[2] On May 30 Jorge Chávez, the president of the constitutional court, resigned in protest of the dismissal of his colleagues.

Street mobilizations continued for several days. On June 4, trade unionists, teachers, student groups, and opposition leaders marched to the hotel where the general assembly of the OAS was meeting to demand action against the Fujimori regime. As the protesters made their way toward the hotel, more than 100 mounted policemen and a police dog squad intercepted the crowd. Though they had a permit to protest, police dispersed the crowd with tear gas and water cannons, and several were arrested.[3] Another protest march took place the following day, culminating in a mass meeting in Plaza Bolívar, outside the congress building. As in the previous day's protest, a broad front of unionists, teachers, student groups, and party leaders from opposition groups from the center-right to the socialist left were present. Riot police again repressed the crowd, resorting to clubs and tear gas.[4]

*On the Front Line: University Students*

The participation of university students in the protests was particularly important. Students have historically been significant actors in prodemocracy protests in Peru as elsewhere. During the Fujimori regime there had been virtually no student mobilization against the regime largely due to the climate of repression and fear. Indeed, early on the Fujimori regime had clamped down on public universities, long seen as a key site of Shining Path recruiting and organizing activities.[5] On some campuses, the armed forces had established military bases, and armed soldiers patrolled campus grounds and controlled who entered and who left the university premises. Reports of students being arbitrarily arrested and in some cases forcibly taken away, as occurred in the case of the abduction and disappearance of nine students and a professor from the campus of La Cantuta, chilled student participation in public life.[6] In the case of the National University of the Center, located in the Andean city of Huancayo and which had an extensive Shining Path presence, over 100 students were detained and either killed or forcibly disappeared between 1989 and 1993 (CVR 2003). Private universities, the haven of middle- and upper-class Peruvians, were less affected, but a handful of high-profile cases had a deep depoliticizing effect on students there as well. In this sense the most illustrative case was that of Ernesto Castillo Páez, a history student at the Catholic University. On October 21, 1990, Castillo Páez was detained while visiting Villa El Salvador; witnesses watched as he was forced into the trunk of a police patrol car in broad daylight and driven away, never to be seen again. A Catholic University student at the time of Castillo Páez's disappearance noted the profound impact this had on him and his classmates:

> The disappearance of Ernesto shocked us all. It was terrifying; it made everyone fearful. We became like little ostriches, burying our heads in our books and not talking to anyone about politics or anything. They put fear in our hearts.[7]

Yet, as political violence waned, and the regime's tactics to ensure its continuation in power became increasingly transparent, some student activists, including those who had been involved in the protests against the amnesty law in 1995, became emboldened to organize antiregime protests.

One of the first cases to ignite broad protest was the regime's effort to impede investigation into the Cantuta murders. The discovery of the students' bodies in 1993 led opposition legislators, human rights groups, and international organizations to demand a full inquiry into the Colina Group, which was presumed responsible for the deaths. The military refused to cooperate, and at one point General Hermoza sent tanks into the streets of Lima to intimidate parliament from pursuing an independent inquiry. As the case advanced in a civilian court, the regime maneuvered to have the case placed under the jurisdiction of military courts. Several members of the Colina Group were found responsible and sentenced to prison, but shortly thereafter proregime legislators rammed through a sweeping amnesty law that freed them and made it impossible for family members to pursue their cases in court. Human rights organizations and family members of several high-profile cases, particularly La Cantuta and the Barrios Altos massacre, became visible critics of the regime and of the Colina Group. They specifically sought to build alliances with other sectors in civil society to support their protests, as Gisela Ortíz, whose brother Luis Enrique was one of the Cantuta victims, notes:

> When the case was moved to the military court we organized a big protest march, which we coordinated with the support of opposition legislators and university students. We went to the Catholic University and talked with the coordinators of the student movement, which were just beginning to organize, and we told them that we were family members of the Cantuta case, and that we opposed the transfer of the case to a military court because this would not guarantee a fair process, and we asked them to accompany us in our protest march. They were very sensitive, and they did join as, as did students from San Marcos and Villareal Universities.... When the impunity law was passed, we also organized two or three big protest marches against the law... that included the key labor organizations as well as university students.[8]

This was the beginning of a synergy between different groups in civil society that would eventually challenge the Fujimori regime head-on in the context of its attempt to ensconce itself in power at any cost in 2000. But there were many hurdles to overcome yet: as noted in the previous chapter, the failure to overturn the amnesty law via a referendum, the repression of the protest marches, and the ongoing climate of fear inhibited civil society action. Nevertheless, the regime's ongoing abuses contributed to generate a shift in the way at least some sectors of civil society perceived the regime and their own role as political subjects. According to Alejandra Alayza, a Catholic University student leader, the regime's abuses, along with its obsession to ensure its perpetuation in power, contributed to this shift in thinking:

> From 1995 to 1997 the regime grew increasingly *duro* (authoritarian) in all aspects.... One of the fundamental aspects of this is the theme of Fujimori's re-election. So in 1997, after the dismissal of the three judges of the Constitutional Court, there was an absolutely spontaneous reaction—because this is part of the massive depoliticization of the [student movement]—and people started to say, "well, they can't just keep on sticking it to us, there must be a limit to this," and we went out [into the streets] and we spoke up.[9]

Many students reported that a series of revelations of regime abuses in early 1997 fueled their indignation and contributed to their decision to participate in the incipient protest movement. For example, in late March the press reported on the brutal murder of army intelligence agent Mariella Barreto, whose decapitated body was found on a roadside on the outskirts of Lima. Just a few weeks later, Leonor La Rosa, a colleague of Barreto, appeared on television in her hospital bed alleging that her torture and Barreto's murder were reprisals for their role in leaking information to the press about the Colina Group's plan to initiate an intimidation campaign against opposition journalists and politicians. Death-squad-style murders of this type were presumably a thing of the past; the brutality of the murder of Barreto and the savage torture to which La Rosa had been subjected seemed to reveal a criminal regime that was completely out of control. The intelligence services were not protecting citizens from subversion, as they claimed, but rather using their power to silence critics and maintain their power at any cost. According to one university student,

> The killing of [Mariella Barreto] was terrible. We thought this type of violence was over. It made us upset, partly because it was a woman, but also because it was a sign that the regime was willing to go to any lengths to silence its opponents.... This was one of those things that made us aware that we were dealing with a criminal government.[10]

These abuses were likely intended to deter any other potential whistle-blowers within the regime—a clear sign of the fraying of the regime's internal cohesion, which will be addressed further below. They also further stoked societal fears over the regime's willingness to use violence to assure its continuation in power. But for some individuals, the cumulative effect of this string of abuses pricked their conscience and prompted them to action.

One of the most well-known incidents fueling this crisis was the regime's heavy-handed treatment of Baruch Ivcher, after his national television station, Frecuencia Latina, began airing a series of news broadcasts exposing these and other serious abuses on the part of the regime. Frecuencia Latina's editorial line had, until this point, been pointedly pro-regime. But, marking a decisive shift in its editorial line, Frecuencia Latina broke the Barreto-La Rosa story, including an exclusive interview of a badly tortured La Rosa in her hospital bed. A string of other news reports detailing the regime's corrupt and criminal behavior followed. In one news program Frecuencia Latina presented copies of Vladimiro Montesinos's income tax returns, demonstrating his high income and suggesting that he was engaged in massive corruption schemes. In mid-July, the channel's news program ran a story exposing a massive government wiretapping scheme to spy on opposition politicians, journalists, and business leaders. An anonymous whistle-blower within the intelligence services leaked 197 taped conversations to Frecuencia Latina, which generated another wave of domestic and international outrage. Frecuencia Latina's new and aggressive criticism of the regime was itself an indication that there were growing rifts between the regime and key civilian allies in the business community. Indeed, rumors traced the shift in Frecuencia Latina's editorial line to a row between Ivcher and Montesinos, who were reportedly once very close friends.

The regime's response to Ivcher's defiance was swift. Just hours after the story of the wiretapping scandal was aired, a decree was issued revoking Ivcher's citizenship. Ivcher was a native Israeli who had become a Peruvian citizen in the early 1980s. This was a clear indication of the regime's intention of punishing Ivcher, since Peruvian law prohibits foreigners from holding a majority share in media companies. Ivcher fled the country in fear for his life. Shortly thereafter, he was dispossessed of his shares in Frecuencia Latina, which were scooped up by the minority shareholder, the Winter Group, owned by brothers Samuel and Mendel Winter.

Until this point, the regime pointed to the existence of freedom of the press in Peru as evidence of its democratic credentials. Newspaper editorials harshly condemned the decision to take away Ivcher's citizenship. "Fujimori's government has taken the grave decision to act on the margins of legality, of respect for fundamental freedoms and even of citizen protest," read the editorial of the conservative Lima daily, *El Comercio,* the next day.[11] Javier Pérez de Cuellar, former UN general secretary who lost his bid to defeat Fujimori in the 1995 elections, also criticized the move as an assault on freedom of the press, and decried the "permanent coup" to which the country was being subjected.[12] The Peruvian Association of Radio and Television, which represents the country's major communications media, called the move to strip Ivcher of his citizenship illegal and "a clear attack on press freedom."[13] Peru's Ombudsman, Jorge Santistevan, as well as the U.S. Congress and the OAS, also joined the chorus of dissent against the regime's muzzling of the press.

A new round of street protests erupted, but now protesters were explicitly linking redress for specific abuses to a broader demand: the removal of Montesinos and the head of the armed forces, General Hermoza. Journalists working at Frecuencia Latina holed up inside the media outlet's offices, promising to continue to report the news despite the clear intimidation tactics against Ivcher. Opposition leaders such as Pérez de Cuellar joined journalists, workers and university students in a small but highly visible series of street demonstrations. On July 15, some 3,000 demonstrators wearing blue ribbons to show their solidarity with Ivcher gathered outside Frecuencia Latina's offices to protest the government's actions. They argued that Montesinos and General Hermoza were also the architects of the Barreto-La Rosa scandals, the wiretapping incident, the retaliation against Ivcher, and a string of other abuses, and should be removed from their positions of power. Over a three-day period, major protests rocked downtown Lima and other important cities, including Trujillo and Cuzco. The protests revealed growing dissatisfaction with regime policies and a citizenry increasingly emboldened to challenge the regime. In the wake of such massive unrest, and growing international concern over the state of press freedom in Peru, Foreign Minister Francisco Tudela quit the government, as did the justice and defense ministers.

The regime showed no sign of bending to such demands, and instead turned to the military to beat back criticism. Two active duty generals were named to head up the Ministries of Defense and of the Interior, a move critics charged was indicative of the ongoing and undue influence of the armed forces in the Fujimori government. Concerns increased after General Hermoza paid a visit to President Fujimori at the presidential palace to declare the loyalty of the army and police forces to the president.[14] Public opinion polls registered the growing concern over the military's role in the government: 53 percent of Lima residents reported that they believed the government was controlled by the military.[15] So intense was the reaction that in his July 28 Independence Day speech to the nation, Fujimori felt compelled to respond to the growing criticism of military tutelage, assuring citizens that he was fully in command of the armed forces.

Hermoza's visit was intended to convey a message both to the regime and to the citizenry. The armed forces were the power behind the regime; citizens challenged it at their peril. A similar message was conveyed in April 1993 when Hermoza ordered military tanks to parade before congress to prevent legislative inquiries into the Cantuta murders. The military's buttressing of Fujimori's leadership helped the regime weather the crisis that erupted in mid-1997. Repression of protest activity and the reassertion of military power forced civil society to retreat. According to Alayza, part of the problem was a certain naïveté about how politics works in an authoritarian regime:

> Everyone really believed that by going out to protest we were going to get the judges reinstated. There was a faith—a premature faith, what you see in a novice, in those who have just started doing things—that the protests would have immediate effects, that there was a capacity for dialogue…and that popular protest would achieve change.[16]

Change was not immediately forthcoming, but there was a crisis in the making, which prompted the regime to implement a series of other measures to intimidate civil society. For example, in May 1998 Fujimori asked congress to pass harsh anticrime legislation. Then, in an effort to avoid legislative delays, he requested and was given by congress decree powers to pass legislation to combat crime. The result was a series of draconian anticrime decrees modeled on the harsh antiterrorism legislation put in place after the 1992 *autogolpe*. The regime seemed to believe that adopting a heavy-handed approach to crime would help it woo public opinion back to its corner. The decree laws defined gang activity, criminal assault, and other such crimes as "aggravated terrorism" and gave military courts jurisdiction over such crimes. The definition of criminal activity was defined so broadly that opposition leaders charged that this legislation was designed to give the regime the legal tools to repress legal opposition activity rather than crime. The decrees gave new powers to the SIN—not the police—to combat crime and gang activity, which opposition leaders feared was a sign of the regime's intention of using this legislation to intimidate students and young people in general from participating in public life.[17]

### Obstacles to Unity: Fractures Within Civil Society

The 1997 protests not only failed to unseat the regime; they seemed to have actually provoked the tightening of military control over the regime. At the same time, they also helped student activists realize that protest activity itself, without broader efforts to mobilize other sectors and without a proactive, rather than merely oppositional, stance, was futile. According to Alayza,

> We didn't know what to do. After this big protest, we were now in the limelight. University students had acquired a public presence but we didn't know what to do with it. [We realized that] we did not have student organizations or clearly defined political groups, nor were we clear about what we really wanted. So again we found ourselves at this point where we didn't know how to handle what was coming.[18]

This prompted renewed efforts to develop coherent student organizations with clear political objectives, and to seek out stronger links with other actors in civil society.

This search for unity was laden with obstacles. Sharp divisions existed within the student movement over different aspects of Fujimori's government. Some, particularly those from the lower-middle class or from Lima's vast *barriadas*, strongly opposed the regime's neoliberal policies, while others held a more ambiguous view. Deep social and ethnic fractures were also evident with the student movement. Interviews with student leaders from private and public universities—with their markedly different socioeconomic backgrounds—revealed profound mistrust of the "other." One student leader from the popular district of Villa El Salvador expressed his concern that some of his middle-class colleagues were concerned with more "bourgeois" issues such as elections and democracy, and less so with bread-and-butter issues that, for people like him, were also of paramount importance. A middle-class student from a private university reflected on the mistrust among students from different social backgrounds:

> For the public university students, [those of us who were from private universities] were engaged in "light" politics. [To them,] we

were rich little snobs whose only demand was democracy. And they questioned who would benefit from the changes we were demanding; the implication was it was only for the middle and upper classes because, well, you cannot eat democracy.[19]

Overlaid on these divisions were concerns about the excessive politicization of the student movement. These concerns reflected both the enormous denigration of organized politics rooted in the crises of the 1980s and fueled by the Fujimori regime's incessant antipolitics discourse, as well as the fear that an overtly political stance, particularly if it took on a radical tone, could be confused with terrorism. According to one student leader,

> I noted, especially in the public universities, a strong ideological presence of the Left. In their discourses they would talk about those of use who were of bourgeois origin, and this was something that scared [middle-class students] a lot. If one of the public university students referred to them as *compañero* they would say, "Oh, no, the next thing you know they are going to be calling me comrade." Or someone would say something radical and they would say, "Oh no, this one is a *terruco* [terrorist]." So there was this underlying fear—it's disgusting but it was real—that class-based divisions opened up other fractures...and created mistrust in which it was no longer the rich or the poor, or what is just or unjust, but rather, the student from a poor background who demanded a series of things with a more radical discourse was a terrorist.[20]

Underlying this discourse are the profound class and racial hierarchies embedded in Peruvian society and politics. The student quoted in chapter nine captured this in her comments about the view she and her fellow students from a private university had about public university students during the first protest movements in 1995:

> We saw the "other"—the student[s] from San Marcos, from La Cantuta—not only as different from us, but also as dangerous.[21]

Gisela Ortíz noted that she and other family members of the Cantuta victims were often met with suspicion because of their frequent and public denunciations of the case. People frequently accepted the government's assertion that the students were members of Shining Path, according to Ortíz, making them as family members guilty by association:

> Some people look at you suspiciously and they label you a terrorist and they call you "senderistas." The only way of making known what happened to our loved ones is going out into the street, but you run the risk of people looking at you the wrong way. Our society is

very fearful... We have lost the ability to feel solidarity. We focus on our own little world, our work, our daily life, and so on.[22]

Thus, though discontent was on the rise, other processes and cross-pressures inhibited collective action. This suggests that while changes in what social movement theorists call the political opportunity structure may create opportunities for social movements to mobilize, resist, and challenge state power, other factors may *simultaneously* inhibit social movement organization.[23] Exogenous factors such as fear and repression may undermine collective action, as may endogenous factors, such as divisions with civil society rooted in specific historic formations and processes. A relational perspective sensitive to changes in the broader structural context and in the constitution of political agency is best suited to tease out such dynamic processes.[24] In the case of Peru, a culture of fear exacerbated by an authoritarian state, coupled with historic divisions rooted in ideology, class, and ethnicity, made civil society organization difficult and challenging. Yet in the context of rising discontent, a series of mistakes made by the Fujimori regime—particularly its determined effort to control the electoral process through fraudulent means—would galvanize diverse social groups and organizations to come together to resist and contest the regime. In the case of the university student movement, this would prompt students and other sectors of civil society of diverse socioeconomic and ideological backgrounds to converge around the one thing they could agree upon: challenging the Fujimori regime's abuse of authority and usurpation of power. This would later become the basis of the prodemocracy discourse articulated in the context of the 2000 elections.

### The Regime Strikes Back

Political society remained weak and sharply divided, impeding its ability to lead a broad-based opposition to the Fujimori regime. Alberto Andrade, an independent who was the mayor of Lima, sought to lead civic protests against the regime in this period. However, the fact that Andrade was preparing to challenge Fujimori in the 2000 presidential elections lent credibility to the regime's charges that his critiques were partisan and that he was manipulating protestors to benefit his campaign. Given the deep discrediting of political parties dating back to the crisis of the 1980s and fueled by Fujimori's antipolitics discourse, this further impeded politicians such as Andrade from being effective leaders of a broad-based opposition movement.

In this context, civil society groups took on the task of organizing a final legal challenge to Fujimori's re-reelection project. Democratic Forum, a nonpartisan civil society group of intellectuals and artists, launched a referendum drive to challenge the Law of Authentic

Interpretation. The referendum option, designed to give citizens a mechanism to challenge unpopular laws, was created by the 1993 constitution; 1.25 million signatures of eligible voters were required to hold a referendum. In July 1998, the opposition presented a petition to hold a referendum on the law signed by 1.4 million citizens. The regime engaged in a series of machinations to prevent the referendum initiative from proceeding, including packing the National Elections Board with cooperative officials, who then voted to uphold a previous law of dubious constitutionality that requires a majority vote in congress in order for a citizen-initiated referendum to proceed. The opposition fell three votes short of the required 48 votes, resulting in the gutting of the referendum initiative.

After the vote was announced, proreferendum supporters holding vigil outside the National Congress reacted angrily, hurling stones, bottles, and eggs against police who were guarding the building. When three opposition congressmen came out to speak to the demonstrators, police refused to allow them back into the building, triggering near-riots. Protests ensued in the days following the gutting of the referendum, again uniting opposition leaders, trade unionists, teachers, and university students in protest of the regime's stifling of dissent. The main union confederation, the CGTP, organized a 48-hour general strike on September 30, which was backed by most opposition parties, including Mayor Andrade. Protests took place in Lima, as well as major cities in Cuzco, Trujillo, Arequipa, Ica, and Puno. Again these protests were brutally repressed by the regime.

*Playing the Terrorism Card*

In the context of this new and more virulent round of opposition protests, the regime once again played the terrorism card, manipulating fear and using intimidation tactics to beat back the opposition. The regime's strategy had two dimensions. The regime sought to use the latent threat of terrorism to induce a fearful citizenry to accept its authoritarian practices as necessary to keep the terrorist threat at bay. At the same time, the regime sought to equate the emerging opposition with terrorism to discredit it and its charges against the regime.

Though it had dealt a deadly blow to the Shining Path insurgency with the arrest of Guzmán and other top leaders in 1992 and 1993, the Fujimori regime did not bring the conflict to a definitive end. Critics charge that the regime in fact allowed the insurgency to fester in order to take advantage of occasional outbursts of terrorist activity to justify its continuation in power (CVR 2003). In effect, the continued threat of terrorism was a useful way of helping to keep the authoritarian consensus intact. In the context of a growing opposition, the arrest of two top Shining Path leaders in 1998 and 1999 permitted the regime to launch a new campaign to affirm its success on the counterinsurgency front. The campaign was designed to remind citizens of the latent terrorist threat as well as of the regime's diligence in combating terrorism. It also sought to portray these captures as the tireless work of the armed forces and the SIN (which was not the case) in order to reassert the regime's efficacy in the war against terror.

On November 1, 1998, a local TV news program presented images of Comrade Rita, who reportedly had been arrested after being turned in by her subordinates. The following day, Fujimori held a press conference affirming that Rita's capture was the result of a military operation led by the armed forces and the SIN. A week later, a regime-friendly news program aired footage it claimed portrayed the heroic capture of Rita by state security forces, followed by interviews with army officials relating details of the operation. An investigative report published a few days later in the daily *La República* presented compelling evidence that the government's story was little more than a montage, and that Rita's arrest was the result not of a military operation but betrayal by her besieged comrades. In essence, the regime—and its media collaborators—had fabricated a military "victory" against the remnants of Shining Path to bolster its image as a relentless fighter of terrorism[25] (Rospigliosi 2000).

A similar show was mounted in July of the following year with the capture of Oscar Ramírez Durand, "Comrade Feliciano," and the presumed leader of Red Path, the faction of the insurgent movement that rejected Guzmán's call for peace talks and continued to pursue armed struggle. The media echoed the regime's claim that Feliciano was arrested in a military operation led by the armed forces and the SIN with support of the police, when in fact he was arrested by a police officer. Critics charged the regime of magnifying the importance of the arrest of Feliciano—and rewriting the story of who was responsible for it—for electoral purposes. The regime sought to use the capture of Feliciano to reinforce its version of history, which ascribed the triumph over terrorism to the army and the intelligence services and that portrayed Fujimori and the military as the saviors of the nation.[26] This paralleled the regime's attempt in 1992 to attribute Guzmán's arrest to the work of Montesinos and the SIN rather than police general Ketín Vidal's DINCOTE.

The second strategy deployed by the regime in this period was to undermine the credibility of the opposition by associating it with terrorism. This affected the social movements that were emerging to contest the regime's authoritarian policies and its human rights abuses, as well as leaders of the democratic opposition who were challenging the regime in elections. This took place in the context of the regime's establishment of virtually complete control over the electronic and print media through a vast web of extortion and influence peddling managed by Montesinos[27] (Rospigliosi 2000; Degregori 2001; CVR 2003). It is also important to note that journalists who maintained their independence and ran stories critical of the regime were often subjected to intimidation and death threats (CPJ 2000).

Fujimori's two key contenders in the upcoming 2000 elections were Alberto Andrade, whose two terms as mayor of Lima had established him as a competent and efficient administrator, and Luis Castañeda Lossio, architect of the successful reform of the national social security system (IPSS). The regime deployed massive propaganda campaigns to discredit both leaders in the eyes of the public. This campaign had multiple dimensions, including character assassination and accusing both opposition leaders of being "soft" on terrorism or virtual terrorist sympathizers. For example, when Castañeda Lossio suggested that the Fujimori government should heed the ruling of the Inter-American Court of Human Rights, which called for new trials for four Chileans linked to the MRTA since the military trials convicting them denied them due process, he was accused of being proterrorist. *El Chino* headlines on September 29, 1999 read: "Chilean terrorists supported Castañeda Lossio. He has promised to impose their demands [on] the country" and on October 15, 1999: "For Castañeda Lossio the terrorists are not our enemies. They must have new trials, 10,000 greenbacks and much comprehension."[28] After several months of such mud slinging, the regime had effectively neutralized both candidates.

The regime also sought to equate social movement protests with terrorism. In the September 30 mobilizations protesting the regime's gutting of the referendum, a small group of protestors broke a police cordon around the presidential palace and entered the building, causing mild disturbances. President of congress Víctor Joy Way portrayed the protestors as subversives whose aim was to destabilize the state.[29] The progovernment media echoed Joy Way's discourse, portraying the protestors as "savages" and "beasts." The daily *Expreso* headline read: "It is barbarity, not protest. Was there terrorist infiltration?"[30] Such media campaigns played deliberately and systematically with existing fears and memories of terrorist violence. There were violent incidents, but independent press reports suggest that this was the result of a government decision to withdraw security forces from downtown Lima in order to generate chaos and discredit the opposition. Rospigliosi (2000) reports that military officers later confirmed that they had been ordered not to act, which directly resulted in a security breakdown.

### The Essential Ingredient: Unity of Purpose

By 1999, there was a growing resolve on the part of different social movement actors to forge unity to be able to confront the Fujimori regime and its abuse of power. The electoral process, scheduled for April 2000, presented opposition groups with an opportunity to reframe the struggle against the Fujimori regime as not simply a defensive struggle against the regime's policies or its authoritarianism but as a proactive struggle in favor of democracy and human rights. The electoral process, in other words, structured a new set of political opportunities for the opposition to challenge the regime's legitimacy. Civil society leaders realized the growing imperative of unity among the diverse opposition groups, as well as developing a discursive formation that was broadly acceptable to all the diverse forces active within the opposition movement. As the 2000 elections neared, the electoral process itself became the terrain upon which civil society could contest the regime on its own terms, while drawing on internationally accepted standards of free and fair elections. Challenging the regime's definition of democracy, denouncing its fraudulent acts, and highlighting the need to reestablish an authentic democracy based on citizenship rights for all became the template upon which civil society could forge greater unity of purpose.

Building a prodemocracy platform would become the common ground for diverse opposition groups to join forces against the regime. Human rights groups had reoriented their work as early as 1997 to focus not only on human rights violations but also on the larger political context. At issue, they argued, were not only individual abuses by state agents, but also the broader authoritarian political system in which these abuses were occurring. As Carlos Basombrío, then director of the Institute for Legal Defense (IDL), one of Peru's most important human rights groups, said,

**Figure 10.1**   Students Protest Fraudulent Elections

University students march in front of the presidential palace in protest of the Fujimori government and the fraudulent electoral process of 2000. These protests were central to undermining the regime's legitimacy domestically and at the international level, contributing to its collapse in November of that year.

*Source*: Photograph by Vera Lentz.

"the question of democracy became the fundamental obstacle for any progress in human rights."[31] Isaías Rojas, also of IDL, further elaborates:

> The link between democracy and human rights is insoluble. Human rights can only be recognized in the framework of democracy, which implies the separation of powers, accountability, transparency, civilian and democratic control over the intelligence services and the armed forces.[32]

Human rights groups, which had developed a highly institutionalized process of collaboration and coordination through the National Human Rights Coordinator (CNDH), thus came to the conclusion that in order to defend human rights, they would have to also address the broader political issue of democracy.[33] Its previous work in defense of human rights gave the CNDH the political capital to challenge the regime, and it became a key point of reference within Peru and internationally as the electoral process of 2000 unfolded.[34] Human rights groups developed a symbiotic relationship with other organizations challenging the regime's fraudulent practices, including the Peruvian affiliate of the international elections observation organization, Transparencia, and the National Ombudsman's Office. Ombudsman Jorge Santistevan was surprisingly outspoken in his criticism of the regime's manipulation of state resources to assure victory in the 2000 elections.[35]

Similarly in the case of the university student movement, the democracy issue came to dominate debate. Student leaders from different universities noted that the previous failures of the student movement to effect change, along with government repression, forced them to recognize the importance of working in a more unified fashion. This led to a series of dialogues among student leaders from public and private universities in an effort to construct a common platform. According to one activist, the students came to realize that despite their differences on some issues, they could find common ground in opposing the Fujimori regime:

> [We realized that] the only way to defeat the dictatorship was through unity... There was not consensus, for example, in terms of opposition to the neoliberal economic model, because some people favored it. But there was consensus in the need to reconstruct democracy and defend human rights.[36]

Key to this was a larger political reality: the justification of the Fujimori regime's use of heavy-handed measures and authoritarian practices was not as convincing now, several years after the arrest of Abimael Guzmán and other top leaders of Shining Path, as it had been in the past. By 1997, acts of violence had decreased dramatically, and terrorism was no longer Peruvians' principal concern; attention shifted to other pressing matters, such as the state of the economy, the lack of jobs, and growing crime rates.[37]

Imperceptibly, but perhaps most significantly, the political conditions that helped create the "authoritarian consensus" were beginning to shift by the end of the 1990s. The abuse of authority, once considered justified in the context of the war against Shining Path, was increasingly viewed by at least segments of civil society, as no longer so. As one university student activist noted in the context of the growing intensity of social protest in 1999 and especially 2000,

> The fear of Shining Path starts to fade, and people are no longer willing to delegate their rights. People are no longer willing to trade away their liberty, and they begin to make demands, and they begin to understand that others can also [legitimately] make demands. . . . There is a growing understanding that this is a repressive regime. Before oppression was stability for all. Today oppression is instability for all.[38]

In its relentless pursuit of reelection, the regime's utter disregard for the rules of the game—rules the regime itself had put in place—actually made the opposition's task easier, at least in terms of framing its discourse as a struggle for democracy. By framing the struggle against the Fujimori regime in this way, civil society groups found a new basis for collaboration as well as an issue that resonated internationally.[39] In the context of the regime's unabashed effort to ensconce itself in power, a new discourse emerged that reframed the regime's abuse of power as no longer a means of defeating a dangerous insurgency but rather a means of maintaining an abusive and corrupt regime in power at any cost. The struggle *against* the regime's abuses became a struggle *for* democracy and human rights.

### Cracks in the Fujimori Regime

The Fujimori regime was sustained by an alliance among state managers, technocrats, and business elites, and the armed forces. The regime could claim legitimacy based on strong public support for Fujimori, rooted in his government's war on inflation and terrorism. But by the late 1990s, cracks in the ruling coalition began to appear that are crucial to understand the vulnerabilities of the Fujimori regime even at what appeared to be the height of its power.

On the one hand, popular support for Fujimori was no longer as solid or as massive after 1997 as it had been in earlier years. The regime's approval ratings were 60 percent or higher until mid-1996, reflecting popular support for concrete policy achievements such as the elimination of hyperinflation, Peru's "reinsertion" into the international economic system and improved macroeconomic performance, and the strategic defeat of Shining Path and the MRTA. Massive social spending in the context of the 1995 elections also proved highly popular (Roberts 1995).

From the year 1997 onward there is a notable decline in Fujimori's approval ratings (though they remained at 40–45 percent), as the regime's inability to address persistent economic issues of poverty and unemployment led to growing disillusionment, and as macroeconomic imperatives forced the regime to cut back on social spending. The material basis of consensus had eroded at least partially, meaning that some segments of society might be open to the appeals of regime challengers. The 2000 electoral process provided the backdrop against which this growing discontent over Fujimori's economic policies—largely a concern of poorer Peruvians— connected with the middle-class groups whose opposition to the Fujimori regime was predicated more on a rejection of its authoritarian practices. As the student activist quoted above pointed out, there was not necessarily agreement on opposition to Fujimori's economic policies, but there were increasing points of convergence from a variety of groups on the need to remove Fujimori.

On the other hand, the internal dynamics of the regime revealed grow- ing fissures that both weakened the regime's internal coherence and hence its stability, and that provided opportunities for opposition groups to press their claims against the regime more effectively. Segments of the business elite had become increasingly skittish over the regime's authoritarianism, its criminal practices, and as we now know thanks to the hundreds of videos documenting the vast webs of graft and corruption that under- girded the Fujimori regime, the massive use of extortion to ensure com- pliance at all levels of society.[40] Further research is needed to understand the complex relationships sustaining the Fujimori regime and how these shifted over time. There is nevertheless clear evidence that some segments of the business elite had withdrawn support from the regime. One exam- ple was the increasingly critical editorial content of some communications media, such as the conservative Lima daily, *El Comercio*, and Ivcher's *Frecuencia Latina*, which prior to 1997 were largely uncritical (and often quite supportive) of the Fujimori regime. The emergence of whistle- blowers such as General Robles, Mariela Barreto, Leonor La Rosa, and others; the withdrawal of support of former regime allies such as Ivcher; and the defection of regime operatives such as Carlos Ferrero, the sole legislator from Fujimori's party to vote in favor of the referendum initia- tive (and who later joined the opposition); also testify to the growing cracks within the ruling coalition.

Perhaps the most evident manifestation of these tensions lie within the ruling triumvirate itself. Since virtually the beginning of the Fujimori regime, power was concentrated in the hands of three men: Fujimori him- self; his security advisor, Vladimiro Montesinos, and General Hermoza. Hermoza was named head of the armed forces in 1991 by Fujimori upon the suggestion of Montesinos (which required the forced retirement of several generals who, according to tradition, should have been named commander in chief) because he was convinced Hermoza would be a compliant ally. Indeed, Hermoza supported Fujimori's *autogolpe* in 1992 in exchange for the regime's full backing of the military's counterinsurgency war. But it soon became evident that Hermoza had developed his own power base independent of Fujimori and Montesinos, and established himself as a full-blown partner in the regime's power structure. This became a symbiotic relationship in which each member of the triumvirate was dependent on the other for their continued power (Obando 1998; Rospigliosi 1996, 1998). Tensions began to emerge over the handling of the border conflict with Ecuador and Hermoza's increasingly emboldened exercise of military power. These tensions exploded in late 1997. On the one-year anniversary of the December 1996 takeover of the Japanese ambassador's residence by the MRTA, *El Comercio* quoted Fujimori saying that Hermoza did not participate in the design or the strategy of the rescue but only in its execution.[41] Fujimori, reportedly irritated with Hermoza's claim in a book he recently published that he was the principal strategist of the rescue operation, hinted at his desire to remove him as head of the armed forces. In response to Fujimori's declarations, Hermoza engineered a massive show of military force, as commanders from around the country, along with the ministers of defense and interior, came together in a public ceremony in Lima to demonstrate their support for Hermoza. The words of General Carlos Pergamino convey the military's full backing of Hermoza's leadership and, in effect, an implicit challenge to Fujimori:

> You, general, personify and represent the army of Peru. Any attempt to discredit your accomplishments is an offense to our institution as a whole.[42]

The message was clear: Hermoza was not going anywhere. Fujimori ordered the generals to return to their command posts, and alleged rumors of a coup subsided. While regime operatives claimed this was a victory for civilian control over the armed forces, critics charged that it was actually further proof of the civil-military alliance governing Peru. But it also demonstrated the deep tensions within that alliance, which erupted again nine months later, in the context of negotiations with Ecuador over simmering tensions from the border dispute. There was intense international pressure to bring the conflict to a peaceful solution, and Hermoza was seen as a hawk and the chief impediment to such an outcome. In the end this gave Fujimori and Montesinos the opportunity to remove Hermoza after an unprecedented seven years as commander in chief of the armed forces.

This contributed to a significant shift in the balance of power: with Hermoza out of the picture, Montesinos acquired virtually complete control over the military. He now had the sole power to determine promotions and dismissals with the armed forces, allowing him to consolidate his personal control over the military institution. Within days Montesinos placed trusted allies in key pots. At least 15 changes in top military ranks occurred within just a few weeks of Hermoza's ouster; all were men who graduated with Montesinos from military training school and whose promotions came outside the normal timetable.[43] Montesinos' classmates now controlled four of the country's six army regions.[44] Without the military to provide a counterweight to Montesinos—and without its vision of a state-building project, albeit a viscerally nationalistic and authoritarian one—the regime quickly degenerated into a kleptocracy of the worst kind. This, in the end, made the regime much more vulnerable and unstable.

## Reclaiming the Streets

It is in this context that the massive social protests around the 2000 electoral process proved to be so debilitating to the façade of legitimacy the Fujimori regime was seeking to obtain by securing a third elected term in office. The opposition's ability to articulate a clear case against the Fujimori regime based on the violation of internationally recognized standards of free and fair elections also prompted international actors to formulate direct criticisms of the regime and its corrupt electoral practices. Indeed, international observers—including the Carter Center/National Democratic Institute, the OAS, and even the U.S. government—played an unusually active and forceful role in denouncing not only the fraud evident on the day of the vote, but also the regime's manipulation of the entire electoral process. As international observers gave credence to the denunciations of fraud by the opposition and local watchdog groups such as Transparencia, resignation over a seemingly inevitable Fujimori victory turned into indignation. And presidential candidate Alejandro Toledo, an unlikely hero, rose to the occasion. Emboldened by massive popular support in the wake of outright fraud during the first round vote on April 9, he launched a frontal attack on the Fujimori regime's authoritarianism, his regime's manipulation of the rules of the game, his political use of state funds, his antipopular economic measures, and his failure to provide a better life for the majority of Peruvians.

The leadership role played by Toledo was central to this process, for it was his willingness to take on this role, and his ability to unite actors in political society with the protest movements on the streets, that gave such force to the resistance movement. Toledo's rise was as surprising as it was swift. He barely registered on public opinion polls in 1999, but two months before the April elections, and as popular opposition grew in the context of mounting evidence of the electoral fraud (and as the other two leading opposition candidates, Andrade and Castañeda Lossio, were discredited due in large part to the regime's mud-slinging campaigns), Toledo's popularity surged. Revelations that one million signatures had been forged in the process of registering different factions of the progovernment alliance— which came to light because an employee hired to forge signatures blew the whistle on the operation—further eroded confidence in the electoral process, creating more favorable conditions for a political alternative to Fujimori. Toledo was in the right place at the right time, and he delighted in his newfound role as leader of the opposition.[45]

On the day of the vote, exit polls gave Toledo a solid lead of 48 percent over Fujimori's 41 percent. Though not an outright victory for Toledo (Peru's electoral laws require 50 percent plus one of the vote, otherwise a second round is held between the top-two vote-getters) this meant that Fujimori would be forced into a second round vote that would be more difficult to manage. Later that evening, however, the quick-count vote reversed the percentage points, giving Fujimori nearly 48 percent and Toledo 41 percent. Though statistically this was within the standard margin of error, the Toledo camp immediately cried foul, suggesting that this was proof positive of the regime's intent to win the elections at any cost. Other opposition leaders joined Toledo in a massive protest at the Sheraton Hotel in downtown Lima and accused the National Office of Electoral Processes (ONPE) of perpetrating "electronic fraud." With Toledo at the lead, 50,000 demonstrators demanded that there be a second round. The following day, the ONPE declared that with tallies from 39 percent of polling stations counted, Fujimori had 49.88 of the vote versus Toledo's 39.88. Transparencia and the OAS mission blasted ONPE for the delays in counting the vote, charging that fraud was in the making to secure a first round victory for Fujimori.

Washington joined the call for a second round to ensure the integrity of the voting process. Secretary of State Madeleine Albright expressed Washington's concern over the "inconsistencies" between the quick count votes and the official counts.[46] Three U.S. senators released a statement declaring that Peru would be an "outcast" if it tampered with the election results in the first round,[47] and the U.S. House of Representatives passed Senate Resolution 43, which urged a review of U.S. aid to Peru if elections were found to be tainted. Civil society groups continued to mobilize on Tuesday and Wednesday in front of the Sheraton Hotel, where international reporters were camped out waiting to hear the official election results, assuring international coverage of the opposition's charges of fraud. Late Wednesday evening ONPE officials declared that Fujimori had obtained 49.84 percent of the vote—less than half a percentage point shy of the 50 percent he needed to win in the first round—and declared that a second round vote would by law follow.

The opposition clearly won this round—though the battle was far from over. But had it not been for massive protests, careful documentation of the electoral fraud by watchdog groups such as Transparencia and the CNDH, and the presence of international observers, Fujimori may have gotten away with his plan to assure victory in the first round by obtaining a majority vote. Instead, the regime was forced to agree to a second round vote. The social opposition to Fujimori found in Toledo an actor in political society—despite the problematic nature of his leadership, and despite the fragility of his movement—who articulated their concerns and challenged the regime head-on. The leadership role played by presidential candidate Alejandro Toledo in bringing disparate groups in civil and political society together to contest the electoral process was central to crystallizing antiregime sentiment into a more coherent and unified movement. Civil society activists report that it was this moment of victory, in which the antiregime protests effectively defeated the regime's plan to secure electoral victory in the first round, that made them perceive the viability of social mobilization to effect social change. As one university activist stated,

> In 1999, part of the debacle of the student movement was due to a sense of frustration that the marches weren't getting us anywhere. Nothing changed, we went out into the streets, wore out our shoes, walked like mad, and nothing changed. But in 2000, with the passage to the second round, this is the first feeling of achievement of the student movement... We reclaimed the streets as a legitimate space for struggle and for social change.[48]

As theorists of democratic transition have noted, the creation of a viable alternative to existing authoritarian arrangements is a crucial step in transition processes (Przeworksi 1986). Toledo's ability to connect the growing social opposition to Fujimori to a concrete political alternative was critical in lending legitimacy to the opposition's cause and isolating the Fujimori regime on the international front.

In the two months between the first and second rounds, the regime deployed similar strategies to those it had used in the past to discredit Toledo: character assassination and portraying Toledo as proterrorist. One headline in the yellow press suggests the virulence of this campaign: "Toledismo continues its campaign of electoral sabotage. In the style of Shining Path, Peru Posible seeks to impede elections with a spiral of violence."[49] Racist allusions were made to Toledo as a *cholo* (a racialized category, often used in a derogatory way, referring to persons of indigenous background who live in the city) who "incites savagery."[50] The regime's discourse blatantly played upon the racial-class ordering of the terrorist "other" that had long dominated popular culture and political discourse in Peru in which Shining Path was associated with "savage" Indians and *cholos* (Mayer 1991; Bourque and Warren 1989).

Toledo, domestic opposition groups, and the OAS mission launched a campaign to ensure a free and fair election on May 28, the designated date for the second round. Toledo requested a delay in the vote to give sufficient time for reforms to be implemented, but the regime refused to budge. When the OAS expressed its concerns that the government was obstructing reforms, Toledo announced his decision to withdraw as a candidate just 10 days before the election in protest of the government's gross manipulation of the electoral process and its refusal to make basic changes to ensure a fair election. International election observers followed suit, pulling their missions from observing the May 28 vote and dealing a serious blow to Fujimori's credibility at home and abroad. Toledo called for a "third round" of civic protest against the regime and to demand new, clean elections, offering to lead peaceful protests in the days leading up to Fujimori's swearing in on July 28, which he dubbed the "March of the Four Suyos." (*Suyo* is a Quechua word meaning direction, and it is a powerful symbolic reference to the four regions of Tahuantinsuyo, the Quechua name for the Incan Empire). The formerly disunited political opposition lined up neatly behind Toledo, whose leadership was now unquestioned. Assuming this new mantle of leadership, Toledo successfully turned protests against fraudulent elections into a new civic movement demanding an end to the manipulations and machinations of the Fujimori regime.

The three days of protest on July 26, 27, and 28 were massive and largely peaceful. The antiregime protests effectively reclaimed public space and helped breathe life into incipient social movements and revive preexisting social networks. Perhaps the most numerous contingent was university students, from state-run and private universities in Lima, such as San Marcos and the Catholic University, as well as from provincial universities such as the National University of the Center. Joining the students in massive social protests were women who had once been active participants in community kitchens, young people who had once organized cultural groups and in political parties, community organizers from Lima's popular districts, and former trade union and peasant federation activists. Middle-class and even some upper-class Peruvians, concerned with the Fujimori regime's abuse of power, also participated. People came from all over the country to participate in the protest marches, and camped out in tents put up by Toledo's business supporters; caravans came from remote Andean villages in Huancavelica and Cuzco as well as the jungle regions of Iquitos and Madre de Dios. As one participant in one of the marches said,

> At the protest march on July 27, [2000] you saw [people like] my aunt, who is very "high society." She said to me, "well here I am alongside the Communist Party and the lesbians." Rich Peruvians like her who go to Markham [a private high school in Lima] or Regatas [an exclusive country club] were there screaming the same slogans as the women from the shantytowns and the communal kitchens. It was unity based on respect for difference.[51]

The protest march on the following day, July 28, coincided with Peruvian Independence Day as well as the presidential swearing-in ceremony. Tens of thousands of people participated in the march. The protestors were met initially by fierce police repression, including tear gas. Later, security forces withdrew from the center of Lima, allowing protestors to advance to the downtown area. The march remained largely peaceful, but as security forces withdrew from the center of Lima, looters and vandals attacked government buildings and set some ablaze. There was no response from the fire department or other security units. In the chaos, a fire at the National Bank blazed out of control, taking the life of six bank guards. Regime supporters immediately accused the opposition of inciting violence, again trying to link them in the public mind with the violent strategies of terrorist groups like Shining Path. The opposition accused the regime of infiltrating the protest and setting the fire itself in order to discredit the opposition—a charge that was later borne out to be true (CVR 2003). The regime's efforts to discredit the protests in this brutal way backfired; few believed the regime's account of the events, revealing the increasing difficulty regime operatives faced, in the context of a more mobilized and informed civil society, of spinning the news in its favor.

Despite massive protests and stinging international criticism of Peru's 2000 electoral process, President Fujimori was sworn in on July 28, 2000. The opposition, dejected at the failure to overturn the outcome of the fraudulent electoral process, nonetheless remained convinced of the necessity of continuing to expose in creative ways the abuses of the Fujimori regime. In the following weeks, a group that called itself simply "Civil Society Collective" organized symbolic events to remind Peruvian citizens of the regime's corruption and abuse of power. Every Friday at one o'clock in the afternoon, dozens and sometimes hundreds of Peruvians gathered in front of the presidential palace to "wash" the Peruvian flag in symbolic protest of the fraudulent electoral process and the usurpation of power by President Fujimori and his cronies. Participants in the protest action took turns washing the red and white flags in large plastic tubs filled with soapy water, then hung them out to dry on make-shift clothing lines set up throughout the Plaza Mayor.

The flag-washing ceremonies were one of a variety of new forms of protest that emerged in Peru and attest to the resurgence of civil society. Women's groups also began taking to the streets, organizing weekly protests in front of the Palace of Justice to denounce the absence of the rule of law and the monopolization of power by Fujimori and his cronies. Students continued to organize frequent protests of the regime. In the Plaza San Martín, a few blocks south of the presidential palace, student and human rights groups erected large banners they called the "Wall of Shame," which displayed the names and images of regime officials, including Fujimori, Montesinos, congresswoman Martha Chávez, as well as others, such as Monseñor Luis Cipriani, an Opus Dei bishop, who were known supporters of the regime. In similar performance-protests, groups of people would walk through the main plazas of downtown Lima with large garbage bags that were imprinted with images of Fujimori and Montesinos dressed in prison garb, along with signs saying "Put the garbage in the garbage." These shaming exercises, and efforts to reclaim both public space and the concept of ethics in government, had a powerful symbolic impact. The often spontaneous participation of Peruvians of all social classes in the flag-washing ceremonies and other protests came to symbolize a reclaiming of public space. They also signaled that the regime's hold on public opinion—despite its hold on the media—was more contested than ever.

## The Revolution Will Not Be Televised

On September 15, 2000, a video was aired on television that showed Montesinos bribing an opposition congressman to quit his party and join the progovernment party. This image provided incontrovertible evidence that the opposition's accusations of massive fraud and corruption of the political process were in fact true. Montesinos immediately went into hiding and later fled the country; Fujimori struggled to do damage control, disbanding the SIN and promising new elections in one year's time. As Cameron (2006) has noted, without Montesinos, Fujimori's power was tenuous, and it soon became clear that Montesinos was not prepared to go down alone. Fujimori realized his own vulnerability and fled the country, faxing his resignation in November from his new safe haven in Japan. Congress, now controlled by the opposition, pronounced Fujimori morally unfit and declared the presidency vacant. An interim government was formed with the president of congress, Valentín Paniagua of the AP, as acting president. The following year, Toledo won a new electoral contest and took office as president in July 2001.

In the end it was not civil society protests that toppled the Fujimori regime, as in the "Velvet Revolutions" in Eastern Europe that brought down communist regimes in that region in 1989. The regime imploded from within, its power base destroyed by the images of corruption on videotape. The scandal that was the catalyst to regime breakdown would likely not have had as explosive an impact, however, had it not been for the massive demonstrations surrounding the 2000 electoral process, which evidenced the fragility of the regime's mandate and the extensiveness of its abuse of authority at the same time that it prompted international condemnation of the regime, isolating it and depriving it of legitimacy. Without the dynamic role played by civil society in denouncing the regime's abuse and corrupt practices, it is conceivable that the Fujimori regime might have weathered this storm, as it had so many others before it. Civil society protests exacerbated tensions within the regime, making it more difficult for regime operatives to manage and control the situation. Civil society protests also helped focus the international spotlight on what was happening in Fujimori's Peru, and led to important withdrawals of international support for the regime. The criticisms of the OAS and the U.S. State Department were especially significant in this regard (though it is also important to note that some sectors of the U.S. government continued to support the Fujimori regime until the bitter end).[52] In this sense, civil society mobilization was central to the demise of the Fujimori regime.

Once the regime collapsed and the interim government was established, political parties came to play a more central role in the political process. As occurred in other transitional societies in which civil society protests were central to the demise of authoritarian regimes, new opportunities opened for political parties to play the key roles of articulating public demands and concerns (Garretón 1989). Civil society groups were increasingly sidelined from the political process, even though in Peru parties remained weak and fragmented. With the unifying principle of opposition to Fujimori no longer relevant, the tenuous movement within civil society toward unity and cohesion was reverted as particularistic interests came to again dominate debates within and among the different civil society organizations involved in the opposition. Civil society groups in Peru today are very active—at times they seemed so powerful that they threatened to unseat President Toledo, as occurred in neighboring Ecuador and Bolivia, at various points during his regime. But civil society in Peru remains heterogeneous, fragmented, and disconnected to the political system. Indeed, the media and on occasion government officials have sought to portray civil society mobilization as no longer a positive element contributing to democracy in Peru, but rather a source of instability, chaos, and "ingovernability" that works against the common good. Peru's weak institutions—gutted by years of authoritarianism and corruption—are hard-pressed to address the multiple demands of the country's newly assertive civil society. Political society, itself still weak and seeking to recover from years of decay, remains largely aloof from the needs and organizations of civil society. Repression and weak efforts at clientelism have been the main tools used by the Toledo government to deal with civil society mobilization, reflecting the ongoing divide between state and society that has fueled social conflict, human rights abuses, and authoritarianism in Peru in the past. On occasion there has also been the tendency to blame societal unrest on the "resurgence" of terrorism, implicitly blurring the distinction between legitimate societal demands and struggles and subversion (Burt 2005).

## State and Society in Peru

In the case of Fujimori's Peru, repression, the instrumentalization of fear, control over the media, and the manipulation of terrorism worked for nearly a decade to undercut opposition movements and keep civil society demobilized. Yet, shifts in both the context in which such methods were so persuasive—the decline in political violence and the dwindling threat of a Shining Path takeover, for example—created opportunities for these discourses and practices to come under greater scrutiny. The regime's authoritarianism and its abuse of authority—long viewed as justified in the context of the war against the Shining Path—by the end of the decade were increasingly being contested. Individuals and civil society groups began to challenge the culture of fear that had so dominated the country. The context of the 2000 elections—and the regime's string of abuses to ensure its victory—also created new opportunities for civil society to challenge the regime's claims to be the legitimate representative of the Peruvian people and their aspirations. In the context of the Fujimori regime's re-reelection project, civil society groups, including electoral watchdog groups, human rights organizations, the student movement, trade unions, and opposition legislators, effectively articulated an ethical stance against the Fujimori regime's authoritarian practices and abuses of authority. They were defining the recuperation of democracy as the solution to Peru's problems. This small and largely middle-class movement created a crucial public space for dissent that facilitated the emergence of a broader opposition movement in the context of the 2000 elections. Peruvian civil society—which had been decimated over the previous decade and a half as a result of economic collapse, state and insurgent political violence, and the political use of fear by the Fujimori regime—was slowly regaining its moorings in the second half of the 1990s and was beginning to challenge the most egregious abuses of the Fujimori government.

While the resurgence of civil society proved to be central to the regime's undoing, civil society today remains weak and fragmented. Poverty and inequality contribute to this process, but so too do ongoing state practices of clientelism, fear mongering, and repression. Facilitating the development of a robust civil and political society remains one of the vital challenges facing Peru's new democracy to ensure that no new despotisms arise. But without democratic state structures that guarantee the rule of law and accountability for public authorities, civil society will continue to be vulnerable to the kind of state practices that had such devastating consequences for democracy and human rights in Fujimori's Peru. To date, Peru's transitional democracy has not pursued a vigorous reform effort in this regard, despite some real headway in some areas, such as police reform.[53] Without a more democratic state that assures horizontal accountability, and a more robust, independent civil society to assure vertical accountability, new cycles of conflict and contestation surely lie ahead.

# NOTES

## Introduction

1. This figure is a statistical projection established by the CVR. In collaboration with the Ombudsman's Office, the International Red Cross, and other organisms, the CVR compiled a preliminary list of 7,168 victims of forced disappearance. Of these, the CVR was able to document 2,144 cases (CVR 2003: Anexo 5).
2. This is documented in the truth commission reports that were written after the dictatorships in each country. For Argentina, see the report of the National Commission on the Disappearance of Persons (CONADEP) entitled *Nunca Más* (Never Again) (1986). For Chile, see the report of the National Commission for Truth and Reconciliation (1991).
3. See the final reports of the UN-sponsored truth commissions in El Salvador and Guatemala (Commission on the Truth for El Salvador 1993; Historical Clarification Commission 1999).
4. Civil society refers to uncoerced collective action around shared interests, purposes, and values. While the institutional forms of civil society are, in theory, distinct from those of the state, family, and market, in practice, the boundaries between state, civil society, family, and market are often complex, blurred, and negotiated.
5. For Keane, for civil society to be *civil*, it must be based on the notions of tolerance, democracy, and civility (nonviolence), otherwise it is *uncivil* society. In Keane's view, the chief obstacle to freedom and democracy is the abuse of state power; in this sense, civil society is central to democracy, since it is civil society that seeks to guarantee that state power is reigned in by horizontal and vertical forms of accountability. On uncivil society in Latin America, see Payne (2000).
6. With the exception of Red Fatherland, all the left-wing parties participated in elections in 1978 and 1980, and eventually Red Fatherland also joined the electoral process.
7. For excellent discussions of racism and the colonial mentality in the context of Peru's internal conflict, see Flores Galindo (1988) and Manrique (2002).
8. With the exception of Colombia, though it could be argued that despite its democratic political system, political exclusion through the National Front pact and other methods, including political violence, contributed to the emergence of insurgent movements. See Gutiérrez and Rueda (2004).
9. In 1990, 32 percent of the national territory, which encompassed 49 percent of the population, had been declared in a state of emergency. In 1991, the respective numbers were 30 percent and 45 percent. In 1990, 10 of Peru's 24 departments, including Lima, were fully under states of emergency. (Comisión Especial de Investigación y Estudio sobre la Violencia y Alternativas de Pacificación 1992:90–93).
10. This argument is made in McClintock (January 1989).
11. This is discussed in more detail in chapter eight. For a full discussion of this military project, see Rospigliosi (1996).
12. On the 1992 coup coalition, see Mauceri (1995).
13. See, for example, Lechner (1992) and Garretón (1992).
14. Tilly has noted that third world states are unlikely to replicate the European experience of state formation. Bright and Harding (1984) highlight state formation as a process rather than an outcome.

15. On the concept of failing states, see Foreign Policy/The Fund for Peace (2005); Rotberg (2003); Herbst (1996/1997); Zartman (1995); and Callaghy (1994).

16. Migdal (2001); Tilly (2003).

17. See, for example, O'Donnell (1993, 1998); Linz and Stepan (1996); Hagopian (1996); McSherry (1997); Aguero and Stark (1998); and Mendez, O'Donnell, and Pinheiro (1999).

18. Some scholars have argued that the forces of globalization—transnational forces such as international financial institutions, transnational corporations, and international capital flows—are resulting in a withering of the state (Strange 1996). Others have argued that globalization alters the shape of the state but does not doom it to irrelevance (Evans 1997).

19. See, for example, the collection of essays by O'Donnell (1999).

20. In reference to insurgent politics, Tilly (1978) once termed this "multiple sovereignty." Others have used the concept of "states within states" to refer to this dynamic of local or regionally based structures of authority and domination within the boundaries of a larger nation-state (Kingston and Spears 2004). Neither seems appropriate in the Peruvian case, since insurgent groups did not establish full territorial control in their zones of influence, but as I argue in chapters six and seven, the insurgents did carry out state-like functions designed to win local support and sympathy.

21. See, for example, Favre (1984); Degregori (1986); Berg (1986/1987, 1992); Manrique (1989); and Isbell (1992).

22. In a 1989 article, Peruvian historian Nelson Manrique pointed out the difficulty of writing about Shining Path. Those seeking to analyze and explain the emergence and expansion of Shining Path would inevitably need to examine local support for the insurgents, but, Manrique noted, raising such issues left analysts open to charges of being guerrilla sympathizers or worse. In the context of war, there is often little space for even scholars to engage in such research without being seen as "taking sides."

23. There is ample literature on these issues, particularly in anthropology. See, for example, Campbell and Brenner (2003); Suarez-Orozco (2000); Sluka (1999); Nelson (1999); Nordstrom (1997); Warren (1993); and Nordstrom and Martin (1992).

24. Interview, Villa El Salvador (December 2002).

25. On racism in Peru, see de la Cadena (2000) and Manrique (1993).

26. For a history of the Peruvian human rights movement, see Youngers (2003) and Youngers and Burt (2000).

27. Few studies exist of victims' and relatives of victims' groups in Peru, which were largely marginalized due to perceptions that they may be linked to Shining Path (Burt 1998).

28. See Degregori (1998); Degregori, Coronel, del Pino and Starn (1996); del Pino (1992); and Starn (1991).

29. This is neither a critique nor an indictment of that literature; it merely reflects the inherent difficulty pointed out by Nordstrom and Robben (1996:13) of writing about violence: any effort to impose order on the disorder of civil conflict through narrative formations is bound to result in an incomplete account of reality.

30. Nordstrom and Robben (1996:5).

31. See Tilly (1975) and Tilly, Tilly and Tilly (1975).

32. See Tilly (1985) and Stanley (1996).

33. Tilly (1978, 1997); Tarrow (1994).

34. Informants were chosen from two basic "types" of shantytown residents: those with leadership experience in some community organization (such as neighborhood associations, community kitchens, women's club, or the "glass of milk" committees); and those who either participated in such organizations as rank-and-file members, or who had no organizational affiliation of this type. To protect the integrity of those interviewed, their names must remain anonymous.

35. Though political violence has waned considerably in Peru since this fieldwork was conducted, I remain bound by my promise of anonymity to these organizations, who were often attacked by both Shining Path and government forces.

36. This survey was carried out by IMASEN, S.A., in January 1994.

37. This involved 25 additional interviews, including some with members of Shining Path currently in prison, as well as community leaders who allegedly had ties to Shining Path. My report on Villa El Salvador was published, in edited form, in the Final Report of the CVR (2003, Vol. 5, Ch. 2.16) and can be found online at: <http://www.cverdad.org.pe>.

## One   The Weak State

1. See, for example, Basadre (1978); Cotler (1978a); Burga and Flores Galindo (1981); and Flores Galindo (1988).
2. Burga and Flores Galindo (1981:91).
3. In effect, Velasco sought to impose a type of state corporatism. On the distinction between state and societal corporatism, see Schmitter (1974). On the corporatist nature of the Velasco regime, see Stepan (1978). For an analysis of the Velasco regime, see McClintock and Lowenthal (1983).
4. Stepan (1988) discusses the inevitable conflicts that arise when militaries govern directly, both with the larger society and within the military as an institution, that often compel sectors of the armed forces to move toward a transition process. For a discussion of the divisions within the Peruvian military during this period, see Pease and Cleaves (1983) and Mauceri (1996).
5. On the emergence of a "classist" labor movement, see Parodi (1986); Rospigliosi (1988); and Balbi (1989). For a discussion of how classist ideologies translated into the barriadas, see Stokes (1995).
6. Oficina Nacional de Estadística, Cuentas Nacionales, as cited in Cotler (1983:21).
7. See Thorp and Bertram (1978); McClintock and Lowenthal (1983); and Mauceri (1996).
8. Richard Webb, cited in Pastor and Wise (1992).
9. While business was pleased at the procapital tone of the Belaúnde administration and eager to regain the ground lost under Velasco's reformist regime, labor was militantly opposed to the administration. The regime's modest attempts to mediate capital and labor interests through the creation of a National Tripartite Commission floundered when the government was unable to persuade business or labor to accept its income and price proposals. The commission fell apart, business lost confidence in the government, and state-capital-labor relations deteriorated. See Pastor and Wise (1992) and Mauceri (1996).
10. Between 1980 and 1983, manufacturing output dropped by nearly 20 percent, and idle capacity in industry rose to over 50 percent (Reid 1985).
11. Private sector gross capital formation fell from 18 percent of GDP in 1980 to 12 percent in 1985, while foreign direct investment hit an all-time low of negative $89 million in 1984 (Pastor and Wise 1992).
12. Heterodox programs were also attempted in newly democratic Argentina under Raúl Alfonsín and Brazil under José Sarney; as in Peru, they resulted in economic recession and dramatic levels of hyperinflation.
13. For Pastor and Wise (1992), this policy was not as dramatic or as ill conceived as has been suggested. The Belaúnde government had already stopped most payments to commercial creditors for simple lack of financial resources. Though more political in nature, APRA's policy was intended to honor selectively obligations that would benefit Peru in terms of trade and development financing; Peru continued to service short-term trade finance and to pay the World Bank and the Inter-American Development Bank. The problem, according to Pastor and Wise, was García's unilateral limiting of debt payments, which prompted the IMF to declare Peru "ineligible" for further loans or credits in 1986, which severely constricted the Peruvian economy and helped feed the hyperinflationary spirals of the late 1980s.
14. APRA won 47.6 percent of the total vote, while IU won 30.8 percent. The continued strength of both APRA and IU seemed to confirm the interpretation that Peru's electorate had made a "critical realignment" toward the center-left.
15. In the end, the banks remained private due to a combination of legal challenges and, in some instances, the devolution of majority ownership to employees, a category exempted from García's nationalization decree. On the revival of the Right in Peru, see Durand (1997).
16. Tax revenues dropped from 14.3 percent of GDP in 1985 to 9.2 percent in 1988 and 5.9 percent in 1989. Tax income in 1989 was 30 percent of what was collected in 1985 (Cáceres and Paredes 1991).
17. This widely accepted estimate was corroborated by official government figures from 1994. In 1994, 54 percent of the population, or 13 million people, lived in critical poverty, defined as insufficient income to cover a basic food basket for a family of 5, while 23 percent of this group suffers from extreme poverty, defined as insufficient income to cover minimum nutritional requirements for a family of 5. See FONCODES (1994).

18. This is based on firsthand observations of responses among residents and local officials in three Lima shantytowns in the days following the "Fujishock."
19. Based on interviews with community kitchen leaders, NGOs, and church leaders in San Juan de Lurigancho, El Agustino, San Martín de Porres, and Villa El Salvador, 1990. In many cases, families would try to stretch rations, since they could not afford even the symbolic cost of community kitchen rations, undermining any attempt to provide quality nutrition through the community kitchens during this period of crisis.

## Two Social Consequences of State Breakdown

1. Statistics on the social costs of the economic crisis are from Graham (1992).
2. In 1990 dollars (Webb and Fernández Baca 1994).
3. Ministry of the Presidency (1993).
4. These include crimes against life, physical integrity and health; property; and "good customs," the family and public tranquility.
5. Comisión Especial sobre las Causas de la Violencia (1989:238).
6. This has been amply confirmed by numerous public opinion polls by IMASEN and Instituto APOYO.
7. Interview with Congressional Deputy Julio Castro, *ideéle*, No. 31 (November 1991), pp. 10–12.
8. Ibid.
9. *El Nacional* (December 13, 1990).
10. The cost of a basic food basket for a family of 6 in 1991 was 486 new soles ($405). See Burt and Panfichi (1992:3).
11. "El Vacío Interior," *Sí*, No. 207 (February 3–10, 1991), p. 12; and the November 1991 issue of *ideéle*, No. 3, p. 31, which examines the crisis of the national police.
12. See "Sicosis en Lima: Delincuencia," *Caretas* (March 25, 1991), p. 39.
13. "La PNP en cifras," *ideéle*, No. 31 (November 1991), p. 11.
14. Ibid.
15. Ibid.
16. Refers to public opinion polls taken annually by Instituto APOYO S.A., and published in the monthly magazine *Debate* ("Encuesta anual sobre el poder en el Perú"), reviewed between 1987 and 1994.
17. 1989 figure from IDL, *Informe Mensual*, No. 9 (December 1989), p. 23; August 1990 through October 1991 figure from "La PNP en cifras," *ideéle*, No. 31 (November 1991), p. 11.
18. "La PNP en cifras," *ideéle*, No. 31 (November 1991), p. 11.
19. Ibid.
20. In 2006, four police officers were tried and convicted of the forced disappearance of Ernesto Castillo. See Rivera (2006).
21. See DESCO (1989a).
22. Data based on review of newspaper accounts from DESCO's database.
23. *Resumen Semanal*, No. 455 (January 29–February 18, 1988).
24. *Resumen Semanal*, No. 458 (March 4–10, 1988).
25. *Resumen Semanal*, No. 455 (January 29–February 18, 1988).
26. See Comisión Investigadora de Grupos Paramilitares (1989).
27. APRODEH (1994a) describes the Cantuta massacre.
28. See Instituto de Defensa Legal, *Informe Mensual*, No. 14 (June 1990), pp. 14–17.
29. See Flores Galindo (1988) for excellent discussions of this issue.
30. See, for example, González (1998).
31. Based on a review of the public opinion polls taken annually by Instituto APOYO, S.A., and published in *Debate* ("Encuesta Anual sobre el Poder en el Perú") between 1987 and 1994.
32. Lynchings have become common in many parts of Latin America, particularly in countries in which governing institutions are perceived as corrupt and ineffective. See the works by Caldeira (2000) and Godoy (2006).

## Three    Terror versus Terror

1. This description is based on newspaper articles reviewed in the days following the attack, as well as IDL (1990) and *Resumen Semanal*, Nos. 512 (March 24–30, 1989) and 514 (April 7–13, 1989).
2. This borrows from the title of McSherry's (1999) book on the Argentine transition to democracy in 1983.
3. For an incisive analysis of this period, see Gorriti (1990).
4. Tapia (1997), for example, argues that this would have led to a quick, if messy, end to the insurgency.
5. Interview, *QueHacer*, No. 20 (1983).
6. Figures on extrajudicial executions from Defense Ministry and Comisión Especial de Investigación y Estudio sobre la Violencia y Alternativas de Pacificación (1989). Figures on disappearances from Commission on Human Rights.
7. For a discussion of national security doctrine, see Weiss Fagen (1992) and Crahan (1982).
8. *Expreso* (August 26, 1984), as cited in DESCO (1989:705).
9. For a full account of the Socos massacre, see Vol. 7, Ch. 7 of the CVR's Final Report (2003).
10. *La República* (August 27, 1984), as cited in DESCO (1989b:585).
11. Law 24150 was widely challenged by the opposition and human rights activists. Interview, Miguel Talavera, Institute for Legal Defense, Lima (June 24, 1989). See also Degregori and Rivera (1993).
12. *Caretas*, No. 813 (August 20, 1984), as cited in DESCO (1989b:680).
13. Alan García, Inaugural Address (July 28, 1985), as cited in DESCO (1989a:124).
14. Alan García, Address before the UN (September 29, 1985), as cited in DESCO (1989a:456–457).
15. Interview, Jorge Salazar, Andean Commission of Jurists, Lima (July 4, 1988). For a fuller analysis of García's human rights policy, see Burt (1989).
16. Amnesty International (1987).
17. For an initial report of the prison massacre, see Amnesty International (1987). See also Vol. 7, Ch. 23 of the CVR's Final Report (2003).
18. The military closed access to the area for 14 days. Once Escobar was allowed entry, he discovered that the corpses had been removed; only empty graves and some body parts were found. A full account of the Cayara massacre can be found in Vol. 7, Ch. 28 of the CVR's Final Report (2003).
19. Investigative reporting by journalist Gustavo Gorriti revealed that Vladimiro Montesinos, de facto head of the SIN since 1991, was responsible for filtering information, including names of witnesses, from the attorney general's office to the military high command to facilitate the elimination of numerous witnesses to the Cayara massacre. See Gorriti (1994).
20. The Human Rights Commission of the Organization of American States (OAS) found the Peruvian security forces culpable of the Cayara massacre in July 1991 and recommended that the case be heard before the Inter-American Human Rights Court.
21. The air force was so incensed that it sent fighter planes to fly over Lima, giving rise to rumors of a coup d'état (Degregori and Rivera 1993).
22. See the congressional report on paramilitaries, Comisión Investigadora de grupos paramilitares (1989).
23. This point and the examples presented here are drawn from Tapia (1997:41).
24. On this history, see Bonilla and Drake (1989).
25. García stated: "We should recognize that Shining Path has active, committed militants who make sacrifices. We should look at them to value the good that they represent, not only to destroy or confront them...These are people who deserve our respect and my personal admiration because, like it or not, they are compañeros, militants. They call them fanatics. I believe that they have mysticism. . . ." As cited in Tapia (1997:41).
26. Comisión Especial de Investigación y Estudio sobre la Violencia y Alternativas de Pacificación (1992).
27. Comisión Especial de Investigación y Estudio sobre la Violencia (1989, 1992).
28. *Resumen Semanal*, No. 542 (October 20–26, 1989).
29. Jurado Nacional de Elecciones, Oficio No. 819-89-P (July 11, 1989).

## Four    The Crisis of Organized Politics

1. On clientelism, see Collier (1976, 1998); Kaufman (1977); and Scott (1977).
2. APRA's dwindling political influence over labor was directly linked to the conservative positions adopted by the party's old guard leadership in the 1950s, which culminated in the 1956 alliance with the oligarchy and the military, known as the *Convivencia* (coexistence) (Bonilla and Drake 1989).
3. The number of people employed by the PAIT program more than doubled in the last trimester of 1986, compared to the same period in 1985 (Paredes 1988).
4. Author's interviews with members of community kitchens in Villa El Salvador, San Juan de Lurigancho, and Pamplona Alta in 1987 and 1989. Many women preferred the increase in family income, however small, to continued participation in the community kitchen, because even though the job program was temporary, they knew that if necessary, they could return to the community kitchen without facing any sanctions in the future. This points to one of the enduring problems of "survival" organizations like community kitchens—the ubiquitous free-rider problem outlined by Olson (1971).
5. See Stepan (1978) for one of the best reviews of the military's corporatist intentions and their shortcomings.
6. See Tovar (1985) and Stokes (1995).
7. A handful of groups decided not to participate, most notably Red Fatherland, which denounced them as an "electoral farce," and Shining Path.
8. See Pásara (1988, 1989) for a closer look at this issue.
9. The APRA party won 35 percent of the vote, while the Popular Christian Party won 24 percent. Among the Left parties, the Trotsky-inspired Worker Campesino Student and Popular Front (FOCEP) won 12.3 percent, the Revolutionary Socialist Party (PSR) won 6.6 percent, the PC-Unity 5.9 percent, and the Popular Democratic Unity (UDP) 4.5 percent (Tuesta 1994).
10. AP took 22 districts; 7 went to independents who were elected on a party ticket but then left their parties; IU won 5; and APRA and PPC took 2 each (Tuesta 1994:192–193, 108–109).
11. Tuesta (1994:188).
12. The IU won 36.5 percent of the total valid votes, compared to APRA's 27.2 percent, PPC's 21.2 percent, and AP's 11.9 percent (Tuesta 1994:187).
13. García won 53.1 percent of the valid vote to Barrantes' 24.7 percent (Tuesta 1994:175).
14. In Lima, APRA won 37.5 percent of the valid vote, to IU's 34.8 percent and the PPC's 26.9 percent; APRA won 19 of 41 districts, while IU held onto only 9, and PPC took 12 (Tuesta 1994: 174).
15. This discussion is based on a review of available IU documents, interviews with IU rank-and-file activists and party leaders, a number of excellent analyses of the development and problems of the IU and the Left in general that are cited below, and my personal observations during fieldwork and visits to Peru since 1986.
16. As cited in Nieto (1983:56).
17. For these groups, the coup against Velasco and the growing repression against the popular sectors revealed the increasingly fascist nature of the military regime; the only solution was revolution. For an excellent review of this period and the different views within the Left, see Nieto (1983). Nieto, who was a participant in the New Left during this period, criticizes its failure to understand what he calls "the democratic aspirations of the Peruvian people" because of dogmatic version of Marxism that dominated the Peruvian Left. See especially pp. 58–65.
18. Pásara (1988) notes that the Left argued that even political democracy was not viable given Peru's deep socioeconomic inequalities.
19. In the case of PUM, these discrepancies culminated in the party's division in 1989.
20. Javier Diez Canseco, former secretary general of PUM and one of the most prominent leaders of the IU, referred to this excessive vanguardism as "hyper-Leninism" (Diez Canseco 1996:55).
21. Chapter seven will explore this dynamic in greater detail, as it relates to the ability of Shining Path to exploit and manipulate such divisions to its own organizational and political purposes.
22. This line of argument is developed in greater detail in Pásara (1988).

23. Hazleton-Woy (1992), for example, emphasizes the distinct strategies pursued by the IU and Shining Path, but fails to appreciate the ambiguity within the IU vis-à-vis Shining Path or the common ideological roots of both movements.
24. Tuesta (1994:106–107).
25. Henry Pease, who ran as the IU candidate, won 7 percent of the vote, while Barrantes, representing the IS, won a mere 4 percent (Tuesta 1994).

## Five   The Iron Belts of Misery

1. Chapters five and six are drawn from "Political Violence and the Grassroots in Lima, Peru" by Jo-Marie Burt, from *The New Politics of Inequality in Latin America: Rethinking Participation and Representation*, edited by Douglas Chalmers et al. New York: Oxford University Press, 1997: 281–309. By permission of Oxford University Press.
2. On the crisis of trade unionism, see Parodi (1986) and Balbi (1997).
3. This account of the strike is based on newspaper articles; see especially López Ricci (1988).
4. The term *barriada*, commonly translated in English as shantytown, not only refers to a physical space of underdeveloped housing and basic services but also denotes a mode of access to housing via organized land invasions and the eventual, often piece-meal, development of housing and other basic services, usually through the self-help efforts of the *barriada* residents (Driant 1991).
5. Lima's explosive growth rate continues. From 1993 to 2005, Lima's population grew by 25 percent, from approximately 6 million to approximately 8 million inhabitants (INEI 2005).
6. National Census of 1961 and 1972 as cited in Driant (1991).
7. The first of these invasions originated on Christmas Eve of 1954 in what would become known as Ciudad de Dios (City of God). Every detail of the invasion was carefully planned. Inhabitants of two inner city slums in the eastern part of Lima formed an association in March 1954 and lobbied for support from government authorities for the land invasion (Matos Mar 1977).
8. Over half of the *barriadas* formed before 1971 occupied land with express authorization of the state (Collier 1976).
9. The most outstanding exception to this laissez-faire policy was Villa El Salvador, which is examined in detail in chapter seven. Though it also started as a grassroots land invasion in 1971, the Velasco regime decided to make it the urban component of its reformist experiment, providing state funds and planners to construct a model urban settlement. A handful of other settlements were modeled on Villa El Salvador's design or some alteration thereof, most notably Huaycán. In general, however, land invasions have continued the ad hoc pattern of previous years and have continued to be the object of clientelistic patronage from ruling elites and other competitors.
10. Census information provided by Driant (1991).
11. Discrepancies existed within Shining Path leadership over this decision. Some party leaders argued that political work in the city was too dangerous and would expose the organization to infiltration.That Guzmán was arrested in Lima, after prolonged police surveillance, would seem to bear out this dissident view.
12. The data, and the broader reconstruction of Shining Path reported activities in Lima, is based on DESCO's database. The database is not without its methodological problems, given it is based primarily on newspaper reports, given both the problem of unreliability of newspaper accounts and the fact than many violent acts were unreported. Despite these limitations it remains an extremely useful source of data for research purposes.
13. *Resumen Semanal* 455 (January 29–February 18, 1988).
14. Though the FMLN in El Salvador sought to establish political and military control over specific areas in El Salvador, they did not engage in massive, indiscriminate terror to do so. The situation in Peru was in many ways more comparable to countries in Africa and Asia, such as Mozambique and Sri Lanka, in which guerrilla movements often engaged in terror in their bid to establish control over civilian populations. See Nordstrom and Martin (1992).
15. See Degregori (1986) for an initial discussion of this nature. Other examples of such arguments can be found in Salcedo (1985); IDS (1989); and Woy-Hazelton and Hazelton (1992).

Significantly, the social bulwark argument was virtually unquestioned among left-wing activists.

16. Poll material gathered by APOYO, S.A. (June 1991). The reaction of Lima-based intellectuals is registered in Balbi (1991).

17. Statement of Bernard W. Aronson, assistant secretary of state for Inter-American Affairs before the Subcommittee on Western Hemisphere Affairs, House Committee on Foreign Affairs (March 12, 1992). The first genocide is the Nazi extermination of the Jews and other groups; the second is the genocide perpetrated by the Khmer Rouge in Cambodia in the 1970s.

18. *Expreso* (July 5, 1992).

## Six   In the Gray Zones: States of Shining Path

1. Popkin (1979) argues that insurgents who deliver specific goods to their desired constituents and who demonstrate self-abnegating leadership are most likely to win support and local trust.

2. On the efforts of the FARC to develop local authority structures in its areas of influence, see Pizarro (1996). For studies on similar strategies developed by Hamas, see Mishal and Sela (2000) and the edited collection by Wiktorowicz (2004).

3. Comisión Especial de Investigación y Estudio sobre la Violencia y Alternativas de Pacificación (1989).

4. These patrols often were established at the initial stage of a land invasion, to protect the community (which was relatively small) from thieves as well as eviction by the police. As invasions became established settlements, these patrols tended to disappear.

5. Refers to public opinion polls taken annually by Instituto APOYO, S.A., and published in *Debate* ("Encuesta Anual sobre el Poder en el Perú"), reviewed between 1987 and 1994.

6. *IMASEN Confidencial*, Lima (August 1993).

7. The *rondas* established in Huaycán were probably the best known during this period, but the particular situation they faced made them unrepresentative of other experiences. The *rondas* were reactivated in Huaycán as crime grew in the settlement during 1990 and 1991. Shortly after the 1992 coup, Fujimori visited the *rondas* in Huaycán and delivered a speech praising the *rondas* as the "first line of defense" against Shining Path in the *barriadas*. While leaders of the communities and the *rondas* tried to distance themselves from the government, the military presence in the district made this extremely difficult. Shining Path thus viewed the *ronderos* as "traitors" to the revolution. At least three *ronda* leaders in Huaycán were killed by Shining Path and numerous others received death threats.

8. Interview, Lima (November 1994).

9. Interview, Lima (April 1994).

10. Interview, Lima (October 1994).

11. Interview, Lima (November 1994).

12. Given the degree of repression against suspected Shining Path members in Peru, it is unlikely that those who sympathize with the organization will say so willingly. Polling experts thus deem it significant when a high number of respondents openly state their approval or comprehension of Shining Path activities (Personal communication, Giovanna Peñaflor, Director of IMASEN [February 1994]). Also significant is the fact that the poll was taken in January 1994, a year and a half after the arrest of Abimael Guzmán. This means that the poll was implemented in a context of reduced Shining Path activity and a government offensive designed to destroy the operational and logistical support structures of Shining Path, which resulted in the detention not only of members of Shining Path but also all those who assisted the organization in any way, even if it was unknowingly or under threat. For these reasons, the fact that 15–33 percent note their approval or comprehension of Shining Path activities including killing or punishing perceived wrongdoers is highly significant.

13. In late 1995, residents of a *barriada* in Caracas killed one man and almost burned another alive after they accidentally shot a six-year-old girl. This was not a unique event; six lynchings were registered in Caracas in 1995 alone. InterPress World News Service (November 27, 1995).

14. On lynchings in Brazil, see Pinheiro (1996) and Caldeira (2000). On lynchings in El Salvador, see Tracy (1995). On Guatemala, see Godoy (2006).

15. *The New York Times* (March 30, 1999).
16. Interview, Lima (July 1990).
17. *IMASEN Confidencial*, Lima (August 1993).
18. *IMASEN Confidencial*, Lima (December 1994).
19. Although much of the literature on the community kitchen movement portrays these as spontaneous expressions of social solidarity, the role of external actors has been key in the formation of most community kitchens, including the Catholic Church and NGDOs. Both the state and political parties have also organized or funded community kitchens in clientelistic fashion as a way of obtaining local support. Much has been written on the community kitchens and the women's movement in general. See, for example, Barrig (1986, 1991); Blondet (1986); Galer and Nuñez (1989); and Delpino (1991).
20. Interview, Lima (February 2004).
21. Interview with the Rev. Gregory Chisholm, Villa El Salvador (July 1993).
22. Interview, Lima (November 1994).
23. Based on a review of DESCO's database.
24. The case of Maria Elena Moyano will be discussed in greater detail in chapter seven.
25. Interview, Lima (November 1993).
26. Interview, Lima (July 2004).
27. Notably 32.5 percent of the lower stratum and 33.6 percent of the lower-middle stratum, ascribed to this view, compared to only 19.1 percent of the upper stratum.
28. As cited in López Ricci (1993).
29. Interview, Lima (October 1994).
30. Interview, Lima (November 1994).

## Seven   The Battle of Villa El Salvador

1. This chapter is based on "The Battle of Lima: The Case of Villa El Salvador," by Jo-Marie Burt, first published in *Shining and Other Paths: War and Society in Peru, 1980–1995*, edited by Steve Stern. Durham, NC: Duke University Press, 1998: 267–306. Reprinted with permission of Duke University Press.
2. This offensive in the capital coincided with Shining Path's announcement in May 1991 that it had achieved "strategic equilibrium" with the armed forces, the intermediate stage of its plan to overthrow the Peruvian state.
3. The Final Report of the CVR (2003) suggests that in some instances, including that of Huaycán and Villa El Salvador, the state may have deliberately sought to recruit local leaders such as Moyano and Pascuala Rosada of Huaycán to confront Shining Path and to lend legitimacy to the state's cause.
4. Census data from INEI (1994).
5. In this respect, Shining Path's attempt to gain influence and control over Villa El Salvador had important parallels in Puno, where similar symbolic issues were at stake in infiltrating the local campesino movement. See Renique (1993, 1998).
6. Interview, Villa El Salvador (December 1992).
7. Velasco's reforms were based on the notion of a "third way" between capitalism and communism for "third world" societies to develop politically and economically. The idea of *autogestión* was based on the Yugoslav model of social property, which would provide the conditions for worker participation and eventually self-management—as well as ameliorate social conflict between capital and labor.
8. The fourth sector did not follow this grid design. The Belaúnde goverment constructed a housing project in this area, which came to be known as Pachacamac.
9. Some of these organizations were promoted by NGOs and/or church organizations such as CARITAS, a Catholic relief agency, which gave food donations to the members of these groups. These organizations later merged into "women's clubs" that continue to exist throughout VES, and many of which are members of the FEPOMUVES.
10. Chapter 3 discusses the Left's ambiguity vis-à-vis electoral democracy in more detail. See also Rospigliosi (1989); Pásara (1990); and Roberts (1999).
11. APRA won 35 percent of the vote, while the PPC won 24 percent. Among the Left parties, the Trotsky-inspired FOCEP won 12.3 percent, the PSR won 6.6 percent, the PCP 5.9 percent, and the Popular Democratic Unity 4.5 percent (Tuesta 1994).

12. Meeting, María Elena Moyano Foundation, Villa El Salvador (March 1993).
13. Several new squatter settlements took Villa El Salvador and the concept of *autogestión* as their model, including Huaycán in Ate-Vitarte and Juan Pablo II in San Juan de Lurigancho.
14. This discussion is based on a review of DESCO's database; a review of newspaper coverage of Villa El Salvador facilitated to me by CIDIAG; and is supplemented by interviews of residents of Villa El Salvador as well as informed observers who live or work in the district.
15. *Sí* (February 24, 1992); Interview with a former San Marcos University student from Villa El Salvador (December 2002).
16. Interviews with several Fe y Alegría students from this period, July and August 1993.
17. The literature that discusses the Left's relationship with Shining Path often misses this ambiguity, focusing instead on the different practices of the legal Left within democracy and Shining Path's armed violence. See, for example, Haworth (1993) and Woy-Hazelton and Hazelton (1992). There were of course many differences, but it is also important to examine the commonalities and ambiguities in order to fully understand the dynamics of the Left vis-à-vis Shining Path.
18. As cited in Pásara (1990).
19. Interview, Santiago Pedraglio, Lima (May 1994).
20. Carlos Tapia, who became a member of the IS, which split from the IU in 1989, maintained this position. See *QueHacer*, No. 70 (1991).
21. Interview, Santiago Pedraglio, Lima (May 1994).
22. Driant (1991) offers an excellent description of the process of consolidation of older land invasions, as squatters slowly build up their homes from cane matting to brick and concrete, basic services such as water and electricity are obtained, and other local infrastructure develops. He contrasts this process to the emergence of new land invasions, largely after 1984, that often encountered greater difficulty in obtaining government assistance to develop their local communities.
23. *El Diario* (January 1992).
24. See *El Plan Integral de Desarrollo de Villa El Salvador*, Lima, DESCO and the Municipality of Villa El Salvador, 1986.
25. Interview, Villa El Salvador (February 1994).
26. *La República* (June 23, 1991).
27. *El Diario*, No. 551 (June 7, 1989).
28. "Whatever happened to the 'projects' and 'programs' of the revisionists and reactionaries? They were only a crass trafficking of the poor that permitted the illicit enrichment of a few at the expense of the poverty of thousands. This is the case of the traffickers Azcueta, Paredes, Moyano, Zazzali, Cáceres, Moreno, and Quintanilla, [IU municipal leaders in popular districts in Lima] among others who work against the Maoist revolution in our country." *El Diario*, No. 613 (1991).
29. Interview, Villa El Salvador (July 1994).
30. In leaflets it distributed in Villa El Salvador, Shining Path disclaimed responsibility for attacking the warehouse, and accused Moyano of orchestrating the attack to cover up her misuse of the organization's resources. In interviews in 1994 and again in 2002, several community leaders speculated that local Shining Path members may have orchestrated the bombing without prior orders from the group's leaders.
31. *La República* (September 22, 1991). The first registered assassination of a female grassroots leader was that of Juana López, leader of a community kitchen in Callao, who was killed on August 31, 1991. Shining Path killed over 100 community activists, including trade unionists, neighborhood council leaders, and women active in the community kitchens and milk program.
32. *La República* (September 22, 1991).
33. Moyano explicitly stated that the *rondas* would be independent of the police or armed forces, since the people lacked confidence in these institutions.
34. *La República* (July 5, 1991).
35. Research on NGDOs carried out in 1993 in Lima, Cusco, and Arequipa revealed a similar pattern of popular responses to development projects, especially after 1989 with the worsening of the economic crisis. The "charity mentality" identified by Delpino (1991) was ably exploited by Shining Path, who used it to attack NGDOs, many of who were linked or sympathetic to the IU.

36. Published in *Ultima Hora* (February 17, 1992).
37. *La República* (February 19, 1992).
38. Interview (December 15, 2002).
39. See, for example, *La República* (February 19, 1992).
40. *El Diario,* No. 551 (1989).
41. *El Diario,* No. 620 (1992).
42. See Delpino (1991) for an excellent discussion of the problem of the fragile institutionality in women's organizations.
43. Roa claimed Azcueta manipulated Moyano and thus placed her in harm's way, a view he reiterated in an interview with the Lima weekly magazine *Sí*: "[Roa]—'Michel Azcueta, with his economic power acquired from [international] donations, uses people and keeps them as his puppets, to use as he pleases.' [Sí]—'Are you saying that María Elena Moyano was a puppet?' [Roa]—'We are perfectly aware that that's the way it was.'" (*Sí*, April 6, 1992).
44. Local residents reported an active Shining Path presence in Pachacamac. The zone was used primarily as a sanctuary and training area.
45. *La República* (March 3, 1992) covered the first march, but mistakenly took the banners against the "militarization" of Villa El Salvador to be a spontaneous popular protest of local residents against the army.
46. See the March 22, 1992 and April 5, 1992 editorials in *Expreso*.
47. Interview, Villa El Salvador (December 2002).
48. For a detailed description of the rivalry between the CUAVES and the municipal government, see Tuesta (1989).
49. "Acuerdos de la VI Convención de la CUAVES," Mimeograph (August 30, 1992).
50. *Expreso* (August 31, 1992).
51. The military was nonetheless relatively restrained in responding to Shining Path's growing influence in Lima's *barriadas*. This will be discussed further in the next chapter.
52. See the statement of Bernard Aronson, assistant secretary of state for Inter-American Affairs before the Subcommittee on Western Hemisphere Affairs, House Committee on Foreign Affairs (March 12, 1992).
53. For an analysis of Shining Path after Guzmán's arrest, see Burt and López Ricci (1994) and Reyna (1996). On current Shining Path activities, see Burt (2005).
54. From the beginning of his tenure in early 1993, Vásquez launched sharp invectives against organizations such as the FEPOMUVES and the former municipal administrations linked to the mainstream Left. In an attempt to discredit the Left, Vásquez allied himself with Roa and Anchita, but his administrative incompetence and blatant corruption led local organizations to demand his ouster. He was arrested on illicit enrichment and other charges in early 1994.

## Eight   The Authoritarian Reconstitution of the State

1. An earlier version of this chapter was first published as "State-Making against Democracy: The Case of Fujimori's Peru." In *Politics in the Andes: Identity, Conflict and Reform*, edited by Jo-Marie Burt and Philip Mauceri. Pittsburgh: University of Pittsburgh Press, 2004: 247–268. Reprinted with permission of University of Pittsburgh Press.
2. On the problem of democratic accountability in delegative democracies, see O'Donnell (1994, 1998). Stokes (2001) addresses directly the issue of democratic accountability and neoliberalism.
3. See his classic statement of this thesis, *The Other Path* (De Soto 1989).
4. World Bank Group Website: http://www.cdinet.com/DEC/wdi98/new/countrydata/.aag/per_aag.pdf.
5. Ibid. We now know that significant portions of the money earned from privatizations were siphoned off into personal accounts of Fujimori, Montesinos, and others.
6. Based on a restricted, procedural definition of democracy, much of the U.S. social science literature discussed the Fujimori regime as a type of democracy "with an adjective" (Collier and Levitsky 1997), referring to it as a semidemocracy, authoritarian democracy, delegative democracy, and even *caudillo* democracy. Thus, with the apparent movement from de facto rule after

the 1992 *autogolpe* to constitutional rule, marked by new congressional elections in November 1992, the approval of a new constitution in 1993, and Fujimori's reelection as president in 1995, Peru was at least a partial democracy (see, for example, Cameron and Mauceri 1997). Other analysts highlight the authoritarian nature of the Fujimori regime. See, for example, Rospigliosi (1996); (Burt 1998, 2004); McClintock (1999, 2005); Levitsky (1999); and Conaghan (2001).

7. On Fujimori and the armed forces, see Obando (1998); Rospigliosi (1998, 1996); Mauceri (1996); and Degregori and Rivera (1993).

8. For an excellent account of the nascent alliance between Montesinos and Fujimori, see Gorriti (1994). According to Gorriti, Alan García ordered the SIN to assist the beleagured candidate in an obvious attempt to help Fujimori get elected and defeat Vargas Llosa, one of García's arch-enemies. This was the first contact between Montesinos and Fujimori.

9. Had such charges been upheld, Fujimori would have been ineligible to run for the presidency.

10. Gorriti (1994) notes that many of the purges were in fact personally motivated, as Montesinos took full advantage of his newly acquired powers to punish those who had forced him out of the army in the 1970s.

11. For Hermoza to be promoted, several prestigious generals ahead of him in seniority were forced into retirement, generating serious discontent within significant sectors of the armed forces. See Obando (1998).

12. Interviews with retired General Jaime Salinas Sedó, and with Fernando Rospigliosi, Lima (June 1998).

13. On the judicial system, see Human Rights Watch (1995).

14. See Gorriti (1994). A Drug Enforcement Agency (DEA) memo leaked to the *Miami Herald* in 1992 corroborates Gorriti's charges that purges within the judiciary were designed to protect military officers linked to drug trafficking.

15. *Caretas,* November 1991.

16. On the decree laws and congressional opposition to them, see Vidal (1993).

17. For an analysis of the 126 decree laws, see Vidal (1993).

18. See, for example, the statement of Bernard Aronson, assistant secretary of state for Inter-American Affairs before the Subcommittee on Western Hemisphere Affairs of the House Committee on Foreign Affairs, March 12, 1992.

19. For an analysis of U.S. policy toward Peru, see McClintock and Vallas (2003).

20. On two previous occasions, DINCOTE had nearly captured Guzmán. In February 1991, the DINCOTE raided a Shining Path safe house in the Lima district of Monterrico and narrowly missed capturing Guzmán. In that raid, police discovered a videotape in which Guzmán and most of the other members of the central committee appeared, all wearing severe gray Mao-like uniforms. This was an invaluable find for the police, who until this point did not know the true identities of the members of Shining Path's central committee. Along with other documents captured, this provided them with several leads, resulting eventually in Guzmán's capture in 1992.

21. These two members were also women. Little research has been done on the role of women in Shining Path, which is remarkable for such a male-dominated society. Kirk (1993) provides an insightful journalistic account of the women of Shining Path.

22. Only six top leaders of Shining Path had been arrested prior to Guzmán's capture in September 1992. Three key leaders, Elena Iparraguirre, Laura Zambrano Padilla, and María Pantoja, were arrested with Guzmán on the evening of September 12. Most members of the central committee had been arrested by May 1998. *Reporte Especial,* No. 85 (May 1998), p. 10.

23. Polay had been arrested in the late 1980s, but regained his freedom along with 140 of his comrades during a daring prison escape in mid-1990. The details of the escape are skillfully treated in Alegría and Flakoff (1996).

24. IMASEN and APOYO polls gave Fujimori 74 and 75 percent approval ratings respectively in the aftermath of the arrest of Guzmán.

25. As cited from most major newspapers, DESCO database (March 31, 1993).

26. See Rospigliosi (1996) and Tapia (1997).

27. Human rights groups and security policy analysts documented this shift in the dynamic of state violence in the early 1990s (see, for example, Degregori and Rivera 1993), and it is corroborated in the Final Report of the CVR (2003).

28. This situation gave rise to the simultaneous uprisings in three Lima prisons in 1986, which was put down with excessive military force. Over 200 prisoners were killed, over half of these after

having surrendered to authorities (Amnesty International 1987; CVR 2003). On Shining Path's use of prisons as sites of indoctrination and recruitment, see Rénique (2003).

29. *Reporte Especial,* No. 13 (May 1992), pp. 6–7. See also Human Rights Watch (1992), pp. 8–11. This is one of the cases for which Fujimori is currently facing indictment by judicial authorities in Peru.

30. *Reporte Especial,* No. 14 (June 1992), pp. 9–11; Human Rights Watch (1992, 1993).

31. "Under this new definition, journalists or human rights activists could be charged with creating a state of anxiety or affecting Peru's international relations through their writings and could face prison terms of *not less than twenty years."* Americas Watch (1992:8). Italics in original.

32. This was later expanded to 30 days. Human Rights Watch (1993).

33. Human Rights Watch (1993); Burt (1994).

34. See Human Rights Watch (1995). The Final Report of the CVR (2003, Vol. I, Chaps. 1 and 3) notes that fully 68 percent of killings committed by government security forces were "targeted" killings, rather than indiscriminate violence. While this does not mean that those killed were in fact subversives, it does reflect a shift in government counterinsurgency policy, since most killings in the early to mid-1980s were primarily the result of indiscriminate violence.

35. On early peasant support for and growing resistance to Shining Path, see Berg (1986/1987); Isbell (1992); and Degregori (1989). On the *rondas campesinas,* see Degregori (1996).

36. According to General Ronaldo Rueda, then military commander of the Ayacucho region, over 5,000 Winchester rifles had been handed out to 1,900 self-defense committees by May 1993. As cited in *The Peru Report* (May 1993).

37. In 1993, 90 percent of recruits in the Ayacucho region were local residents (*The Peru Report,* May 1993). This new policy is also noted in Degregori and Rivera (1993). For a comprehensive discussion of the racist dimensions of the counterinsurgency during the mid-1980s, see the chapter "La Guerra Silenciosa" in Flores Galindo (1988).

38. On the cult of personality surrounding Guzmán, see Gorriti (1992, 1998). Degregori (1998) argues that Shining Path was so dependent on Guzmán as its leader and "guiding thought" that his arrest was a devastating and irrevocable blow to the organization.

39. These observations are based on interviews with shantytown residents; newspaper and electronic media accounts of these civic-action programs; and APRODEH (1994b).

40. With its declaration of Raucana as a "popular support base" and a number of provocative actions in the district (including street fights with police), Shining Path was clearly expecting the police and armed forces to act violently and arbitrarily against the local population, which they calculated would further polarize the situation and ultimately prove to their advantage. The armed forces, however, seemed to have learned that such arbitrary behavior was counterproductive and ultimately played into the hands of insurgent groups. In this sense, the civic-action campaigns were a crucial component to the modified counterinsurgency strategy adopted in the early 1990s.

41. APRODEH (1994b) notes that rural communities are often less approving of the civic-action campaigns than the urban poor.

42. These quotes are from the APRODEH study.

43. Interview, Lima (August 1994).

44. For an analysis of the role of FONCODES in building regime support, see Roberts (1995). Schady (1997) provides an analysis of FONCODES as a clientelistic device.

45. On the repentance law, see Rivera (1993) and Burt (1994).

46. Democracies must not be subject to the arbitrary power of nonelected officials, including the armed forces. This criteria was not considered in the original formulations of polyarchy as articulated by Dahl (1974) and others, but has been incorporated in new definitions of democracy such as those elaborated by Karl and Schmitter (1996).

47. On the concept of delegative democracy, see (O'Donnell 1994). On Peru as an example of illiberal democracy, see Zakaria (1997). On neopopulism, see Roberts (1995) and Weyland (1996).

48. This draws on Linz's typology of authoritarianism, which includes civil-military regimes as a broad category of authoritarian regime that may not contain all the elements of other similar types, such as bureaucratic authoritarianism. Rospigliosi (1996) makes a similar point about the imperatives of creating the semblance of democracy for international purposes given Washington's imperative in favor of elected governments.

49. Regime supporters sought to justify the Cantuta murders as a revenge killing by state security agents against Shining Path. According to this explanation, incensed over a Shining car bomb on Tarata Street in the residential district of Miraflores that resulted in the deaths of nearly two dozen people, individual members of the state security forces responded in kind by abducting and disappearing the Cantuta students, who they believed to be the Shining Path militants responsible for the car bomb attack. This argument sought to exploit and reinforce the growing "common sense" in favor of heavy-handed measures against the insurgency. This argument is made in General (ret.) Gastón Ibañez O'Brien, "Amnistía y unidad nacional," *Expreso* (Lima) (June 22, 1995). Congresswoman Martha Chávez, of the ruling Cambio 90-Nueva Mayoría party, repeated this explanation during an interview with the author (Lima, July 2, 1998).

50. Statement read by General Howard Rodríguez Málaga, commander of the First Military Region, to the Army High Command the day the tanks paraded Lima, April 21, 1993, as cited in APRODEH (1994a:23).

51. A few weeks later, from exile in Buenos Aires, Robles made public the name of his source— General Willy Chirinos, director of army intelligence when the Cantuta kidnappings took place. Robles said Chirinos attempted to deactivate the Colina death squad, but was dismissed by Montesinos. See *Caretas* (May 27, 1993).

52. The remains were discovered thanks to a map that, as was later discovered, was leaked to the press by a member of the SIE who was involved in the Cantuta operation. That agent, Mariella Barreto, was found decapitated on the streets of Lima in late 1996, presumably in retaliation for her revelation of the location of the bodies. Another agent, Leonor La Rosa, was severely tortured at the hands of her superiors, also in retaliation for her leaks to the press about the activities of the Grupo Colina.

53. Security forces arrested a young Evangelist claiming he was the author of the map and a member of Shining Path; Attorney General Blanca Nélida Colán threatened to sue the independent newspaper that discovered the bodies at Cieneguilla based on the map that, it was later revealed, was leaked by a member of the intelligence services.

54. The bodies were virtually unrecognizable. However, a set of keys found on one of the bodies discovered in Cieneguilla was recognized by Raida Cóndor as belonging to her son, one of the disappeared students. One of the keys effectively opened the door to her son's dorm room, proving that these were the bodies of the Cantuta students. Interview with Raida Cóndor, Lima (July 1998); see also APRODEH (1994a).

55. Based on polls from IMASEN and Instituto APOYO.

56. Concerns about the role of the military and the SIN in the electoral process were voiced as early as 1998. See, for example, Coordinadora Nacional de Derechos Humanos (1998).

# Nine   *Quien Habla es Terrorista*: The Politics of Fear

1. This chapter was first published as "'Quien habla es terrorista': The Political Use of Fear in Fujimori's Peru," by Jo-Marie Burt, from *Latin American Research Review* 41:3 (2006): 32–62. Reprinted with permission.

2. This widespread support for the Fujimori regime has been amply documented and analyzed (Stokes 2001; Carrión 1999; Panfichi 1997; and Roberts 1995).

3. Interview, Villa El Salvador (May 1994).

4. Civil society refers to uncoerced collective action around shared interests, purposes, and values. While the institutional forms of civil society are, in theory, distinct from those of the state, family, and market, in practice, the boundaries between state, civil society, family, and market are often complex, blurred, and negotiated.

5. These concepts are drawn from social movement theory. See, for example, McAdam, Tarrow, and Tilly (2001).

6. On the free-rider problem in collective action, see Olson (1971).

7. For an analysis of the Fujimori regime's interactions with women's groups, see Blondet (2002).

8. For Keane's notion of civil and uncivil society, see note 5, p. 243.
9. There is a vast literature on Shining Path; see especially the essays in Palmer (1992) and Stern (1998). McClintock (1998) offers an insightful comparative discussion of Shining Path. Degregori (1990) and Gorriti (1990, 1999) provide compelling analyses of the insurgency's early years.
10. For an analysis of Shining Path's attempts to destroy such alternative projects, see Rénique (1998) and Burt (1998).
11. The policy of arming the *rondas* actually began in the last year of the García administration, but became a systematic aspect of the state's counterinsurgency policy under Fujimori (Tapia 1997; CVR 2003).
12. This assertion is based on interviews with human rights activists in 1988 and 1989, and review of numerous human rights reports. See Comité de Familiares (1985); Amnesty International (2003, 1996, 1990, 1989); Human Rights Watch (1997, 1995, 1992); and CVR (2003).
13. Interview, Villa El Salvador (December 2002).
14. This observation is based on interviews and informal discussions with IU activists in 1988 and 1989.
15. One prevailing hypothesis, known as the "theory of two demons," suggests that left-wing guerrilla violence is equally responsible for the massive human rights violations committed by the military regimes in the Southern Cone. This view is widely criticized, however, given that violence was primarily exercised by state agents against unarmed civilians. See Izaguirre (1998).
16. For literature on this period, see Ballón (1986); Degregori et al. (1986); Stokes (1995); and Schönwälder (2002).
17. Interview, Sofia Macher, Coordinadora Nacional de Derechos Humanos, Lima (June 24, 1998).
18. An important exception is Conaghan (2002), which analyzes the regime's control over the print and electronic media.
19. On the regime's antipolitics discourse, see Panfichi (1997) and Degregori (2001).
20. As cited from major Lima newspapers, DESCO database (March 31, 1993).
21. As quoted in *The San Francisco Chronicle* (April 11, 1995).
22. As quoted in *The Dallas Morning News* (November 28, 1993), p. B5.
23. As cited, *La República,* DESCO Database (May 27, 1996).
24. Society-centered explanations of support for Fujimori emphasize the regime's policy successes (Carrión 1999) while other explanations focus on the regime's provision of material goods in exchange for votes (Roberts 1995). Both are important yet they do not account for the ways in which state power and official discourse may constitute—or in the words of Herman and Chomsky (1988), manufacture—consent.
25. As quoted in *Latin American Weekly Report*, WR-91-41 (October 24, 1991), p. 11.
26. As cited in APRODEH (1995).
27. *Oiga* (December 21, 1992).
28. Coordinadora Nacional de Derechos Humanos, "Percepción de los derechos humanos en los estratos populares," 1995. This document reports on the findings of eight focus groups of men and women randomly selected from Lima's popular sectors between September 12 and 19, 1995.
29. Ibid.
30. In the 1980s, while there was no formal amnesty law, the handful of cases involving accusations of human rights violations by military or police personnel were transferred to military courts, where impunity was assured. Often military courts would claim jurisdiction over cases being pursued in the regular judicial system; the supreme court would routinely rule in favor of military jurisdiction, thus providing institutional cover for impunity.
31. Interview, Susana Villarán, Lima (August 1, 2000).
32. Interview, Lima (August 8, 2000).
33. Severe human rights violations occurred in the context of Operation Aries. See Coordinadora (1995).
34. Interview, Anel Townsend, Lima (June 24, 1998).

35. Interview, Jorge Salazar, Instituto de Prensa y Sociedad, Lima (August 2000). Cable TV station Canal N was one of the few broadcast agencies that maintained an independent profile and televised reports critical of the regime, but few Peruvians have access to Cable TV, limiting its reach and therefore its impact. Its impact on middle-class sectors, however, was probably quite significant in crystallizing antiregime sentiment.
36. Interview, Miguel Jugo, Director, APRODEH, Lima (June 25, 1998).
37. Interview, congresswoman Anel Townsend (June 24, 1998).
38. Interview, Susana Villarán, Lima (June 23, 1998).

## Ten   The Authoritarian State and the Resurgence of Civil Society

1. Conaghan (2001) describes this process.
2. On the IACHR statement, see Agence France Press (June 5, 1997). On the U.S. response, see *The Washington Times* (June 17, 1997). According to the *Times* report, a shocked Fujimori pressed President Clinton's special envoy to Latin America, Thomas McLarty, on whether Jett's comments represented official U.S. policy, to which McLarty replied that they did.
3. America Television, Lima, in Spanish (June 5, 1997) as reported in BBC Summary of World Broadcasts (June 6, 1997).
4. *Latin American Weekly Report*, WR-97-23 (June 10, 1997), p. 268.
5. For a detailed study of the impact of violence on the universities, see CVR (2003: Vol. 3, Ch. 3.6).
6. Each of these cases is extensively documented in the Final Report of the Truth CVR. On the case of the university students of Huancayo, see CVR (2003: Vol. 5, Ch. 2.21). On the case of Castillo Páez, see CVR (2003: Vol. 3, Ch. 3, p. 6). On the Cantuta case, see CVR (2003: Vol. 5, Ch. 2.19). As of this writing, the Ernesto Castillo Páez case is the sole instance in which agents of the state who committed human rights violations have been tried and convicted; notably this case involved members of the national police, not members of the armed forces (Rivera Paz 2006).
7. Interview, Lima (December 16, 2002).
8. Interview, Gisela Ortíz, Lima (August 2, 2000).
9. Interview, Alejandra Alayza, Lima (August 8, 2000).
10. Interview, Lima (August 14, 2000).
11. As cited, Agence France Presse (July 14, 1997).
12. As cited, Agence France Presse (July 14, 1997).
13. As cited, Associated Press (July 14, 1997).
14. For Hermoza's full statement, see Radioprogramas del Perú, Lima (July 17, 1997), cited in BBC Summary of World Broadcasts (July 19, 1997) .
15. Poll by Apoyo, cited in Agence France Presse (July 19, 1997).
16. Interview, Alejandra Alayza, Lima (August 8, 2000).
17. Interview, Anel Townsend, Lima (June 24, 1998).
18. Interview, Alejandra Alayza, Lima (August 8, 2000).
19. Interview, Lima (August 12, 2000).
20. Interview, Lima (August 8, 2000).
21. Interview, Lima (August 8, 2000).
22. Interview, Gisela Ortíz, Lima (August 2, 2000).
23. The classic work on political opportunity structure is Tarrow (1994).
24. For a discussion of the utility of relational analysis for understanding revolutions and other forms of collective action, see Emirbayer and Goodwin (1996) and Tilly (2003).
25. Rospigliosi (2000) notes that this was not a case of government manipulation of the media but of active media collusion in the preparation of disinformation. The numerous videotapes documenting Montesinos's interactions with many of Peru's top media moguls have confirmed this.
26. Degregori (2001) analyzes the manipulation of the Feliciano arrest and the regime's broader attempt to portray Fujimori and the military as saviors of the nation. See also Burt (1998).

27. While some of the print media was able to maintain independence, as was the case with *La República* and *El Comercio*, for example, virtually all the electronic media came under governmental control. One important exception was Canal N, which aired only on Cable TV and thus was accessible only to those who paid for it. The yellow press that emerged in this period was largely the creation of the SIN. See Rospigliosi (2000).

28. As cited in Degregori (2001:159).

29. Some speculated that the ease with which protestors were able to enter the courtyard of the presidential palace was a set-up meant to incite protestors into violence and so discredit them in the eyes of the broader population. It may have also been designed to instigate divisions within the opposition, which remained fragmented and divided over tactics and over who should lead the struggle against Fujimori. *Latin American Weekly Report*, WR-98-39 (October 6, 1998), p. 461.

30. *Expreso* (October 1, 1998).

31. Interview, Carlos Basombrío, Lima (August 8, 2000).

32. Interview, Isaías Rojas, Lima (August 17, 2000).

33. Interview, Sofía Macher, Lima (August 10, 2000).

34. Youngers (2003) provides a detailed study of the evolution of the human rights movement in Peru.

35. For an analysis of the Defensoría in Peru and elsewhere in the Andean region as a counterweight to state abuses, see Ungar (2004).

36. Interview, Lima (August 8, 2000). The interviewee also noted, however, that political divisions within the different student organizations—including discrepancies with the national level Federation of Peruvian Students, which has long been controlled by the Maoist Red Fatherland—made such unity virtually impossible. Overlaid were class-based differences, diverse political tendencies, and individual desires to use the organization as a springboard for their own political career.

37. Based on a review of monthly public opinion polls by Instituto APOYO.

38. Interview, Alejandra Alayza, Lima (August 8, 2000).

39. The framing of social protest—the way in which issues are framed, or rhetorically articulated and presented in the public realm—is a central aspect of successful social mobilization. See Tarrow (1994).

40. On the relationship between the business elite and the Fujimori regime over time, see Durand (1997 and 2002).

41. NotiSur, *Latin American Data Base*, 8:1 (January 9, 1998).

42. NotiSur, *Latin American Data Base*, 8:1 (January 9, 1998).

43. NotiSur, *Latin American Data Base*, 8:31 (August 28, 1998).

44. NotiSur, *Latin American Data Base*, 8:31 (August 28, 1998).

45. For a detailed analysis of this process, see Conaghan (2005).

46. Agence France Press (April 11, 2000).

47. Agence France Press (April 12, 2000).

48. Interview, Alejandra Alayza (August 8, 2000).

49. *Referendum* (May 23, 2000), as cited in Degregori (2001:174).

50. *LaChuchi* (May 30, 2000) as cited in Degregori (2001:174).

51. Interview, Lima (August 12, 2000).

52. On U.S. policy toward Peru, see McClintock and Vallas (2003).

53. For an analysis of Peru's police reforms since 2001, see Costa (2006) and Costa and Neild (2005).

# BIBLIOGRAPHY

Abugattás, Juan. "El Leviatán apedreado: la polémica sobre el estado en el Perú." In *Estado y Sociedad: Relaciones Peligrosas*, edited by Juan Abugattás. Lima: DESCO, 1990: 81–107.

Adelman, Jeremy. "Unfinished States in the Andes." In *State and Society in Conflict: The Andes in Comparative Perspective*, edited by Paul Drake and Eric Hershberg. Pittsburgh: University of Pittsburgh Press, 2006: 41–73.

Afflito, Frank. "The Homogenizing Effects of State-Sponsored Terrorism: The Case of Guatemana." In *Death Squad: The Anthropology of State Terror*, edited by Jeffrey A. Sluka. University Park, PA: University of Pennsylvania Press, 2000: 114–126.

Aguero, Felipe and Jeffrey Stark, eds. *Fault Lines of Democracy in Post-transition Latin America*. Coral Gables, FL: North-South Center Press, 1998.

Alegría, Ciro. *Broad and Alien is the World*. New York: Farrar & Rinehart, 1941.

Alegría, Claribel and Darwin Flakoll. *Tunnel to Canto Grande: The Story of the Most Daring Prison Escape in Latin American History*. Willimantic, CT: Curbstone Press, 1996.

Americas Watch. *Abdicating Democratic Authority*. New York: Human Rights Watch, 1984.

Amnesty International. *The Prison Massacres in Peru*. New York: Amnesty International, 1987.

———. *Peru: Human Rights in a State of Emergency*. New York: Amnesty International, 1989.

———. *Peru: Attacks on Human Right's Defenders 1988–1990*. New York: Amnesty International, 1990.

———. *Peru: Summary of Amnesty International's Concerns 1980–1995*. New York: Amnesty International, 1996.

Arendt, Hannah. *On Violence*. New York: Harcourt Bruce Jovanovich, 1970.

Armony, Ariel. *The Dubious Link: Civic Engagement and Democratization*. Stanford, CA: Stanford University Press, 2004.

Asociación Pro-Derechos Humanos (APRODEH). *De la tierra brotó la verdad. Crimen e impunidad en el caso La Cantuta*. Lima: APRODEH, 1994a.

———. "Informe Final: Rastrillajes y Acción Cívica." Mimeograph. January 1994b.

Atwood, Roger. "Democratic Dictators: Authoritarian Politics in Peru from Leguía to Fujimori." *SAIS Review* 21:2 (2001): 155–176.

Azarya, Victor. "Reordering State-Society Relations: Incorporation and Disengagement." In *The Precarious Balance: State and Society in Africa*, edited by Donald Rothchild and Naomi Chazan. Boulder: Westview Press, 1988: 2–21.

Azarya, Victor and Naomi Chazan. "Disengagement from the State in Africa: Reflections on the Experience of Ghana and Guinea." In *The Precarious Balance: State and Society in Africa*, edited by Donald Rothchild and Naomi Chazan. Boulder: Westview Press, 1988: 106–131.

Balbi, Carmen Rosa. *Identidad Clasista en el Sindicalismo*. Lima: DESCO, 1989.

———. "Una inquietante encuesta de opinión." *QueHacer* 71 (1991): 40–45.

———. "Sendero en las Fábricas. Encendiendo la Mecha." *QueHacer* 77 (1992): 76–88.

———. "Politics and Trade Unions in Peru." In *The Peruvian Labyrinth: Polity, Society, Economy*, edited by Maxwell Cameron and Philip Mauceri. University Park, PA: Pennsylvania State University Press, 1997: 134–151.

Ballón, Eduardo, ed. *Movimientos Sociales y Democracia: La Fundación de un Nuevo Orden*. Lima: DESCO, 1986.

———. *Movimientos Sociales: Elementos para una Relectura*. Lima: DESCO, 1990.

Barrig, Maruja. "Democracia Emergente y el movimiento de mujeres." In *Movimientos Sociales y Democracia: La Fundación de un Nuevo Orden,* edited by Eduardo Ballón. Lima: DESCO, 1986: 143–183.

———. *De vecinas a ciudadanas: la mujer en el desarrollo urbano.* Lima: SUMBI, 1988.

———. "The Difficult Equilibrium between Bread and Roses: Women's Organizations and the Transitions from Dictatorship to Democracy in Peru." In *The Women's Movement in Latin America: Feminism and the Transition to Democracy,* edited by Jane S. Jaquette. Boulder: Westview Press, 1991: 114–148.

Basadre, Jorge. *Perú: Problema y posibilidad.* 3rd ed. Lima: Banco Internacional del Perú, 1978.

Bedoya, Jaime. "Más inseguros que nunca." *Debate* 11:55 (March/May 1989).

Berg, Ronald. "Sendero Luminoso and the Peasantry of Andahuaylas." *Journal of Inter-American Studies and World Affairs* 28 (Winter 1986/1987): 164–196.

———. "Peasant Responses to Shining Path in Andahuaylas." In *Shining Path of Peru,* edited by David Scott Palmer. New York: St. Martin's Press, 1992: 83–104.

Blondet, Cecilia. *Muchas vidas construyendo una identidad: Las mujeres pobladoras de un barrio limeño.* Lima: Instituto de Estudios Peruanos, 1986.

———. *El encanto del dictador. Mujeres y política en la década de Fujimori.* Lima: Instituto de Estudios Peruanos, 2002.

Bonilla, H. and P. Drake, eds. *El APRA: De la ideología a la praxis.* Lima: CLAHES, CILAS, and Nuevo Mundo Editoriales, 1989.

Bourque, Susan C. and Kay B. Warren. "Democracy without Peace: The Cultural Politics of Terror in Peru." *Latin American Research Review* 24:1 (1989): 7–34.

Bourricaud, François. *Poder y sociedad en el Perú.* Lima: Instituto de Estudios Peruanos/Instituto Francés de Estudios Andinos, 1989.

Bright, Charles and Susan Harding. *State-Making and Social Movements.* Ann Arbor, MI: University of Michigan Press, 1984.

Burga, Manuel and Alberto Flores Galindo. *Apogeo y crisis de la república aristocrática.* 2nd ed. Lima: Ediciones Rikchay, 1981.

Burt, Jo-Marie. "Convulsion in the Andes: Promises and Repression in Peru." *Sojourners* 18:2 (1989): 8–10.

———. "Peru: Facade of Democracy Crumbles." *NACLA Report on the Americas* 26:1 (July 1992): 3–6.

———. "La Inquisición pos-senderista." *QueHacer* 92 (1994): 30–35.

———. "Peruvian Politics Beyond the Raids." *Newsday* (April 27, 1997a): G5.

———. "Political Violence and the Grassroots in Lima, Peru." In *The New Politics of Inequality in Latin America. Rethinking Participation and Representation,* edited by Douglas A. Chalmers, Carlos M. Vilas, Katherine Hite, Scott B. Martin, Kerianne Piester, and Monique Segarra. London: Oxford University Press, 1997b: 281–309.

———. "Shining Path and the 'Decisive Battle' for Lima's *Barriadas*: The Case of Villa El Salvador." In *Shining and Other Paths. War and Society in Peru, 1980–1995,* edited by Steve Stern. Durham: Duke University Press, 1998: 267–306.

———. "State-Making against Democracy: The Case of Fujimor's Peru." In *Politics in the Andes: Identity, Conflict, Reform,* edited by Jo-Marie Burt and Philip Mauceri. Pittsburgh: University of Pittsburgh Press, 2004: 247–268.

———. "Plotting Fear. The Uses of Terror in Peru." *NACLA Report on the Americas* 38:6 (May/June 2005): 32–37.

———. "The Political Uses of Terror: The Case of Peru." *Playing Politics with Terrorism,* edited by George Kassimeris. New York: Columbia University Press, 2007: 62–100.

Burt, Jo-Marie and César Espejo. "The Struggles of a Self-built Community." *NACLA Report on the Americas* 28:4 (January/February 1995): 19–25.

Burt, Jo-Marie and José López Ricci. "Peru: Shining Path after Guzmán." *NACLA Report on the Americas* 28:3 (November/December 1994): 6–9.

Burt, Jo-Marie and Aldo Panfichi. *Peru: Caught in the Crossfire.* St. Louis, MO: Peru Peace Network, 1992.

Cáceres, Armando and Carlos E. Paredes. "The Management of Economic Policy, 1985–1989." In *Peru's Path to Recovery: A Plan for Economic Stabilization and Growth,* edited by Carlos E. Paredes and Jeffrey D. Sachs. Washington, DC: Brookings Institute, 1991: 80–113.

Caldeira, Teresa. *City of Walls: Crime, Segregation and Citizenship in Sao Paolo.* Berkeley: University of California Press, 2000.

Calderón, Julio and Rocío Valveavellano. *Izquierda y Democracia entre la Utopia y la Realidad: Tres municipios en Lima.* Lima: Instituto de Desarrollo Urbano, 1991.

Callaghy, Thomas. "Africa: Back to the Future." *Journal of Democracy* 5:4 (October 1994): 133–145.

Cameron, Maxwell A. *Democracy and Authoritarianism in Peru: Political Coalitions and Social Change.* New York: Palgrave MacMillan, 1994.

———. "Political and Economic Origins of Regime Change in Peru: The Eighteenth Brumaire of Alberto Fujimori." In *The Peruvian Labyrinth: Polity, Society, Economy,* edited by Maxwell Cameron and Philip Mauceri. University Park, PA: Pennsylvania State University Press, 1997: 37–69.

———. "Exogenous Regime Breakdown: The Vladivideo and the Fall of Peru's Fujimori." In *The Fujimori Legacy: The Rise of Electoral Authoritarianism in Peru,* edited by Julio Carrión. University Park, PA: Pennsylvania State University Press, 2006: 268–293.

Cameron, Maxwell and Philip Mauceri. "Introduction." In *The Peruvian Labyrinth: Polity, Society, Economy,* edited by Maxwell Cameron and Philip Mauceri. University Park, PA: Pennsylvania State University Press, 1997: 1–11.

Campbell, Bruce B. and Arthur D. Brenner, eds. *Death Squads in Global Perspective: Murder with Deniability.* New York: Palgrave Macmillan, 2003.

Caro, Nelly. *Democracia interna y las organizaciones de sobrevivencia en Lima.* MA Thesis, Sociology Department, Catholic University of Peru, 1993.

Carr, Barry and Steve Ellner, eds. *The Latin American Left: From the Fall of Allende to Perestroika.* New York: Westview Press, 1993.

Carrión, Julio. "La popularidad de Fujimori en Tiempos Ordinarios, 1993–1997." In *El juego político: Fujimori, la oposición y las reglas,* edited by Fernando Tuesta Soldevilla. Lima: Fundación Friedrich Ebert, 1999: 231–246.

Chalmers, Douglas. "The Politicized State in Latin America." In *Authoritarianism and Corporatism in Latin America,* edited by James M. Malloy. Pittsburgh: University of Pittsburgh Press, 1977: 47–87.

Chávez de Paz, Dennis. *Juventud y Terrorismo: Características sociales de los condenados por terrorismo y otros delitos.* Lima: Instituto de Estudios Peruanos, 1989.

Chazan, Naomi. "Patterns of State-Society Incorporation and Disengagement in Africa." In *The Precarious Balance: State and Society in Africa,* edited by Donald Rothchild and Naomi Chazan. Boulder: Westview Press, 1988: 121–148.

Cohen, Jean. "Strategy or Identity: New Theoretical Paradigms and Contemporary Social Movements." *Social Research* 52:4 (Winter 1985): 663–716.

Collier, David. *Squatters and Oligarchs: Authoritarian Rule and Policy Change in Peru.* Baltimore: Johns Hopkins University Press, 1976.

Collier, David and Steven Levitsky. "Democracy with Adjectives: Conceptual Innovation in Comparative Research." *World Politics* 49:3 (1997): 430–451.

———. "Trajectory of a Concept: 'Corporatism' in the Study of Latin American Politics." In *Latin America in Comparative Perspective. New Approaches to Methods and Analysis,* edited by Peter Smith. Boulder: Westview Press, 1998: 135–162.

Comisión de la Verdad y Reconciliación (CVR). *Final Report.* Lima: CVR, 2003.

Comisión Especial de Investigación y Estudio sobre la Violencia y Alternativas de Pacificación. *Violencia y Pacificación.* Lima: DESCO/Comisión Andina de Juristas, 1989.

———. *Violencia y pacificación en 1991.* Lima: Senate of the Republic, 1992.

Comisión Investigadora de grupos paramilitares. *Una lucha cívica contra la impunidad.* Lima, October 26, 1989.

Comité de Familiares de Presos Políticos de Izquierda Unida e independientes y el Sindicato de Trabajadores de Editora La República. *Presos políticos y derechos humanos: razones para una amnistía.* Lima, 1985.

Commission for Historical Clarification. *Guatemala: Memory of Silence. Report of the Commission for Historical Clarification, Conclusions and Recommendations.* Guatemala City: UN Office of Project Services, 1999.

Commission on the Truth for El Salvador. *From Madness to Hope: The 12-Year War in El Salvador: Report of the Commission on the Truth for El Salvador.* New York: UN Publications, 1993.

Committee to Protect Journalists (CPJ). "Peru." *Report on the Americas 2000.* New York: CPJ, 2000.

Conaghan, Catherine. "Making and Unmaking Authoritarian Peru: Re-election, Resistance and Regime Transition." *The North-South Agenda Papers* 47 (2001).

———. "Cashing in on Authoritarianism: Media Collusion in Fujimori's Peru." *Harvard International Journal of Press/Politics* 7:1 (2002): 115–125.

———. *Fujimori's Peru: Deception in the Public Sphere.* Pittsburgh: University of Pittsburgh Press, 2005.

Coordinadora Nacional de Derechos Humanos (CNDH). *Informe anual 1994. Informe sobre la situación de derechos humanos 1994.* Lima: CNDH, 1995.

———. *Informe anual 1996.* Lima: CNDH, 1997.

———. *Informe anual 1997. Situación de los derechos humanos en el Perú en 1997.* Lima: CNDH, 1998.

Coronel, José and Carlos Loayza. "Violencia política: formas de respuestas comunera en Ayacucho." In *Perú: el problema agrario en debate,* edited by Carlos Iván Degregori. Lima: Universidad Nacional de la Amazonía Peruana and Seminario Permanente de Investigación Agraria, 1992: 509–537.

Costa, Gino. "Two Steps Forward, One and a Half Steps Back: Police Reform in Peru, 2001–2004." *Civil Wars* 8:2 (June 2006): 215–230.

Costa, Gino and Rachel Neild. "Police Reform in Peru." *Australian and New Zealand Journal of Criminology* 38:2 (August 2005): 216–229.

Cotler, Julio. *Clases, Estado y Nación en el Perú.* Lima: Instituto de Estudios Peruanos, 1978a.

———. "A Structural-Historical Approach to the Breakdown of Democratic Institutions: Peru." In *The Breakdown of Democratic Regimes: Latin America,* edited by Juan J. Linz and Alfred Stepan. Baltimore: Johns Hopkins University Press, 1978b: 178–206.

———. "Military Interventions and 'Transfer of Power to Civilians' in Peru." In *Transitions from Authoritarian Rule: Latin America,* edited by Guillermo O'Donnell, Philippe C. Schmitter, and Laurence Whitehead. Baltimore: Johns Hopkins University Press, 1986.

———. "Los partidos políticos y la democracia en el Perú." In *Democracia, Sociedad y Gobierno en el Perú,* edited by Luis Pásara and Jorge Parodi. Lima: Centro de Estudios de Democracia y Sociedad, 1988: 151–191.

Crahan, Margaret. *Basic Needs and Human Rights in the Americas.* Washington, DC: Georgetown University Press, 1982.

CUAVES/CIDIAG. *Un Pueblo, Una Realidad: Villa El Salvador. Resultados del II Censo organizado por la CUAVES el 8 de abril de 1984.* Lima: CUAVES/CIDIAG, 1984.

Cueto, Marcos. *El Regreso de las Epidemias: Salud y Enfermedad en el Perú del Siglo XX.* Lima: Instituto de Estudios Peruanos, 1997.

Dahl, Robert. *Polyarchy.* New Haven: Yale University Press, 1971.

———. *After the Revolution? Authority in a Good Society,* 2nd rev. ed. New Haven: Yale University Press, 1990.

Degregori, Carlos Ivan. *Sendero Luminoso: I. Los hondos y mortales desencuentros; II. Lucha armada y utopía autoritaria.* Documento de trabajo No. 4 y 6. Lima: Instituto de Estudios Peruanos, 1986.

———. *Qué difícil es ser Dios. Ideología y violencia política en Sendero Luminoso.* Lima: El zorro de abajo ediciones, 1989.

———. *Ayacucho 1969–1979: El Surgimiento de Sendero Luminoso.* Lima: Instituto de Estudios Peruanos, 1990.

———. "Jóvenes y Campesinos ante la Violencia Política: Ayacucho 1980–1983." In *Poder y Violencia en los Andes,* edited by Henrique Urbano. Cuzco: Centro de Estudios Regionales Andinos Bartolomé de Las Casas, 1991a: 395–417.

———. "La Estrategia Urbana de Sendero: Al filo de la navaja." *QueHacer* 73 (1991b): 26–34.

———. "The Origin and Logic of Shining Path: Two Views." In *Shining Path of Peru,* edited by David Scott Palmer. New York: St. Martin's Press, 1992: 33–58.

———. "Harvesting Storms. Peasant *Rondas* and the Defeat of Sendero Luminoso in Ayacucho." In *Shining and Other Paths. War and Society in Peru, 1980–1995,* edited by Steve Stern. Durham: Duke University Press, 1998: 128–157.

———. *La década de la antipolítica. Auge y huida de Alberto Fujimori y Vladimiro Montesinos.* Lima: Instituto de Estudios Peruanos, 2001.

Degregori, Carlos Iván, José Coronel, Ponciano del Pino and Orin Starn. *Las rondas campesinas y la derrota de Sendero Luminoso.* Lima: Instituto de Estudios Peruanos, 1996.

Degregori, Carlos Iván and Carlos Rivera. *Fuerzas Armadas, Subversion y Democracia: 1980–1993, Documento de Trabajo No. 53*. Lima: Instituto de Estudios Peruanos, 1993.

Degregori, Carlos Iván and Romeo Grompone. *Elecciones 1990. Demonios y redentores en el nuevo Perú*. Lima: Instituto de Estudios Peruanos, 1991.

Degregori, Carlos Iván, Cecilia Blondet, and Nicolas Lynch. *Conquistadores de un nuevo mundo. De invasores a ciudadanos en San Martin de Porres*. Lima: Instituto de Estudios Peruanos, 1986.

de la Cadena, Marisol. *Indigenous Mestizos: The Politics of Race and Culture in Cuzco, Peru, 1919–1991*. Chapel Hill: Duke University Press, 2000.

de la Jara Basombrío, Ernesto. *Memoria y batallas en nombre de los inocentes. Perú 1992–2001*. Lima: Instituto de Defensa Legal, 2001.

de Soto, Hernando. *The Other Path: The Invisible Revolution in the Third World*. New York: Harper and Row Publishers, 1989.

del Pino, Ponciano. "Los campesinos en la guerra. O de como la gente comienza a ponerse macho." In *Perú: El problema agrario en debate*, edited by Carlos Iván Degregori. Lima: Universidad Nacional de la Amazonía Peruana and Seminario Permanente de Investigación Agraria, 1992: 487–508.

Delpino, Nena. "Las organizaciones femeninas por la alimentación: un menú sazonado." In *La Otra Cara de la Luna: Nuevos Actores Sociales en el Perú*, edited by Luis Pásara. Lima: Centro de Estudios de Democracia y Sociedad, 1991: 29–72.

Delpino, Nena and Luis Pásara. "El otro actor en escena: las ONGDs." In *La Otra Cara de la Luna: Nuevos Actores Sociales en el Perú*, edited by Luis Pásara. Lima: Centro de Estudios de Democracia y Sociedad, 1991: 154–173.

DESCO. *Violencia Política en el Perú, 1980–1988* (Tomo I). Lima: DESCO, 1989a.

———. *Violencia Política en el Perú, 1980–1988* (Tomo II). Lima: DESCO, 1989b.

Diez Canseco, Javier. "Reconozco errores pero no soy un arrepentido." *idéele* 88 (July 1996): 53–56.

Driant, Jean-Claude. *Las Barriadas de Lima: Historia e Interpretacion*. Lima: IFEA/DESCO, 1991.

Durand, Francisco. "The Growth and Limitations of the Peruvian Right." In *The Peruvian Labyrinth: Polity, Society, Economy*, edited by Maxwell Cameron and Philip Mauceri. University Park, PA: Pennsylvania State University Press, 1997: 152–175.

———. "Business and the Crisis of Peruvian Democracy." *Business and Politics* 4:3 (2002): 319–341.

Emirbayer, Mustafa and Jeffrey Goodwin. "Symbols, Positions, Objects: Toward a New Theory of Revolution and Collective Action." *History and Theory* 35:3 (October 1996): 358–374.

Evans, Peter. "The State as Problem and Solution: Predation, Embedded Autonomy and Structural Change." In *The Politics of Economic Adjustment: International Constraints, Distributive Conflicts, and the State*, edited by Stephen Haggard and Robert R. Kaufman. Princeton: Princeton University Press, 1992: 139–181.

———. "The Eclipse of the State? Reflections on Stateness in an Era of Globalization." *World Politics* 50:1 (1997): 62–87.

Evans, Peter, Deitrich Rueschemeyer, and Theda Skocpol, eds. *Bringing the State Back In*. Cambridge: Cambridge University Press, 1985.

Favre, Henri. "Perú: Sendero Luminoso y horizontes oscuros." *QueHacer* 31 (1984): 25–35.

Fernández Baca, Jorge and Jeanice Seinfeld, "Gasto social y políticas sociales en América Latina." *Desarrollo Social* 5 (June 1993).

Flores Galindo, Alberto. *Buscando un Inca*, 3rd ed. Lima: Editorial Horizonte, 1988.

———. *Reencontremos la dimensión utópica. Carta a los amigos*. December 14, 1989. Available at: <http://www.andes.missouri.edu/andes/Especiales/AFG_CartaAmigos.html>.

FONCODES, *El Mapa de la Inversión Social: Pobreza y Actuación de FONCODES a nivel departamental y provincial*. Lima: Instituto Cuanto and UNICEF, 1994.

Foreign Policy/The Fund for Peace, "The Failed States Index." *Foreign Policy* (July/August 2005). Available at http://www.foreignpolicy.com/story/cms.php?story_id=3098.

Foucault, Michel. *Discipline and Punish. The Birth of the Prison*. New York: Vintage Books, 1979.

Franco, Carlos. *Acerca del modo de pensar la democracia en América Latina*. Lima: Fundación Friedrich Ebert, 1998.

Galer, Norma and Pilar Nuñez, eds. *Mujer y Comedores Populares*. Lima: Servicios para el Desarrollo, 1989.

García, Alan. *A la inmensa mayoría*. Lima: Emi Ediciones, 1989.

Garretón, Manuel Antonio. "Fear in Military Regimes: An Overview." In *Fear at the Edge: State Terror and Resistance in Latin America*, edited by Juan E. Corradi, Manuel Garretón, and Patricia Weiss Fagen. Berkeley: University of California Press, 1992: 13–25.

Geertz, Clifford. *Negara: The Theater State in Nineteenth-Century Bali*. Princeton: Princeton University Press, 1980.

Godoy-Snodgrass, Angelina. *Popular Injustice: Violence, Community and Law in Latin America*. Stanford: Stanford University Press, 2006.

Goldstone, Jack A. "Theories of Revolution: The Third Generation." *World Politics* 32:3 (April 1980): 425–453.

Gonzales, José. "Guerrillas and Coca in the Upper Huallaga Valley." In *Shining Path of Peru*, edited by David Scott Palmer. New York: St. Martin's Press, 1992: 105–125.

González, Eduardo. "Heroes or Hooligans: Media Portrayals of Peruvian Youth." In *NACLA Report on the Americas* 32:1 (July/August 1998): 30–35.

González de Olarte, Efraín and Lilian Samamé. *El Péndulo Peruano: Políticas económicas, gobernabilidad y subdesarrollo, 1963–1990*. Lima: Consorcio de investigación económica y el Instituto de Estudios Peruanos, 1991.

Gorriti, Gustavo. "Sendero: ¿Qué Hacer?" *Posible* (1987).

———. *Sendero Luminoso: Historia de la Guerra Milenaria en el Perú*. Lima: APOYO, 1990.

———. "The Betrayal of Peru's Democracy: Montesinos as Fujimori's Svengali." *CovertAction Quarterly* 49 (Summer 1994): 4–12, 54–59.

———. *Shining Path: A History of the Millenarian War in Peru*. Chapel Hill: University of North Carolina Press, 1999.

Graham, Carol. "The APRA Government and the Urban Poor: The PAIT Programme in Lima's Pueblos Jóvenes." *Journal of Latin American Studies* 23 (February 1991): 91–130.

———. *Peru's APRA. Parties, Politics, and the Elusive Quest for Democracy*. Boulder: Lynne Rienner Publishers, 1992.

———. *Safety Nets, Politics, and the Poor. Transitions to Market Economies*. Washington, DC: Brookings Institute, 1994.

Gramsci, Antonio. *Selections from the Prison Notebooks*, 9th ed. New York: International Publishers, 1987.

Granados, Manuel Jesus. "El PCP Sendero Luminoso: Aproximaciones a su ideología." *Socialismo y Participación* 27 (March 1987): 15–30.

Grindle, Merilee. *Challenging the State: Crisis and Innovation in Africa and Latin America*. New York: Cambridge University Press, 1996.

Grompone, Romeo. *El velero en el viento: Política y sociedad en Lima*. Lima: Instituto de Estudios Peruanos, 1991.

Guzmán, Abimael. "La entrevista del siglo: El Presidente Gonzalo rompe el silencio." *El Diario* (July 1988): 2–47.

Guzman Bouvard, Marguerite. *Revolutionizing Motherhood: The Mothers of the Plaza De Mayo*. New York: Scholarly Resources, 1994.

Hagopian, Frances. "After Regime Change: Authoritarian Legacies, Political Representation, and the Democratic Future of South America." *World Politics* 45 (1993): 464–500.

———. *Traditional Politics and Regime Change in Brazil*. New York: Cambridge University Press, 1996.

Harding, Colin. "Antonio Díaz Martínez and the Ideology of Sendero Luminoso." *Bulletin of Latin American Research* 7:1 (1988): 65–73.

Haworth, Nigel. "Radicalization and the Left in Peru, 1976–1991." In *The Latin American Left: From the Fall of Allende to Perestroika*, edited by Barry Carr and Steve Ellner. New York: Westview Press, 1993: 41–59.

Herbst, Jeffrey. "Responding to State Failure in Africa." *International Security* 21:3 (Winter 1996/1997): 120–144.

Herman, Edward S. and Noam Chomsky. *Manufacturing Consent. The Political Economy of the Mass Media*. New York: Pantheon,1988.

Hoy-Wazelton, Sandra and William H. Wazelton. "Shining Path and the Marxist Left." In *Shining Path of Peru*, edited by David Scott Palmer. New York: St. Martin's Press, 1992: 225–242.

Huber Stephens, Evelyne. "The Peruvian Military Government, Labor Mobilization, and the Political Strength of the Left." *Latin American Research Review* 18:2 (1983): 57–93.

Huggins, Martha K. *Vigilantism and the State in Modern Latin America. Essays on Extralegal Violence.* New York: Praeger, 1991.

Human Rights Watch. *Peru under Fire: Human Rights since the Return to Democracy.* New York: Human Rights Watch, 1992.

———. *Human Rights in Peru: One Year after Fujimori's Coup.* New York: Human Rights Watch, 1993.

———. *Peru: The Two Faces of Justice.* New York: Human Rights Watch, 1995.

———. *Torture and Political Persecution in Peru.* New York: Human Rights Watch, 1997.

Huntington, Samuel P. *Political Order in Changing Societies.* New Haven: Yale University Press, 1968.

IACHR. *Caso Huilca Tecse vs. Perú.* Washington DC: Inter-American Commission on Human Rights (March 2005). Available at http://www.corteidh.or.cr/seriecpdf/seriec_121_esp.pdf.

International Commission of Jurists (ICJ). *Report of the International Commission of Jurists on the Administration of Justice in Peru.* Lima: ICJ, 1993.

Instituto Cuánto. *Niveles de Vida: Subidas y Caídas. ENNIV 1991.* Lima: Instituto Cuánto, 1993.

Instituto de Defensa Legal (IDL). *Peru 1989: En la espiral de la violencia.* Lima: IDL, 1990.

———. *Peru Hoy: En el oscuro sendero de la guerra.* Lima: IDL, 1992.

———. "Policía Nacional. ¿Reforma integral o retoque cosmético?" *ideéle* 79 (September 1995).

Instituto Democracia y Socialismo (IDS). *Peru: La Violencia Política vista desde el pueblo.* Lima: IDS, 1989.

Instituto Nacional de Estadística e Informática (INEI). *Mapa de Necesidades Básicas Insatisfechas de los Hogares a Nivel Distrital.* Lima: INEI, 1994.

———. *Perú: Compendio Estadístico 2005.* Lima: INEI, 2005.

Isbell, Billie Jean. "Shining Path and Peasant Responses in Rural Ayacucho." In *Shining Path of Peru,* edited by David Scott Palmer. New York: St. Martin's Press, 1992: 59–82.

Izaguirre, Inés. "Recapturing the Memory of Politics." *NACLA Report on the Americas* 31:6 (July/ August 1998): 28–34.

Jelín, Elizabeth. "The Minefields of Memory." *NACLA Report on the Americas* 32:2 (September/ October 1998): 23–29.

Karl, Terry Lyn and Philippe Schmitter. "What Democracy Is…and What It Is Not." In *The Global Resurgence of Democracy,* edited by Larry Diamand and Marc F. Plattner, 2nd ed. Baltimore: Johns Hopkins University Press, 1996: 49–62.

Kaufman, Robert. "Corporatism, Clientelism, and Partisan Conflict: A Study of Seven Latin American Countries." In *Authoritarianism and Corporatism in Latin America,* edited by James M. Malloy. Pittsburgh: University of Pittsburgh Press, 1977: 109–148.

Keane, John. "Despotism and Democracy." In *Civil Society and the State: New European Perspectives,* edited by John Keane. New York: Verso Press, 1988: 35–71.

———. *Reflections on Violence.* New York: Verso, 1996.

Kenney, Charles. "¿Por qué el autogolpe? Fujimori y en congreso, 1990–1992." In *La política bajo Fujimori: Partidos políticos y opinión pública,* edited by Fernando Tuesta. Lima: Fundación Friedrich Ebert, 1996: 75–104.

———. *Fujimori's Coup and the Breakdown of Democracy in Latin America.* Notre Dame: University of Notre Dame Press, 2004.

Kingston, Paul and Ian S. Spears, eds. *States-within-States: Incipient Political Entities in the Post–cold war Era.* New York: Palgrave Macmillan, 2004.

Kirk, Robin. *The Decade of Chaqwa: Peru's Internal Refugees.* Washington, DC: U.S. Committee for Refugees, 1991.

———. *Grabado en piedra: Las mujeres de Sendero Luminoso.* Lima: Instituto de Estudios Peruanos, 1993.

Lechner, Norbert. "Some People Die of Fear: Fear as a Political Problem." In *Fear at the Edge: State Terror and Resistance in Latin America,* edited by Juan E. Corradi, Manuel Garreton, and Patricia Weiss Fagen. Berkeley: University of California Press, 1992: 26–35.

Leeds, Elizabeth. "Cocaine and Parallel Polities in the Brazilian Urban Periphery: Constraints to Local-Level Democratization." *Latin American Research Review* 31:3 (Fall 1996): 47–83.

Leger, Kathryn. "Delincuencia y Desarrollo Urbano en el Perú." *El CIID informa* (October 1994): 26–27.

Levi, Margaret. *Of Rule and Revenue*. Berkeley: University of California Press, 1988.

Levitsky, Steven. "Fujimori and Post-party Politics in Peru." *Journal of Democracy* 10:3 (1999): 78–96.

Linz, Juan J. and Alfred Stepan. *Problems of Democratic Transition and Consolidation: Southern Europe, South America, and Post-communist Europe*. Baltimore: Johns Hopkins University Press, 1996.

Lipset, Seymour Martin and Stein Rokkan, eds. *Party Systems and Voter Alignments: Cross-National Perspectives*. New York: Free Press. 1967.

Lopez-Alves, Fernando. *State Formation and Democracy in Latin America, 1810–1900*. Chapel Hill: Duke University Press, 2000.

López Maya, Margarita and Luis Lander. "The Struggle for Hegemony in Venezuela." In *Politics in the Andes: Identity, Conflict, Reform*, edited by Jo-Marie Burt and Philip Mauceri. Pittsburgh: University of Pittsburgh Press, 2004: 207–227.

López Ricci, José. "Las Organizaciones Populares en San Martin de Porres." Informe de Investigación (MSS). Lima: Centro Alternativa, 1993.

Lowenthal, Abraham, ed. *The Peruvian Experiment: Continuity and Change under Military Rule*. Princeton: Princeton University Press, 1975.

Lynch, Nicolás. *La Transición Conservadora: Movimiento Social y Democracia en el Perú, 1975–1978*. Lima: El zorro de abajo ediciones, 1992.

Mainwaring, Scott. "Parties, Politicians and Electoral Systems: Brazil in Comparative Perspective." *Comparative Politics* 24:1 (October 1991): 21–44.

Mainwaring, Scott and Timothy R. Scully. *Building Democratic Institutions: Party Systems in Latin America*. Stanford: Stanford University Press, 1996.

Mainwaring, Scott and Frances Hagopian, eds. *The Third Wave of Democratization in Latin America: Advances and Setbacks*. New York: Cambridge University Press, 2005.

Mallon, Florencia E. *Peasant and Nation: The Making of Post-colonial Mexico and Peru*. Berkeley: University of California Press, 1995.

Malloy James M. and Catherine M. Conaghan. *Unsettling Statecraft: Democracy and Neoliberalism in the Central Andes*. Pittsburgh: University of Pittsburgh Press, 1995.

Mann, Michael. "The Autonomous Power of the State: Its Origins, Mechanisms and Results." In *States in History*, edited by John A. Hall. New York: Basil Blackwell, 1986: 109–136.

Manrique, Nelson. "La Década de la Violencia." *Márgenes* 5 (1989): 137–182.

———. *Vinieron los sarracenos: El universo mental de la conquista de América*. Lima: DESCO, 1993.

———. *El tiempo del miedo. La violencia política en el Perú, 1980–1996*. Lima: Fondo Editorial del Congreso del Perú, 2002.

Mao, Zedong. *Four Essays on Philosophy*. Honolulu, Hawaii: University Press of the Pacific, 1937; rpt. 2001.

March, James and Johan Olsen. *Rediscovering Institutions*. New York: Free Press, 1989.

Mariátegui, José Carlos. *Siete ensayos de interpretación de la realidad peruana*, 57th ed. Lima: Biblioteca Amauta, 1992.

Marshall, T.H. *Class, citizenship, and Social Development*. New York: Doubleday Press, 1965.

Marx, Karl. "The Eighteenth Brumaire of Louis Bonaparte." In *The Marx-Engels Reader*, edited by Robert C. Tucker, 2nd ed. New York: W.W. Norton and Co., 1978: 594–617.

Matos Mar, José. *Las barriadas de Lima 1957*, 2nd ed. Lima: Instituto de Estudios Peruanos, 1977.

———. *Desborde Popular y Crisis del Estado*. Lima: Instituto de Estudios Peruanos, 1984.

Mauceri, Philip. "State Reform, Coalitions, and the Neoliberal Autogolpe in Peru." *Latin American Research Review* 30:1 (1995): 7–37.

———. *State under Siege. Development and Policy Making in Peru*. New York: Westview Press, 1996.

———. "The Transition to 'Democracy' and the Failures of Institution Building." In *The Peruvian Labyrinth: Polity, Society, Economy*, edited by Maxwell Cameron and Philip Mauceri. University Park, PA: Pennsylvania State University Press, 1997: 13–36.

May, Rachel A. *Terror in the Countryside: Campesino Responses to Political Violence in Guatemala, 1954–1985*. Athens: Ohio University Press, 2001.

Mayer, Enrique. "Peru in Big Trouble: Mario Vargas Llosa's 'Inquest in the Andes' Reexamined." *Cultural Anthropology* 6:4 (1991): 466–504.

McAdam, Doug. "Conceptual Origins, Current Problems, Future Directions." In *Comparative Perspectives on Social Movements: Political Opportunities, Mobilizing Structures, and Cultural Framings*, edited by Doug McAdam, John D. McCarthy, and Mayer N. Zald. Cambridge: Cambridge University Press, 1996: 23–40.

McAdam, Doug, John D. McCarthy, and Mayer N. Zald. "Introduction: Opportunities, Mobilizing Structures and Framing Processes—Toward a Synthetic, Comparative Perspective on Social Movements." In *Comparative Perspectives on Social Movements: Political Opportunities, Mobilizing Structures, and Cultural Framings*, edited by Doug McAdam, John D. McCarthy, and Mayer N. Zald. Cambridge: Cambridge University Press, 1996: 1–22.

McAdam, Doug, Sidney Tarrow, and Charles Tilly. *Dynamics of Contention*. New York: Cambridge University Press, 2001.

McClintock, Cynthia. "Why Peasants Rebel: The Case of Peru's Sendero Luminoso." *World Politics* 3 (October 1984): 48–84.

———. "Peru's Sendero Luminoso Rebellion: Origins and Trajectory." In *Power and Popular Protest: Latin American Social Movements*, edited by Susan Eckstein. Berkeley: University of California Press, 1989a: 61–101.

———. "The Prospects for Democratic Consolidation in a 'Least Likely' Case: Peru." *Comparative Politics* 21:2 (January 1989b): 127–149.

———. "La voluntad política presidencial y la ruptura constitutional de 1992 en el Perú." In *Los enigmas del Poder: Fujimori 1990–1996*, edited by F. Tuesta Soldevilla. Lima: Fundación Friedrich Ebert, 1996: 53–72.

———. *Revolutionary Movements in Latin America: El Salvador's FMLN and Peru's Shining Path*. Washington, DC: U.S. Institute of Peace Press, 1998.

———. "Es autoritario el gobierno de Fujimori?" In *El juego político: Fujimori, la oposición y las reglas*, edited by F. Tuesta Soldevilla. Lima: Fundación Friedrich Ebert, 1999: 65–95.

McClintock, Cynthia and Abraham Lowenthal, eds. *The Peruvian Experiment Reconsidered*. Princeton: Princeton University Press, 1983.

McClintock, Cynthia and Fabian Vallas. *The United States and Peru: Cooperation at a Cost*. New York: Routledge, 2003.

McCormick, Gordon. *The Shining Path and the Future of Peru*. Santa Monica, CA: Rand Corporation, 1990.

———. *From the Sierra to the Cities: The Urban Campaign of the Shining Path*. Santa Monica, CA: Rand Corporation, 1992.

McSherry, J. Patrice. "Military Power, Impunity, and State-Society Change in Latin America." *Canadian Journal of Political Science* 25:3 (1992): 463–488.

———. *Incomplete Transition: Military Power and Democracy in Argentina*. New York: St. Martin's Press, 1997.

McSherry, J. Patrice and Raul Molina Mejia. "Introduction to Shadows of State Terrorism: Impunity in Latin America." *Social Justice* 26:4 (1999): 1–12.

Mendez, Juan E., Guillermo A. O'Donnell, and Paulo Sergio Pinheiro, eds. *The (Un)Rule of Law and the Underprivileged in Latin America*. Notre Dame: Helen Kellogg Institute of International Studies, University of Notre Dame Press, 1999.

Migdal, Joel. *Peasants, Politics, and Revolution. Pressures toward Political and Social Change in the Third World*. Princeton: Princeton University Press, 1974.

———. *Strong State and Weak Societies. State-Society Relations and State Capabilities in the Third World*. Princeton: Princeton University Press, 1988.

———. "The State in Society: An Approach to Struggles for Domination." In *State Power and Social Forces: Domination and Transformation in the Third World*, edited by Joel Migdal, Atul Kohli, and Vivienne Shue. Cambridge: Cambridge University Press, 1994: 7–34.

———. *State in Society. Studying How States and Societies Transform and Mutually Constitute One Another*. New York: Cambridge University Press, 2001.

Minc, Alain. *Le Nouveau Moyen Âge*. Paris: Gallimard, 1993.

Ministerio de la Presidencia. "Lineamientos Básicos de la Política Social." Mimeograph, Lima, November 1993.

Mishal, Shaul and Avraham Sela. *Palestinian Hamas: Vision, Violence, and Coexistence*. New York: Columbia University Press, 2000.

Montoya, David and Carlos Reyna. "Sendero: Informe de Lima." *QueHacer* 76 (1992): 34–55.

Moore, Barrington. *The Social Bases of Democracy and Dictatorship. Lord and Peasant in the Making of the Modern World.* Boston, MA: Beacon Press, 1966.

———. *Injustice. The Social Bases of Obediance and Revolt.* New York: M.E. Sharp, 1978.

Moulián, Tomás. "A Time of Forgetting: The Myths of the Chilean Transition." *NACLA Report on the Americas* 32:2 (September/October 1998): 16–22.

National Commission on the Disappearance of Persons. *Nunca Más: Informe de la Comisión Nacional sobre la Desaparición de Personas.* 14th ed. Buenos Aires: Editorial Universitaria de Buenos Aires, 1986.

National Commission for Truth and Reconciliation. *Informe de la Comisión Nacional de Verdad y Reconciliación.* Santiago, Chile: Ministerio Secretaría General de Gobierno, 1991.

Nelson, Diane. *A Finger in the Wound: Body Politics in Quincentennial Guatemala.* Berkeley: University of California Press, 1999.

Nieto, Jorge. *Izquierda y Democracia en el Perú, 1975–1982.* Lima: DESCO, 1983.

Nordstrom, Carol. "The Backyard Front." In *Paths to Domination, Resistance and Terror*, edited by Carol Nordstrom and Joann Martin. Berkeley: University of California Press, 1992: 260–274.

———. *A Different Kind of War Story.* University Park, PA: University of Pennsylvania Press, 1997.

Nordstrom, Carol and Antonius C.G.M. Robben, eds. *Fieldwork under Fire: Contemporary Studies of Violence and Culture.* Berkeley: University of California Press, 1996.

Nordstrom, Carolyn and Joann Martin, eds. *The Paths to Domination, Resistance, and Terror.* Berkeley: University of California Press, 1992.

Obando, Enrique. "Civil-Military Relations in Peru, 1980–1996: How to Control and Coopt the Military (and the Consequences of Doing So)." In *Shining and Other Paths. War and Society in Peru, 1980–1995*, edited by Steve Stern. Durham: Duke University Press, 1998: 385–410.

O'Donnell, Guillermo. "On the State, Democratization, and Some Conceptual Problems: A Latin American View with Glances at Some Postcommunist Countries." *World Development* 21 (1993): 1355–1369.

———. "Delegative Democracy." *Journal of Democracy* 5:1 (January 1994): 55–69.

———. "Horizontal Accountability in New Democracies." *The Journal of Democracy* 9:3 (1998): 112–126.

———. *Counterpoints. Selected Essays on Authoritarianism and Democratization.* Notre Dame: Helen Kellogg Institute of International Studies, University of Notre Dame Press, 1999.

O'Donnell, Guillermo, Philippe C. Schmitter, and Laurence Whitehead. *Transitions from Authoritarian Rule: Latin America.* Baltimore: Johns Hopkins University Press, 1986.

Offe, Clause. *Disorganized Capitalism.* Oxford: Oxfor d University Press, 1985.

Oliart, Patricia. "'A President Like You': Fujimori's Popular Appeal." *NACLA Report on the Americas* 30:1 (July/August 1996): 18–19.

———. "Alberto Fujimori: The Man Peru Needed?" In *Shining and Other Paths. War and Society in Peru, 1980–1995*, edited by Steve Stern. Durham: Duke University Press, 1998: 411–424.

Olivera, Luis and Eduardo Ballón. "Lima y su organización popular." Paper presented at the Foro de Iberoamérica, Participación Ciudadano y Movimientos Sociales en las Metropolis Latinoamericanos, Salamanca, October 1993.

Olson, Mancur. *The Logic of Collective Action: Public Goods and the Theory of Groups.* Cambridge, MA: Harvard University Press, 1971.

Otárola Peñaranda, Alberto. "El otro desborde popular: Violencia urbana." *PeruPaz* 3:18 (January 1994).

Palmer, David Scott. "Rebellion in Rural Peru: The Origins and Evolution of Sendero Luminoso." *Comparative Politics* 18:2 (January 1986): 127–146.

Palmer, David Scott. *Shining Path of Peru.* New York: St. Martin's Press, 1992.

Panfichi, Aldo. "The Authoritarian Alternative: Anti-politics among the Popular Sectors of Lima." In *The New Politics of Inequality in Latin America. Rethinking Participation and Representation,* edited by Douglas A. Chalmers, Carlos M. Vilas, Katherine Hite, Scott B. Martin, Kerianne Piester, and Monique Segarra. London: Oxford University Press, 1997.

Parodi, Jorge. "*Ser obrero es algo relativo.*" *Obreros, clasismo y política.* Lima: Instituto de Estudios Peruanos, 1986.

————. "Entre la utopía y la tradición: izquierda y democracia en los municipios de los pobladores." In *Los pobres, la ciudad y la política*, edited by Jorge Parodi. Lima: Centro de Estudios de Democracia y Sociedad, 1993: 121–203.

Parodi, Jorge and Walter Twanama. "Los pobladores, la ciudad y la política: un estudio de actitudes." In *Los pobres, la ciudad y la política*, edited by Jorge Parodi. Lima: Centro de Estudios de Democracia y Sociedad, 1993: 19–89.

Pásara, Luis. "La libanización de la democracia en el Perú." In *Democracia, Sociedad y Gobierno en el Peru*, edited by Luis Pásara and Jorge Parodi. Lima: Centro de Estudios de Democracia y Sociedad, 1988: 19–52

————. *La izquierda en la escena pública.* Lima: Centro de Estudios de Democracia y Sociedad / Fundación Freidrich Ebert, 1989.

————. "El doble sendero de la izquierda peruana." *Nueva Sociedad* 106 (1990): 58–72.

Pásara, Luis and Alonso Zarzar, "Ambigüedades, Contradicciones e Incertidumbres." In *La Otra Cara de la Luna: Nuevos Actores Sociales en el Perú*, edited by Luis Pásara. Lima: Centro de Estudios de Democracia y Sociedad, 1991: 174–203.

Pastor, Manuel, Jr. and Carol Wise. "Peruvian Economic Policy in the 1980s: From Orthodoxy to Heterodoxy and Back." *Latin American Research Review* 27:2 (1992): 83–117.

Payne, Leigh. *Uncivil Movements: The Armed Right Wing and Democracy in Latin America.* Baltimore: Johns Hopkins University Press, 2000.

Pease García, Henry. *Los años de la langosta: La escena política del fujimorismo.* Lima: La Voz Ediciones, 1994.

Pedraglio, Santiago. "Violencia y pacificación." *ideéle* 78 (August 1995).

Pinheiro, Paolo Sérgio. "Democracy without Citizenship." *NACLA Report on the Americas* 30:2 (September/October 1996): 17–23.

Pizarro, Eduardo. *Insurgencia sin revolución: La guerrilla colombiana en una perspectiva comparada.* Bogotá: Tercer Mundo Editores/IEPRI, 1996.

Pizzorno, Alejassandro. "Interest and Parties in Pluralism." In *Organizing Interests in Western Europe. Pluralism, Corporatism and the Transformation of Politics*, edited by Suzanne Berger. Cambridge: Cambridge University Press, 1981: 249–284.

Popkin, Samuel. *The Rational Peasant: The Political Economy of Rural Society in Vietnam.* Berkeley: University of California Press, 1979.

Portes, Alejandro. "Latin American Urbanization in the Years of Crisis." *Latin American Research Review* 24:3 (1989): 7–45.

Przeworski, Adam. "Some Problems in the Study of the Transition to Democracy." In *Transitions from Authoritarian Rule: Comparative Perspectives,* edited by Guillermo O'Donnell, Philippe C. Schmitter, and Laurence Whitehead. Baltimore: Johns Hopkins University Press, 1986: 47–63.

Przeworski, Adam with Pranab Bardhan, Luiz Carlos Presser Pereira, László Bruszt, Jang Jip Choi, Ellen Turkish Comissio et al. *Sustainable Democracy.* New York: Cambridge University Press, 1995.

Reid, Michael. *Peru: Paths to Poverty.* London: Latin American Bureau, 1985.

Rénique, José Luis. "La Batalla por Puno." Seminario sobre la Violencia Política en el Perú: Analisis y Perspectivas. Organizado por el Centro Peruano de Estudios Sociales (CEPES) y el Instituto de Estudios Peruanos (IEP). Lima, de julio de 12–14, 1993.

————. "Apogee and Crisis of a 'Third Path': Mariateguismo, 'People's War,' and Counterinsurgency in Puno, 1987–1994." In *Shining and Other Paths. War and Society in Peru, 1980–1995,* edited by Steve Stern. Durham: Duke University Press, 1998: 307–338.

————. *La Voluntad Encarcelada: Las "Luminosas Trincheras de Combate" de Sendero Luminoso del Perú.* Lima: Instituto de Estudios Peruanos, 2003.

Reyna Izaguirre, Carlos. "Shining Path in the 21st Century: Actors in Search of a New Script." *NACLA Report on the Americas* 30:1 (July/August 1996): 37–40.

Riofrío, Gustavo. *Se busca terreno para próxima barriada.* Lima: DESCO, 1978.

Rivera, Carlos. "Arrepentidos: Luces y sombras." *ideele* 57 (October 1993).

————. "Una sentencia histórica: la condena por la separación de Castillo Páez." *ideele-mail* 487 (March 22, 2006). Available at: <http://www.justiciaviva.org.pe/nuevos/2006/marzo/23/idlmail487.doc.>

Roberts, Kenneth. "Neoliberalism and the Transformation of Populism in Latin America: The Peruvian Case." *World Politics* 48 (1995): 82–116.

———. *Deepening Democracy? The Modern Left and Social Movements in Chile and Peru.* Stanford: Stanford University Press, 1999.

Roberts, Kenneth and Mark Peceny. "Human Rights and United States Policy in Peru." In *The Peruvian Labyrinth: Polity, Society, Economy,* edited by Maxwell Cameron and Philip Mauceri. University Park, PA: Pennsylvania State University Press, 1997: 192–222.

Rochabrún, Guillermo. "Crisis, Democracy, and the Left in Peru." *Latin American Perspectives* 15 (1988): 77–96.

Roht-Arriaza, Noami. "Combatting Impunity." *Law and Contemporary Social Problems* 59:4 (1996): 93–102.

Rojas Pérez, Isaías. "Sendero(s) Luminoso(s): Guerra de supervivencia." *ideéle* 82–83 (December 1995): 98–105.

Rospigliosi, Fernando. *Juventud obrera y partidos de izquierda de la dictadura a la democracia.* Lima: Instituto de Estudios Peruanos, 1988.

———. "Izquierdas y clases populares: Democracia y subversión en el Perú." In *Clases populares, crisis y democracia en América Latina,* edited by Julio Cotler. Lima: Instituto de Estudios Peruanos, 1989: 103–142.

———. *Las fuerzas armadas y el 5 de abril. La percepción de la amenaza subversiva como una motivación golpista.* Documento de Trabajo No. 73. Lima: Instituto de Estudios Peruanos, 1996.

———. *La Operación Chavín de Huántar. Un caso ilustrativo de cómo funcionan las relaciones cívico militares en el Perú a las puertas del siglo XXI.* Lima: Instituto de Defensa Legal, 1998.

———. *El Arte del Engaño. Las relaciones entre los militares y la prensa.* Lima: Tarea, 2000.

———. *Montesinos y las Fuerzas Armadas.* Lima: Instituto de Estudios Peruanos, 2001.

Rotberg, Robert. *When States Fail: Causes and Consequences.* Princeton: Princeton University Press, 2003.

Salcedo, José María. "Puno. ¿Esperando a Sendero?" *QueHacer* 36 (1985): 51–64.

Sanborn, Cynthia. *The Democratic Left and the Persistence of Populism in Peru: 1975–1990.* PhD Dissertation, Harvard University, 1991.

Sartori, Giovanni. *Parties and Party Systems: A Framework for Analysis.* New York: Cambridge University Press, 1976.

———. "Comparing and Miscomparing." *Journal of Theoretical Politics* 3:3 (1991): 243–257.

SASE-Instituto APOYO. *El Desarrollo Institucional de las Organizaciones No-Gubernamentales de Desarrollo (ONGDs) en el Perú.* Unpublished manuscript. Lima: SASE/Instituto APOYO, 1993.

Schady, Norbert R. "The Political Economy of Expenditures by the Peruvian Social Fund (FONCODES), 1991–1995." *American Political Science Review* 94:2 (1997): 289–304.

Schmitter, Philippe C. "Still the Century of Corporatism?" In *The New Corporatism: Social-Political Structures in the Iberian World,* edited by Fredrick B. Pike and Thomas Stritch. Notre Dame: University of Notre Dame Press: 85–131.

Schönwälder, Gerd. *Linking Civil Society and the State: Urban Popular Movements, the Left, and Local Government in Peru, 1980–1992.* University Park: Pennsylvania State University Press, 2002.

Scott, James. *The Moral Economy of the Peasant. Rebellion and Subsistence in Southeast Asia.* New Haven: Yale University Press, 1976.

———. "Patron-Client Politics and Political Change in Southeast Asia." In *Friends, Followers, and Factions: A Reader in Political Clientelism,* edited by Steffen W. Schmidt. Berkeley: University of California Press, 1977: 123–146.

———. *Weapons of the Weak: Everyday Forms of Peasant Resistance.* New Haven: Yale University Press, 1985.

———. *Domination and the Arts of Resistance: Hidden Transcripts.* New Haven: Yale University Press, 1990.

Selbin, Eric. "Revolution in the Real World: Bringing Agency Back In." *Theorizing Revolutions,* edited by John Foran. London: Routledge, 1997: 123–136.

———. *Modern Latin American Revolutions.* New York: Westview Press, 1999.

Skocpol, Theda. *States and Social Revolutions: A Comparative Analysis of France, Russia, and China.* Cambridge: Cambridge University Press, 1979.

Sluka, Jeffrey, ed. *Death Squad: The Anthropology of State Terror*. University Park, PA: University of Pennsylvania Press, 1999.

Smith, Michael. "Shining Path's Urban Strategy: Ate-Vitarte." In *Shining Path of Peru*, edited by David Scott Palmer. New York: St. Martin's Press, 1992: 127–148.

Starn, Orin. "Sendero, soldados y ronderos en el Mantaro." *QueHacer* 74 (1991): 60–68.

———. "'I Dreamed of Foxes and Hawks': Reflections on Peasant Protest, New Social Movements, and the *Rondas Campesinas* of Northern Peru." In *The Making of Social Movements in Latin America. Identity, Strategy and Democracy*, edited by Arturo Escobar and Sonia E. Alvarez. Boulder: Westview Press, 1992: 89–111.

Steinmo, Sven, Kathleen Thelen, and Frank Longstreth. *Structuring Politics: Historical Institutionalism in Comparative Analysis*. Cambridge: Cambridge University Press, 1992.

Stepan, Alfred. *State and Society: Peru in Comparative Perspective*. Princeton: Princeton University Press, 1978.

———. *Rethinking Military Politics: Brazil and the Southern Cone*. Princeton: Princeton University Press, 1988.

Stern, Steve, ed. *Resistance, Rebellion, and Consciousness in the Andean Peasant World, 18th to 20th Centuries*. Madison: University of Wisconsin Press, 1987.

———. *Shining and Other Paths: War and Society in Peru, 1980–1995*. Durham: Duke University Press, 1998.

Stokes, Susan. "Hegemony, Consciousness and Political Change in Peru." *Politics and Society* 19:3 (September 1991): 265–290.

———. *Cultures in Conflict: Social Movements and the State in Peru*. Berkeley: University of California Press, 1995.

———. "La opinión pública y la lógica política del neoliberalismo." In *El juego político: Fujimori, la oposición y las reglas*, edited by Fernando Tuesta Soldevilla. Lima: Fundación Friedrich Ebert, 1998: 201–230.

———. *Mandates and Democracy: Neoliberalism by Surprise in Latin America*. Cambridge: Cambridge University Press, 2001.

Strange, Susan. *The Retreat of the State: The Diffusion of Power in the World Economy*. New York: Cambridge University Press, 1996.

Stanley, William. *The Protection Racket State: Elite Politics, Military Extortion, and Civil War in El Salvador*. Philadelphia: Temple University Press, 1996.

Suarez-Orozco, Marcelo and Antonius Robben. "Interdisciplinary Perspectives on Violence and Trauma." In *Cultures under Siege: Collective Violence and Trauma*, edited by Antonius Robben and Marcelo Suarez-Orozco. New York: Cambridge University Press, 2000: 1–42.

Sulmont, Denis, Javier Mujica, Vicente Otta, and Raúl Aramendy. *Violencia y Movimiento Sindical*. Lima: Red Peruana de Educación Popular y Sindicalismo, 1989.

Tanaka, Martin. *Los espejismos de la democracia : El colapso del sistema de partidos en el Perú en perspectiva comparada*. Lima: Instituto de Estudios Peruanos, 1998.

Tapia, Carlos. *Las Fuerzas Armadas y Sendero Luminoso. Dos estrategias y un final*. Lima: Instituto de Estudios Peruanos, 1997.

Tarrow, Sidney. *Power in Movement: Social Movements, Collective Action and Politics*. Cambridge: Cambridge University Press, 1994.

———. "The Europeanisation of Conflict: Reflections from a Social Movement Perspective." *West European Politics* 18:2 (1995): 223–251.

Taussig, Michael. "Culture of Terror—Space of Death. Roger Casement's Putumayo Report and the Explanation of Torture." *Comparative Studies in Society and History* 26:3 (1984): 467–497.

Thorp, Rosemary. "Trends and Cycles in the Peruvian Economy." *The Journal of Development Economics* 27:1–2 (1987): 355–374.

Thorp, Rosemary and Geoffrey Beltram. *Peru 1890–1977: Growth and Policy in an Open Economy*. New York: Columbia University Press, 1978.

Tilly, Charles. *Formation of National States in Western Europe*. Princeton: Princeton University Press, 1975.

———. *From Mobilization to Revolution*. Reading, MA: Addison-Wesley Publishing Co., 1978.

———. "War making and State making as Organized Crime." In *Bringing the State Back In*, edited by Peter B. Evans, Dietrich Rueschemeyer, and Theda Skocpol. New York: Cambridge University Press, 1985: 169–191.

Tilly, Charles. "A Primer on Citizenship." *Theory and Society* 26:4 (1997): 599–602.

———. *The Politics of Collective Violence.* Cambridge: Cambridge University Press, 2003.

Tilly, Charles, Louise Tilly and Richard H. Tilly. *The Rebellious Century, 1830–1930.* Cambridge, MA: Harvard University Press, 1975.

Tovar, Teresa. *Otra historica prohibida: Velasquismo y movimiento popular.* Lima: DESCO, 1985.

———. "Barrios, Ciudad, Democracia y Política." In *Movimientos Sociales y Democracia: La Fundación de un Nuevo Orden,* edited by Eduardo Ballón. Lima: DESCO, 1986: 143–184.

Tracy, Terry. "Death Squads Reemerge in El Salvador." *NACLA Report on the Americas* 29:3 (November/December 1995): 2.

Tuesta, Fernando. "Villa El Salvador: Izquierda, Gestión Municipal y Organización Popular." Unpublished manuscript. Lima: Centro de Estudios de Democracia y Sociedad, 1989.

———. *Perú Político en Cifras.* Lima: Fundación Friedrich Ebert, 1994.

Ungar, Mark. "Human Rights in the Andes: The Defensoría del Pueblo." In *Politics in the Andes: Identity, Conflict, Reform,* edited by Jo-Marie Burt and Philip Mauceri. Pittsburgh: University of Pittsburgh Press, 2004: 164–184.

Vargas Meza, Ricardo. "The FARC, the War and the Crisis of the State." *NACLA Report on the Americas* 31:5 (March/April 1998): 22–27.

Vega-Centeno B., Imelda. *Aprismo Popular: Cultura, Religion y Política.* Lima: CISEPA-Catholic University of Peru and Tarea, 1991.

Vidal, Ana María. *Los decretos de la guerra. Dos años de políticas antisubversivas y una propuesta de paz.* Lima: Instituto Democracia y Sociedad, 1993.

Walton, John. "Debt, Protest, and the State in Latin America." In *Power and Popular Protest: Latin American Social Movements,* edited by Susan Eckstein. Berkeley: University of California Press, 1989: 299–328.

Warren, Kay, ed. *The Violence Within: Cultural and Political Opposition in Divided Nations.* Boulder: Westview Press, 1993.

Webb, Richard. "Prologue." In *Peru's Path to Recovery: A Plan for Economic Stabilization and Growth,* edited by Carlos E. Paredes and Jeffrey D. Sachs. Washington, DC: Brookings Institute, 1991.

Webb, Richard and Graciela Fernández Baca. *Perú en Números 1993.* Lima: Instituto Cuánto, 1994.

Weber, Max. "Politics as a Vocation." In *From Max Weber: Essays in Sociology,* edited and translated by H.H. Gerth and C. Wright Mills. New York: Oxford University Press, 1958: 77–128.

Weiss Fagen, Patricia. "Repression and State Security." In *Fear at the Edge: State Terror and Resistance in Latin America,* edited by Juan E. Corradi, Manuel Garreton, and Patricia Weiss Fagen. Berkeley: University of California Press, 1992: 39–71.

Werlich, David. *Peru: A Short History.* Carbondale: Southern Ilinois University Press, 1978.

Weyland, Kurt. "Neopopulism and Neoliberalism in Latin America: Unexpected Affinities." *Studies in Comparative International Development* 31:3 (1996): 3–31.

———. "The Rise and Decline of Fujimori's Neopopulist Leadership." In *The Fujimori Legacy: The Rise of Electoral Authoritarianism in Peru,* edited by Julio Carrión. University Park, PA: Pennsylvania State University Press, 2006: 13–38.

Wiktorowicz, Quintan, Ed. *Islamic Activism: A Social Movement Theory Approach.* Bloomington, IN: Indiana University Press, 2004.

Wise, Carol. "Democratization, Crisis, and the APRA's Modernization Project in Peru." In *Debt and Democracy in Latin America,* edited by Barbara Stallings and Robert Kaufman. Boulder: Westview Press, 1989: 163–180.

———. "State Policy and Social Conflict." In *The Peruvian Labyrinth: Polity, Society, Economy,* edited by Maxwell Cameron and Philip Mauceri. University Park, PA: Pennsylvania State University Press, 1997: 70–103.

Wood, Elisabeth Jean. *Insurgent Collective Action and Civil War in El Salvador.* New York: Cambridge University Press, 2003.

Woy-Hazelton, Sandra and William A. Hazelton. "Shining Path and the Marxist Left." In *Shining Path of Peru,* edited by David Scott Palmer. New York: St. Martin's Press, 1992: 207–224.

Youngers, Coletta. *Violencia Política y Sociedad Civil en el Perú. Historia de la Coordinadora Nacional de Derechos Humanos.* Lima: Instituto de Estudios Peruanos, 2003.

Youngers, Coletta and Jo-Marie Burt. "Defending Rights in a Hostile Environment." *NACLA Report on the Americas* 34:1 (July/August 2000): 43–46.

Zakaria, Fareed. "The Rise of Illiberal Democracy." *Foreign Affairs* (November/December 1997): 22–43.

Zartman, William, ed. *Collapsed States. The Disintegration and Restoration of Legitimate Authority*. Boulder: Lynne Rienner Publishers, 1995.

# INDEX

through implementation of
austerity measures, 29–32, 36–40,
41–51; persistence during and after
democratic transition, 29–31; *see
also* Shining Path in Lima
Stein, Eduardo, 215
strategic equilibrium, 67, 95, 97, 99, 141
structural adjustment, *see* neoliberalism
SUTEP, *see* Peruvian Education Workers'
Union

Temporary Income Support Program
(PAIT), 33, 43, 75–7, 248n3
Toledo, Alejandro, 213, 235–41
Townsend, Anel, 210
Transparencia, 215, 231, 235–6
Trujillo, 66, 222, 227
Truth and Reconciliation Commission
(CVR), 2, 20, 56, 193–4, 208 243n1,
255n34
Túpac Amaru Revolutionary Movement
(MRTA), 2, 49, 66, 82, 139, 165,
173, 175–6, 181, 199, 204, 207–8,
232, 234

Uchiza, 53–54, 66
United Left (IU) (*also* Left)
ambiguity vis-á-vis democracy, 80–1,
133, 139, 143, 248nn17–18
ambiguity vis-á-vis Shining Path,
138–9, 141, 242n17, 249n23,
252n17
division of, 86–7, 186, 248n19
origins and development of, 14,
28–9, 31, 33, 77–80, 132–4,
171, 196, 245n14, 248nn9–10,
248n12, 248n14, 249n25,
251nn10–11
relationship with social movements,
41–2, 51, 69–72, 74–85, 99–102,
112, 122–3, 127–9, 134–6, 145–7,
192–3
Shining Path targets members of, 1–2,
4, 14, 91, 95–6, 114–15, 119,
125–8, 130, 140, 142–53, 194–6,
252n28, 252n35: *see also* Villa El
Salvador
state security forces target members of,
4, 58–9, 195–6

tensions within, 81–7, 136, 139, 143–4,
148, 152
United Mariateguista Party (PUM), 80–3,
85–6, 143–4, 148, 152, 248nn19–20
university students
government repression of, 47, 65, 84,
181, 195, 219, 258n6: *see also*
Ernesto Castillo Páez, Cantuta
massacre, National University of
the Center
participation in opposition protests, 189,
192, 216, 218–22, 230–2, 238:
divisions among inhibiting, 207,
224–6; alliance building with other
sectors of civil society, 220–1
Shining Path and, 84, 219, 225
urbanization, 21, 92–4, 119, 131, 139–40,
249n6
*see also barriadas,* land invasions
U.S. Congress (*also* U.S. House of
Representatives, U.S. senators), 170,
222, 236
U.S. Government, *also* U.S. State Department,
11, 101, 153, 170, 172, 181–2, 215–16,
218, 235–6, 240, 258n1

Vargas Llosa, Mario, 34, 104, 162–3, 167,
254n8
Velasco Alvarado, General Juan, 26–30,
33, 59–60, 71, 75, 77, 80, 164, 192,
245n3, 245n9, 248n17, 251n7
role in formation of Villa El
Salvador, 128, 131–3,
249n9
Venezuela, 38, 110, 170
Villa El Salvador, 7, 14, 19–22, 75
as a model of popular participation, 79,
127–8
origins of, 128, 131–4
resistance to Shining Path infiltration
of, 145–52, 154–5
strategic importance for Shining Path,
101, 129–30
Shining Path and: presence in, 107–10,
115, 118–19, 137–41;
confrontational politics in, 1,
141–2, 146–52; limits to Shining
Path's advance in, 153–5
United Left (IU) in, 133–7, 142–6